The End of the Cold War and the Third World

This book brings together recent research on the end of the Cold War in the Third World and engages with ongoing debates about regional conflicts, the role of great powers in the developing world, and the role of international actors in conflict resolution.

Most of the recent scholarship on the end of the Cold War has focused on Europe or bilateral US–Soviet relations. By contrast, relatively little has been written about how the end of the Cold War affected the Third World: in Asia, Africa, and Latin America. How did the great transformation of the world in the late 1980s affect regional conflicts and client relationships? Who 'won' and who 'lost' in the Third World and why do so many Cold War-era problems remain unresolved? This book brings to light evidence from recently-declassified archives in Russia, the US, Eastern Europe, as well as from private collections, recent memoirs and interviews with key participants. It goes further than anything published so far in systematically explaining, both from the perspectives of the superpowers and Third World countries, what the end of bipolarity meant not only for the underdeveloped periphery, so long enmeshed in ideological, socio-political and military conflicts sponsored by Washington, Moscow or Beijing, but also for the broader patterns of international relations.

This book will be of great interest to students of the Cold War, war and conflict studies, Third World and development studies, international history, and international relations in general.

Artemy M. Kalinovsky is Assistant Professor of East European Studies at the University of Amsterdam and a Research Associate at the London School of Economics IDEAS. **Sergey Radchenko** is Lecturer at the University of Nottingham, China Campus, Ningbo, China.

Cold War History Series
Series Editors: Odd Arne Westad and Michael Cox.

In the new history of the Cold War, forming since 1989, many of the established truths about the international conflict that shaped the latter half of the twentieth century have come up for revision. The present series is an attempt to make interpretations and materials available that will help further the development of this new history, and it will concentrate, particularly, on publishing expositions of key historical issues and critical surveys of recently-available sources.

Reviewing the Cold War
Approaches, Interpretations, Theory
Edited by Odd Arne Westad

Rethinking Theory and History in the Cold War
The State, Military Power and Social Revolution
Richard Saull

British and American Anticommunism before the Cold War
Marrku Ruotsila

Europe, Cold War and Coexistence, 1953–1965
Edited by Wilfried Loth

The Last Decade of the Cold War
From Conflict Escalation to Conflict Transformation
Edited by Olav Njølstad

Reinterpreting the End of the Cold War
Issues, interpretations, periodizations
Edited by Silvio Pons and Federico Romero

Across the Blocs
Cold War Cultural and Social History
Edited by Rana Mitter and Patrick Major

US Internal Security Assistance to South Vietnam
Insurgency, subversion and public order
William Rosenau

The European Community and the Crises of the 1960s
Negotiating the Gaullist challenge
N. Piers Ludlow

Soviet–Vietnam Relations and the Role of China, 1949–64
Changing alliances
Mari Olsen

The Third Indochina War
Conflict between China, Vietnam and Cambodia, 1972–79
Edited by Odd Arne Westad and Sophie Quinn-Judge

Greece and the Cold War
Frontline state, 1952–1967
Evanthis Hatzivassiliou

Economic Statecraft during the Cold War
European responses to the US trade embargo
Frank Cain

Macmillan, Khrushchev and the Berlin Crisis, 1958–1960
Kitty Newman

The Emergence of Détente in Europe
Brandt, Kennedy and the formation of Ostpolitik
Arne Hofmann

European Integration and the Cold War
Ostpolitik–Westpolitik, 1965–1973
Edited by N. Piers Ludlow

Britain, Germany and the Cold War
The search for a European Détente 1949–1967
R. Gerald Hughes

The Military Balance in the Cold War
US perceptions and policy, 1976–85
David M. Walsh

The Cold War in the Middle East
Regional conflict and the superpowers 1967–73
Edited by Nigel J. Ashton

The Making of Détente
Eastern and Western Europe in the Cold War, 1965–75
Edited by Wilfried Loth and Georges-Henri Soutou

Europe and the End of the Cold War
A reappraisal
Edited by Frédéric Bozo, Marie-Pierre Rey, N. Piers Ludlow, and Leopoldo Nuti

The Baltic Question during the Cold War
Edited by John Hiden, Vahur Made and David J. Smith

The Crisis of Détente in Europe
From Helsinki to Gorbachev, 1975–85
Edited by Leopoldo Nuti

Cold War in Southern Africa
White power, black liberation
Edited by Sue Onslow

The Globalisation of the Cold War
Diplomacy and local confrontation, 1975–85
Edited by Max Guderzo and Bruna Bagnato

Yugoslavia and the Soviet Union in the Early Cold War
Reconciliation, comradeship, confrontation, 1953–1957
Svetozar Rajak

The End of the Cold War and the Third World
New perspectives on regional conflict
Edited by Artemy M. Kalinovsky and Sergey Radchenko

The End of the Cold War and the Third World

New perspectives on regional conflict

Edited by Artemy M. Kalinovsky and Sergey Radchenko

Routledge
Taylor & Francis Group
LONDON AND NEW YORK

First published 2011
by Routledge
4 Park Square, Milton Park, Abingdon, Oxon OX14 4RN
605 Third Avenue, New York, NY 10017

Routledge is an imprint of the Taylor & Francis Group, an informa business

British Library Cataloguing in Publication Data
A catalogue record for this book is available from the British Library

Library of Congress Cataloging-in-Publication Data
The end of the Cold War and the Third World : new perspectives on regional conflict / [edited by] Artemy Kalinovsky, Sergey Radchenko.
p. cm. – (Cold war history)
1. Developing countries–Foreign relations. 2. World politics–1945-1989. 3. Cold War. I. Kalinovsky, Artemy. II. Radchenko, Sergey.
D887.E53 2011
909'.097240829–dc22
2010049143

ISBN: 978-0-415-60054-5 (hbk)
ISBN: 978-0-203-81674-5 (ebk)

Typeset in Baskerville
by Wearset Ltd, Boldon, Tyne and Wear

Contents

Contributors

Editors

Dr Artemy M. Kalinovsky is Assistant Professor of Eastern European Studies at the University of Amsterdam. He is the author of *A Long Goodbye: The Soviet Withdrawal from Afghanistan* (Harvard University Press, 2011). Artemy M. Kalinovsky has a PhD and an MA in International History from the London School of Economics and a BA from the George Washington University. His publications include "Soviet Decision-making during the War in Afghanistan, from Intervention to Withdrawal." *Journal of Cold War Studies* (Fall 2009) and "Politics, Diplomacy and the Soviet Withdrawal from Afghanistan: From National Reconciliation to the Geneva Accords," *Cold War History* 8:3 (August 2008), 381–404. His articles have also appeared in *Foreign Policy, National Journal* (nj.com), and *NeoAmericanist*. He is currently working on a history of Soviet advising in the Third World and a study of the effects of the Afghan War on Central Asia and the Caucasus.

Dr Sergey Radchenko has written on the history of the Cold War, on Soviet foreign policy during the Cold War years, and on the regional history of North East Asia, including China, Mongolia, Korea (North and South) and Japan. He has a PhD from the London School of Economics. Besides numerous articles, he is the co-author, with Campbell Craig, of *The Atomic Bomb and the Origins of the Cold War* (Yale University Press, 2008) and the author of *Two Suns in the Heavens: The Sino-Soviet Struggle for Supremacy, 1962–67* (Woodrow Wilson Center Press and Stanford University Press, 2009). He currently teaches at the University of Nottingham in China.

Contributors

Dr Dima Adamsky is a fellow at the National Security Studies Program at Harvard University. He has been a visiting fellow at the Institute of War and Peace Studies, Columbia University and at the Norwegian

Institute for Defense Studies. His research interests include strategic and intelligence studies, ideational approach to international security, jihadi military thought, nuclear proliferation, American, Russian and Israeli security policy. He has published on these topics in the Journal of Strategic Studies, Intelligence and National Security, Studies in Conflict and Terrorism, Journal of Cold War History, Defense and Security Studies and has contributed chapters to edited volumes and encyclopedias on contemporary military and international history. His first book *Operation Kavkaz* (Hebrew) won the prize for the best academic work on Israeli security in 2006. His second book *The Culture of Military Innovation: Comparing the RMA in Russia, the US and Israel* was published by Woodrow Wilson Center Press and Stanford University Press in 2010.

Dr Duccio Basosi teaches History of North America at the University of Florence, Italy. He has published several articles on US foreign policy in the 1970s and 1980s. He also authored a monograph on the Nixon administration and the fall of Bretton Woods (*Il governo del dollaro*, Firenze, 2006) and coedited, with Alessandra Lorini, a forthcoming volume on Cuba's foreign relations (*Cuba in the world, the World in Cuba*, Firenze, 2009).

Dr Victor Figueroa Clark has a PhD from the London School of Economics. His current research focuses on the Chilean Left in exile, and upon its relationship with the Sandinista Revolution. He is also interested in Latin American history, the US–Latin American relationship, the history of the Soviet Union and that of Cold War era national-liberation struggles. Victor Figueroa Clark is a graduate of the POLIS department at the University of Leeds, and of the Institute for the Study of the Americas of the University of London, where he studied Globalisation and Latin American Development.

Professor Chen Jian holds the Michael J. Zak Chair of the History of US-China Relations at Cornell University and is a distinguished research scholar, writer and teacher. He is the author of *Mao's China and the Cold War* (University of North Carolina Press, 2001) and *China's Road to the Korean War: The Making of the Sino-American Confrontation* (Columbia University Press, 1995), and shared honours for the 2005 Emmy Award for Outstanding Achievement in News and Documentary Research for *Declassified: Nixon in China*.

Professor Mark Kramer is Director of the Cold War Studies Program at Harvard University and a Senior Fellow of Harvard's Davis Center for Russian and Eurasian Studies. He has taught at Harvard, Yale, and Brown Universities and was formerly an Academy Scholar in Harvard's Academy of International and Area Studies and a Rhodes Scholar at Oxford University.

Dr Sue Onslow is Co-Head of the Africa International Affairs programme at LSE IDEAS and Administrator for the Executive Masters programme International Strategy and Diplomacy. She has lectured at the LSE since 1994. She is also the programme coordinator of the Southern Africa Programme. She recently organised a conference, Rhodesian UDI: 40 Years On, which addressed the entirety of the Rhodesia UDI experiment in the context of the Cold War in Southern Africa in the 1960s and 1970s, followed by a framing seminar on broader aspects of Southern Africa in the Cold War. Her current main areas of research are: British foreign policy and decolonisation since 1945; Southern Africa in the Cold War (the domestic context of the struggle between white domination and black liberation, the role of the regional and superpowers, the end of the white minority imperialism, and its legacy). She is co-editor of the forthcoming, *Britain and Rhodesia: Road to Settlement 1977–1980*, (to be published by the Institute of Historical Research) which draws on her extensive interviews with leading British politicians and civil servants involved in the Rhodesian question. She is also currently preparing a monograph on South Africa and the Rhodesian UDI period.

Dr Svetlana Savranskaya received a PhD in Political Science from the Emory University in Atlanta in 1998. She published "New Sources on the Role of Soviet Submarines in the Cuban Missile Crisis" and "Theoretical Approaches to the Concept of National Interest" in 1990. Since 2000 she has been a Director of Russia Programs at the National Security Archive, Washington, DC. In 2001 she became an Adjunct Professor at the American University in Washington, DC.

Dr Chris Saunders is Emeritus Professor in the Department of Historical Studies at the University of Cape Town. He is the author of 'The Angola/Namibia Crisis of 1988 and its Resolution' in S. Onslow (ed.), *Cold War in Southern Africa. White Power, Black Liberation* (Routledge, 2009) and of a chapter on the Cold War in Southern Africa co-authored with Sue Onslow in M. Leffler and O.A. Westad (eds), *The Cambridge History of the Cold War*, Vol. 3 (Cambridge University Press, 2010).

Professor Vladimir Shubin received his doctorates from the Academy of Social Sciences and Moscow State University as well as a PhD Honoris Causa from the University of the Western Cape. He is Deputy Director of the Institute of African Studies, Russian Academy of Sciences and a Professor at the Russian State University for the Humanities. Before joining academia he was involved in political and practical support of the liberation struggle in Southern Africa. He authored several books including (in English) *Social Democracy and Southern Africa* (under a pen name, Vladimir Bushin); *ANC: a View from Moscow* and *the Hot "Cold War": the USSR in Southern Africa*. He was awarded the South African Order of Companions of Oliver Tambo (silver).

Dr Matias Spektor is coordinator of the Center for the Study of International Relations at Fundação Getulio Vargas (Rio de Janeiro, Brazil), where he is Assistant Professor in International Relations. His first book was entitled *Henry Kissinger and Brazil* (in Portuguese, Zahar, 2009). His main current research projects are a history of emerging countries in international society and a study of US–Brazil relations since the end of the Cold War. Matias also manages the one-year professional graduate degree in International Relations at FGV, and an oral history programme on the Foreign Relations of Brazil since the End of the Cold War. He is managing editor with FGV Press for a new pocket series in International Relations. Previously he worked as an official for the UN and as a consultant for the Tavistock Institute in London. He earned his doctorate from the University of Oxford in 2007.

Dr Balázs Szalontai earned his PhD in 2003 from Central European University in Budapest, Hungary, and is the author of *Kim Il Sung in the Khrushchev Era: Soviet–DPRK Relations and the Roots of North Korean Despotism, 1953–1964* (Woodrow Wilson Center Press and Stanford University Press, 2005), as well as the co-author, with Sergey Radchenko, of "North Korea's Efforts to Acquire Nuclear Technology and Nuclear Weapons: Evidence from Russian and Hungarian Archives," in *the Cold War International History Project Working Paper*, No. 53. He has published articles about the economic policies of the Vietnamese and Mongolian Communist regimes and the global impact of the Stalinist model of repression. His other research interests include Cambodia, Laos, Albania, and North Korea's relations with Cuba and the Middle East. Currently, he teaches at East China Normal University.

Introduction

The end of the Cold War in the Third World

Artemy M. Kalinovsky and Sergey Radchenko

In October 1990 the US Congress voted to curb covert aid to some of Washington's long-time clients in the Third World – UNITA guerrillas in Angola, mujahadeen in Afghanistan and anti-Communist rebels in Cambodia. Unimpressed with the increasingly outdated efforts to defend the Reagan doctrine in the struggle with revolutionary regimes and movements in Latin America, the lawmakers halved the aid package destined for El Salvador. The use of humanitarian aid for express political purposes was explicitly prohibited. As Congress increasingly attached conditions to aid packages, obtaining loans from the US became ever more difficult for countries like Pakistan, Kenya, and Zaire. The prevailing sentiment on Capitol Hill was that, with the Cold War peacefully winding down, it was time for Washington to quietly end its various Third World commitments.

Moscow's retreat from the Third World began even earlier; its most potent symbol was the semi-dignified withdrawal from Afghanistan following the signing of the Geneva Accords, in April 1988. Soviet advisers who had labored on behalf of the socialist promise in distant places were recalled or, unpaid or altogether abandoned, returned on their own account. Soviet economic collapse reduced the flow of aid to the Third World to a mere trickle by 1990. Mikhail Gorbachev, who had gone cap in hand from summit to summit asking for aid, lost interest in former clients, although on occasion he called on his Western partners to join hands in offering multilateral aid to the Third World.[1] Ideas of a similar kind were floated in academia and broader policy circles in the US and the Soviet Union alike; one paper, co-written by an American and a Russian academic (a sign of the times!), wrote of "a growing sense that Soviet and US interests converge in the long run on peaceful alternatives to the political instability and economic deprivation that now characterize many developing countries."[2]

And who could argue with that! The end of the Cold War seemed to herald a bright new future for the Third World, for at last, it seemed, bloodshed inspired by ideological zeal and supported by the flow of arms from, or by interventions on the part of, the two superpowers, could be set aside in the name of development, of the struggle against poverty, disease and hunger. Unfortunately, these expectations did not always bear fruit. Misery and want continued to plague the smoking ashes of former Cold War battlefields in Africa and the Middle East, and some of these conflicts were only exacerbated as the superpowers disengaged, leaving desperate clients to their own devices. The 1990s heralded the marginalization of the Third World, and many of its lingering problems, including poverty and inequality, have remained painfully neglected, although 9/11 offered a stark reminder of the hefty price tag of this neglect.

By the 1960s, the European continent had entered into what historian John Lewis Gaddis famously called "The Long Peace."[3] It was still a tense time – several million Warsaw Pact and NATO troops stood ready to go into battle. The enormous stockpile of nuclear weapons on either side meant that war, if it broke out, for instance, because of an accidental confrontation in the divided city of Berlin, could have truly apocalyptic results. But the prospect of apocalyptic war also made any such confrontation less likely. Equally important for the "Long Peace" was that both sides recognized (or at least grudgingly accepted) the other's spheres of influence in Europe. This was evident in the mild western response to the Soviet invasions of Hungary (1956) and Czechoslovakia (1968), or to the Moscow-encouraged crackdown in Poland in 1981. With Europe divided, the focus of Cold War competition shifted to Asia, Africa and Latin America. This shift was already taking place by 1949/1950; it was hastened by the surge of de-colonization in the 1950s. The last 30 years of the Cold War were fought out in the jungles, deserts and mountains of what was loosely termed the Third World.

The very term "Third World" has inspired so much controversy that it might take another book to explain what it means, and any such volume would be bound to obscure as much as it explained, for the Third World has meant different things to different people.[4] In 1952 the French demographer and economic historian Alfred Sauvy first wrote of nations "ignored, exploited, despised" aspiring, like the third estate of the French Revolution, "to be something." The Third World of the 1950s was not just economically deprived, in was also "non-aligned" in the sense of not belonging to either the US-led capitalist First World or the Second World of the Soviet Union and its allies. The Cold War-inspired notion of "non-alignment" of the Third World was useful, once upon a time, as a way to define a political agenda for countries, some of which had very little in common. Not all less-developed countries were non-aligned, and not all non-aligned countries were less-developed. Many, but not all had just emerged from anti-colonial struggles.

This obscurity of terminology was not helped by China's two yuan's worth of three worlds theory, elaborated by Mao Zedong and proclaimed by Deng Xiaoping from the UN podium in April 1974, as Chen Jian discusses in his chapter on China and the Third World. The Chinese placed the two superpowers, the US and the Soviet Union in the First World category, with Western Europe and Japan comprising the Second World. The Third World, then, referred to countries in Asia, Africa and Latin America. The Chinese notion of the Third World was an intellectual successor to Mao's theory of an intermediate zone, first formulated in the late 1940s; and it also shared ground with another former hallmark of Beijing's foreign policy, the defunct idea of Afro-Asian solidarity. All of these terms were premised on China's self-proclaimed membership of this ill-defined community of poor nations. China shared many social and economic difficulties with post-colonial countries. However, Beijing's efforts to place China in the ranks of the Third World, and, indeed, as the leader of the Third World, suggested that, since the late 1950s at least, China was neither. For much of the Cold War it was a key player in a three-way competition, with the US and the Soviet Union, for the loyalties of the Third World.

The bipolarity of international politics between the late 1940s and the early 1960s encouraged efforts on behalf of geographically disparate, and in other respects dissimilar, nations to forge a common front of "non-alignment." The outlines of the Non-Aligned Movement did not fully correspond to what we would now term the "Third World," and, in fact, one of the key co-sponsors of the movement was Yugoslavia, a European country that did not belong to the Third World in any meaningful sense. Although the viability of this movement was severely constrained by differences among the main participants, non-alignment played an important role in the eventual conceptualization of the North–South divide. Similar ideas underpinned the "Bandung Discourse," and the short-lived movement of Afro-Asian Solidarity (1955–1965). Thus, the 1950s and the early 1960s witnessed the emergence and the consolidation of the Third World in an ideological sense. This ideology of the Third World was both a part of, and a counter-narrative to, the Cold War.

For the purposes of this book, the Third World is simply that part of the world (Latin America, Africa, the Middle East, and virtually all of Asia) where competition between the US, the Soviet Union and other contestants was played out during the course of the Cold War. This vague definition – especially the use of the term "other contestants" – provides an additional layer of intellectual complexity, for Cold War competition in the Third World was not just a Soviet–US competition, nor even a Sino–Soviet–US competition. Representing the Third World simply as an analytical Cold War battleground also allows one to skirt the question of economic development, for it serves no useful purpose here to delve into detailed discussion of what precisely constitutes underdevelopment. Of course, for the most part, the countries of the Third World were poor and technologically unsophisticated. The Third World was, by and large, pre-industrial though often well-endowed with natural resources which could be traded away, unprofitably, to the other worlds in exchange for much-needed equipment or consumer goods. These were countries in need of lasting recognition and developmental aid. Many were looking to the great powers for weapons, to fight their neighbors or domestic opponents.

Soviet involvement in, and courtship of, the Third World is often traced back to the visit of Nikita Khrushchev and Nikolai Bulganin to India, Burma, and Afghanistan in 1955. Of course, the Soviet Union had a long tradition of helping the "toilers of the East" – in particular, through the training of revolutionaries, covert funneling of funds and weapons, and occasional military interventions (e.g. Mongolia and China) in the name of "liberation" of neighboring peoples from the yoke of feudalism and colonial exploitation. But, for all these continuities, the mid-1950s represented a new beginning: in part because Moscow now had both capability and willingness to project its influence far beyond its borders, and in part because of the dramatic expansion of opportunities for doing so with the increasing pace of decolonization. Khrushchev's 1956 speech, declaring that Soviet foreign policy would now be guided by the principle of "peaceful coexistence" simultaneously heralded the start of a superpower competition that would be primarily ideological and economic.[5] Soviet involvement in the Third World became a crucial element of that competition, one by which, in Khrushchev's imagination, the world would judge which system – socialist or capitalist – commanded the destiny of mankind.

Almost from the outset, even as they found themselves preoccupied with events in Europe, US policy makers realized that the underdeveloped postcolonial world mattered in the global struggle against International Communism. This realization underpinned Harry S. Truman's Four Point Program, promulgated in January 1949, the aim of which was to "help free peoples through their own efforts to produce more food, housing, and power to lighten their burdens."[6] Although the Program languished in obscurity for the first few years, by the early 1950s the US had become more actively involved in efforts to contain Communism, even in places where Moscow's influence was more imaginary than real (e.g. Iran in 1953 and Guatemala in 1954). US involvement in the Korean War and its security guarantees to Taiwan were potent indicators of the shifting grounds of the Cold War, and of the increasing involvement of the Third World in the superpower contest.

The US had a long legacy of involvement in the affairs of its own little "third world" in the Western hemisphere. The imperative of maintaining unchallenged positions in Latin America was hardly a function of Washington's Cold War. It was a fundamental tenet of US foreign policy that had been 150 years in the making. True, the Cold War made an early impact on Latin America but only as an ideological backdrop to indigenous developments – that is to say, retrenchment of democracy and resurgence of the conservative elites. Indeed, Latin America did not truly become a Cold War battlefield until the Cuban revolution of 1959.[7] At that point, the reality of a Communist regime 90 miles off the coast of Florida called for a reappraisal of US policies in the Third World, not least in

America's own backyard. The intellectual framework for this reappraisal was furnished by modernization theorists like Walt Rostow who set the liberal development agenda with his *Stages of Economic Growth: A Non-Communist Manifesto.* Modernization theory, underpinned by ideological proclivities borne of US exceptionalism, offered the Third World a pathway to prosperity laden with policy choices, which had proven successful for the US, that is – democracy and the market. Modernization theory informed John F. Kennedy's Alliance for Progress, announced amid fanfare in March 1961 as a "vast cooperative effort, unparalleled in magnitude and nobility of purpose, to satisfy the basic needs of the [Latin] American people for homes, work and land, health and schools."[8]

In the meantime, in the Soviet Union, political scientists and economists worked to offer a coherent theory that would explain and channel aid to newly independent states that were not necessarily ready to adopt Communism full-stop. In newly established institutes, often focused on area studies, they coined terms like "national democracies" to denote socialist-leaning states that would make good partners for the Soviet Union.[9] Their acceptance of Soviet aid and advice would itself, it was hoped, prove to be a major boon in the competition with the western capitalist model. The Soviets advised state-led industrialization (with a considerable, if not exclusive, emphasis on heavy industry), which would, presumably, allow their third world clients to break free of the shackles of world capitalism. In the longer term, Soviet engagement with the Third World, it was hoped, would produce a transition to "socialism" in these countries, "bypassing the capitalist stage of development"; Lenin himself had toyed with the idea as early as 1920.

The development policies and philosophies of the late 1950s and early 1960s shared a profound confidence and optimism that the respective systems had something to offer to the newly independent states and that the models, either capitalist or socialist, were replicable. By the 1970s this enthusiasm had waned. Both Moscow and Washington had become disenchanted with their erstwhile allies, who seemed incapable of absorbing the lessons and aid being offered them were too quick to take offense at perceived transgressions on national sovereignty, and were too ready to jump into the arms of the enemy. The inability of Latin America to "modernize" along the lines previously predicted by Walt Rostow, and painful setbacks for the US in Indochina, prompted soul-searching among the American theorists and practitioners of Third World development; modernization theory was contested and partly discredited as a disguise for quasi-imperialism. For their part, by the end of the 1970s, the Soviets had been "burned" by Egypt and Somalia, and, in a lesser way, by Indonesia, Algeria, and a host of other countries.

The competition in the Third World was far from peaceful. Although, aside from the Cuban Missile Crisis and Soviet Premier Nikita Khrushchev's vague threats during the Suez fiasco, the threat of nuclear war was rarely associated with the superpower competition there, prolonged and deadly conflict nevertheless ensued in a number of places: Indochina, Afghanistan, Angola, and the Horn of Africa are only a few examples of local conflicts multiplying in scale and lethality as a result of superpower involvement or intervention.

In the meantime, the flare-up of Sino–Soviet disagreements added a layer of complexity to the struggle for hearts and minds of the Third World. Moscow and Beijing competed for influence in Asia, Africa and Latin America, each claiming to represent the true aspirations of national liberation movements. China made important gains in this competition in the early 1960s, in part because Mao's revolutionary rhetoric had a greater appeal in the Third World than Khrushchev's timid platitudes of peaceful coexistence. But the Soviets made a comeback after 1964, and by the early 1970s the struggle for the Third World truly assumed the character of a three-way competition, with Washington, Moscow and Beijing supporting different factions in local conflicts – a condition which served to perpetuate these conflicts. Cuba's involvement in Africa and Latin America, from the 1960s until the very end of the Cold War, was yet another ingredient in the explosive mixture of national liberation struggles. Itself a Third World country, effectively a client of Moscow's (but often acting independently), Cuba bravely charted a course of its own in aiding revolutions from the Congo to Angola to Nicaragua alongside, but sometimes in spite of, the Soviet Union.

If the first post-Cold War years saw an explosion of studies, enabled by unprecedented archival access, of the conflict as seen in Moscow, Washington, or the capitals of Europe, the last decade has seen a plethora of work that reoriented Cold War historiography towards the Third World. Many of these new histories were still written with a "north-south" perspective: i.e., they were studies of Moscow's or Washington's policies in the Third World, rather than studies of the Third World in the Cold War as such. But there were notable exceptions: studies that kept Washington and Moscow in the picture, but made the main protagonist Havana, Luanda, or Cairo.[10] The process culminated in Odd Arne Westad's *Global Cold War: Third World Interventions and the Makings of our Times*.[11] Even since the publication of that book, however, new studies have continued to emerge.[12]

And yet, in the anniversary year of 2009, the dozens of books about the end of the Cold War barely mentioned the Third World.[13] In the media, too, all of the focus was on Europe. (The one exception was Afghanistan, where the Soviet withdrawal was mentioned with increasing frequency against a background of US and NATO involvement there.) Perhaps this is not surprising – the end of the Cold War in the Third World did not have a neat end-date like it did in Europe. There was no march of revolutions – weeks or at most months apart from each other – bringing down one order and replacing it with another. Nevertheless, the end of the Cold War did mean tremendous changes for the Third World: old sources of arms or aid were drying up, networks disappearing, ideologies losing their currency. None of the front-line Third World states emerged from the end of the Cold War unchanged.

The purpose of this book is to lay the groundwork for future studies of the end of the Cold War in the Third World and to contribute to ongoing debates about regional conflicts, the role of great powers in the developing world, and the role of international actors in conflict resolution. How did the great transformation of the world in the late 1980s affect regional conflicts and client relationships? Who "won" and who "lost" in the Third World and why do so many Cold War-era problems remain unresolved? This book, featuring contributions by prominent and promising scholars, and bringing to light evidence from recently declassified archives in Russia, the US, Eastern Europe, as well as from private collections, recent memoirs and interviews with key participants, goes further than anything published so far in systematically explaining, from both the perspectives of the superpowers and those of the Third World countries, what the end of bipolarity meant not only for the underdeveloped periphery, so long enmeshed in ideological, socio-political and military conflicts sponsored by Washington, Moscow or Beijing, but also for the broader patterns of international relations.

In effect, the world witnessed, in the space of a few years: Soviet retrenchment, the bankruptcy of socialist developmental discourse and the triumph of market economics, the winding down of some regional conflicts and the remarkable persistence of others, the growing prominence of the North-South divide, the rise of unipolarity and the stirrings of new Regional Blocs. As this book shows, many of these developments were rooted in tendencies which preceded the Cold War, continued during the Cold War, and, indeed, outlived the Cold War. And yet, the Cold War was central to the postwar history of the Third World; the Cold War was fought, to some extent, for and in the name of the Third World.

Of course, different countries experienced the superpower confrontation in different ways. Angola and Afghanistan, Korea and Vietnam, the Congo and Mozambique, to take a few examples, were soaked in blood. Brazil mostly watched from the sidelines. China abandoned revolutionary discourse in favor of quasi-capitalist development years before fall of the Berlin Wall heralded the bankruptcy of Soviet socialism. Conflicts in Southeast Asia, Southwest Asia, and in the Middle East had a dynamic quite apart from Cold War tides.

This book does not provide – and does not attempt to provide – an overarching theoretical framework. It makes no effort to explain where the Third World is heading, or engage with the ongoing North–South debate, or even make specific policy recommendations, the preserve of voluminous International Relations literature on the persistent woes of the Third World.[14] Contributors to this volume are, primarily, historians, and the constituent chapters aim, in large part, to explain what happened and why, a task informed less by elaborate theoretical constructs than by nitty-gritty work with evidence in archives the world over, and by rigorous historical analysis. The book relies upon a wealth of historical record to explain and interpret the problems that the Third World faces today; in this respect, it is a roadmap to the present, an effort to highlight legacies and inescapable continuities and inform contemporary policy debate, bringing it to a new level of sophistication.

In Chapter 1 Svetlana Savranskaya writes about the Soviet retrenchment from the Third World in what is, presently, the only comprehensive overview of Mikhail Gorbachev's Third World policies in the existing literature written on the basis of the declassified archival record. The emerging picture shows a different Gorbachev – Gorbachev at pains to understand the Soviet role in the Third World, support old clients and yet define new Soviet interests in Asia, Africa and Latin America. Savranskaya argues that Gorbachev's policy towards the Third World went through two distinct phases. From 1985 to 1988 he continued to provide Soviet support to long-time clients – Cuba, Angola, Syria, Vietnam, among others. His only major concern was to promptly patch up the "bleeding wound" of Afghanistan. In the meantime, however, Gorbachev's reform-inclined advisers and the voices in the broader policy community urged him to curb Soviet aid to militant, and mostly self-serving, regimes. From 1988 Gorbachev adopted a much more proactive attitude towards the Third World, seeking to settle long-running conflicts in the spirit of the "new thinking." Soviet Third World policy became a function of Gorbachev's efforts to improve relations with the US and bring the Cold War to a close.

Savranskaya's argument that there were, in effect, two Gorbachevs, before and after 1988, is supported by other authors in this volume. Vladimir Shubin sees a different Gorbachev (in relation to the conflict in southern Africa) from about 1989; Sergey Radchenko finds that Gorbachev's policies in South Asia changed sharply half-way through *perestroika*. Overall, the evidence presented in this volume offers a more refined view of Gorbachev who, far from rushing headlong to mend fences with his Cold War foes, trod the ground carefully, in full awareness of the Soviet Union's global strategic interests, and with a remarkable commitment to the Soviet Third World clientele. What happened then, in 1988, that led to rapid Soviet retrenchment from all those commitments? Relevant chapters in this volume agree that Gorbachev's investment in the rapprochement with the West, especially with the US, increasingly dictated his foreign policy choices towards the end of the 1980s. Moreover, serious resistance to domestic reforms, persistent economic woes, and a growing conservative backlash encouraged Gorbachev to take bold measures in foreign policy.

But, to what extent was Soviet retrenchment from the Third World a function of an ideological reorientation (that is to say, Gorbachev's "new thinking"), and to what extent – simply a result of an interplay of particular circumstances? In Chapter 2, Mark Kramer, disagreeing in important respects with Savranskaya's account, argues that Soviet arms transfers to the Third World – one of the most effective levers of Moscow's influence – declined (and ultimately almost collapsed) for reasons which had little to do with the changes occasioned by "new thinking" in Soviet foreign policy. At the time of Gorbachev's accession to power, in 1985, Soviet arms transfers to its clients in the Socialist Bloc and the Third World were at all time highs and accounted for 45 percent of the world's arms trade. The volume of transfers continued to increase significantly until 1988–1989, at which time Soviet fortunes in the trade were reversed, but not for lack of trying. Indeed, as the Soviet military faced financial constraints in the face of Gorbachev's efforts to redirect the military-industrial complex towards civilian needs, the prospect of new arms deals appeared all the more desirable from Moscow's perspective, and the Soviets went out of their way, in 1989–1991, to boost sales, even as far as putting sensitive technologies on the market and arming former enemies. These efforts failed, in the end, because of the downturn in the global arms trade due to the oversaturation of the market and the difficult financial circumstances faced by Soviet clients in the Third World.

Chen Jian offers a very different approach to the end of the Cold War in the Third World. In Chapter 3 he begins with a broad overview of the genesis and the development of China's Third World policies, from Mao Zedong's early conceptualization of the "intermediate zone" through the Bandung Discourse and China's engagement with the anti-colonial movement in Asia and Africa, which Mao connected to his revolutionary visions of a world, gripped by struggle and chaos, an anti-imperialist revolution in which China played the leading role.[15] The turning point for China's relationship with the Third World was Mao's formulation of his own "three worlds theory" in 1973–1974, which, by and large, dispensed with the rhetoric of class struggle (formerly, the key theme of the Chairman's view of world politics) in favor of development as the principal element in the demarcation of the three worlds. Mao's late shift from class struggle to developmental discourse, in large part due to the failure of his "continuous revolution" model, paved the way to China's embrace of the "four modernizations" in subsequent years.

As the country's domestic climate shifted from revolution to modernization, so did China's Third World policies shift from opposing imperialism to promoting development. This, in Chen Jian's view, marked a turning point in international politics and the beginning of the end of the Cold War – at least a decade before the Berlin Wall fell. Chen Jian's argument has an important implication: if, by the end of the 1970s, China had "departed" from the Cold War (in the sense that Beijing embraced the non-socialist path to modernity), when did the Cold War end for the Third World? Although the current state of scholarship does not permit a confident answer to this question, there is an intuitive ring of truth to Chen's assertion that "Beijing's repudiation of the Soviet model discouraged other

Third World countries from taking Communism as a useful and competitive path toward modernity." If so, just as the policy makers in the Soviet Union thought that the Third World was going "their way" (to evoke the title of a recent book on the subject),[16] the Third World was going precisely the opposite way – away from Soviet-style economic solutions. One can take this argument forward: perhaps, by the time Gorbachev took power, the Soviet Union had already lost the struggle for the Third World, although it maintained an illusion of influence by providing weapons to militant clients.

Although not all the contributors to this volume would agree with Chen Jian's assessment, one provocative possibility suggested by his chapter as well as by Duccio Basosi's, is that in order to understand how the Cold War ended in the Third World, we should look not to so much to the 1980s, and not to the impact of the Soviet retrenchment, or to the influence of Gorbachev's "new thinking," but to the 1970s, which, in spite of the oil crisis, stagflation and financial tremors in the West, increasingly signaled the bankruptcy of Soviet-style socialism as a viable path to modernity. The Cold War had yet to see some of its hottest years with the breakdown of détente, but it was in the 1970s that the dynamic of North-South relations began to transcend the dynamic of the Cold War; seen from that light, the 1980s were merely an epilogue for the unsuccessful Soviet effort to win the hearts and minds of the developing world.

Chen Jian's take on the subject suggests the appropriateness of disentangling Cold War politics from the parallel strands of international and local politics – in China's case, developmental discourse. It is only by keeping in mind the complexity and interconnectedness of these various strands that we may begin to appreciate why the end of the Cold War did not lead to the "end of history." Dima Adamsky's treatment of the Arab–Israeli conflict in Chapter 4 is a case in point. The causes of this conflict, he notes, go deeper than the Cold War, and while US and Soviet relations with their clients influenced regional politics in important ways, developments in the Middle East had a logic of their own, a logic which derived from a complex interplay of ethnic, religious and territorial grievances, a product of conflicting nationalisms which survives to this day.

Yet, even as Adamsky points to certain perennial qualities of Arab–Israeli relations, which easily transcend the historical particularities of the Cold War era, he shows that the end of the superpower confrontation had an important transformative effect on the conflict, reflected not only in renewed opportunities for peace talks but also in the changes to the strategic outlook and alliance politics of Israel and its neighbors. Adamsky argues that Israel's military superiority and a moment of confidence inspired by the US triumph in the Cold War in fact encouraged the Israelis to give peace talks a chance; by the same token, Soviet retrenchment from the Middle East, and a more evenhanded approach in dealing with Israel and former Soviet clients, served to encourage peace talks, although not, Adamsky points out, to guarantee their success, which was anyway unrelated to superpower relations. The end of the Cold War, in other words, helped to make peace talks possible but it did not bring peace to the Middle East.

In the chapter on the Afghan endgame following the signing of the Geneva Accords in April 1988, Artemy M. Kalinovsky examines the motives, perceptions and tactics of the Soviet Union, the Kabul regime, the US and Pakistan, the Afghan resistance and the UN. Kalinovsky shows why the end of the Cold War did not lead to a satisfactory political settlement in Afghanistan. He accounts for Najibullah's ability to survive for longer than anyone expected through stop-gap political manipulation and pay-offs, but also shows how these tactics did not add up to anything like a lasting solution to the conflict. Kalinovsky highlights growing Soviet impotence to influence events in Afghanistan, and Gorbachev's hopes that the UN might play a constructive role in the settlement. He also examines US policies in Afghanistan, noting the apparent contradiction between the White House's growing disinterest in the region, and the efforts of CIA operatives, alongside Pakistan's intelligence agency, the ISI, to subvert the Kabul regime and see the mujahadeen to their triumph in Afghanistan. Ultimately, the withdrawal of both superpowers from the conflict allowed the local actors to fight it out among themselves in a war that continues to this day.

In Chapter 7 Sergey Radchenko continues the discussion of the Cold War endgame in South Asia with an account of India's foreign policy under the premiership of Rajiv Gandhi. He looks at the reasons why Gandhi, who had set out in November 1984 to reshape India's foreign relations and reassert its central role in a refashioned world order, failed to achieve his aims, and why India, by the late 1980s, found itself not only at odds with its neighbors (with the important exception of an improving relationship with China) but also largely marginalized, internationally, at a time when global realignment of forces and ideas rendered non-alignment old-fashioned and even irrelevant. Rajiv Gandhi never developed anything approaching a grand strategy; he sought to raise India's profile by improving relations with both the US and the Soviet Union. From the US he expected to receive much needed technology to propel India on a course of modernization but he underestimated the degree of Washington's suspicion of India's relationship with the Soviet Union. This relationship, especially as Gorbachev took the reins of power, appeared exceedingly promising in Rajiv's eyes – it was to become the backbone of a new and more equitable international order. Yet he read too much into what, in reality, was a temporary alignment of his and Gorbachev's interests and their personal rapport; true, Gorbachev looked East at the outset of his tenure but, before too long, he turned to the West. Outpaced by events at the end of the Cold War, India entered the 1990s without a clear international strategy, or a clear role to play.

If in South Asia and in the Middle East the end of the Cold War was by no means synonymous with the end of conflict – rather the opposite, in fact – the story was very different for Southeast Asia, as Balázs Szalontai persuasively demonstrates in Chapter 6. According to Szalontai, well before the political settlement of the Cambodian conflict was reached at the Paris conference of 1991, tensions were subsiding in Indochina, as regional actors eyed opportunities for extending economic cooperation. Cambodian leaders, defying Vietnam's suspicions, reached out to Thailand, while Bangkok increasingly opted for lucrative trade deals with the Hun Sen regime to the disadvantage of a long-time client, the Khmer Rouge. Landlocked Laos had launched itself on a path of economic reform, upsetting the Vietnamese. Ultimately, Hanoi, upon inspecting the sad consequences of years of economic mismanagement, embarked on a reform program, the "doi moi," encouraged in this by the glitter of promising opportunities in Southeast Asia, and the radical curtailment of Soviet aid. For Indochina, Szalontai asserts, the winding down of the Cold War meant bringing former enemies from the battlefield and into the marketplace.

This regional metamorphosis, in Szalontai's view, was accomplished for two main reasons. On the one hand, Hanoi was increasingly drawn to emulate the economic experience of its Southeast Asian neighbors. In this respect, Szalontai shares ground with Chen Jian (in terms of their argument that Asian capitalism discredited Soviet-style economic practices in the eyes of the Third World audience) except that Szalontai believes that policy makers in Hanoi looked to Thailand rather than China for inspiration, and this inspiration clearly did not register until the late 1980s, even though the Vietnamese had expressed a strong interest in developing relations with ASEAN at least a decade prior to the end of the Cold War. On the other hand, Soviet pressure on Vietnam to withdraw troops from Cambodia and the drying-up of Soviet economic aid to the region served to erode the basis for Hanoi's relations with the Soviet Union and the countries of Eastern Europe, prompting political and economic reorientation towards ASEAN in Vietnam, as well as in Laos and in Cambodia. This reorientation was facilitated by the abhorrence with which the Vietnamese and (to a lesser extent) the Laotians greeted the political upheaval in Eastern Europe and the Soviet Union.

Three chapters in the book address the under-researched subject of the impact of the end of the Cold War on Latin America. No other chapter is as much at odds with the notion of the ideological bankruptcy of socialism in the Third World as Chapter 8, written by Victor Figueroa Clark. This is, in part, because Figueroa Clark plays down the connections between Soviet-style socialism and the "revolutionary process" in Latin America, which, far from being a Soviet import, reflected indigenous reaction to political and socio-economic inequalities in countries like Chile and Nicaragua, as well as popular dissatisfaction with Washington's heavy-handed meddling and unabated hegemony in the region. The US policy makers, especially during the Reagan Administration, which had an ideological blind spot in this respect, completely misconstrued the nature of Latin

American revolutions, propping up deeply repressive regimes (as in Chile) or reverting to blatant subversion (as in Nicaragua) in an effort to keep the Soviets out, even though, as Figueroa Clark demonstrates, the Soviet influence in the region was as, at best, minimal.

The Cubans, on the other hand, played a more prominent role in the revolutionary process, not least by training cadres for the Sandinistas in Nicaragua, who included not only Nicaraguans but also volunteers from elsewhere in Latin America, especially from Chile. In other words, Figueroa Clark portrays the closing years of the Cold War in the region as a period marked by a collaborative endeavor by the Latin American Left to beat back US hegemonic policies – an endeavor which, he asserts, still continues (it may be added that in crucial respects it predated the Cold War). Figueroa Clark also points out that the Reagan Administration eventually recognized the fallacy of direct subversion and began to promote transition in countries like Chile (to what he calls limited democracy with free market capitalism) and to peace talks in battlegrounds like Nicaragua. As for the Soviet role, like other contributors to this volume (for example, Vladimir Shubin's chapter on southern Africa), Figueroa Clark emphasizes Moscow's support for the aims of the Latin American Left until the end of the Cold War.

In Chapter 9 Duccio Basosi discusses the consequences of the 1982 debt crisis in Latin America, from the perspectives of both the debtor nations and the policy-makers in the White House. Basosi shows that the Reagan Administration's tough stand on debt repayment, even as imposed austerity measures threatened social stability in the economically fragile Latin and South American countries, did not produce a backlash in the form of Soviet penetration of the region. In fact, Moscow failed to capitalize on opportunities presented by the crisis, and US policy makers privately recognized Soviet impotence, even if their public rhetoric remained alarmist to a high degree. The only challenge to US preponderance in Latin America was Fidel Castro, who, with limited success, attempted to rally debt-ridden countries to his banner of anti-imperialism. Basosi explains Reagan's success at maintaining a unipolar order in Latin America not only by overall Soviet weakness and the unappealing sight of the stagnating Soviet economy, but also by the attitudes of the ruling elites in Latin America who, despite domestic difficulties and chafing at Washington's policies, continued to follow the US lead through the 1980s. In that sense, the end of the Cold War in 1989 was anticlimactic for Latin America. There, the Cold War had been won by the US a decade before the fall of the Berlin Wall.

In Chapter 10, Matias Spektor writes about Brazil's response to the end of the global Cold War in 1989. The response, he argues, was not that of euphoria but rather concern with the consequences of a US-led unipolar world for Brazil's ability to maintain its relative economic and political autonomy in the face of the relentless onslaught of triumphant neoliberalism. The military regime that ran the country after 1964 was never tempted by the promise of Soviet-style socialism (quite to the contrary) but, although Brazil was lodged securely within the Western alliance, it kept out of Washington's shadow; for the better part of the Cold War period, Brasilia did what it wanted where it mattered, and often against US resistance (as in the case of Brazil's recognition of Angola). However, by the late 1980s, policy makers in Brasilia, realizing the increasing constraints of a changing world, looked for ways to oppose unilateralism through regional cooperation in South America, by reaching out to other global players, not least the Soviet Union and China. In his succinct analysis, Spektor shows the intellectual roots of Brazil's present-day multipolar diplomacy – roots closely bound up with the challenges and opportunities of 1989. That having been said, Spektor places the end of the Cold War in a broader perspective to argue that for Brazil, the end of the Cold War was anticlimactic. By the late 1980s, there was a firm consensus in Brazil on what constituted a successful path to development and modernization.

The final three chapters in the book concern the end of the Cold War in Africa. In Chapter 11 Vladimir Shubin assesses the Soviet role in the Angolan/Namibian peace settlement (1988), and explores Soviet relations with South Africa in the final years of the Cold War. Shubin argues that the Soviet Union, far from twisting the arms of its allies in Luanda and Havana to force a diplomatic settlement of the conflict when its grand strategy so required, continued to maintain a high level of political and military support for the Angolans until the agreement was reached, at last, to bring hostilities to an end. The African National Congress maintained close relations with Moscow until at least 1989, even as confidential contacts were being set up with the apartheid regime in Pretoria. The ANC knew about some of these Soviet contacts but understood that these were needed to find a way out of the Angolan conflict. In the meantime, until very late in perestroika, the Soviet Union continued to provide overt political and covert support to the ANC. It was only after Gorbachev's foreign policy underwent a radical reorientation in 1989 that Moscow abandoned its erstwhile allies, to the detriment of the ANC's struggle with apartheid. Looking back at the results of Soviet involvement in the conflict in South Africa and its neighborhood, Shubin argues that the Soviet presence was beneficial for the region because of Moscow's consistent opposition to racism and social inequality. The value of Shubin's perspective on the events in southern Africa is underscored by the fact that he is not only a scholar of the region but was an official of the Communist Party of the Soviet Union with responsibility for the countries in question.

In Chapter 12 Chris Saunders argues that, while the end of apartheid was a consequence of internal developments, lessening superpower tensions greatly facilitated a peaceful transfer of power to the ANC. The acceptance, by F. W. de Klerk's, of the ANC and the South African Communist Party as indigenous players rather than proxies for Moscow's regional expansion, paved the way for political dialogue, while the collapse of Soviet socialism encouraged Pretoria to renounce its nuclear program. At the same time, South Africa was coming under US pressure, for now that the Cold War was fading, Washington was increasingly disinclined to support an apartheid regime for the purpose of containing the Communist threat. The fall of the Berlin Wall and events in Eastern Europe, Saunders finds, also contributed to the political settlement in Namibia, not only in the sense of achieving broad peace accords and the withdrawal of South African troops, but also in that the leaders of newly independent Namibia embraced democracy and a market economy as the only plausible socio-political path in the post-Cold War world.

Reading Shubin and Saunders shows the importance of continued research on the subject. Clearly, the two authors disagree on a number of important points, not least with regard to the role the superpowers played in the winding down of the Cold War in southern Africa. Saunders finds that both superpowers positively prodded their allies towards a negotiated settlement once leaders in Moscow and Washington realized that their global interests were no longer in conflict in Africa. "South African officials," writes Saunders, "meeting their Soviet counterparts for the first time [in 1988], found them working for similar goals, for the Soviets put pressure on Cuba and Angola to continue talking and negotiate an agreement." For the ANC and the South African Communist Party, Saunders argues, the fall of Communism in Eastern Europe produced a reorientation away from Soviet-style economic ideology towards free market solutions.

In the final chapter Sue Onslow (with a contribution by Simon Bright), looks at the role the media played in Angolan conflict. One of the integral components of the unraveling of Cold War tensions, and regional power politics in the Third World, was the "battle of images and words." This chapter looks at the debate about the presentation of the story of Cuito Cuanavale in Southern Angola, as an integral part of the military and propaganda war between the South African/UNITA forces, and their Cold War and rival liberation movement antagonists, Cuba, the Soviet Union and the MPLA. It examines the manner in which the global media space was manipulated and exploited by both sides.

Although Onslow's analysis centers on one particular aspect (media coverage) of just one battle in the long-running Angolan conflict, her methodological approach has wider implications. The drama of the Cold War was played out on television screens (consider the role of television in the Vietnam War). Exploitation of the media space was nothing new in the 1980s. But there was something different in the way media was being exploited here: increasing globalization of communications and media allowed hitherto unheard voices to be heard. The story of Simon Bright's brave encounter with besieged Cuito Cuanavale, recounted in Onslow's chapter, is a telling example of how local players consciously sought, and managed, to project their views and agendas to a large international audience. In this respect, media coverage of Cuito Cuanavale was a harbinger of things to come.

This book does not cover every conceivable angle on the end of the Cold War in the Third World. It covers most of the key regions, mostly from the perspective of local and regional players, although Soviet and Chinese Third World policies are also discussed at length. By contrast, while several chapters touch on the US role in the Third World in the 1980s, none offers a thorough treatment of that subject. A few words should be said about the subject here.

For the US, the 1980s were a recovery period from the 1970s and the scars that decade had left. The Vietnam war had divided American society, and the subsequent fall of Saigon had shattered US confidence. The détente practiced by Henry Kissinger under Presidents Nixon and Ford was increasingly under attack from both Republicans and conservative Democrats like Henry "Scoop" Jackson. Meanwhile, the string of Soviet successes across the Third World only seemed to highlight US weakness.[17] The Carter and Reagan administrations were determined to reverse those Soviet advances and to reassert US influence in the Third World.

President Jimmy Carter and his National Security Adviser, Zbigniew Brzezinski, attempted to draw new lines in the sand. Carter and Brzezinski saw Soviet advances in the Third World as a violation of the spirit of détente, a threat to US interests, and, ultimately, a source of instability. The US increased its involvement with very unlikely allies, so long as they could stem Soviet advances. During the Ogaden crisis in 1977, the Carter administration supported socialist Somalia against Soviet-aligned Ethiopia. After the Soviet intervention in Afghanistan, US aid flowed to the mujahadeen and brought Washington close to the dictatorship of Zia ul Haq. In Latin America, and in particular in Central America and the Caribbean, the Reagan administration acted to assert its traditional influence. US aid went to support the right-wing Contras against the democratically elected, and popular, Sandinista government of Nicaragua. It reversed the Carter administration's suspension of aid to the right-wing government of El Salvador, although it did make some attempts to exert pressure on that government about human rights and to stop it from supporting death squads. And in 1983, it launched an invasion of Grenada, where a vaguely socialist government had been in power for several years. US influence was being reasserted with bravado and determination, such that even Congressional opposition to the administration's policies was to be circumscribed: the root of the Iran–Contra scandal.

Military aid to anti-Soviet governments and guerrillas was only one aspect of US involvement in the Third World during the 1980s. Perhaps equally important, by the early 1980s the US had moved away from the New Deal-inspired aid programs that had been prevalent under the Kennedy and Johnson administrations. The neoliberal agenda would now be exported. The Carter administration had tied respect for human rights to extension of US aid, pushing a number of countries to rely, instead, on loans from private commercial banks. The Reagan administration, continuing to speak the language of human rights, nevertheless offered aid to regimes of various stripes. But its aid came with a new twist: countries accepting loans would have to accept the neoliberal prescription in favor with the administration and with the IMF and the World Bank (see Chapter 9).[18]

Many of Reagan's policies had the feeling of a "crusade" because of the emotional commitment he seemed to make and the hyperbolic language he used, either in denouncing Soviet Communism, supporting the "freedom fighters in Afghanistan," or the Contras fighting against the Sandinista government in Nicaragua. Some of his staff members, among them Reagan's first Secretary of State, Alexander Haig, arguably shared this trait. Equally characteristic of the 1980s, however, was that at least some of Reagan's "crusades" were picked up by both parties in Congress, who sometimes pushed US policies further than even the administration had intended. Thus, in the case of Afghanistan, Reagan found, to his chagrin, that his agreement to the Geneva Accords was being attacked by both Democrats and Republicans in Congress, who accused him of selling out the "Freedom Fighters." When the US began taking part in a multilateral effort to end the civil war in Angola, groups like the Heritage Foundation attempted to mobilize support to keep aid flowing to Jonas Savimbi.[19] In this general atmosphere, Reagan found it difficult to collaborate with the Soviet Union on resolving Third World conflicts until he was practically on his way out.

Reagan was succeeded by his Vice President, George H. W. Bush. A technocrat who had served in the course of his career as Ambassador to the UN, Chief of the Liaison Office in the People's Republic of China, and CIA chief, Bush was, in some ways, the anti-Reagan. A pragmatist, he eschewed the rhetorical flourishes that were Reagan's staples. Bush, and his administration, are credited with overseeing the peaceful end of the Cold War, the fall of Communism in Eastern Europe, and the re-unification of Germany, all without gloating or rubbing new US predominance in Gorbachev's face. He refrained from cheering for the nationalist independence movements, to the chagrin of domestic critics.

But even if Bush can be credited with helping to manage a smooth transition in Europe, the administration's record on the Third World is murkier. The domestic coalition of moderates and hard-liners was breaking up, meaning that aid for allies like Savimbi was increasingly difficult to secure.[20] In Afghanistan, the US reduced its aid to the mujahadeen, but failed to play a constructive role, continuing to insist that the Soviet client could not participate in a transition government. In its own back yard, it was largely business as usual, as Bush ordered the invasion of Panama and the overthrow of Manuel Noriega, a one-time US ally who had fallen out of favor. As Jeffrey Engel pointed out in a recent assessment of Bush's foreign policy, "the 41st President believed that democracy was on the march and US force could and should be deployed to help it along where possible."[21]

The administration's biggest foreign involvement, of course, was Operation Desert Storm, launched to push Saddam Hussein's forces out of Kuwait. The US operation was truly evidence that the Cold War had ended. The Soviet Union tried to play the role of mediator with its ally, but when it failed, stepped back and endorsed the US-led operation. The efforts of Gorbachev, veteran Arabist Evgeny Primakov, and other Soviet diplomats, failed to convince Bush to avoid a land war; the compromises they had secured from Hussein were "totally unacceptable" to Bush.[22] It was in this context that Bush declared that humanity stood on the threshold of a "new world order." The entire operation, carried out with relative ease and with minimal casualties for the US military, seemed to highlight the triumph of advanced US technology over the Iraqi military's Soviet weapons. Saddam Hussein's forces were not the only enemy being slain: once again, and as with the Panama invasion, the ghost of Vietnam was itself a target.[23]

Desert Storm has recently been discussed wistfully as an example of the kind of prudent, multilateral leadership that the US was meant to exercise as the sole superpower, and contrasted favorably with the unilateral, divisive policies of the more recent President Bush. But Desert Storm was, arguably, as much a precedent for later US arrogance as for wise leadership. It is clear that although George H. W. Bush sought congressional approval before going to war, he was prepared to launch his operation without it; that although he consulted with the Soviets, and allowed them to try to persuade Hussein to pull back before it was too late, neither he nor his advisers ever doubted that in the end force should and would be used. Moreover, the relatively easy military victory only confirmed the views of those, first in the Clinton and then later in the George W. Bush administration, who thought that the emerging overwhelming US predominance was something that needed to be deployed to assure overwhelming US influence, even in far flung regions of the world.

Today the Cold War is receding into the past, even as so many of its legacies are not only with us but dominate the headlines on a regular basis. At the same time, at least some of the patterns that existed prior to 1989 seem to be re-emerging. China is returning to the Third World in force, with a fat check-book instead of Mao's Little Red Book. Russia is once again becoming a player in Latin America and Africa. Unlikely alliances and associations are being forged between the cats and mice of Cold War times – Shanghai Cooperation Organization and BRIC (Brazil-Russia-India-China) are but two examples. US influence is, thus, being challenged where the idea of a New World Order once rang true. In the Middle East, the relationship between the great powers is uneasy: nominally they are cooperating on issues like containing Iranian nuclear ambitions, but in practice follow different policies, vying for influence and checking each other's moves. But, crucially, the ideological competition, which had offered Third World countries divergent paths to modernity during the Cold War, is no longer in place. And so there is no more "winning" the Third World – just, for the most part, keeping it at bay, with all of its unsolvable problems and nightmare scenarios. The Cold War is history but the chaos and conflict in the Third World which it sometimes caused, often exacerbated and invariably internationalized, will continue to vex international politics for many years to come.

Notes

1 For example, in a public letter to the French President, Francois Mitterand; see Jim Hoagland, "Summit Leaders Vow to Aid East Europe; Declaration Condemns China Crackdown," *Washington Post*, 16 July 1989, p. A1.
2 David Francis, "Soviet, US economists propose joint foreign aid projects," *The Christian Science Monitor*, 30 May 1990, p. 7.
3 John Lewis Gaddis *The Long Peace: inquiries into the history of the Cold War* (New York: Oxford University Press, 1987).
4 For a useful discussion of the various meanings of the term "Third World" see Leslie Wolf-Phillips, "Why 'Third World?': Origin, Definition and Usage," *Third World Quarterly*, Vol. 9, No. 4 (October 1987), pp. 1311–27. Also, Peter Worsley, *The Three Worlds: Culture and World Development* (Chicago, IL: University of Chicago Press, 1984), esp. ch. 5. A more recent effort to tackle the terminology is Louise Fawcett and Yezid Sayigh (eds.), *The Third World beyond the Cold War: Continuity and Change* (Oxford: Oxford University Press, 1999), pp. 5–7, 18–22.
5 Nikita Khruschev's speech to the 20th Party Congress (February 1956). Reproduced in Robert V. Daniels, *A Documentary History of Communism*, Vol. 2 (London: I. B. Tarius & Co., 1986), p. 223.
6 Dean Acheson, *Present at the Creation: My Years in the State Department* (New York: W. W. Norton & Co., 1969), p. 265.
7 For in-depth analysis see Hal Brands, *Latin America's Cold War* (Cambridge, MA: Harvard University Press, 2010). See also a relatively dated but convincing volume, Leslie Bethell and Ian Roxborough (eds.), *Latin America between the Second World War and the Cold War* (Cambridge: Cambridge University Press, 1992).
8 Walt Rostow, *The stages of economic growth: a non-communist manifesto* (Cambridge: Cambridge University Press, 1960). On US development and modernization projects during the Cold War, see Nils Gilman, *Mandarins of the Future: Modernization theory in Cold War America* (Baltimore, MD: John Hopkins University Press, 2003). On the ideology behind modernization theory see Michael Latham, "Ideology, Social Science, and Destiny: Modernization and the Kennedy-Era Alliance for Progress," *Diplomatic History*, Vol. 22, No. 2 (Spring 1998), pp. 199–229 and *Modernization as ideology: American social science and "nation-building" in the Kennedy era* (Chapel Hill, NC: University of North Carolina Press, 2000).
9 See Margot Light (ed.), *Troubled Friendships: Moscow's Third World Ventures* (London: Royal Institute of International Affairs, 1993), pp. 7–9. See also Sergey Mazov, *A Distant Front in the Cold War: The USSR in West Africa and the Congo, 1956–1964* (Washington, DC and Stanford, CA: Woodrow Wilson Center Press and Stanford University Press, 2010).
10 For example, Piero Gliejeses, *Conflicting Missions: Havana, Washington, and Africa* (Chapel Hill, NC: University of North Carolina Press, 2002).

11 Odd Arne Westad, *The Global Cold War: Third World interventions and the making of our times* (Cambridge: Cambridge University Press, 2005).
12 Recent examples include the excellent study on revolutionary Ethiopia, Gebru Tareke, *The Ethiopian revolution: war in the Horn of Africa* (New Haven, CT: Yale University Press, 2009).
13 For an overview of this literature, see Timothy Garton Ash, "1989!" *New York Review of Books*, Vol. 56, No. 17, 16 November 2009.
14 An excellent sample of this literature is Fawcett and Sayigh (eds.), *The Third World beyond the Cold War.*
15 This subject is addressed in greater detail in Chen Jian, "China and the Bandung Conference: Changing Perceptions and Representations," in See Seng Tan and Amitav Acharya (eds.), *Bandung Revisited: A Conference's Legacy and Relevance for International Order* (Singapore: National University of Singapore Press, 2008), pp. 132–59.
16 Christopher Andrew and Vasili Mitrokhin, *The World Was Going Our Way: the KGB and the Battle for the Third World* (New York: Basic Books, 2005).
17 Sean Willentz, *The Age of Reagan: A History, 1974–2008* (New York: Harper Collins, 2008), pp. 48–72; Mario Del Pero, *The Eccentric Realist: Henry Kissinger and American Foreign Policy* (Ithaca, NY: Cornell University Press, 2010), pp. 111–44.
18 David S. Painter, *The Cold War: An International History* (London: Routledge, 2003), p. 101.
19 James M. Scott, *Deciding to Intervene: The Reagan Doctrine and American Foreign Policy* (Durham, NC: Duke University Press, 1996), p. 126.
20 Ibid., 143.
21 Jeffrey Engels, "A Better World ... But Don't Get Carried Away: The Foreign Policy of George H. W. Bush Twenty Years On," *Diplomatic History*, Vol. 34, No. 1 (January 2010), p. 35.
22 Christopher Maynard, *Out of the Shadow: George H. W. Bush and the End of the Cold War* (College Station, TX: Texas A&M University Press, 2008), p. 89.
23 Jeffrey Engels, "A Better World ...," p. 33.

1 Gorbachev and the Third World

Svetlana Savranskaya

Between 1985 and 1991, the Soviet Union retreated voluntarily from its overseas empire, thus ending several decades of competition and confrontation that had been central to the Cold War.[1] In the late 1970s, the Soviet leaders found themselves overextended and overtaxed by the burden of supporting regimes which proclaimed themselves to be socialist-oriented but were mainly economically underdeveloped dictatorships, and by the serious deterioration of relations with the US after the Soviet invasion of Afghanistan. Some retrenchment would be expected after such expansion. However, what actually happened went beyond the imagination of most perceptive analysts – to a complete redefinition of Soviet and then Russian relationships with the developing world. The Soviet Union withdrew from Afghanistan and worked together with the UN and the US to bring peace and national reconciliation to Angola, Ethiopia, Cambodia, and Nicaragua. The Soviets drastically cut their military aid and withdrew almost all military facilities from Vietnam and Cuba. The central arms control relationship with the US and the transformation in Europe lowered the importance of the developing countries for the Soviet Union, at the same time as it could no longer afford the costs of extended commitments.

This chapter does not presume to provide a comprehensive analysis of Third World conflicts at the end of the Cold War, but has a rather limited scope – focusing on Gorbachev and his policies in the Third World using the new evidence available on this topic from Russian archives.[2] Rather than concentrating on the resolution of specific conflicts during the perestroika period, I will try to address the following questions: how did Gorbachev's views about the Third World evolve and where did it fit in his priorities? What did he hope to accomplish in the Third World, what were his strategic goals, and what was he able to accomplish?

Gorbachev's priorities in 1985

One important element to be mentioned from the outset is the lack of knowledge about issues in the Third World with which Gorbachev came to power. Coming from the Stavropol Krai in Southern Russia and serving for most of his time in Moscow as Secretary for Agriculture, Gorbachev was not really aware of all the intricacies of Soviet policy in the Third World, and saw them mostly in the context of the global competition with the US and the ideology of national liberation. At the same time, Gorbachev was a true student and a protégé of Yuri Andropov, who had a keen interest in the Third World as the place where the ultimate competition between the two systems would be decided. Andropov also, as the head of the KGB, knew the real state of the Soviet economy and the burden the allies put on his country. That knowledge and also the experience of the 1970s made Andropov critical of the almost automatic support of Third World regimes which proclaimed themselves Marxist.

Gorbachev's main priorities were domestic economic reform, ending the Cold War, and stopping the arms race, without which reform would be impossible. The main, pressing, issue in the Third World, as he saw it, was the war in Afghanistan, which he called the "bleeding wound" at the 27th Party Congress. Ending the war in Afghanistan was at the top of his list. Gorbachev took his Leninism, if not his Marxism, seriously, constantly going back to Lenin for ideas. As far as the Third World was concerned, he believed both in competition with the US, but also in the self-determination of developing countries. The real change that the "new thinking" contained in this sphere was reducing the role of ideology in international relations and abandoning the goal of building socialism in every possible location. In his presentation to the Politburo on Afghanistan on 13 November 1986 he said:

> We don't seek socialism there. Our objective is to have a friendly neutral neighbor [...] What we don't want is the Americans with their bases. If there are no US air or military bases, they can decide everything else on their own.[3]

Gorbachev's rhetoric on the Third World showed early signs of change, but also continuity with the old policy. At the Warsaw Pact's Political Consultative Committee meeting in Sofia on 22 October 1985, Gorbachev, following the usual ritual of such meetings, devoted a section of his speech to the situation in the Third World, calling on the allies to pay special attention to states of "socialist orientation," putting them into the larger context – "their successes are perceived in the world as confirmation of the ... socialist choice. And to the contrary – their failures are used to discredit it." He mentioned the situation in Angola, Ethiopia and Zimbabwe in the context of the need to help them defend against external aggression, but it was India that drew his attention most, as the biggest country of the Non-Aligned Movement and as a key to building collective security structures in Asia. In a way, his treatment of the developing world was more about security and competition with the US than it was about socialist choice. In the same speech, he mentioned the role of developing countries in the anti-war and anti-imperialist struggle, but not in terms of progress toward socialism, only as far as the arms race was concerned.[4] All in all, Gorbachev was calling for holding Soviet positions but not expanding them, and he gave no encouragement to the idea of world revolution.

Thus, Gorbachev started with a gradual redefinition of Soviet interests – away from supporting Marxist-Leninist regimes and towards cultivating strategic allies in the Third World. There was little new in that approach. It was more in line with the traditional realpolitik views about foreign policy – in other words, capitalist orientation of prospective allies was fine if there were common anti-US grievances. It was very much in line with Andropov's thinking – Gorbachev's mentor talked about cutting costs and avoiding overextension in the Third World – which Gorbachev must have internalized at least to some extent. According to Karen Brutents, deputy head of the International Department of the Central Committee, already under Andropov superpower interests came to the fore of Soviet policy in the Third World, and Brutents connected this development directly to the origins of Gorbachev's "new thinking."[5] This approach meant that now the important countries were not Ethiopia and Mozambique, but India, Argentina, Brazil, Egypt, Iran, and Saudi Arabia. In the Third World the goal became to remove excessive financial obligations and burdens and correct the most outrageous mistakes like Afghanistan. In the beginning of the Gorbachev administration, he basically relied on the same strategy as Andropov would have, just with reduced expenses and scaled down ideological rhetoric. That way, it fitted well with Gorbachev's overarching strategy, which placed domestic reforms at the forefront.

Criticism of Soviet Third World policy before Gorbachev

Already in the 1970s, along with Soviet expansionism in the developing world and especially in Africa, criticism of this policy started to emerge within the Central Committee and in influential research institutes in Moscow. Senior Soviet decision makers, with the important exception of the head of the International Department, Boris Ponomarev, shared a somewhat paternalist approach to the Third World and looked at it as a periphery of world politics.[6] The key Cold War relationship was with the US and NATO. Local situations in the developing countries were often evaluated in terms of class struggle and the competition between the two visions of the future – how many regimes called themselves Marxist, or socialist-oriented. Expectations from such countries were quite primitive – if they followed the socialist model, they could count on Soviet assistance. At the same time, geostrategic considerations were also prominent – Soviet military bases clearly followed Soviet ideas – in Cuba, Vietnam, Angola, Ethiopia – resulting in a sort of socialist colonialism.

The Soviet understanding of détente included freedom of competition in the Third World while stabilizing and improving the central relationship with the US and engaging in arms control. This notion was never accepted by the US, and détente began disintegrating in the late 1970s precisely because of Soviet expansionism in the Third World. As Zbigniew Brzezinski famously said, referring to the war in Somalia, "SALT lies buried in the sands of Ogaden."[7] This fact did not go unnoticed among Soviet foreign policy specialists, and elicited a negative reaction among the more progressive part of the elite. Karen Brutents was especially vocal in his criticism, calling for the reorientation of Soviet Third World policy away from "insignificant" allies to large states with important geostrategic locations – even if they were capitalist-oriented. This approach, obviously, was gaining ground with the Soviet leadership, especially after the invasion of Afghanistan in 1979. In late 1983, Andropov had a long conversation with Brutents about the Third World and asked him to draft a memo about a new approach to the developing world.[8] People like Georgii Mirskii and Kiva Maidanik at Moscow's Institute of World Economy and International Relations (Russian acronym: IMEMO) argued that the Soviet Union should stop being a hostage to irresponsible leaders proclaiming themselves Marxist, who were becoming dependent on bigger and bigger subsidies from the Soviet Union.[9] It was understood among Soviet Third World watchers that the attractive power of the socialist idea had begun to grow dull. Most often, the socialist-oriented regimes were poorer and less developed than their neighbors, and often could not feed their own citizens, which made them appeal for more Soviet aid in return for ideological purity and support for the Soviet Union at the UN. No wonder there were anti-Communist rebels in almost all of those countries. Something had to be done.

A fresh start in Soviet policy to the Third World, 1985–1987

As mentioned above, Gorbachev came to power with very little exposure to the Third World, and no particular strategy other than the general Andropovian approach. However, over the first two years of his tenure, he developed a more systematic policy guided by a coherent set of ideas, which, however, he did not have time to implement fully. Gorbachev's early Third World policy was driven by anti-imperialism and the spirit of competitiveness, and by the need to revive the appeal of socialism.

As in many other spheres of foreign policy, Gorbachev wanted a new start which would invigorate Soviet foreign policy and benefit domestic reform. The new policy was designed to be proactive; in no way did it envision a retreat from established geopolitical gains like Angola or Mozambique. It was decided to make a new breakthrough in relations with Latin America, create new security structures in Asia in partnership with India, improve relations with China, and keep supporting Cuba, Nicaragua,

Vietnam and most important revolutionary regimes in Africa. In one important initiative, Eduard Shevardnadze traveled alone to Brazil, Argentina and Uruguay in 1987 in preparation for a Gorbachev visit to Latin America. His predecessor, the formidable Foreign Minister Andrei Gromyko, had never visited Latin America. Central America was seen as especially important both strategically and politically – strong leftist movements right at the back door of the US. The Soviet Union was not going to abandon Cuba and Nicaragua, and in fact it increased its assistance to Nicaragua in 1985 by 40 percent and, initially, the decision was made to supply MiG fighter planes and other military equipment to fight the US-backed Contras, as a measure countering US trade embargo against Nicaragua.[10]

From the start, India became one of the most important countries for Gorbachev. He envisioned a strong partnership with India based on a commonality of problems and aspirations. He saw an overriding need for the two countries to ensure peaceful conditions for internal modernization, which would not be undermined by the drain of an arms race. Gorbachev believed that this relationship "became one of the generators of those ideas, which constitute the 'theoretical skeleton' of the new world order."[11] India held a special appeal as the leader of Non-Aligned Movement, as the country with a strong tradition of good friendly relations with the Soviet Union. Gorbachev found an ideal partner in Rajiv Gandhi – a young reformist leader with global aspirations, who came to power not much earlier than Gorbachev himself. As in many bilateral settings, the personal communication and chemistry were crucially important for Gorbachev, the ability to talk openly and sincerely about domestic and global problems was the key to success in any joint endeavor. Pavel Palazchenko noted that "Gorbachev found it much easier to talk with Gandhi than with Reagan or some other leaders. Their rapport was total and their discussions were genuinely frank."[12] Rajiv Gandhi, who made his first foreign trip as Prime Minister to Moscow, became an important peer for the Soviet leader. One can understand many of Gorbachev's views and hopes for the Third World by reading memoranda of his conversations with the Indian leader available at the Gorbachev Foundation in Moscow.

In May 1985, during Rajiv Gandhi's visit to Moscow, Gorbachev emphasized the common interests of all countries and peoples in questions of war and peace. Those interests would allow us "to create some sort of common front of pressure on the American imperialism and its allies in order to induce it to engage in genuine negotiations." Gorbachev proposed countering US military expansion in Asia by constructing a new security system for the continent, along the lines of the European security system, creating a zone of peace in the Indian Ocean. He also noted great prospects for Soviet–Indian economic cooperation and trade.[13] It was an energetic and ambitious conversation, very characteristic of early Gorbachev policy in the Third World. Gorbachev's arguments were quite anti-American, and sounded like a call for bringing India closer to the Soviet side of the Cold War, and building a separate regional security system. During the visit, the Soviet and Indian leaders signed several agreements on trade, economic and scientific-technological cooperation for the period to 1990, and on building several big industrial enterprises in India. Gorbachev gave his full public support to the initiative of six non-aligned countries – India, Argentina, Greece, Mexico, Tanzania, and Sweden – calling for a comprehensive ban on nuclear testing, production and deployment of nuclear weapons and delivery means, prevention of an arms race in space, and signing of a treaty banning nuclear weapons. While this initiative was hailed in the Soviet Union, Gorbachev lamented that it was completely ignored by the US.[14]

Another strong theme in Gorbachev's rhetoric about Third World countries was the unequal trade and economic relations between them and capitalist countries, and the exploitation of the developing world. Gorbachev developed this theme in June 1986 with Indian Foreign Minister Shiv Shankar, when they touched, specifically, on the US policy of robbing developing countries and the need to fight it globally. This theme was not just invented by the Soviets; in fact, in the mid-1980s, it was one of the major issues raised by developing countries in international organizations.

The strong connection to India and its new leadership manifested itself most significantly during Gorbachev's visit to India in November 1986, after the Reykjavik summit with Ronald Reagan. During this visit, Gorbachev and Gandhi signed the Delhi Declaration on a nuclear-free world, another set of trade agreements, and Gorbachev spoke to the Indian parliament. The Delhi Declaration can be seen as an early declaration of "new thinking," which included emphasis on universal human values, calls to abolish nuclear weapons by the year 2000, and to replace the "equilibrium of fear" with comprehensive international security based on non-violence.[15] The Soviet leader's speeches and conversations in Delhi sounded like he was trying to appeal to the world, over the head of Ronald Reagan, to put an end to the arms race.[16] The failure to reach an agreement in Reykjavik was very close to Gorbachev's heart, and he shared his frustration with the US in his conversations with the Indians while also hoping that developing Asian countries would respond to his call against the arms race. Unfortunately, by now the Reagan administration was preoccupied with the Iran–Contra scandal and nobody there heard Gorbachev's appeal from Delhi.

Argentina was another priority ally, with its strong Communist Party, strong economy and large population. In his meetings with General Secretary Athos Fava, Gorbachev agreed that reinvigoration of the Communist movement was necessary and the Latin American Communists represented a large potential force in the movement. In Gorbachev's view, one particularly important forum for discussion of the experience and the future of the movement would be the gathering of representatives of all Communist and left parties in Moscow to celebrate the 70th anniversary of the Great October Revolution, in the fall of 1987.[17] At the meeting itself, attended by 187 delegations from Communist, socialist and green parties, Gorbachev spoke at length about the need for the left movements to unite on the basis of universal human values, which did not help to clarify what the new goals of the movement were.

As exemplified in the Soviet–Indian conversations, beginning in 1986, the Soviets embarked on a search for a new strategy in the Third World. This strategy was still very competitive and anti-imperialist, but it no longer had the ideological underpinnings of the previous 40 years. As in the case with India, many new initiatives were announced in relation to particular countries, but there were real economic limits to their implementation. The change was not immediate, as Gorbachev himself was learning and changing his own views of the Third World in the process. And there were also political constraints on him, just as there were in other spheres of policy, so he had to move gradually, looking over his shoulder. In 1986, the old cadres still dominated the Central Committee, and Gorbachev had to be careful not to look as if he was abandoning Third World allies. He was especially sensitive to such charges about Cuba, Vietnam and Angola. At the same time, where he could cut assistance without bearing direct political cost, he started doing it in a rather cold-blooded fashion.[18]

As was the tradition, new policy directions were outlined at party congresses. At the 27th Party Congress, in late February 1986, Gorbachev gave surprisingly little attention to the developing world, which usually occupied a lengthy section filled with ideological jargon about gains of socialist-oriented regimes and the progress of the "national liberation struggle" in earlier congresses, in especially stark contrast with the last, 26th Party Congress in 1981. The General Secretary's report to the congress hardly mentioned the "national liberation movement," but instead used a new term – "regional conflicts." Gorbachev's speechwriter and adviser, Andrei Grachev, puts the main responsibility for this shift in the speech on Alexander Yakovlev, who drafted Gorbachev's report.[19] Rather than expanding on the ideological substance of each of the conflicts and how each was tied into the global conflict between Communism and imperialism, the Soviet leader spoke about the need to resolve them. At the same Congress, Gorbachev spoke about ending the war in Afghanistan as his top priority, and called the war "the bleeding wound." While this change in terminology and emphasis was overlooked by the Soviet public, it was quickly noticed by observers both at home and in the West, such as Francis Fukuyama in his 1986 article in *Foreign Affairs.*[20]

In his conversation with Fidel Castro during the 27th Party Congress, on 2 March, Gorbachev discussed the role that the Soviet Communist Party should play in the International Communist movement. Castro encouraged Gorbachev to preserve and strengthen the CPSU role as the leader in the global revolutionary movement. To the Soviet leader's question on how he saw the Soviet role, Castro replied that he disagreed with the Comintern methods, when the CPSU commanded the Communist movement like an army, but that now the Soviet Union could be a genuine "moral leader, political leader, ideological leader," on Leninist principles, and that, in fact, it "is the leader of the revolutionary movement whether you want it or not."[21] From the conversation, one could see that Gorbachev shared Castro's view at the time, and did not intend to abandon the movement. He believed in the Leninist principles, and was hoping to make them more cost-effective. The Soviet leader quoted Castro regarding the objective and unavoidable leadership role at a Central Committee conference on the results of the 27th Party Congress on 10 March 1986 and stressed the need for the CPSU to lead by example. Gorbachev was calling for a "soft power" approach.

This change of tone was persistent in several of the post-Congress Politburo sessions. Gorbachev spoke about the Third World quite often and, one could even say, enthusiastically. The main theme was the need to reinvigorate and make more dynamic Soviet relations with developing countries, and to create some order of priorities, so that the Third World allies would not be a drain on the Soviet economy but real promoters of Soviet interests and ideals globally. Gorbachev repeatedly emphasized the need to develop a new Soviet strategy towards the Third World. Often, discussions of Third World issues were accompanied by strong anti-imperialist rhetoric and competitive tones, showing that the Soviets did not intend to lose to the West in the competition in the developing world. At a Politburo session on 15 May 1986, Gorbachev asked the new head of the International Department Anatolii Dobrynin to write a report on the real situation in the International Communist movement – "not a routine one like under Ponomarev, but a sincere one and such that everything would become absolutely clear."[22]

The months of May and June 1986 were crucial for the Soviet reassessment of commitments in the Third World. At the end of May, at a discussion of Third World indebtedness to the Soviet Union, Gorbachev told his colleagues, "We need to outline the stages in our relations with the Third World, and to calculate precisely, where our presence is justified and where it is not."[23] He made a strong statement on Third World policy in his speech to the Ministry of Foreign Affairs on 28 May 1986 – the Soviet Union needed to develop a new strategy to "unblock" regional conflicts, make its policy in this direction more dynamic, but also to "calculate all the pluses and minuses of economic assistance to the developing countries and to bring them in synch with our capabilities and political motives."[24] In June 1986, Gorbachev asked the Politburo and several ministries to focus on the situation in the socialist camp, to prepare a detailed and realistic analysis of the situation, and called for a development of a new strategy toward socialist allies as well.

The Middle East was an especially important region where Gorbachev wanted Soviet influence to be extended. Some of the Soviet policy toward the region was quite controversial and inconsistent – trying to keep old allies as long as possible, but really embarking on new relations with big conservative countries like Saudi Arabia to the detriment of established radical allies like Syria and Libya. On 28 May 1986 Gorbachev met with Syrian Foreign Minister Abdel Halim Haddam. The Soviet leader praised the Soviet–Syrian military cooperation, mentioning that "it is no longer limited to just supplies of new types of weaponry, but encompasses also improvements in management and automatization." He mentioned that the future could bring on some trials and challenges for the Soviet–Syrian relationship, but expressed his hope that those would be resolved in the prevailing "atmosphere of trust."[25] In the same conversation he spoke critically about the Palestinian leader Yasser Arafat, and asked the Syrian leader not to allow events in the Middle East to get to the state of another military conflict.

In one of more unusual discussions of the Middle East at the Politburo on 11 July 1986 the Deputy Foreign Minister in charge of the Middle East, Iulii Vorontsov, presented a draft of new Soviet positions on the Middle East – to include all five representatives of the UN Security Council in the Middle Eastern mediation, and to convene an international conference on the Middle East. The most radical proposal mentioned by Vorontsov was that the Soviet Union might give up the idea of an independent Palestinian state if it was necessary for a peaceful settlement in the region. In the discussion of the new proposals, Gromyko spoke strongly against giving up the demand for a Palestinian state, but Shevardnadze supported Vorontsov. Gorbachev weighed in by removing this proposal from the text of the draft and suggested that the Politburo "take Vorontsov's ideas just as a basis for consultations at this time. Because otherwise we can blow up the previous policy and not get anything in exchange … And this is not for the public statement."[26] This and other discussions show Gorbachev and his closest allies speaking negatively and condescendingly about Yasser Arafat and other pro-Soviet Arab leaders, emphasizing the need to reorient Soviet policy towards more significant states like Egypt, Saudi Arabia and Iran.

However, as the year wore on, Gorbachev found himself bogged down in the Afghanistan quagmire, unable to deliver on many of the promises he made regarding expansion of trade relations, and limited in his impact in the developing world. At the same time, in 1987, the only sphere in which Gorbachev was able to deliver on expectations, and where "new thinking" actually brought some dividends, was the arms control relationship with the US. In 1987, one saw hesitation in his pronouncements on Third World issues – still ardent desire not to retreat or make concessions, but slow realization of the inability to actually pursue the ambitious policy in the developing world. In late March 1987, during his meeting with the Foreign Ministers of socialist countries, Gorbachev called for persistence in the Third World: "If we lose Mozambique, if we lose in Ethiopia,

Angola, then we will lose Africa. ... We cannot afford to lose. Even if we cannot move decisively ahead, we still can and should keep what we already have."[27] This was a watershed realization – we cannot move decisively ahead, but we should keep what we already have. Very soon, even that priority would be replaced by the overriding desire to resolve regional conflicts in cooperation with the US.

In the summer of 1987 the Soviets generally adhered to the line of support and strengthening – with all available means – the regimes in Ethiopia, Mozambique, Angola, Zimbabwe and other countries while disengaging ideologically and toning down the rhetoric of the socialist choice. A similar policy prevailed in Afghanistan, too – trying to strengthen the regime, applying a technocratic non-ideological approach, while preparing for the eventual withdrawal of troops. But apparently, economic factors were becoming more pressing. Gorbachev called several times for a comprehensive overview of Soviet Third World policy, and finally, in October 1987, the International Department prepared an extensive memorandum with a review of the issues of economic effectiveness of cooperation with developing countries. The memo, prepared by Brutents, listed the existing shortcomings in economic cooperation with developing countries and argued that the "economic situation of our partners is worsening, the competitive pressure of western countries is growing, and in this connection, the tendency to see the solution in developing cooperation with the latter [is growing too]."[28]

In December 1987, Gorbachev and Reagan signed the INF treaty in Washington at the peak of US–Soviet arms control cooperation. In their conversations they touched upon Third World issues as the main impediment to further progress in arms control and bilateral relations. These two factors – limits of economic leverage and the linkage to US–Soviet relations – meant that the Soviet policy towards the Third World was about to change.

Reassessment of commitments and change of policy in 1988–1991

In 1988 Soviet Third World policy entered a new stage with distinct characteristics. The initial stage of competitiveness with the US seemed to be over, anti-US and anti-imperialist rhetoric had almost disappeared, and the main focus was on the resolution of local conflicts in cooperation with the US, applying the model of national reconciliation to each conflict. Soviet analysis and rhetoric now emphasized the local roots of every conflict and rejected class-based or even superpower interest-based descriptions of conflicts. Instead of class interests, Soviet leaders now spoke of broader interests – building new cooperative international security in close interaction with the US. As Brutents described the turn,

> the USSR undertook reorientation of all its relationships with the Third World [...] radically curtailing everything that in the past was

> dictated by ideological or superpower considerations. [...] The sign of the times was the rejection of military engagement in the Third World, the course toward resolution of regional conflicts set in the context of ending the confrontation with the United States."[29]

This disengagement meant withdrawal from bases which made little strategic sense in the absence of superpower conflict and were expensive to keep. It meant ending support for opposing factions in local conflicts.

Of course, the importance of Third World countries for the Soviet leadership became very low as a result, they mattered only as long as those regional conflicts were being resolved and only to the extent that they affected the central relationship. Now the priority for ambassadors and foreign ministry officials was to put an end to the conflicts above all else. Deputy Foreign Minister Anatolii Adamishin described the instructions he received from Gorbachev and Shevardnadze:

> I was told to "assure the smooth progress of Namibia towards its independence on the basis of cooperation with the West, put an end to the civil war in Angola, and establish constructive dialogue with South Africa in order to assist the process of ending the apartheid." It was not an easy assignment since on the one hand we had to get the Cubans out of Africa as they no longer had anything to do there. On the other, I had problems convincing the Americans that our talk about ending confrontation was serious and had to reassure the South Africans, explaining that we had no intention of dragging Communism to their part of the world and that we were absolutely inclined to let them choose their own way of life.[30]

What was important was that similar discussions were happening not only at the top echelon of the policymaking community, but in institutes, mass media – practically in the street. In August 1988 the future Russian Foreign Minister, Andrei Kozyrev wrote in an influential foreign policy magazine:

> The myth that the class interests of socialist and developing countries coincide in resisting imperialism does not hold up to criticism at all, first of all because the majority of developing countries already adhere to or tend toward the Western model of development, and second, because they suffer not so much from capitalism but from a lack of it.[31]

What is most fascinating in the records of conversations between Soviet and Third World leaders of that period is the practically complete disappearance of the language of competition. The main principles mentioned often were freedom of choice (self-determination) and national reconciliation involving all local parties in the political process without outside arms supplied to any of the factions. This approach worked for most regional conflicts, especially where the US provided real support for reconciliation, but resulted in growing domestic opposition to Gorbachev's policy. Some turnarounds in the late 1980s were quite unexpected and costly.

In April 1988 Gorbachev signed the Geneva Accords on Afghanistan and the withdrawal of Soviet troops began in May. The Geneva Accords meant that the US would be the Soviet partner in bringing the conflict to an end, however, the US continued to supply money and arms to the Afghan mujahadeen through Pakistan. Nevertheless, the Soviet model of national reconciliation was moderately successful – the Najibullah regime stayed in power even after Soviet troops left. Withdrawal was accomplished ahead of schedule notwithstanding Najibullah's pleading for help and the warnings of the regime's impending collapse, and even the domestic opposition to the fast withdrawal expressed by none other than Foreign Minister Shevardnadze himself.[32]

Two important examples of breakthroughs in the Middle East after 1988 were the development of cooperation with Iran and the Persian Gulf War where the Soviet Union decided to support the US against its own former ally.

Even though the Soviet Union never openly supported either side in the Iran–Iraq war, Iraq was the recipient of Soviet military equipment, and many Soviet specialists worked there on contracts in military and civilian industries. From 1986, Gorbachev was trying to reach out to Iran, realizing that it was the most strategically important country in the region. Starting in 1988, contacts with Iran grew substantially, including cooperation on building nuclear power stations. There was a proliferation of Iranian visits to Moscow. Just in 1989, the following meetings took place: in January, Gorbachev met with Javadi-Amoli (personal representative of Imam Khomeini), and in March the Politburo discussed the question of sales of "special equipment" to Iran. In March, Gorbachev met with Foreign Minister Ali Akbar Velayati, and in June, Gorbachev met for two days with soon-to-be President of Iran Akbar Hashemi Rafsanjani. In the last meeting, the two specifically discussed cooperation in building reactors. The Iranian complained that many Western firms had canceled contracts, and then directly told the Soviet leader that now the Iranians would prefer cooperation with the Soviets. When he asked Gorbachev for assistance in building a nuclear power station, the Soviet leader responded simply: "*khorosho.*"[33]

The ultimate expression of change and the puzzle of the Soviet policy in the Middle East was the US–Soviet cooperation in the Gulf War. To make the initial decision to denounce Saddam Hussein's invasion of Kuwait in early August 1990, Gorbachev and Shevardnadze had to effectively isolate themselves from the Politburo. This decision was especially important because eventually the chain of events led to the use of force against Iraq – something that Gorbachev declined to do in his foreign policy as a matter of principle. The Gulf War and other cases, where cooperation with the US meant abandoning former allies, cost Gorbachev a lot – economically and in terms of his political standing at home. Supporting the US in the Middle East had some real hard currency costs. According to the Defense Ministry and the Ministry of Foreign Affairs, the Soviet Union lost $2.1 billion annually in forfeited arms sales to Iraq and $0.6 billion annually as a result of supporting US sanctions against Libya.[34]

The bulk of Soviet aid went to Cuba and Vietnam – and that relationship began changing quite soon. In both cases direct aid and trade were cut and in the case of Vietnam, Gorbachev kept telling his Vietnamese visitors not to hurry in building socialism. Just in terms of "special equipment" supplies, the Soviet Union provided Vietnam with 2,202.8 million rubles worth of equipment in 1986–1990, but was planning to provide only 199.8 million rubles in 1991; and for Cuba it was 3,866.4 and 467 million rubles respectively.[35]

In his conversation with the General Secretary of the Vietnamese Communist Party Nguyen Van Linh, on 3 May 1989, Gorbachev talked about the need for economic reform along the lines of Lenin's new economic policy. On Cambodia, they spoke about the need for genuine national reconciliation and stopping outside weapon supplies. Earlier, the Vietnamese agreed, under Soviet pressure, to complete withdrawal of their troops from Cambodia by October 1989, and they abided by their promise. In the same conversation, the Vietnamese leader expressed his real concern for the fate of socialism globally and asked the Soviet Union not to abandon it. He also expressed concern for the events in Eastern Europe, especially Poland and Hungary. In response, Gorbachev mentioned his conversation with Castro, his faith in socialism, but also in freedom of choice and radical economic reform.[36]

Latin America, with its strong tradition of anti-imperialist and indigenous Communist movements was one of Gorbachev's early hopes, but by 1988, policy there was dominated by the issues of Central American reconciliation and the pressure from the US regarding the Cuban role in Nicaragua and El Salvador. As was characteristic of Gorbachev in foreign policy, he found some leaders especially close to his point of view and enjoyed quite sincere discussions with them. Rodney Arismendi, General Secretary of the Communist Party of Uruguay, was one such peer who shared Gorbachev's views on the abolition of nuclear weapons. In his conversation with Gorbachev on 29 April 1988, Arismendi addressed the need for changes in the International Communist movement and presented the struggle for peace and nuclear disarmament as the key goal of the movement – an argument that fitted precisely with Gorbachev's priorities at the time.[37]

Cuba was a difficult but very important ally for Gorbachev. It was the most important ally in Latin America, but still in 1985–1987 trade was cut by about 15 percent and the price of oil and sugar cane approached the world level – the shift to economic priorities was noticeable. Castro was uneasy and critical of perestroika and weary of abandoning positions internationally. His version of the reform Cuba needed was rectification – almost the opposite of what Gorbachev was trying to do. And yet, Gorbachev had a great respect for the Cuban leader, and sincerely wanted to engage him in reconciliation efforts in Latin America and Africa. It was not easy for Gorbachev to tell Castro that Soviet commitments around the globe were being reviewed, so he used competitive and ideological rhetoric while speaking with him longer than with other world leaders. One could sense Gorbachev's unease in a telephone conversation with Castro on 5 April 1988. The bulk of the conversation was devoted to Soviet–Cuban cooperation in support of progressive regimes in Africa soon after Castro made a major military commitment to Angola. In response to a letter from Fidel expressing concern about perestroika and abandoning positions in Africa, Gorbachev said, somewhat defensively,

> I received your big letter – your very important and sincere letter. Frankly speaking, it made me worried. My first impulse was to immediately write to you – Fidel – everything is good between us. [...] You and we have a common concern – the progressive regimes in Africa. I have in mind Angola, Ethiopia, Mozambique. We need to do everything to hold them. It is not an easy task, but we need to act in such a way that the imperialists would not be able to make a comeback. Taking into account the fact that there are also Algeria and Libya in the north of Africa, and to the south we have the People's Republic of Southern Yemen and Madagascar, our base [platsdarm] is quite impressive. By holding that [territory] we will be able to project influence on the whole of Africa. The imperialists understand the importance of those regimes and of their strengthening.[38]

Gorbachev's advisers, especially Cherniaev, were very critical of Castro. Cherniaev tried to delay Gorbachev's planned visit to Cuba and probably suspected that Castro had influence on Gorbachev and found that influence disagreeable. On 15 January 1989 Cherniaev summarized his view of Castro in his diary the following way: "the Beard has destroyed his own revolution and now is trying to destroy his country."[39]

However, Gorbachev did go to Cuba in April 1989 and the visit became a significant breakthrough on Central America and probably started Cuba's turn away from the support of revolutionary movements around the globe. The series of most fascinating conversations, very different in tone and substance from the earlier conversations on record, took place on 3–5 April 1989 during Gorbachev's visit to Cuba, just before his visit to London. The first one-on-one session was tense and uncomfortable for Gorbachev, as he reported to the Politburo, but the second and subsequent sessions became an open deep discussion of domestic economy, political reform, US–Soviet relations and Nicaragua.[40]

A large portion of the conversation was devoted to the US, the Bush "pause," as the period of reassessment of the US policy toward the Soviet Union was called, and how it was hurting the progress of arms control. But then, as the trust started to build between the Soviet and the Cuban leaders, Gorbachev shared the text of Bush's letter dealing with Central America and US–Cuban relations with Castro. In this conversation, Castro essentially asked Gorbachev to act as a channel between him and Bush (and Thatcher, since the Soviet leader was on his way to London) for improving relations with the US, and for resolving the conflict in Central America. The most important part dealt with Nicaragua. Gorbachev suggested that Cuba should announce that it would stop supplying weapons to Nicaragua and El Salvador and support the Contadora Group. Castro agreed with the idea and suggested that he would even stop sending advisers. Castro recommended that instead of going public with these proposals, Gorbachev should outline them in a personal letter to Bush, in response to his earlier letter. Over the two days, Gorbachev and Castro developed a tentative plan of national reconciliation for Nicaragua – by that time the Soviets had practically stopped weapon supplies. The plan – Cuba would announce an end to weapon supplies, the US would become a guarantor of no outside supplies of weapons to warring parties, and all three parties would express their support for a democratic election in Nicaragua – worked in its main details, and free elections took place in Nicaragua in February 1990.

Role of advisers and domestic politics

As mentioned earlier, Gorbachev did not come to power with strong views about the Third World. However, he was an eager if unsystematic learner and relied on a rather narrow circle of advisers and allies who shared his overall goals and ideals about ending the Cold War and reforming the international system. Most important of those were Alexander Yakovlev, Anatolii Cherniaev, Vadim Zagladin, Georgii Shakhnazarov and Karen Brutents – the last four coming from the International Department of the Central Committee – the department which had primary responsibility for relations with Communist parties in capitalist and developing countries. These individuals had tremendous experience of and expertise on the Third World. What connected these people was their unorthodox views and hope for change even in the years of stagnation. Brutents was one of the main critics of Soviet Third World policies in the 1970s and one of the minds behind the reassessments of the ideological commitments. They also carried institutional memory, since most of them were working in the department in the late 1970s and then under Andropov, when the most interesting debates about the Soviet role in the Third World were taking place.[41] As early as the late 1970s they believed that Soviet policy in the Third World should be more pragmatic, that it should be based on national interest and economic benefit rather than ideology.

The International Department provided Gorbachev with a constant flow of criticism of existing Third World policy. It gave Gorbachev both a reality check and a tone check on his policies, especially after Anatolii Dobrynin replaced Boris Ponomarev as head of the department in the spring of 1986. A former Ambassador to the US, he understood better than others how detrimental Third World involvements could be to the most important relationship the Soviet Union now had and how they had already derailed détente in the 1970s. New thinking in the Third World could save money for the Soviet Union, save lives in developing countries, and produce real dividends in the superpower relationship.

These advisers wrote bold notes warning Gorbachev not to take steps that would contradict his own "new thinking," especially when they sensed that their boss did not feel comfortable with some of the leaders involved or might be influenced by them and unable to say "no." They found ways to speak to him in public and in private calling attention to how adherence to the old dogma might undermine his public standing. For example, Cherniaev, as noted above, was trying to delay or even prevent Gorbachev from meeting with Castro, and regularly sent his boss memos warning him about what his Cuban ally was up to. He was quite critical of Castro's internal "rectification" campaign and his generally suspicious attitude to perestroika. Loyal and sensitive to his boss's feelings, Cherniaev was probably concerned that Castro would be able to influence Gorbachev and either get him to commit to some reckless act in Africa or to tone down his decisiveness to disengage from conflicts there. At the Politburo meeting on 15 January 1989, Cherniaev argued strongly against the visit to Cuba, about which he wrote in his diary:

> [Castro] will not stop in his demagoguery about orthodox Marxism-Leninism and going "to the end;" since this is the last thing he can use to preserve his "revolutionary halo." But this halo is already a myth ... Nobody reckons with Cuba in South America, it is no longer setting any kind of example. The Cuban factor has waned.[42]

This influence of liberal advisers also helped to counteract the pressure of the Soviet military-industrial complex to continue and expand military and economic aid to developing countries. The interests of the uniformed military and the military-industrial complex remained strong and followed the old patterns many years into perestroika. Defense was a sacred cow in the Soviet Union under Brezhnev, and so was the slogan of proletarian internationalism, which obliged the Soviet Union to come to the aid of revolutionary regimes in danger or facing imperialist aggression. Resistance to the new policies of cutting unnecessary obligations was quite powerful also because the flow of military assistance and the leverage that went with it gave a much desired superpower identity to the military and made it possible for them to be posted abroad. Naturally, it was in their interest to produce more weapons to sell, and ideology was a useful tool to justify those priorities. When leaders' attention was focused on other issues, the military kept pressing the Politburo to grant requests from "socialist-oriented" states for more military equipment, like the constant requests from Afghanistan, Nicaragua and Ethiopia. Sometimes, it took strong interference from advisers combined with support from other Politburo members to push back on such proposals as in the case with Ethiopia's Haile Mariam Mengistu's requests described by Cherniaev in his diary. He wrote a memorandum arguing against sending additional weapons to Ethiopia on 1 April 1988, pointing Gorbachev to his own duplicity – talking about the need to resolve regional conflicts to the Politburo and at the same time as soon as a "friend" was asking, rushing to fulfill his requests. "Our weapons will not change anything, and this aid would push Mengistu even more toward a hopeless affair – to try to solve everything military force."[43]

There was a certain pattern that was becoming more visible in 1989 – the advisers persistently "intercepted" such requests from the military and then drew Gorbachev's attention to the profound contradictions between continuing to supply weapons to the Third World and the expressed goals of the "new political thinking." These themes were raised in a memo by Shakhnazarov on 28 July 1988 regarding a request from the military for more assistance to Cuba: "I would like to call your attention to the memo on the issue of strengthening our military assistance to Cuba. I think that the proposed solutions do not fit our new thinking in the world arena."[44] Another example of this is a memo written together by Shakhnazarov and Cherniaev, which starts with "the contradiction between our international policy and the practice of export of Soviet weapons is becoming more shocking". The memo argued strongly against continuing weapon sales to the self-proclaimed socialist-oriented allies.[45] And in Zagladin's memo of 24 January 1989, he reminded the General Secretary of the fact that if democratic principles are to be implemented, the Soviet parliament should consider the issues of military assistance after a careful and comprehensive review of all obligations the Soviet Union assumed so far:

> We need to review all our existing obligations on military assistance to foreign countries. We undertook extensive obligations over time, which now, if we had to act upon them, could undermine and even throw back everything that had been achieved in terms of perestroika in the entire international system [...] In the future, any commitments regarding military assistance should be approved by the Supreme Soviet.[46]

Not just military assistance, but even preparation of military officers in Soviet military academies was called into question. Cherniaev on 16 August

1991 wrote to Gorbachev about students from the African National Congress describing such assistance as an unnecessary burden for the Soviet Union. "Since 1964 we prepared 1,500 officers for the ANC, 44 are still studying," what should be done with them? Cherniaev argued for the need to minimize this kind of assistance in the future.[47]

Very often these memoranda made an explicit connection between Soviet pronouncements or policies on a certain Third World issue and the harm they could do to US–Soviet relationship. Cherniaev especially felt that the most important global issues were being decided in the US–Soviet dialog and acted protectively of this relationship while pushing Third World issues away from Gorbachev's schedule or downgrading their importance. Thus, in a way, the advisers as a group kept Gorbachev focused and consistent with his "new thinking" even when he was under pressure from the domestic conservatives or demanding "socialist-oriented" allies.

Interaction with foreign leaders and policy change

Some observers have noted that many of the changes in Soviet policy towards the Third World were implemented in connection with negotiations with the US if not under direct pressure from them, Cuba and Nicaragua being the two most obvious cases. Evidence supports a slightly more nuanced explanation – interaction with people whom he considered his partners was one of the main, if not the main factor of change in Gorbachev's views and subsequently policies on the Third World. That included the advisers discussed above but it was especially his interaction with leaders of democratic western countries, who were his main partners in arms control. Gorbachev believed in his own ability to persuade his interlocutor, but documents show that he also responded to persuasion and exhibited a surprising capacity for empathy unusual for a Communist apparatchik. He took his partners' views seriously and devoted a lot of thought and subsequent discussion to what was said in those conversations. Personal chemistry and trust mattered a lot.

British Prime Minister Margaret Thatcher was the one who claimed to have "discovered" Gorbachev and announced to the outside world that he was the one with whom she could do business. She became an early important influence on his thinking about the Third World. In April 1987, when Thatcher visited Moscow, she accused her Soviet counterpart of spreading revolution around the world, striving for Communist domination. It was quite an emotional speech:

> The Soviet Union follows the doctrine of global dominance of Communism, the Brezhnev Doctrine. [...] we see the aspiration of Communism to dominate everywhere. Take for example Yemen, Ethiopia, Mozambique, Angola, Nicaragua, the Cuban troops in several African

> countries. [...] And Afghanistan? That is why we are saying that foreign policy of Communism is aimed at the global domination.[48]

Gorbachev denied any effort to spread Communist domination, but as in most of their conversations, the emotional directness of the British Prime Minister impressed him and led to serious rethinking of some of Soviet policies in the Third World. In the same meeting she explained to Gorbachev how the Soviet Union was seen as a threat in Western Europe because of its history of invasions in 1956, 1968 and 1979 – the issue he then raised at the Politburo after the visit and linked it to the need to reformulate the Soviet military doctrine.[49]

It would be an overstatement to attribute the start of the turn in the Soviet Third World policy to this conversation, but it certainly reinforced the already forming trend in Gorbachev's own thinking. Both Grachev and Cherniaev point to the importance of Thatcher in the development of Gorbachev's view of the world. Indeed, while that first meeting between Gorbachev and Thatcher in Moscow included a genuinely heated discussion about the Third World, Gorbachev's meetings with Thatcher in London in April 1989 show a complete turn-around from confrontation to cooperation in settling regional conflicts. Thatcher talked with Gorbachev about the need to take more decisive action to end proxy conflicts in Africa and to put pressure on the Cubans to withdraw their troops (she alleged Cuba had a military presence in 14 African countries):

> I visited a camp in Zimbabwe where a small unit of British troops teaches Mozambique citizens how to fight RENAMO terrorists following a request from the government of Mozambique. I saw a completely unbelievable picture there: the British training the Mozambique [people] with Kalashnikov automatic rifles in Zimbabwe.

This conversation also included a fascinating discussion with Gorbachev about his visit to Cuba immediately before he came to London. Instead of ideological antagonists on the subject of the Third World, in April 1989, one sees two partners and friends, trying to find solutions to complex situations in the framework of their "special relationship."[50]

As much as Thatcher's views mattered to Gorbachev personally, it was the US Presidents who constantly pressed the Soviet leader to focus on the regional issues, and linked those issues successfully with the outcomes of arms control negotiations and with US support for the Soviet withdrawal from Afghanistan. However, perhaps not surprisingly, Gorbachev did not see Thatcher's arguments as simply ideological rhetoric, as he saw Reagan's statements on the Third World and, therefore, it was easier for him to engage with the British Prime Minister than with Reagan, who often read prepared statements.

US–Soviet summits really mattered for the formulation of Soviet Third World policy. As Andrei Grachev pointed out,

> At every US–Soviet summit, the American administration raised the issue of 'regional conflicts' with almost the same regularity as the subject of human rights violations within the Soviet Union; for Gorbachev this represented another embarrassing legacy inherited from the former Soviet leadership from which he wanted to free himself as soon as possible.[51]

Starting with Geneva, Reagan always raised the issue of regional conflicts. In fact, he raised it in their first private conversation in Geneva accusing the Soviet Union of "helping socialist revolutions around the world."[52] Reagan spoke of the American belief in the idea of self-determination, which, ironically, was the core Marxist idea about the Third World and anti-colonialism, and which Gorbachev sincerely shared.

The most important conflicts for the US were the war in Afghanistan and the conflict in Central America – Soviet and Cuban support for the Nicaraguan revolution. Afghanistan was seen by many in the US as a test case for the seriousness of Soviet reform, and the Soviet leadership was aware of that. In his turn, Gorbachev saw the success of a peaceful resolution in Afghanistan as a starting point for resolving other regional conflicts – in cooperation with the US and the UN. While Gorbachev's hope that the US would play a constructive role in cutting support for the mujahadeen never materialized, the Soviet Union still carried out the withdrawal in close coordination with the US and according to the Geneva Accords.

Third World issues were always present in Soviet–US conversations, regardless of the main topic of the discussion. In 1985–1986 Gorbachev usually responded to US criticism by discussing global inequality and exploitation of the Third World by imperialist powers (for example, he did so during his summit with Reagan in Geneva), but later on, the need for cooperation with the US in resolving regional conflicts through national reconciliation became Gorbachev's dominant theme. In one such conversation, during Gorbachev's meeting with the US Secretary of State George Shultz in Moscow in February 1988 (which included a detailed discussion of the Iran–Iraq war), Gorbachev defined the need for Soviet–US cooperation in settling regional conflicts: "Since we [both] are present [involved] everywhere, we are simply bound together in search of a balance of interests."[53]

In the fall of 1988, in a major breakthrough, the situation in Southern Africa yielded to a joint US–Soviet mediation led by Anatolii Adamishin and Chester Crocker – Cuba agreed to withdraw its troops from Angola, and South Africa eventually withdrew its troops from Namibia.[54] Successful resolution of this long-standing and bloody conflict set Gorbachev firmly on the path of Soviet–US cooperation in resolving Third World conflicts.

The most spectacular case of US–Soviet discussion of regional conflicts took place during the Malta summit, where Gorbachev acted as a channel between Castro and Bush expressing Castro's wish to improve relations with the US. Bush, on the other hand, dismissed Castro's assurances and instead warned Gorbachev against supplying weapons (helicopters) to Nicaragua and El Salvador through Nicaragua. Bush also expressed a new US position: if the Sandinistas allowed democratic elections with international observers, the US would support the outcome – provided the Soviet Union did the same. The basic understanding that was reached during this meeting eventually led to the acceptance of the results of the Nicaraguan elections of February 1990 and the end of the conflict there.[55]

According to Anatolii Cherniaev, for some time in 1989 Gorbachev believed in the possibility of achieving a breakthrough in US–Cuban relations and saw himself as the best mediator. If successful, Gorbachev would have been playing the role of a lifetime, and that would provide the ultimate proof that ideological conflicts could be peacefully resolved. The Soviet leader took all the requirements and conditions of the US side, conveyed them to Soviet allies in Central America, ensured cessation of arms deliveries and encouraged free elections in Nicaragua. However, after practically all the conditions were met, and Violetta Chamorro was inaugurated as the first democratic President of Nicaragua, President Bush explained to Gorbachev during their Washington/Camp David summit in May-June 1990 that the real problem for the US was Castro's domestic regime and, therefore, there could be no improvement of relations or lifting of the Cuban embargo for as long as this regime remained in place.[56] In this area, Soviet good will and cooperation was not enough to resolve the conflict. Gorbachev's design for Central America proved to be too ambitious or too naïve.

The 1990 Washington summit included an extensive discussion of Soviet–US cooperation in the Third World. The two leaders spoke as close partners engaged in a productive project to put out local fires around the globe. Gorbachev was very attached to the idea of a US–Soviet partnership in resolution of regional conflicts, and in fact, practically all conflicts mentioned above saw such successful resolution in 1988–1991 due, in large part, to US–Soviet cooperation, but also due to the fact that the disappearance of the central US–Soviet rivalry removed one of the most significant causes of those conflicts.

Conclusion: imperial withdrawal based on ideas

The end of the Cold War in the Third World became possible as the result of an unprecedented turn in Soviet foreign policy that led to the withdrawal of Soviet troops from Afghanistan, normalization of Soviet relations with China and the gradual abandonment of many Soviet commitments in the Third World, which had seemed to be core to its superpower status in the 1970s. In place of the ideological struggle and geostrategic competition, the Soviet leadership now offered models of national reconciliation domestically, and US–Soviet cooperation internationally for resolution of regional conflicts. Ideas and interaction, not power balances, accounted for the turn.

For most of the time, the Third World was not truly important to Gorbachev. His priorities lay in ending the Cold War and improving relations with the US and Europe. Lack of previous exposure and minimal experience with the region did not prepare him well for developing a clear strategy for Third World countries. And yet, one can distinguish two periods of Soviet policy towards the Third World during the perestroika period. Initially, in 1985–1987, the goal was to invigorate Soviet Third World policy and make it more competitive while cutting the economic burden of aid by concentrating on bigger, more important, countries. In the second period, from 1988 onwards, the Soviet priority shifted to trying to resolve regional conflicts in cooperation with the US and international institutions. Many of the changes were made in a conscious linkage to US–Soviet relations or the arms control process. Soviet leaders saw the national reconciliation model applicable universally as a part of the new, transformed, post-Cold War world.

The importance of advisers was crucial. The most influential people, who shaped Gorbachev's views, helped him to stick to his proclaimed principles, and warned him against yielding to "socialist-oriented" friends' requests for assistance, were Alexander Yakovlev, Anatolii Cherniaev, Georgii Shakhnazarov, and Karen Brutents. Often, on the issues of the Third World, Eduard Shevardnadze was running a separate game, as with Afghanistan, keeping old commitments for too long and being more willing to satisfy requests for arms. The International Department played an indispensable role in formulating Soviet Third World policy in the perestroika years – practically all the reformers came from it, bringing the ideas that had been germinating there back in the 1970s.

Gorbachev's Third World policy was, essentially, interactive. One cannot understand it without understanding how deeply the interaction with US Presidents and other Western leaders shaped Gorbachev's Third World priorities. The Soviet leader wanted to show genuine cooperation and progress in the Third World so that it would create trust and thus influence, positively, the central issues like arms control and his efforts to build the "Common European Home." Interaction with the US was especially important – it provided proof that Gorbachev's "new thinking" was actually working, created a positive image of Soviet Union around the world and made the Soviet leader feel like a truly valuable partner to the West in the new, transformed, world. The new New Soviet policy towards the Third World was not, in any way, a withdrawal under US pressure, it was, rather, a partnership with the West in resolving the deadliest conflicts and, thus, in building this new world.

The ideas really mattered, and, as they changed gradually, the policy changed too. Gorbachev was sincerely committed to his belief in self-determination and in non-use of force for solving international disputes and to his ideas of a new world order with primacy of universal human values over balance of power politics and class interests. One of the most important direct reasons for the change in Soviet policy towards the Third World was idealistic, or as Arne Westad expressed it, "the Soviet President practiced what both liberals and revolutionaries had been calling for at the beginning of the century – a firm and idealist dedication to letting the people of the world decide their own fates without foreign intervention."[57] As Gorbachev's perception of security changed from more ideological to more cooperative, his Third World policy put more and more stress on international cooperation and national reconciliation. However, the strong perception of Soviet failures in the Third World, and of the unbearable economic burden of aid, had a direct impact on decisions made by the Soviet leadership.

The Third World was central to the Cold War and to the end of the Cold War, but it was not seen as a central priority by the Gorbachev leadership. The reassessment of the importance of Third World allies began in the late 1970s, but real change only became possible when the new leader came to power and brought with him individuals who shared and implemented the ideas developed in the International Department and the academic institutes in the period 1975–1985. Advisers became the conduits of those ideas, and in the strictly hierarchical and closed system of the Soviet Union, their influence on policy was much greater than it would have been in a democratic system.

The achievements and breakthroughs in the Third World during the Gorbachev period were significant, but many of them were soon forgotten – because they were seen as a rushed retreat from a global presence – something Russia is trying to undo nowadays. The real turn in policy followed the evolution of Gorbachev's views regarding the Third World as a result of learning and especially his interaction with foreign partners on arms control and the building a new, cooperative, security system. Ideas drove the change in policy. With the Soviet and US withdrawal of military assistance from their proxies, processes of national reconciliation started working in such diverse places as Afghanistan, Angola, Ethiopia, Cambodia and, most successfully, Nicaragua. However, in none of those places were the deep domestic conflicts resolved completely just by superpower withdrawal, in fact, in most of those cases, some fighting continued after the end of the Cold War. In Afghanistan, superpower withdrawal actually resulted in the coming to power of religious fundamentalists and led to another long war. The unprecedented cooperation between the Soviet Union and the US in resolution of regional conflicts in the late 1980s is unlikely to be replicated under modern conditions.

Notes

1 For the best document-based overview of the Cold War in the Third World see O. A. Westad, *The Global Cold War: Third World interventions and the making of our times* (Cambridge: Cambridge University Press, 2005).
2 My special thanks to Sergey Radchenko and Artemy M. Kalinovsky, who shared their sources on the Third World with me and pointed me to more available documents at GARF.
3 Minutes of CC CPSU Politburo meeting, 13 November 1986, www.gwu.edu/~nsarchiv/NSAEBB/NSAEBB272/Doc%205%201986–11–13%20Politburo%20on%20Afghanistan.pdf.
4 Gorbachev speech at the Political Consultative Committee (PCC) meeting in Sofia, 22 October 1985, Archive of the Gorbachev Foundation, Moscow [AGF], F. 2, Op. 1, p. 13.
5 Karen Brutents, *Nesbyvsheesia: Neravnodushnye zametki o perestroike* (Moscow: Mezhdunarodnye otnosheni'ia, 2005), p. 129.
6 See the testimony of Anatolii Dobrynin at the conference of the Carter-Brezhnev project in Fort Lauderdale, Florida, Transcript, pp. 16–17.
7 Raymond Garthoff, *Détente and Confrontation: American-Soviet Relations from Nixon to Reagan* (Washington, DC: Brookings Institution Press, 1994), p. 716.
8 Brutents, *Nesbyvsheesia*, p. 450.
9 Interview with Kiva Maidanik, July 1993, Moscow.
10 Westad, *Global Cold War*, p. 370.
11 M. S. Gorbachev, *Zhizn' i reformy* (Moscow: Novosti, 1995), Vol. 2, p. 108.
12 Pavel Palazchenko, *My Years with Gorbachev and Shevardnadze: The Memoir of a Soviet Interpreter* (University Park, PA: Pennsylvania State University Press, 1997), p. 59.
13 Mikhail Gorbachev's statements to Rajiv Gandhi, 21 May 1985, AGF, F. 3, Document 4766.
14 Gorbachev, *Zhizn' i reformy*, Vol. 2, p. 110.
15 Shrinath Sahai, *The Delhi Declaration, Cardinal of Indo-Soviet Relations* (New Delhi: D. B. Offset Press, 1990), pp. 14–17.
16 Record of Conversations between Mikhail Gorbachev and Rajiv Gandhi, 25–27 November 1986, AGF, F. 1, Op. 1.
17 Record of Mikhail Gorbachev's conversation with Athos Fava, 3 March 1987, AGF, F. 1, Op. 1.
18 Andrei Grachev, *Gorbachev's Gamble: Soviet Foreign Policy and the End of the Cold War* (Cambridge, MA: Polity Press, 2008), p. 112.
19 Ibid.
20 Francis Fukuyama, "The Reagan Doctrine: Gorbachev and the Third World," *Foreign Affairs*, Vol. 64, No. 4 (1986).
21 Record of Mikhail Gorbachev's Conversation with Fidel Castro, 2 March 1986, AGF, F. 5, Document 4797.
22 Anatolii Cherniaev *et al.* (eds.), *V Politbiuro TsK KPSS* (Moscow: Gorbachev-Fond, 2008), p. 39.
23 Ibid., p. 41.
24 Mikhail Gorbachev, Speech to the Ministry of Foreign Affairs, 28 May 1986, in Mikhail Gorbachev, *Gody Trudnykh Reshenii* (Moscow: Alfa-Print, 1993), p. 53.
25 Record of Conversation between Mikhail Gorbachev and Abdel Halim Haddam, 28 May 1986, AGF, F. 1, Op. 1.
26 Minutes of the Politburo Session, 11 July 1986, AGF, F. 10, Op. 2.
27 Record of Gorbachev's conversation with Foreign Ministers of socialist countries, 25 March 1987, AGF, F. 10, Op. 2.
28 Brutents, *Nesbyvsheesia*, p. 170.
29 Ibid., p. 452.

30 Adamishin quoted in Grachev, *Gorbachev's Gamble*, p. 113.
31 Andrei Kozyrev quoted in Westad, *Global Cold War*, p. 386.
32 For a document-based account of Soviet withdrawal from Afghanistan see Artemy M. Kalinovsky *A Long Goodbye* (Cambridge, MA: Harvard University Press, 2011). See also Kalinovsky's chapter in this volume.
33 Record of conversation between Mikhail Gorbachev and Hashemi Rafsanjani, 21 June 1989, AGF, F. 1, Op. 1.
34 State Archive of the Russian Federation, Moscow (GARF), F. 10026, Op. 1, D. 3060.
35 Katushev memo to Cherniaev, undated, 1991, AGF, F. 2, Op. 1, Document 8997.
36 Record of conversation between Mikhail Gorbachev and Nguyen Van Linh, 3 May 1989, AGF, F. 1, Op. 1. See also Balázs Szalontai's chapter in this volume.
37 Record of conversation between Mikhail Gorbachev and Rodney Arismendi, 29 April 1988, AGF, F. 1, Op. 1.
38 Record of Telephone Conversation between Mikhail Gorbachev and Fidel Castro, 5 April 1988, AGF, F. 5, Document 20686.
39 Anatolii Cherniaev's diary, entry for 15 January 1989.
40 Record of conversation between Mikhail Gorbachev and Fidel Castro, 3–4 April 1989, AGF, F. 5, Document 20700.
41 Brutents, *Nesbyvsheesia*, pp. 152–5.
42 Anatolii Cherniaev's diary, entry for 15 January 1989.
43 Anatolii Cherniaev, *Shest' let s Gorbachevym* (Moscow: Kul'tura, 1993), p. 192. Anatolii Cherniaev's diary, entry for 1 April 1988.
44 Georgii Shakhnazarov, Memorandum to Gorbachev, 28 July 1988, AGF, F. 5, Document 18099.
45 Anatolii Cherniaev and Georgii Shakhnazarov, Memorandum to Gorbachev, 30 September 1988, AGF, F. 2, Op. 1, Document 1547.
46 Vadim Zagladin, Memorandum to Gorbachev, 24 January 1989, AGF, F. 3, Document 7179.
47 Anatolii Cherniaev, Memorandum to Gorbachev, 16 August 1991, AGF, F. 2, Op. 1.
48 Record of conversation between Mikhail Gorbachev and Margaret Thatcher, 30 March 1987, AGF, F. 1, Op. 1.
49 Minutes of the Politburo Session, 8 May 1987, *V Politbiuro TsK KPSS*, p. 177.
50 Record of Conversation between Mikhail Gorbachev and Margaret Thatcher, 5 April 1989, AGF, F. 1, Op. 1.
51 Grachev, *Gorbachev's Gamble*, p. 111.
52 Geneva Summit Memorandum of Conversation. 19 November 1985, 10:20–11:20 a.m., First Private Meeting, www.gwu.edu/~nsarchiv/NSAEBB/NSAEBB172/Doc15.pdf.
53 Record of conversation between Mikhail Gorbachev and George Shultz, 22 February 1988, AGF, F. 1, Op. 1.
54 See chapters by Chris Saunders and Vladimir Shubin in this volume.
55 Soviet transcript of the conversation between Mikhail Gorbachev and George H. W. Bush, Malta summit, 2–3 December 1989, www.gwu.edu/~nsarchiv/NSAEBB/NSAEBB298/Document%2010.pdf.
56 Record of Conversation between Mikhail Gorbachev and George H. W. Bush, First Conversation, Camp David, 2 June 1990, AGF, F. 1, Op. 1.
57 Westad, *Global Cold War*, p. 387.

2 The decline in Soviet arms transfers to the Third World, 1986–1991

Political, economic, and military dimensions

Mark Kramer

From the mid-1950s through the end of the Cold War, arms transfers played a crucial role in Soviet relations with the Third World.[1] During this period, the Soviet government supplied weapons to 47 less-developed countries (LDCs) and at least six "national liberation" guerrilla movements in the Third World.[2] The Soviet Union's emphasis on military aid to LDCs stemmed as much from necessity as from design: Soviet leaders tried to establish close ties with Third World countries through a variety of non-military means, including economic assistance, foreign trade, higher educational programs, and political cooperation; but by the late 1970s the Soviet Union in most cases was providing only a modest amount of economic aid and was no longer widely seen as a "model" for development. The training of students from Third World countries at Soviet universities increased steadily in the 1960s and 1970s, but the political gains for Moscow were often elusive.[3] Consequently, arms supplies were one of the few instruments that still enabled the Soviet Union to compete with Western countries and China for influence in the Third World.

By the time Mikhail Gorbachev became General Secretary of the Communist Party of the Soviet Union (CPSU) in March 1985, the salience of arms transfers in Soviet–Third World relations was greater than ever. Military exports at that point were the most important vehicle of Soviet influence in the developing world and were also a key source of hard currency for the Soviet Union. From the late 1970s through the late 1980s, the Soviet Union dominated the global arms trade, accounting for roughly 46 percent of all weapons transfers to the Third World, compared with only about 16 percent for the United States.[4] In the first few years after Gorbachev took office, from 1985 to 1988, Soviet military deliveries to the Third World rose from $16.8 billion to roughly $21.6 billion, and new Soviet arms agreements with Third World states reached a peak of $29.8 billion in 1986, representing more than 57 percent of all new military agreements with LDCs.[5] Having commanded an overwhelming share of the global arms market for more than a decade, the Soviet Union in the mid to late 1980s seemed destined to remain the world's largest supplier of weapons.

From that point on, however, Soviet military shipments to the Third World steadily declined. From 1986 to 1988, new Soviet arms export agreements with LDCs decreased by 58 percent, and in 1989 they declined by a further 12 percent. Soviet arms deliveries, which had continued upward in 1987–1988, fell by almost 15 percent in 1989, to $18.8 billion.[6] These reductions corresponded with the general downturn in the world's arms trade in 1988–1989 that resulted in part from the saturation of the market in the mid-1980s and the severe financial problems confronting most Third World countries. Despite a slight upturn in global arms transfer agreements in 1990 (caused mainly by Saudi Arabia's new purchases from the United States), Soviet weapons exports fell by some 25 percent.[7] The continuing decline in Soviet military deliveries and agreements was spurred by the UN arms embargo against Iraq starting in August 1990, the cuts in Soviet military assistance to erstwhile clients such as Nicaragua and Ethiopia, and the settlement of long-standing conflicts in southern Africa. In 1991, Soviet arms transfers contracted by a further 60 percent, from $11.8 billion to $5 billion, the lowest total since the early 1970s.[8] This precipitous decline was even more dramatic than it seemed, for it came after Soviet military exports to the Third World had already shrunk by some 60 percent compared to their peak in 1986, the year after Gorbachev came to power.

This trend coincided with the rise of "new political thinking" in Soviet foreign policy and a broad Soviet retrenchment in the Third World, including the withdrawal of all Soviet combat forces from Afghanistan in 1988–1989. Unlike in the past, when the Soviet Union had fueled civil wars and interstate violence in the Third World, Soviet leaders in the late 1980s began encouraging the political resolution of armed conflicts in Latin America, Southeast Asia, Africa, and the Middle East.[9] This shift of policy was in keeping with Gorbachev's basic effort to improve East-West relations. The conceptual rationale for the "new thinking" vis-à-vis the Third World was elucidated in 1988 by Andrei Kozyrev, who was then a Soviet Foreign Ministry official responsible for policy planning (and who later became Russian Foreign Minister):

> Our direct and indirect involvement in regional conflicts [in the Third World] has resulted in colossal losses by increasing general international tension, justifying the arms race, and hindering the establishment of mutually advantageous ties with the West.... The notion that any conflict between developed Western countries and developing countries must be assessed primarily in the context of the "suppression of national liberation aspirations" became obsolete long ago. In actual fact, what is most often at stake are complex international conflicts that need to be settled in a way that takes both sides' interests into account.... Blind "anti-imperialism" is a poor guidepost when working to improve the situation in the world as a whole and in its individual regions.[10]

In southern Africa in 1988, the Soviet government was instrumental in obtaining Cuban support for a resolution of the war involving Angola, Cuba, and South Africa.[11] The following year, Gorbachev and Soviet Foreign Minister Eduard Shevardnadze not only pressured Vietnam to end its occupation of Cambodia but also pushed Ethiopia's Communist regime to seek a resolution of its bloody 30-year war in Eritrea.[12]

This quest for political solutions to Third World military conflicts was accompanied by a sharp decline in Soviet overseas naval deployments and large-scale naval exercises. Declassified US intelligence documents reveal that the Soviet Navy by 1989 had ceased its submarine patrols near Great Britain and off the west African coast and drastically curtailed its submarine and surface patrols in the Indian Ocean, South China Sea, and western Atlantic Ocean.[13] The contraction of Moscow's global naval presence in the late 1980s and early 1990s mirrored the sharp downward trend in Soviet arms exports to the Third World.

These concurrent trends caused some observers to conclude that Gorbachev's acceptance of "new political thinking" and his reorientation of Soviet policy in the Third World were what led to the reduction of Soviet arms transfers to LDCs.[14] This view, however, is not borne out by declassified top-secret Soviet documents that have recently come to light. These newly available materials indicate that the sharp reduction in Soviet weapons shipments to the Third World stemmed not from Gorbachev's "new political thinking" but from underlying trends in the global arms market, which had turned distinctly unfavorable for major suppliers. To the extent that the "new political thinking" affected Soviet arms transfer policy, the impact was only limited and transitory. The Soviet Union's promotion of diplomatic settlements of regional conflicts did eventually contribute to the decline in Soviet weapons exports, which were no longer needed for countries that had ceased being at war. The "new political thinking" also facilitated proposals for greater caution with arms transfers, and these proposals made some headway in 1989. But soon thereafter, the Soviet government began running so short of hard currency that it launched a vigorous effort to *increase* its military exports to Third World countries. By endeavoring to sell more weapons abroad for hard currency, Soviet officials hoped not only to deal with financial problems but also to minimize the disruption from Gorbachev's military conversion program. The drive to expand Soviet arms transfers failed in the end, but not for lack of trying. The further drop in Soviet weapons exports occurred solely because of circumstances in the global economy that induced Third World governments to forgo new arms purchases.

This chapter examines Soviet weapons transfers and military aid to the Third World during the Gorbachev era. Because arms exports since the 1960s had been such an important component of Soviet policy toward the developing countries, an analysis of these exports in the latter half of the 1980s and early 1990s should be useful in casting light on broader aspects of Soviet–Third World relations under Gorbachev. The first part of the chapter briefly lays out the historical context of Soviet arms transfer policy, noting the conditions in the late 1960s and early 1970s that permanently changed the nature and level of Soviet arms exports. The chapter then discusses the way Soviet arms transfers to the Third World evolved in the 1980s, looking at the quantitative and qualitative trends in arms supplies and the nature of the main recipients both before and after Gorbachev came to power. Following that, the chapter explores the domestic and external factors that stimulated and constrained Soviet arms transfers to the Third World during the Gorbachev era, including the Soviet Union's primary motivations for supplying arms, the way these motivations shifted in relative importance over time, the advantages the Soviet Union enjoyed over the West as a supplier, and the problems it encountered with its arms exports during the Gorbachev era.

The chapter shows, among other things, that Soviet arms transfer policy went through three distinct phases during the Gorbachev era – the first from 1985 through mid-1988, the second from the latter half of 1988 through the latter half of 1989, and the third from the beginning of 1990 through the end of 1991. Only during the second phase did the "new thinking" in Soviet foreign policy contribute to the reduced level of Soviet arms exports to the Third World. During the first phase, Soviet leaders were still seeking to maintain the large volume of Soviet arms transfers and to attract new customers, especially those that would pay in hard currency. During the final phase, the Soviet Union returned to a policy of actively promoting weapons sales to LDCs. The all-out drive to sell arms for hard currency in 1990–1991 was largely unsuccessful for the reasons mentioned above, but it continued under the Russian government after 1991.

The chapter draws not only on primary sources available at the time (US government publications, Soviet public statements, Soviet articles, etc.) but also on a wide range of formerly classified materials, including recently released US Central Intelligence Agency (CIA) documents and declassified Soviet documents from the Gorbachev Foundation archive, from Fond 89 at the Russian State Archive of Recent History, and from the invaluable collection of Vitalii Kataev's documents now stored at Stanford University's Hoover Institution Archive. Kataev, a long-time senior official in the Soviet military-industrial complex, was deputy head of the CPSU Defense Industry Department and an adviser to Gorbachev on defense issues from 1985 to 1991. Prior to his death in 2001, he and his daughter agreed to transfer 20 large boxes of his photocopied papers to the Hoover Institution. Most of the boxes have been made accessible.[15] They contain a wealth of documents about all aspects of Soviet military and defense-industrial issues during the Gorbachev era, including questions of arms transfers to Third World countries.

Historical context

Soviet weapons exports to LDCs began in the early to mid-1950s and expanded significantly over the next decade as Nikita Khrushchev avidly courted newly independent Third World countries. Until the mid-1960s, however, the volume of Soviet arms supplied was relatively modest. A small number of states, especially China (before 1960), Egypt (until 1972), India, Indonesia, Iraq, and Syria, did receive substantial quantities of Soviet arms; but in most cases Khrushchev's overtures focused primarily on economic assistance and trade, rather than military exports. From 1955 until Khrushchev's removal in October 1964, Soviet economic assistance to the Third World averaged $425 million annually, some $50 million higher than the average annual level of military aid.[16] Soviet trade with LDCs during that same period also grew rapidly, facilitated by Moscow's willingness to subsidize its exports and loans. Thus, until the mid-1960s, the economic dimension of the Soviet Union's relations with Third World countries overshadowed the military dimension.

By the late 1960s, however, Soviet arms transfer policy began to change. The quantity and quality of Soviet weapons supplied to developing countries increased, and the number of Third World recipients of those weapons burgeoned, especially in the Middle East and Africa. That pattern continued, with minor fluctuations, throughout the 1970s and 1980s, including the early years of the Gorbachev era. Eight factors, in particular, were initially responsible for the expansion of Soviet military deliveries to the Third World.

First, by the mid to late 1960s, serious doubts had arisen about the economic aid programs favored by Khrushchev. Long delays and poor implementation hindered many projects; a backlog of unallocated credits had built up; and numerous Western countries, particularly the United States and West European countries, had shown themselves to be far more capable of promoting economic development in the Third World than the Soviet Union was.[17] Moreover, economic assistance required extensive preparation and detailed planning and implementation before it could produce any results. Arms transfers, by contrast, often yielded immediate political benefits and required much less preparation. Hence, military aid was increasingly viewed by Moscow as more effective than economic assistance in gaining influence with key Third World states.

Second, the major expansion of Soviet military production that began in the early to mid-1960s, especially after Khrushchev's ousting in 1964, enabled Soviet factories to assure a steady output of military goods and services for shipment abroad, even while domestic requirements (i.e., those for the Soviet armed forces) were being met. Although surplus stocks of Soviet military equipment had been available earlier, the military buildup under Leonid Brezhnev ensured that modern Soviet weapons were readily available for export.

Third, vast improvements in the Soviet Union's ability to ship over thousands of miles, through the development of long-range transport aircraft and expanded sealift, opened up new opportunities for Soviet arms transfers to distant Third World states.[18] As Soviet airlift capacity grew, Soviet leaders were increasingly able to dispatch arms rapidly in an emergency. Soviet military transport aviation (*Voenno-transportnaya aviatsiya*) played a crucial role during the October 1973 Arab–Israeli War for the rapid resupply of Egypt and Syria. Similarly, in 1975–1976, Soviet An-22 transport aircraft ferried vast amounts of weapons, equipment, and Cuban troops to the Communist guerrilla forces in Angola. In 1977–1978, during the decisive stage of the Ogaden conflict in Ethiopia, the Soviet Union used 225 long-range Antonov and Ilyushin aircraft (nearly 15 percent of the Soviet military transport fleet) to turn the tide of the war. The aircraft took off almost continuously for three weeks, carrying weapons, 1,500 Soviet advisers, and 15,000 Cuban troops to support the Ethiopian government.[19] Such a feat would have been impossible less than a decade earlier. The expansion of Soviet sealift capacity in the late 1960s and 1970s was equally impressive, with the acquisition of an ocean-going navy and the fourth largest merchant marine in the world. The Soviet merchant fleet and sea transport forces played a major role in ferrying arms during the October 1973 Middle East War, the 1975–1976 Angolan Civil War, and the 1977–1978 war between Ethiopia and Somalia.

Fourth, the continuing process of decolonization and the emergence of many new Third World countries provided a much broader range of customers for Soviet armaments. The dissolution of the French and British empires by the mid-1960s, and the breakup of the Portuguese empire in the 1970s, led to the creation of a plethora of states (Algeria, South Yemen, Mozambique, Angola) that were eager to receive Soviet armaments. Other Third World governments, spurred on by anti-Western sentiments and a desire to avoid dependence on the United States for weapons supplies, regarded the Soviet Union as a natural alternative. Revolutions and conflicts in the Third World produced additional opportunities for Soviet military exports, as in Indochina and Ethiopia. Although the number of states receiving Soviet weapons (47) was still small compared to the number of countries receiving arms from the United States, the Soviet Union, by the mid-1970s, had expanded its Third World clientele from a mere handful of countries to a truly global network.

Fifth, the 1965 Indo-Pakistani War and the 1967 Middle East War – in which some 80 percent of Egypt's weapons were destroyed or captured – led to requests from India, Egypt, Iraq, and Syria for a full-scale resupply of their depleted arsenals. With the means now available to fulfill these requests, the Soviet government agreed, and Soviet arms transfers soared in the late 1960s as a result. The resupply operations firmly established the Soviet Union as a source of modern weaponry for key states in the Middle East and South Asia.

Sixth, Israel's deep bombing strikes against Egypt during the War of Attrition in 1970 prompted the Soviet Union to allow the Egyptians to buy much more advanced weapons than they had previously. Soviet policy thus underwent an important shift: Instead of supplying old, outdated equipment as in the past, the Soviet Union became willing to provide its closest Third World allies with modern, sophisticated armaments. The Frog missiles, ZSU-23–4 mobile anti-aircraft guns, and SA-2 and SA-3 air-defense missiles that were supplied to Egypt in 1970–1971 were accompanied by 7,500 Soviet combat troops – another important shift as Soviet combat personnel had not previously been dispatched in such large numbers to a Third World country to operate modern weaponry.

Seventh, the emergence of strategic nuclear parity between the superpowers by around 1970 (and its codification in the 1972 US–Soviet strategic arms control accords) inspired Soviet leaders to seek parity in other areas as well. Soviet officials believed that, as a coequal superpower, they could compete on an equal basis with the United States in the Third World. As one Soviet diplomat later put it, the superpowers should have had "an equal right to meddle in third areas."[20] Because the United States had long maintained an extensive network of arms supply relationships with Third World countries, officials in Moscow viewed military exports both as a natural concomitant of superpower status and as a means of undercutting US influence.[21]

Eighth, the growing confidence and buoyancy among Soviet officials in the early to mid-1970s, reflected in Andrei Gromyko's boast that no major international issue could be decided without the Soviet Union's participation or against its interests, were reinforced by the post-Vietnam disillusion and "neo-isolationism" in the United States. US diplomacy in the 1970s was marred by uncertainty and a lack of resolve, which enabled the Soviet Union to exploit opportunities that arose in the Third World, most notably in Angola and Ethiopia. Soviet leaders were quick to fill the vacuum that had been left by the temporary US retrenchment, as they shipped in large numbers of arms and advisers. In the absence of active US opposition, the Soviet Union was free to establish itself as an arms supplier in entirely new markets.

The result of these eight factors – mounting problems with Soviet economic aid, increased Soviet military production, expanded Soviet transport capacity, the emergence of new Third World countries, the resupply operations needed after the Indo-Pakistani and Middle East Wars, the growing sophistication of Soviet-supplied weapons, the advent of strategic nuclear parity, and the post-Vietnam disillusion in the United States – was that the Soviet Union began to rival the United States in arms transfers to the Third World from the late 1960s onwards. Two further factors in the early to mid-1970s contributed to the sharp rise in Soviet arms transfers that occurred in the latter part of the decade: the 1973 Middle East war, and the steep increase in oil prices that followed. The war itself depleted the arsenals of most Arab states and, thus, spurred huge purchases of Soviet weapons over the next few years, at roughly the same time that Israel's armed forces were being replenished by the United States. Soviet military exports to Arab countries in the period 1974–1979 were five times greater than in 1967–1973.[22] The new oil wealth of many Arab states (especially the major oil producers) allowed most of these purchases to be transacted directly in cash, bringing a lucrative windfall for the Soviet Union. With the opportunity to earn hard currency so easily, Soviet officials were even more eager to sell sophisticated, and thus more costly, armaments to the Third World.

Soviet motivations for supplying arms

The central role of military supplies in Soviet relations with the Third World meant that decisions about arms transfers through the late 1980s were determined mainly by political-military considerations rather than economic concerns. Starting in the mid-1970s, however, the economic dimension of Soviet weapons sales became increasingly salient in Soviet decision-making. The weight given to economic considerations increased still further after Gorbachev came to office, particularly during his final two years, when Soviet arms export policy (like numerous other aspects of Soviet foreign policy) was driven almost entirely by economic pressures. The discussion here points to several discrete Soviet motivations, but in reality most decisions on military shipments to the Third World were shaped by several (or, at times, all) of the factors mentioned.

Political-military

Both before and during the Gorbachev era, the Soviet Union used arms transfers to advance key political and military objectives, with varying degrees of success. Some Soviet arms exports were intended primarily to curry favor with local states and compete with the West for political influence in the Third World. This aspect of Soviet policy was most conspicuous with regard to Communist countries such as Cuba, Vietnam, Ethiopia, and South Yemen and was also a prominent factor in the Middle East, where large-scale shipments of Soviet weapons to radical Arab states were intended to counterbalance US support for Israel and for moderate Arab regimes. Much the same was true of Soviet arms transfers to India, which were largely designed to gain influence with the Indian government and offset US support for Pakistan. The Soviet Union's desire to maintain good relations with key states such as India and Syria was evident from the sophistication of the hardware Moscow was increasingly willing to supply to them, including MiG-29 fighters, SS-21 surface-to-surface missiles, and SA-5 and SA-8 air defense interceptors. For their part, the recipients of Soviet weapons – India, Libya, Syria, Iraq, and Ethiopia, among others – offered diplomatic support for the Soviet Union at the UN and refrained from criticizing the Soviet war in Afghanistan.

A second motivation for Soviet arms transfers to the Third World, especially after 1960, was to attenuate Chinese influence. In Angola and Rhodesia, for example, Soviet military support for Marxist guerrillas was oriented predominantly against Chinese-backed rivals (in the former case successfully for the Soviet Union, in the latter case unsuccessfully). Likewise, Soviet military assistance to India and Afghanistan from the early 1960s was intended, at least in part, to "contain" China in South Asia. Much the same was true of Soviet support for Vietnam. The Vietnamese depended on Soviet military aid both in their occupation of Cambodia and in preparing for a possible renewal of direct hostilities with China, as in 1979. Moscow's desire to mitigate Chinese influence also spurred arms shipments to North Korea, including an agreement in 1985 for 50 MiG-23 Flogger fighters, 30 SA-3 Goa surface-to-air missiles, and AA-7 Amos air-to-air missiles to go to Pyongyang to wean it away from Beijing as well as to counter US backing for South Korea.[23]

Another goal for Soviet military shipments was to obtain overflight and landing rights, port facilities, bases, and pre-positioning of equipment. In the 1960s and 1970s, Soviet arms transfers to West African countries (Congo, Benin, Guinea-Bissau, Mali, etc.) enabled the Soviet Union to gain access to airfields that proved crucial during the supply operation in Angola in 1975–1976. Soviet weapons shipments to South Yemen were even more fruitful in allowing Soviet forces to use the base at Khormaksar and the port facilities at Aden, to obtain anchoring rights at the islands of Socotra and Perim, and to land at Yemeni airfields. These facilities played a central role in the Soviet intervention in Ethiopia in the late 1970s.[24] Soviet arms transfers to other African and Middle Eastern states, including Syria, Angola, Libya, Mozambique, Ethiopia, and the Seychelles, proved equally effective in securing access for Soviet forces to air and naval bases. In East Asia, too, the Soviet Union used weapons supplies to gain regular use of military facilities. The base at Cam Ranh Bay in Vietnam, for example, was opened to the Soviet Navy at the end of the 1970s in exchange for regular arms shipments and economic aid. Similarly, in 1985, the Soviet Union shipped MiG-23 fighters, SA-3 surface-to-air missiles, and AA-7 air-to-air missiles to North Korea in return for overflight rights and port facilities. The prospect of gaining access to foreign facilities in return for arms transfers was increasingly important for leaders in Moscow as they sought to establish the Soviet Union as a global superpower and to project force through an expanded military presence in the Third World.

Soviet weapons shipments were also frequently geared toward supporting Third World allies engaged in warfare. Short of the direct involvement of Soviet combat troops, arms transfers were the most visible means of demonstrating the Soviet Union's commitment and helping allied states to achieve their military objectives, whether offensive (as in the case of Vietnam's occupation of Cambodia) or defensive (as in the case of Angola's battle against US-supported guerrillas). A side-benefit of this aspect of Soviet arms transfer policy was that Soviet military planners often could gain valuable information about the performance of their weapons in combat. The Middle East, in particular, provided extensive data about how the latest Soviet armaments fared against comparable Western systems – often with disconcerting results.

Another motivation for Soviet arms transfers was to provide assistance to guerrilla movements and terrorist groups that were fighting pro-Western regimes in the Third World. In some cases this was done directly, in other cases indirectly. Appropriate types of weapons shipped to countries like Libya, Syria, South Yemen, Nicaragua, and Cuba could be retransferred to insurgents and terrorists in the Middle East, Africa, and Latin America. Although the Soviet Union provided arms directly to some subnational groups (such as the Palestine Liberation Organization, the African National Congress, and the Southwest Africa People's Organization) and offered training for guerrillas at camps in the southern Soviet Union and near Moscow, the more common procedure was for this sort of assistance to be provided indirectly.[25] Weapons and training would be supplied by the Soviet Union or other Warsaw Pact countries (especially East Germany and Bulgaria) to Third World regimes and then secretly (or not so secretly) redirected to terrorists. The use of intermediaries enabled Soviet officials to claim, disingenuously, that they did not "support international terrorism."

Soviet arms transfer policy was also intended to preserve the dependence of Third World states on the Soviet Union for new weapons, training, expertise, servicing, and spare parts. Partly for this reason and partly because of concerns about the compromise of sensitive technology, the Soviet Union was usually reluctant to export plans or equipment for co-production of major weapons. Transfers of manufacturing technology for major arms were granted only to India, North Korea (through the early 1970s), and China (before 1960). Numerous other Third World states, including Egypt, Peru, and South Yemen, received manufacturing technology for small arms, some spare parts, ammunition, and maintenance.[26] In general, though, without facilities for indigenous production of a whole range of weapons and spare parts, Third World states had no alternative but to depend on the Soviet Union for supplies, modernization, and even proper maintenance. This dependence could, at least in principle, augment Soviet bargaining leverage on other matters.

Finally, arms transfers were a valuable means for the Soviet Union to carry out espionage through the dispatch of advisers and technicians to accompany the weapons. The Soviet government almost always sent advisers along with its arms shipments – a practice that was understandable in view of the complex weapons that were being provided to states that had few technically skilled personnel. However, the number of these Soviet "advisers" was often so large that at least some of them were clearly sent there for intelligence-gathering and covert activities, rather than to provide advice. Such was the case, for example, in Afghanistan in the late 1970s, when Soviet "advisers" helped to shape the policies of the Kabul regime after the Communist coup in April 1978 and then laid the groundwork for the Soviet invasion 20 months later.[27] Likewise, in South Yemen in early 1986, the presence of Soviet military personnel enabled the Soviet Union to regain control of events after bloody fighting erupted between rival units of the local Communist Party.[28]

The many thousands of other Soviet advisers and technicians who were stationed throughout the Third World included a sizable number whose chief purpose was to ensure the maintenance of pro-Soviet regimes (or what in Soviet parlance were known as "states with a socialist orientation"). The influence that Soviet military advisers were able to exert in Third World states was of particular significance in the wake of the setbacks the Soviet Union experienced in Indonesia, Ghana, and Egypt in the 1960s and 1970s. The training of indigenous security forces in the Third World – by East German and Cuban as well as Soviet advisers – was perhaps even more important, from the Soviet perspective, in preserving the "socialist orientation" of "progressive" regimes. Indeed, Soviet military writers regarded the development of a strong internal security apparatus as indispensable to the survival of a Marxist-Leninist government in the Third World.

In addition to sending advisers and technicians to provide guidance and carry out other functions in Third World countries, the Soviet Union and its East European allies provided training on their own soil for military personnel from the LDCs. From 1955 to 1984, nearly 80,000 military officers from some 45 Third World countries were trained on Warsaw Pact territory, primarily in the Soviet Union. The trainees learned a wide range of military skills, with a special emphasis on surface-to-air missile operations, combat pilot training, tank operations, and weapons maintenance and repair.[29] Although experiences of this sort might occasionally have produced greater tension between Third World officers and their Soviet Bloc counterparts, the training in most cases seems to have spawned a sense of camaraderie and a greater affinity of political-military views. Military personnel who were trained in the Soviet Union or Eastern Europe tended, upon returning home, to be among the staunchest advocates of a pro-Soviet orientation for their own countries.

Economic

Soviet arms transfers were also motivated by economic considerations. In particular, the sale of weapons was a means of earning hard currency. By the mid to late 1980s, some 70 percent of all Soviet military deliveries to the Third World were paid for in hard currency.[30] The earnings from Soviet arms exports were increasingly important as Soviet revenues from oil and other raw materials waned. The precipitous decline in the prices of oil and natural gas in the mid-1980s undercut the Soviet Union's other main source of revenue, and the prices of other commodities (gold, for example), also plummeted. By 1986, hard currency from military exports represented 25–30 percent of total Soviet foreign trade earnings.[31] By comparison, US arms sales generated only about 3 percent of trade revenue for the United States.

Arms transfers also benefited both the Soviet economy and the Soviet armed forces by allowing for the maintenance of excess capacity in Soviet defense manufacturing plants at minimal cost. A 1986 US intelligence report noted that in Soviet military factories, "most weapons for export are manufactured concurrently with those for Soviet forces, [though] the Soviets have often dedicated entire production lines and runs to export variants."[32] The revenue from Soviet arms transfers defrayed the expense of maintaining the additional capacity to produce military goods for sale abroad. In the event of a crisis or conflict, Soviet facilities that manufactured arms for export could have been swiftly diverted to war production. Thus, arms transfers bolstered the readiness and wartime "surge" capacity of the Soviet military industrial base, without necessitating the large, costly allocation of resources that such improvements normally would have entailed.

In addition, arms transfers helped to spread the burden of the Soviet Union's research and development (R&D) costs for particular weapons.[33] Prices for most Soviet armaments included a surcharge that was intended to recoup R&D expenses. The surcharge was supposed to be small enough to avoid warding off potential customers but large enough, when taken cumulatively, to defray a significant portion of R&D expenses. Although it is difficult, even in retrospect, to estimate how much the Soviet Union actually spent on R&D, the revenue from the surcharge on arms transfers undoubtedly led to important savings.

In a similar vein, arms transfers generally reduced the unit cost of Soviet weapons by allowing for longer production runs. The quantity of Soviet tanks and combat helicopters sold to the Third World from 1980 to 1986 was equivalent to 32 percent of all such weapons produced in the Soviet Union during that period. For submarines the percentage was 17 percent, and for fighter aircraft nearly 39 percent.[34] The manufacture of extra weapons for shipment abroad enabled Soviet military industries to achieve greater economies of scale. As a result, the Soviet armed forces were able to save on procurement costs for their own weapons, allowing them to buy more weapons without boosting overall expenditures. For complex weapons like the MiG-29, which had very high unit costs, the sale of even small quantities to states such as India and Syria significantly reduced the unit costs. Much the same applied to aircraft like the MiG-23, which, though far less expensive than the MiG-29, were sold in large quantities to numerous Third World countries.

Finally, arms transfers could occasionally lead to economic concessions for the Soviet Union akin to the political benefits discussed in the previous section. In the case of Peru, for example, the $1.6 billion worth of military goods and services provided by the Soviet Union in the 1970s and 1980s prompted the Peruvian government to allow some 200 Soviet fishing vessels to use Peruvian ports. By the mid-1980s, the revenue from these fishing vessels amounted to roughly $120 million per year for the Soviet Union. In addition, Peru, unlike most other Latin American countries, accepted regular air service from the Soviet state airline, Aeroflot.[35] Economic concessions of this sort, though obviously not a dominant motivation behind Soviet weapons transfers, reinforced the other political and economic factors that induced the Soviet government to export arms.

Shift in orientation

Until the early 1970s, Soviet motivations for arms transfers to the Third World were almost entirely military and political, rather than economic. The highly favorable terms of financing provided by the Soviet Union (including a substantial number of outright grants) meant that arms transfers in earlier decades were a net economic drain – a burden that was considered tolerable only because it was outweighed by political and military benefits. By the early to mid-1970s, however, the situation had changed dramatically: the Soviet Union had begun experiencing hard-currency trade deficits when it had to import large quantities of Western grain to make up for a series of crop failures. These trade deficits were particularly unwelcome because Moscow needed hard currency to purchase Western machinery and high technology. Consequently, Soviet officials were eager to earn hard currency from whatever source they could, including increased military sales to the Third World. The prices for Soviet weapons were raised, and the terms of financing were tightened. Military exports to some countries that had failed to repay the credits extended to them in the 1970s, such as Zambia, were halted in the early 1980s pending the outcome of talks on the regulation of payments.[36] Moreover, the geographical distribution of Soviet arm supplies shifted disproportionately to the Middle East, where oil-producing states were able to pay promptly in hard currency.

The results of this shift in orientation were striking: in the early 1970s, arms transfers accounted for only about 3 percent of Soviet hard currency revenues; by the end of the decade they brought in 10–15 percent of such earnings. With the decline in the price of oil in the mid-1980s and the consequent drop in Soviet oil revenues, the share of hard currency coming from arms sales rose to 25–30 percent. This fundamental economic realignment confronted Gorbachev when he took over as CPSU General Secretary. To the extent that Gorbachev's economic modernization program depended on imports of high technology from the West, he undoubtedly realized at the outset that hard currency revenues from arms transfers would, potentially, be of huge benefit to the Soviet economy. Over the next few years the economic destabilization that resulted from his policies gave an even greater incentive to rely more heavily on revenue from military exports.

Trends in the 1980s

From the late 1970s through the late 1980s, the Soviet Union was by far the largest supplier of weapons, military equipment, and military services to the Third World, having dislodged the United States from the top position. Soviet arms shipments to developing countries in the decade from 1978 to 1988 were many times larger than in the previous three decades combined. As noted earlier, the Soviet Union during this period accounted for roughly 46 percent of all weapons exported to the Third World, nearly three times the quantity supplied by the United States. Moreover, although Soviet arms transfers to most regions leveled off in the early 1980s as a result of the reduced demand for weapons among indebted LDCs, the volume of Soviet military shipments overall remained very high.[37] Soviet weapons deliveries to the Third World as a whole totaled $121 billion from 1980 to 1986 (measured in constant 1987 dollars), compared with $56 billion from 1973 to 1979. New Soviet arms agreements with Third World countries in 1980–1986 exceeded $129 billion, compared to only around $56 billion for the United States. Thus, by the start of the Gorbachev era, the Soviet Union had firmly established itself as the dominant supplier in the global arms trade.

This trend could be seen in all categories of major weapon systems except subsonic combat aircraft. Soviet deliveries in 1980–1986 consistently exceeded those of the United States, in most cases by a very wide margin. Soviet deliveries accounted for more than half the total quantity of supersonic combat aircraft, surface-to-air missiles, and military helicopters provided to developing countries in the early 1980s from all suppliers. The Soviet Union also transferred vastly larger numbers of tanks, armored personnel carriers, submarines, and anti-aircraft artillery than did any other supplier. The sheer quantity of Soviet military exports to the Third World from the mid-1970s to the mid-1980s is perhaps best understood in terms of the numbers of specific weapons supplied in 1974–1985: 14,775 tanks, 18,760 armored vehicles, 5,600 fighter aircraft, 17,020 artillery pieces, 1,805 combat helicopters, 18 submarines, 66 surface ships, and 93 missile attack boats.[38] With military shipments on a scale this large, it is scarcely surprising that the dollar value of Soviet arms deliveries to the developing countries rose as sharply as it did from the late 1970s through the mid-1980s.

The increased number of weapons exported was not the only factor responsible for the growth of Soviet arms transfers. Along with the large quantitative increases in Soviet arms shipments came striking qualitative improvements in the types of weapons the Soviet Union agreed to provide. For many years, particularly in the 1950s and early 1960s, the Soviet government had transferred old, and in many cases obsolete, military equipment to Third World recipients. Starting in the mid-1970s, though, the quality of the weapons provided by the Soviet Union to key Third World countries improved dramatically. Some countries, most notably Syria and India, began receiving top-of-the-line weaponry and sophisticated communications gear, at times even before the equipment was supplied to the Soviet Union's Warsaw Pact allies in Eastern Europe. The upgraded quality of Soviet-made armaments exported to the Third World was evident in nearly all categories of conventional weapons, including fighters, ground-attack aircraft, medium-range bombers, combat helicopters, naval systems, surface-to-surface missiles, air defense missiles, main battle tanks, other armored vehicles, transport aircraft, and reconnaissance and early warning aircraft.

Impressive as the aggregate totals of Soviet arms transfers were, they tended, if anything, to understate the impact of Soviet weapons in the Third World in the first half of the 1980s. At the regional level, Soviet military exports were often of decisive importance, particularly in South Asia, where roughly three-fifths of all arms sold came from the Soviet Union. From 1981 to 1985, the Soviet Union accounted for 77 percent of the tanks shipped to South Asia, 87 percent of the armored personnel carriers, 72 percent of the surface-to-air missiles, 93 percent of the combat helicopters, and 60 percent of the field artillery. The Soviet Union's role in sub-Saharan Africa was nearly as dominant, with roughly half of all arms supplies coming from Moscow. The Soviet Union provided all five submarines that were exported to Africa in 1981–1985, 51 percent of the tanks, 82 percent of the supersonic combat aircraft, 90 percent of the surface-to-air missiles, and nearly 75 percent of the anti-aircraft artillery.[39] With such a disproportionate share of the market, the Soviet Union was well situated to determine the outcomes of conflicts in South Asia and Sub-Saharan Africa via weapons shipments.

The role of Soviet arms transfers was also crucial in the Middle East, which, from the mid-1970s, was the most heavily militarized region in the world. Middle Eastern countries, especially Syria, Iraq, and Libya, were by far the largest recipients of Soviet weapons in the 1980s. From 1980 to 1985, countries in the Middle East and South Asia received approximately 74 percent of total Soviet arms shipments. The bulk of the remaining Soviet military exports during this period went to East Asian states, primarily Vietnam, North Korea, and Malaysia. Military deliveries to Syria more than tripled in the 1980–1985 period compared to 1974–1979, rising from $4.8 billion to $16.3 billion.[40] Shipments to all other leading recipients of Soviet arms in the Middle East and South Asia underwent similar increases (with the exception of Libya and Iraq, whose purchases rose less sharply, in part because they started at such high levels).

Not only was the volume of Soviet arms transfers to the Middle East much larger in the 1980s than in the 1960s and early 1970s, but so too were the risks that Moscow was willing to take, if the resupply of Syria after the 1982 Lebanese conflict is any indication. Previous Soviet resupplies of Arab states, after the 1967 and 1973 Middle East Wars and during the War of Attrition, had been aimed at restoring a balance with Israel while eschewing supplies that might induce the Arabs to escalate hostilities. Soviet officials had been particularly cautious about introducing top-of-the-line weapons that might aggravate a volatile situation. The resupply of Syria in 1982–1983 was not a radical departure from these earlier practices, but it did entail risks that went beyond anything in the past. At the time of the resupply, there was ample reason to believe that hostilities between Syria and Israel might soon resume. Indeed, by providing the Syrians with the latest SS-21 surface-to-surface missiles and SA-5 air defense missiles, the Soviet government almost seemed to be encouraging a new round of warfare.[41] The danger inherent in the Soviet move was augmented by the thousands of Soviet combat troops who had been sent to operate the new systems.[42] If, as appeared likely for a while, the conflict had flared up anew, the Israelis would have been openly attacking front-line Soviet soldiers. The resupply of Syria was thus fraught with serious risks that exceeded those of previous Soviet actions in the region. Even though the 1982–1983 resupply operation did not herald a sweeping change of Soviet arms transfer policy in the Middle East, it did indicate a greater Soviet willingness to risk the escalation of conflicts in the region through the introduction of new weapons and troops.

Soviet arms transfer policy vis-à-vis the Iran–Iraq War reflected the same pattern. During the first two years after Iraq started the war, the Soviet government sharply curtailed its arms shipments to both sides and exerted pressured on the Iraqis to bring the fighting to an end. By the summer of 1982, however, as the Iranian position strengthened and the prospect of a humiliating Iraqi defeat loomed, the Soviet Union resumed large-scale arms supplies to Baghdad. Some Soviet weapons also began to flow to Iran via third parties, including Syria, Libya, North Korea, and South Yemen. The Soviet Union thus found itself in the position of arming both sides in the war. But toward the end of 1983, the Soviet government abandoned its "even-handed" approach and clearly began "tilting" to the Iraqi side.[43] From 1983 through 1987, Soviet weapons shipments to Iraq exceeded those to any other country, and the shipments included some of the most advanced weapons available, such as the MiG-29 Fulcrum fighter and the Su-25 Frogfoot fighter-bomber. The shift in Soviet arms transfer policy toward Iraq was due in part to Moscow's desire to remain the dominant supplier of military hardware to Baghdad; but it was also due to the Soviet authorities' willingness to tolerate greater risks when exporting advanced weaponry to the Middle East and Southwest Asia.

Problems encountered by the Soviet Union

By the time Gorbachev came to power, Soviet arms transfers to the Third World had been encountering numerous problems. Although some of these problems plagued other weapons suppliers as well, many were unique to the Soviet Union. The problems can be grouped into two broad categories: political-military, and economic.

Political-military

First, and most important, the political and military influence that the Soviet Union hoped to gain from arms transfers to the Third World often proved ephemeral. Soviet weapons shipments to China were futile in the 1920s and just as futile in the 1950s. Large-scale supplies of Soviet armaments did not win a lasting presence in Egypt or permanent basing rights at Berbera in Somalia. The failure to convert arms supplies into genuine and enduring influence in the Third World was hardly a problem unique to the Soviet Union, as the US experience with Iran in the 1970s demonstrated. Nevertheless, the Soviet government seemed to encounter particular difficulty in acquiring lasting influence with Third World states on the basis of military exports alone. The sudden rift with Egypt in 1972 was perhaps the best illustration of this, coming as it did despite the infusion of huge quantities of Soviet weapons and the presence of some 21,000 Soviet military advisers.

Soviet arms transfer policy was further hindered by the poor showing of Soviet weaponry in the 1982 Lebanon conflict and the favorable showing of US and Israeli armaments in Lebanon and of French and British equipment in the Falklands War. To be sure, the performance of these weapons was probably due at least as much to the skills of those using them as to the characteristics of the arms themselves.[44] If Israel and Syria had fought with each other's arsenals, the Israelis might still have won decisively because of their superior training, cohesiveness, military prowess, and morale. Even so, the important thing is that many Third World governments after the 1982 Lebanon conflict came to believe (or at least to fear) that the quality of Soviet-manufactured arms was at best problematic. The performance of Soviet-made air defense missiles during the US bombing strikes against Libya in April 1986, and the unhindered flight of a small Cessna-172 into Red Square in May 1987, reinforced those perceptions and further narrowed Gorbachev's options.

These concerns about the quality of Soviet-made weapons were reinforced by the Soviet Union's tendency to produce arms that were intended exclusively for export to the Third World. Echoing the complaints of Egypt in the early 1970s, several Third World governments (e.g. Algeria) objected in the mid-1980s that the weapons they were receiving from

Moscow were nearly obsolescent and did not measure up to the sophisticated armaments deployed by potential adversaries. Complaints of this sort were hard to dispel because Soviet military-industrial officials had long been averse to providing top-of-the-line equipment to more than a few select countries.[45] Among other things, they were aware that even if the Soviet Union did export higher-quality weapons more widely, the situation might not permanently improve. After all, Syria had been receiving advanced arms for many years before it suffered its humiliating defeat in 1982.[46]

Another obstacle to increased Soviet military exports was the behavior of Soviet military advisers. The intrusiveness and overbearing manner of Soviet advisers had created friction numerous times in the past, most notably in Egypt in the early 1970s. The friction was compounded by local concerns that many of the advisers were there to conduct espionage rather than to provide genuine advice.[47] By the same token, a large number of Third World countries – even long-time clients such as India, Syria, and Iraq – were reluctant to have their officers trained in the Soviet Union because of concerns about what the training would include. Such concerns were heightened after the April 1978 coup in Afghanistan, which was carried out by a small group of Afghani officers who had been trained in the Soviet Union, and after the January 1986 coup in South Yemen.

One final problem that hampered Soviet arms transfers was the poor quality of servicing, training, and technical support provided by Soviet advisers and technicians. Soviet personnel were often ill-qualified and unfamiliar with the weapons they were supposed to be servicing. The training that Soviet advisers offered to foreign personnel was so deficient at times that it provoked bitter complaints from countries such as Syria (in 1967 and 1982), Egypt (1970–1972), and Libya (1986). Moreover, logistical support for Soviet weapons was constrained by shortages of spare parts and by a lack of indigenous maintenance facilities. Although some developing countries sought to remedy this problem by stocking up on supplies of spare parts and support equipment, the Soviet Union generally discouraged such practices.[48] The dubious quality of Soviet weapons-servicing and training made it difficult for Soviet political and military officials to convince Third World governments to rely exclusively (or even heavily) on Soviet armaments.

Economic

Of the economic problems that plagued Soviet arms transfer policy in the latter half of the 1980s, the most significant was the sharp and sustained decline in the world price of oil. The drop in revenues for the main oil exporters meant that Middle Eastern states, which were by far the largest purchasers of Soviet weapons, were no longer able to buy the quantity of arms they once did from the Soviet Union unless they received highly concessionary terms. This compounded the adverse effect that the declining price of oil had on the Soviet foreign trade ledger: Soviet oil revenues, which provided more than half the Soviet Union's total export earnings, contracted sharply from the mid-1980s; yet the one thing that might have made up for those lost revenues – an increase in weapons sales abroad – was itself made more difficult by the drop in oil prices.

To make matters worse, most countries outside the Middle East began finding it harder to buy Soviet weapons because of the enormous debts they accumulated in the 1970s and early 1980s. Loans from Western banks to the Third World in the 1970s facilitated the purchase of both civilian and military goods at a time when most arms suppliers (including the Soviet Union) had begun to emphasize hard-currency sales rather than outright grants. Arms purchases accounted for more than 5 percent of total Third World imports in the 1970s. By the early 1980s, with the mounting debt burden in the Third World and the sharp contraction of Western credits, many developing countries found themselves compelled to cut back precipitously on imports, including weapons purchases.[49] By the mid-1980s, the economic problems and continued indebtedness of most developing countries had resulted in a notable reduction in the demand for arms among Third World states. Consequently, fewer opportunities were available for Soviet military exports.

Another problem for Soviet military sales in the mid to late 1980s was the trend toward a buyers' market for weapons, with many Western and Third World arms suppliers vying for customers. By the mid-1980s, many of the largest recipients of Soviet weapons, such as India and Iraq, were turning increasingly to Western suppliers to diversify their arsenals. The French government used sales of the Mirage 2000 aircraft to make inroads into what formerly were exclusive (or nearly exclusive) markets of the Soviet Union. In addition, some Third World arms producers like Brazil and Taiwan began capturing an ever larger share of the market, as did Israel, which benefited from the results of the 1982 Lebanese conflict. Combined with the economic problems facing most developing countries, the growing competitiveness of the world arms market prompted many Third World purchasers to demand highly concessionary terms, including low interest rates, long repayment periods, and permission to pay in local currency. The Soviet government was very reluctant to go along with these demands because Soviet leaders wanted to make money on their arms exports, not to lose it. Gorbachev's advisers warned him that his plans for industrial revitalization and economic reform would suffer if resources had to be diverted to finance large-scale arms exports.[50]

The growing desire of many Third World states to work out "offsets," of both a direct and an indirect nature, to mitigate the costs of buying arms from the Soviet Union (and from other suppliers) created further problems for Gorbachev.[51] Indirect offsets usually amounted to barter arrangements, or "non-monetary" compensation for military equipment. In the

1980s, numerous LDCs exchanged local commodities for Soviet weapons. For example, Ethiopia traded coffee for arms, and Nicaragua traded sugar and fruit as well as coffee. Other states, such as Libya, "paid" for Soviet weaponry with shipments of oil or grain (which the Soviet Union then re-sold on the world market). Occasionally, the offsets involved "triangular" trade, whereby developing countries retransferred Western goods (especially high technology not exported by Western countries to the Soviet Union) to the Soviet Union in exchange for arms. India was the most notable example of a country that worked out arrangements along these lines, retransferring both technology and grain to the Soviet Union, including transshipments of American wheat during the US grain embargo in 1980. When Third World states insisted on indirect offsets (barter, countertrade, reciprocal investment, and triangular trade), the Soviet Union went along with them only reluctantly.[52] Such arrangements were obviously less desirable from Moscow's perspective than were direct payments in hard currency.

More troubling still for Soviet policymakers were the growing expectations among Third World countries that they would receive "direct" offsets. Direct offsets most often took the form of co-production agreements for weapon systems or weapons components. In a typical co-production venture, the Soviet Union transferred technical data and equipment that enabled the recipient country to manufacture weapons or components on its own. Well before the 1980s, the Soviet Union allowed China, North Korea, and Egypt to co-produce major weapons as well as components and small arms. In the 1980s, the Soviet Union granted India co-production rights for the T-72 tank, for MiG-21, MiG-23, MiG-25, and MiG-27 aircraft, and for components and add-ons for the MiG-29. Other countries, such as Peru, Afghanistan, and South Yemen, received co-production licenses for small arms, ammunition, spare parts, and (for Peru's Su-22s) local overhaul and maintenance.

During Gorbachev's early years, Third World demands for direct offsets were on the rise, leaving him little choice but to transfer manufacturing technology for spare parts and small arms to a larger number of states. Technology to produce major weapons, however, was more of a sticking point. Although the experience with India (and earlier with China and North Korea) indicated that Soviet officials were occasionally willing to provide Third World countries with the capacity to produce top-of-the-line weaponry, the widespread diffusion of Soviet arms-manufacturing technology was a worrisome prospect for Moscow – a prospect that Soviet military-industrial officials frequently warned against.[53] These officials were concerned about the possible compromise of Soviet military technology: when, for example, SA-5s were first deployed in Syria and Libya, Soviet personnel maintained strict control over the missiles until local troops were deemed sufficiently reliable to operate them. Officials in Moscow were aware that if several Arab states gained co-production rights for the latest Soviet weapons (e.g. the MiG-29), the Israelis might be able to capture the weapons-manufacturing plans and technologies during a future conflict, as they did with older Soviet equipment in the 1967, 1973, and 1982 wars. The capture of facilities that could produce advanced Soviet weapons would be far more damaging to the Soviet Union than the seizure of weapons alone ever was. Thus, Gorbachev came under pressure at home not to grant co-production rights for major arms to additional Third World countries, for fear of compromising Soviet technology.[54]

Furthermore, on purely economic grounds, direct offsets would have been disadvantageous for the Soviet Union, at least in most cases. The granting of co-production licenses tended to convert purchasers of Soviet arms into competitors, as happened with China and to a lesser extent with North Korea and even India. If Gorbachev had allowed many more LDCs to co-produce major Soviet weapons, the demand for such items from the Soviet Union itself undoubtedly would have shrunk. A further drawback to co-production arrangements was that, by failing to lead to longer production runs for Soviet military factories, they precluded a reduction of the unit costs of Soviet weapons. The greater economies of scale that arms transfers normally would have produced were absent in co-production ventures. Thus, Soviet military-industrial officials were quick to point out that, from an economic standpoint, direct offsets were bound to be detrimental to Soviet interests.

Nevertheless, despite Soviet officials' reluctance to accede to Third World requests for financial concessions and offsets, Gorbachev had to balance political-military considerations against economic concerns, especially in light of the competitiveness of the international arms market. During Gorbachev's early years, political-military considerations seemed to take priority, as Soviet weapons shipments continued in large quantities to countries that could not pay in hard currency and had to be granted highly concessionary terms of purchase (Cuba, Vietnam, North Korea, Afghanistan, Mongolia, etc.). Not until 1989 did the "new political thinking" begin to influence the CPSU Politburo's deliberations about arms transfer policy. But this influence proved to be short-lived. The growing severity of domestic economic pressures in 1990–1991 reoriented Soviet arms export policy toward an all-out campaign for hard-currency sales.

Formulation and reformulation of Soviet Arms Transfer Policy, 1985–1991

The three phases of Soviet policy on military supplies to the Third World during the Gorbachev era – from 1985 to late 1988, from late 1988 to late 1989, and from 1990 through the dissolution of the Soviet Union in December 1991 – witnessed some notable areas of continuity but also some salient differences. In each case, policymaking was influenced by both internal and external factors, though with varying weights over time.

Initial phase: 1985–1988

During Gorbachev's first three-and-a-half years in office, Soviet arms transfer policy was shaped almost entirely by the trends of the preceding decade, notably the enormous quantities of Soviet weapons flowing to Third World countries (or already in the pipeline) and the nettlesome political and economic problems resulting from some of these exports. The Soviet Politburo and Defense Council, both headed by Gorbachev, sought to rectify these problems and to maintain or even expand the total volume of Soviet arms shipments. In August 1986 the Soviet Defense Council adopted a key decision affirming that "military supplies to developing countries are an important, fundamental component of the foreign policy activity of the CPSU and the Soviet government."[55] The Defense Council expressed dismay at the "serious shortcomings that have arisen in this sphere" and chastised the agencies that had failed to carry out "timely and complete supplies" of weaponry "in accordance with [Third World countries'] purchase orders and requests." The Defense Council emphasized that

> the failure to provide timely supplies of spare parts and repairs of combat equipment has done *grave damage* to the authority of our country. Especially appalling are the shortcomings in arrangements for repairs of aviation equipment and air defense systems.

The Council members demanded "a thorough-going improvement of military cooperation with socialist and developing countries" and warned that "the leaders of the USSR ministries and departments that handle this type of cooperation will bear personal responsibility for ensuring that their ministries and departments successfully carry out" a "drastic improvement" and devise a workable program to "eliminate all existing shortcomings" (especially those pertaining to supplies of spare parts and repairs of armaments) within three months.[56]

The Defense Council decision, with its emphasis on bolstering "the quality of weaponry, spare parts, and other materials that are supplied," illustrates Soviet priorities on arms transfer policy during the initial phase of Gorbachev's tenure. Far from seeking to curtail military shipments to the Third World, Soviet leaders were demanding fundamental improvements to ensure that weapons exports could be increased and could enhance, rather than detract from, "the authority of the CPSU and Soviet government." The Defense Council decision was thus fully in keeping with the foreign policy objectives of earlier Soviet leaders.

The continued importance of political-military considerations in Soviet arms transfer policy during Gorbachev's first few years was highlighted by the resumption of military shipments to Zambia and other Third World countries to which exports of weapons had been halted in 1980 after a prolonged lack of debt repayment.[57] The resumption of this aid, combined with a drop in hard-currency arms sales, led to a sharp increase in the percentage of Soviet military assistance provided in the form of grants, rising from 25–30 percent in 1986 to more than 40 percent in 1988.[58] The persistence of long-standing patterns of Soviet arms transfer policy during this period was also reflected in the continued provision of weapons and equipment to Middle Eastern guerrilla and terrorist groups via Syria, Libya, and other radical Arab states.[59] In the aftermath of the US bombing raids against Libya in April 1986, the Soviet Union promptly resupplied the Libyan armed forces with highly advanced air defense systems and large stocks of munitions, a gesture that, according to a high-ranking Soviet official involved in the transfer, was intended to convey "a clear political message" both to the United States and to Soviet allies and friends in the Third World.[60]

Soviet leaders were also still as intent as ever on using military exports to cement bilateral ties with key Third World allies such as India and Algeria. In late October 1986 the CPSU Politburo reaffirmed its earlier decision to transfer a Charlie-class nuclear-powered submarine to India for training purposes.[61] No arms-exporting country had ever before provided a nuclear submarine to a Third World government, but Soviet Politburo members believed that the transfer, originally scheduled to take place in mid-1987, would be valuable in "demonstrating the continuity of Soviet policy and the Soviet leadership's continuing deep interest in strengthening India's influence in the Indian Ocean region." Soviet leaders also were confident that India's acquisition of a nuclear-powered submarine would "considerably boost the personal prestige of [Indian Prime Minister Rajiv] Gandhi," who had been staunchly supportive of close strategic ties with the Soviet Union.[62]

Privately, some officials in Moscow expressed unease about the "serious negative political consequences" and "malicious rumors" that might result from the transfer of a nuclear-powered submarine to India.[63] They warned, for example, that "the Soviet Union might be accused of violating the Nuclear Nonproliferation Treaty" and that the United States might "retaliate by supplying a similar vessel to Pakistan." They also warned that "sensitive technical data about [Soviet] submarine systems and the specific parameters of our nuclear propulsion equipment might fall into the hands of the Americans" and that "the Soviet Union and its leadership might be accused of political inconsistency and of failing to match words with deeds" by first "calling for a resumption of negotiations to convert the Indian Ocean into a zone of peace" (a proposal broached by Gorbachev in his major speech in Vladivostok in July 1986) and then seeming to undermine that proposal by giving a nuclear-powered submarine to India, a step that would "increase the militarization of [the Indian Ocean] to a qualitatively new level."[64] They recommended that Soviet leaders "in meetings at the highest level with the Indian side once again discuss the far-reaching repercussions of such a step and determine once again whether it is advisable in light of our recent peace initiatives."[65]

These concerns were not enough to induce the Soviet Politburo to refrain from supplying a Charlie-class submarine to India. When Gorbachev made a highly publicized visit to India in late November 1986, he gave no indication to Rajiv Gandhi that the proposed transfer of the submarine would have to be reconsidered "in light of [the USSR's] recent peace initiatives."[66] On the contrary, Gorbachev pledged that "relations with India [would] be infused with new dynamism" under his leadership. Soviet military-industrial officials took seriously the risk of a possible compromise of Soviet propulsion technology, and they sought to develop safeguards to forestall it. This work resulted in a brief delay in the transfer of the submarine, but the new vessel, christened the *INS Chakra*, began patrols with the Indian Navy in early February 1988, attracting wide attention in the international media.[67] A month later, India acquired the latest of several advanced Kilo-class submarines it had bought from the Soviet Union, further bolstering the regional dominance of the Indian Navy.[68] (The Kilo-class submarines, unlike the Charlie-class, were diesel-powered.) Although the Soviet government did its best to "offset the [adverse] consequences of [these steps] by emphasizing in the press that the nuclear submarine will be used only for training purposes and that combat missile systems will not be transferred," the leasing of the Charlie-class submarine to India was indicative of Soviet priorities during the first few years under Gorbachev.[69] Despite being warned that the transfer of a nuclear submarine to a potential combatant in a volatile region of the Third World would set an ominous precedent, the Soviet Politburo concluded that the political-military benefits outweighed the risks.

The policymaking framework for Soviet weapons exports during this period was adjusted to allow for smoother coordination with other foreign economic activities, but the impact of these changes was very limited. Nearly all of the Soviet Union's long-standing procedures for arms transfers remained intact. In August 1986 the CPSU Politburo authorized the formation of a State Foreign Economic Commission, but this new agency was not given any responsibility for military exports. In October 1986, at the Politburo's behest, the CPSU Defense Industry Department and CPSU Economic Department worked out a joint program to coordinate weapons sales with the agencies in charge of foreign economic activities.[70] The program, devised with assistance from the Ministry of Defense, the State Planning Commission, and the Ministry of Foreign Trade, stipulated that responsibility for arms transfers to the Third World should remain with the State Commission on the Defense Industry (VPK), which was to work with the 10th Directorate of the Soviet General Staff and the technical and engineering directorates of the State Committee on Foreign Economic Ties. The VPK also was to retain jurisdiction over civilian goods produced in the military-industrial complex, although the export of such goods was to be overseen by the Ministry of Foreign Trade. Finally, the VPK was to work with the Soviet KGB in reviewing proposals for joint ventures between foreign firms and Soviet defense-industrial enterprises involving civilian goods manufactured under the VPK's auspices. This basic institutional framework for arms transfers, with all key decisions ultimately subject to approval by the CPSU Politburo or Soviet Defense Council, remained in place over the next two years.[71]

Overall, then, Soviet policy on military exports to the Third World during Gorbachev's initial years as CPSU General Secretary displayed a high degree of continuity with the policies of earlier Soviet leaders. Even when some officials in Moscow raised concerns about specific transfers of weaponry, the CPSU Politburo ultimately moved ahead with the transfers in order to achieve crucial political and military objectives. The goals and processes of Soviet arms deliveries to the Third World remained almost wholly intact.

Second phase: 1989 (part 1)

The reservations expressed by some Soviet officials about the provision of a nuclear submarine to India did not derail the supply of the vessel, but the exchanges about this matter augured a gradual shift in Soviet policy that became evident in 1989. This shift was reflected in several ways. First, by March 1989, Soviet officials were proposing to call for negotiations to achieve multilateral limits on the quantity and quality of weapons exported to the Third World. Second, Soviet leaders took greater account of the "new thinking in foreign policy" as they formulated their approach on arms transfers to LDCs. Third, at least one or two specific proposals for Soviet weapons supplies to Third World countries were put on hold. In particular, India's persistent efforts to obtain additional nuclear-powered submarines from the Soviet Union and to receive material and technical help in developing nuclear propulsion systems for India's own submarines came to naught – a striking reversal of the much more open-ended policy that had been in place through mid-1988. Fourth, the policymaking process for military exports was gradually reconfigured to give a prominent role to agencies responsible for foreign economic relations. Fifth, the Soviet Union in late 1988 and 1989 began informing some long-time Third World recipients of Soviet weapons that military assistance would no longer be provided in the form of grants and would be supplied only on a cash basis. Even though these sundry changes in Soviet arms transfer policy ultimately had only a transitory impact and did not generate lasting pressure to restrict weapons exports, they were important departures from past policies.

The reorientation of Soviet military assistance programs began gradually in the last months of 1988 and then accelerated in the first half of 1989 when, at Gorbachev's behest, the CPSU Politburo and Soviet Council of Ministers re-evaluated Soviet arms transfer policy and adopted several far-reaching measures. In late January 1989, after Gorbachev asked his chief national security aides to prepare a detailed assessment of Soviet "obligations connected with military assistance" to Third World governments, the relevant agencies and ministries began exploring the issue in depth. In late March, Gorbachev received a 10-page memorandum from Foreign Minister Eduard Shevardnadze, Defense Minister Dmitry Yazov, and State Foreign Economic Commission Chairman Vladimir Kamentsev reviewing different aspects of the Soviet Union's "obligations to strengthen the defense capacity" of developing countries. "These obligations," the officials wrote,

> are carried out in accordance with intergovernmental agreements that provide for the supply of weapons and military equipment for national armies, the provision of technical assistance for the production of weapons through Soviet licenses and the construction of military facilities, the dispatch of Soviet military advisers and specialists to friendly countries, the training of foreign cadres at academies of the USSR Ministry of Defense, and the conduct of maneuvers and combat exercises by units of friendly armies at Soviet training grounds.[72]

The three officials noted that "agreements on weapons supplies occupy a special place in the framework of our obligations regarding military-technical cooperation" with Third World countries, and they argued that such agreements must henceforth reflect the changing goals and images of Soviet foreign policy:

> Although these agreements in themselves would not be able to embroil the Soviet Union in an armed conflict, they are factors that in numerous instances could cause a dangerous development of the military-strategic situation in certain regions [of the Third World] or a sharpening of the [global] military-political situation overall. This sort of problem could arise if we were to provide the most dangerous types of offensive weapons and military technology, including ballistic missiles (as well as transfers of the means of producing them) and nuclear-powered submarines, which might spur a regional arms race on a qualitatively new level and provoke other states [in the region] to take retaliatory measures, thus leading to a dangerous destabilization of the regional situation that would be fraught with conflict.[73]

The references to ballistic missiles (including production technology) and nuclear submarines were particularly important because the Soviet Union had long been supplying ballistic missiles to key countries (Iraq, Libya, Syria, Afghanistan, and, until 1973, Egypt), had aided India in producing ballistic missiles, and had leased a nuclear submarine to India barely a year earlier, with promises of more such submarines to come.

The memorandum stressed that

> when determining the nature and volume of cooperation with friendly countries in the military-technical sphere, we should be guided by the priorities of the USSR's foreign policy interests and the principle of reasonable sufficiency for the defense of these countries.[74]

The phrase "reasonable sufficiency for defense" had become one of the major concepts and slogans of the "new thinking in foreign policy," a concept that justified reductions of Soviet military forces, including unilateral cuts of the sort announced by Gorbachev in his landmark speech at the UN only a few months earlier.[75] The idea was that as long as the remaining Soviet military forces were "sufficient" for defense, the Soviet Union would be both militarily secure and economically better off with lower levels of forces.

The application of this concept to Soviet arms transfer policy implied that the Soviet Union should export only the weapons needed for a recipient country to defend itself at a minimum level of forces. The authors of the memorandum stressed that "although military-technical cooperation [with Third World countries] should obviously continue, it must be based on precise and reasonable criteria." Specifically, this would mean that

> in quantitative terms our assistance must not lead to the over-arming of our friends in comparison to their neighbors, and in qualitative terms we must refrain from supplying weapons and military equipment of great destructive power that could spark unintended action, above all ballistic missiles, nuclear-powered submarines, and other types of weapons that could have a negative influence on the strategic situation in a region.[76]

Shevardnadze, Yazov, and Kamentsev said that any decision to supply advanced weaponry to recipients in a volatile region of the Third World "would be particularly unacceptable if other countries in the region do not possess such types of arms." The three officials urged a "more thorough assessment of our long-term programs of military-technical cooperation with other countries, especially countries like India and North Korea."[77]

In addition, the memorandum recommended curbs on "Soviet licensing of production of weapons and military technology in friendly countries" and emphasized that new guidelines on this matter "should take account of the political and economic expediency of concluding such agreements and of carrying them out on a commercial basis." The three officials called for a "strengthening of control over special items from the USSR licensed for production" in order to "prevent the technology from being transferred to third countries without the consent of the Soviet side." This proposal to "tighten contractual provisions" on re-exports would have affected countries such as Libya, Syria, Egypt, and North Korea, all of which had transferred major weapons or Soviet-licensed manufacturing capacity (including ballistic missiles in the case of Libya, Syria, and Egypt) without first gaining Moscow's approval. The recent experience of the Iran–Iraq war, when Iraq had used Soviet-made ballistic missiles and then Iran had retaliated in kind after acquiring Soviet-made missiles from Libya and Syria, was undoubtedly one of the factors that inspired this proposal.

The authors of the memorandum argued that even as the Soviet Union asserted greater control over its own military exports, it should "actively seek to achieve the beginning of negotiations on limiting the sale of weapons around the world, particularly the most destabilizing types of weapons."[78] Four rounds of talks on this matter had been held by Soviet and US officials from December 1977 to December 1978, but the talks ultimately achieved nothing and broke down, in part because of bureaucratic disagreements within the US administration and in part because of continued hostility and competition between the Soviet Union and the United States.[79] The Shevardnadze–Yazov–Kamentsev proposal to seek new negotiations on multilateral limits came at a much more propitious time, amid rapid improvements in US–Soviet relations. Placing this matter back on the superpower agenda would signal the growing scope of Soviet "new political thinking."

Shevardnadze, Yazov, and Kamentsev left no doubt that their proposals could significantly affect Soviet military assistance to India. They argued that

> in connection with the initiatives laid out by the USSR at the UN [in December 1988], our efforts to stabilize the situation around the globe as rapidly as possible compels us to reassess our obligations for military-technical cooperation with India in the building of its own nuclear-powered submarines.[80]

A year earlier, on 11 March 1988, Soviet leaders had tentatively decided to help India produce the requisite nuclear-propulsion technology, but the passage of a year had altered the calculus in Moscow. Although the memorandum did not demand an immediate end to the assistance, it directed the VPK and relevant ministries to submit within two months a "comprehensive review of our obligations in providing military-technical aid to India in the construction of nuclear-powered submarines."[81]

Finally, the memorandum proposed important changes in the policy-making process for military exports to the Third World. Shevardnadze,

Yazov, and Kamentsev argued that "the most reliable guarantee for adopting optimal decisions about supplies of combat equipment" to developing countries would be a "specially created system of control for the adoption of decisions and the conclusion and implementation of appropriate treaties and agreements by the USSR Supreme Soviet." Even though Gorbachev was chairman of the Supreme Soviet, this proposal to give the parliament oversight of arms transfer policy was a far-reaching change from the past. Until 1989, the Supreme Soviet was only a figurehead legislature with no meaningful role in Soviet foreign policy. Gorbachev, however, was seeking to strengthen the parliament as he weakened and scaled back the central party apparatus. In support of that effort, the memorandum's authors stressed that "only by establishing a legislative basis for the implementation of military-technical cooperation will we be able to guarantee that we will not be dragged into foreign conflicts that would undermine our interests and security."[82] Their recommendation was consonant with a resolution adopted by the Soviet Council of Ministers a few weeks earlier, which had stipulated that the Supreme Soviet would determine which types of weapons and military technology could be exported by Soviet organizations and firms.[83]

The projected bolstering of the Supreme Soviet's role complemented other changes under way in the institutional framework of Soviet arms export policy that reflected Gorbachev's broader political and economic priorities. A directive adopted by the Soviet government in March 1988 and approved by the CPSU Politburo stipulated that the newly formed Ministry of Foreign Economic Ties (MVES) should be given responsibility for the "practical implementation" of Soviet military assistance to the Third World.[84] The MVES had been set up two months earlier as a successor to the Ministry of Foreign Trade and the State Commission for Foreign Economic Ties, both of which were abolished. The proposal to give the MVES jurisdiction over weapons exports was designed to help "forge a unified foreign economic policy for the USSR and to uphold Soviet state interests on foreign arms markets and the benefits accruing from [military] assistance."[85] Although the VPK, the Soviet General Staff, and the ministries responsible for national security and the defense industry were supposed to retain important roles in weapons exports decisions, the devolution of authority to the MVES for implementing the decisions was an unprecedented departure.

This reconfiguration took effect at the end of February 1989 when the Soviet Council of Ministers adopted a resolution "specifying the functions to be carried out by the MVES jointly with the USSR Defense Ministry, the USSR Foreign Ministry, the USSR Finance Ministry, USSR Gosplan, and other relevant ministries and departments in implementing military-technical cooperation."[86] The ministry's functions covered all stages of the arms transfer process, starting with assessments of requests from Third World governments for weapons, training, construction, and the like.

After deciding which requests to fulfill, the MVES and other agencies were supposed to provide the appropriate items and services and collect payments from the foreign governments; while ensuring that no classified information was compromised. The export prices for all goods and services were supposed to be "based on world prices."[87] Three separate parts of the MVES – the Main Engineering Directorate, the Main Technical Directorate, and the Main Directorate for Cooperation and Interaction – were chiefly responsible for handling military assistance.

Second phase: 1989 (part 2)

The impact of these changes – both substantive and procedural – on Soviet arms transfer policy had barely been felt by the time the CPSU Politburo undertook a further detailed review of Soviet military assistance to the Third World in June 1989. On 23 June, the nine highest-ranking officials responsible for national security affairs and the defense industry, several of whom were also Politburo members, submitted a memorandum to the full Politburo introducing and explaining a newly drafted "Conception of Military Cooperation with Foreign Countries (Other Than Socialist Ones) for the Period 1990–1995," which they attached to their cover memorandum.[88] The authors of the cover memorandum declared at the outset that

> the new political thinking, based on all-human values, the primacy of law, and the impossibility of resolving international problems through forceful means, and the new model of security put forth by M. S. Gorbachev at the 43rd Session of the UN General Assembly, demand that we devise a new approach to military cooperation with Third World countries.

The nine officials averred that it was "essential to eliminate the increasingly glaring contradiction" between, on the one hand, "the Soviet Union's line supporting the limitation and reduction of armaments and the political regulation of conflicts" and, on the other hand, "our ongoing and in some cases expanding cooperation with foreign countries through weapons supplies."[89]

The cover memorandum said that "special anxiety" had arisen about the tendency of some recipients of Soviet weapons to use them "for purposes ranging beyond defense" and about "the diffusion of technology to produce armaments, including missile technology, as a result of our military assistance." Not only did these problems threaten to "destabilize the situation" in key regions of the Third World, they also gave "the West a pretext to step up its interference in regional conflicts and increase its own arms supplies," thus "severely detracting from the effectiveness of our attempts to improve the situation in the world and to strengthen relations between the USSR and the USA and reduce the West-East confrontation overall."[90]

The nine officials also expressed practical concerns about Soviet arms transfers. On the one hand, they voiced dismay at the "imbalance of our relations with developing countries" and the numerous cases in which "our relations with friendly states are dominated by military forms of cooperation" and "the basis of relations between the USSR and friendly countries in the Third World remains very narrow." On the other hand, they worried that "the inadequate effectiveness of our military cooperation has done significant political and economic damage to our long-term policy" and "has not been suitable for the tasks of radical reform of the USSR's national economy and foreign economic activity." They also lamented the "inadequate performance of our advisers and specialists" and the "weak results" of Soviet arms and spare parts.[91]

The authors of the cover memorandum emphasized that they were not proposing sharp cuts in arms transfers, at least in the near term:

> Of course, as long as the USA and other NATO countries continue to rely on force, including military force, in their relations with countries of a progressive orientation, and as long as regional conflicts remain unregulated, states friendly to us will be compelled to strengthen their defense capability, which in turn means that our military cooperation with them must continue on a certain scale. We must also take account of the fact that up to now the USSR's military cooperation with numerous [Third World] countries has defined our foreign policy positions in those regions.[92]

The nine officials argued that it was "thanks mainly to the USSR's assistance that the armed forces of friendly states [in the Third World] have been able to uphold their countries' defense capacity." They also pointed to other benefits the Soviet Union had gained from weapons exports, including "opportunities for the USSR Navy to gain access to the ports [of recipient countries] and for [Soviet] military aircraft to land at their airfields." Most significant of all, "military cooperation with certain [Third World] states has been an important source of hard currency revenue for the Soviet Union." The role of arms sales in generating hard currency became increasingly exigent for Soviet leaders over the next few months, eclipsing everything else.

The cover memorandum indicated that the Conception was designed to "ensure the closest possible link between military cooperation and our country's foreign policy course" and was "aimed at increasing the quality and effectiveness of military cooperation while subsequently reducing the volume of military assistance and limiting supplies of offensive weaponry." The nine officials emphasized that arms transfers to developing states would be "based on the recipients' priority in the Soviet Union's policy and also on the conditions of providing them with military assistance."[93] The memorandum indicated that the Conception would be the guidepost for all aspects of Soviet weapons exports to the Third World for the first half of the 1990s.

The Conception itself began by proclaiming that Soviet military assistance to the Third World must "correspond to the USSR's main foreign policy tasks" and must serve "our country's economic interests."[94] These criteria, the document said, had to be judged "in the context of our all-encompassing approach to international security and our line pushing for a halt to the arms race, for disarmament, and for the political regulation of regional conflicts." Hence, military assistance to the Third World "must not provoke regional tension and an arms race" and "must not result in the political and economic militarization of the recipient-countries."

Echoing the March 1989 memorandum, the Conception affirmed that "the volume and nature of military assistance should be determined by the principle of reasonable sufficiency for defense of friendly countries without giving them the potential for aggressive, offensive operations." The document stressed that the Soviet Union must "pursue a long-term policy seeking limits on military assistance to foreign countries and on supplies of offensive weaponry to them, especially in regions of international tension, if possible on a mutual basis with the West." The Conception called for "stepped-up efforts within the UN to forge international agreement among all the major suppliers of weaponry regarding limits on arms exports and even a full cessation of them." But the document made clear that curbs on weapons supplies would be desirable only if international reciprocity were forthcoming:

> As a first step we should strive to achieve agreement with the USA and other leading producers of weaponry about the possibility of displaying mutual restraint to avoid stoking potential conflicts, including those of an internal nature. But in doing this, we must seek to avoid a situation in which a vacuum emerges in the absence of our military supplies and the countries most important for us turn elsewhere, especially to Western suppliers, to fulfill their needs.[95]

The document indicated that the major arms suppliers (including the Soviet Union) should make a particular effort to "avoid supplies or leases to developing countries of any weapons of great destructive power that could spark unintended actions, especially ballistic missiles and other types of armaments that can influence the strategic situation." They must also "refrain from transferring the technology to produce such weapons."

When discussing the Soviet Union's own approach to the transfer of production technology, the Conception said that "we should continue our policy of reducing assistance involving the manufacture of armaments and military technology in friendly countries under Soviet licenses." But the document made clear that the licensing of military production technology would continue – and indeed possibly even increase – when it could be "arranged on commercial terms" and was "economically worthwhile." In such cases, the document added, the Soviet Union should be "ready to sell licenses for [the manufacture of] the latest models of weapons, provided that the recipient-countries have sufficient productive and technical potential."[96]

This emphasis on economic criteria was typical of the entire Conception, which repeatedly stressed the importance of military exports for the Soviet economy and highlighted the need to increase the gains derived from these exports:

> The economic profitability of military assistance must be assessed not only by looking at the revenue that comes directly from it but also by taking account of all the national economic expenses and consequences it entails. To bolster the economic effectiveness of military-technical cooperation, we must pursue a policy of reducing the volume of military assistance provided as grants and on preferential terms. Our military cooperation must be determined first and foremost by political criteria, but when military cooperation allows us to earn major hard-currency revenue, we need to take full account of this important factor as we consider whether to limit the volume of such assistance.[97]

The document called for a strictly commercial approach, with "terms of payment no less stringent than those now existing" for all categories of purchasers.[98] The Conception urged the CPSU Politburo to "intensify efforts to secure repayment of earlier credits by making wider use of different forms of debt scheduling," and it recommended a firm moratorium on the "extension of further credits to countries that have not fulfilled the terms of their debt repayments and are seeking to make new purchases of our military goods."[99]

This emphasis on the economic benefits of arms transfers adumbrated the trend in Soviet policy over the next two-and-a-half years, as Soviet officials increasingly promoted arms sales around the world as a means of generating hard currency. The recommendations in the Conception to curtail grants and concessionary loans were quickly reflected in Soviet policy. The Soviet Union's ongoing efforts to promote settlements of regional conflicts in which some of its closest Third World allies were involved – in Cambodia, southern Africa, and Central America – had been inspired in part by a desire to reduce the volume of weapons shipped to these countries to help them sustain their combat operations. By the summer of 1989, in accordance with a resolution adopted by the Soviet Council of Ministers on 26 June, the Soviet Union had informed several of its staunch allies in the Third World as well as the governments of less important grant recipients (Benin, Burundi, Congo, Tanzania, etc.) that Soviet military assistance would no longer be provided on a strictly grant basis after existing contractual commitments came to an end in 1990–1991.[100]

This pattern, according to the document, could be modified as needed to take account of the "priority that countries enjoy in receiving [Soviet] military assistance." The degree of priority was supposed to reflect

> the content of their foreign policy and the extent to which it corresponds with the new political thinking, the degree of friendly relations they have established with us, the development of their political, economic, and other ties [with the USSR], our interests in particular regions, and other factors.

The document acknowledged that "determining long-term priorities right now is exceptionally difficult because of the fluidity of the international situation and of the internal conditions in specific countries." Even so, the Conception stipulated that "the current ranking of priorities in our military cooperation with foreign countries (other than socialist) is that requests from India, Syria, Ethiopia, Algeria, and Libya will be handled with the greatest urgency."[101] In particular, the document urged the CPSU Politburo to do whatever was necessary to "ensure the preservation of the Soviet Union's role as the main partner in [military] cooperation with India." India, along with Syria, Algeria, Libya, and Iraq, was to be "supplied with state-of-the-art weapons systems and military technology," even if "deliveries of offensive weaponry to them are somewhat reduced." Lower (though still high) in priority were Angola, Ethiopia, South Yemen, North Yemen, Nicaragua, and Mozambique, all of which were to be "supplied with armaments of a defensive nature, primarily to replace obsolete models and depleted weaponry." The new systems were mostly heavy weapons, except in the case of Mozambique, which was "to be supplied primarily with light arms."[102]

The Conception indicated that Afghanistan, from which all Soviet troops had been withdrawn in February 1989, would receive all "the military assistance it needs, taking account of the development of the military-political situation in that country."[103] Over the next two years, as Soviet officials concluded that the pro-Soviet ruler of Afghanistan, Najibullah, would need continued infusions of weaponry to keep the insurgency at bay, Soviet military assistance poured in, making Afghanistan one of the largest recipients of Soviet arms during the final three years of the Soviet Union.[104] Most of the weapons supplied to Afghanistan came from the Soviet Defense Ministry's surplus stocks. Although the Afghan government could not pay for the shipments, the Soviet military-industrial official Vitalii Kataev later explained that the arrangement was "economically advantageous [for the USSR] because the costs of dismantling and disposing of these armaments would have been greater than the costs of exporting them, even without any hope of receiving payment."[105]

The Conception offered a dual message on Iraq and Iran, the former of which had been the largest recipient of Soviet arms during most of the 1980s: "Now that the Iran–Iraq conflict has been settled, we should stress the desirability of achieving international agreement to limit weapons supplies to these two countries." But the document emphasized that until firm agreement on the matter was achieved, the Soviet Union "must provide military assistance to Iraq, without excluding the possibility of giving assistance to Iran as well."[106]

The document likewise indicated that Soviet supplies of weaponry to both South Yemen and North Yemen were intended to preserve a "military equilibrium" between the two countries. With respect to Angola and Mozambique, the Soviet Union should "preserve friendly relations" with them while "seeking to achieve political settlements of the conflicts in southern Africa." The goal of these settlements, according to the Conception, was to allow "the Soviet Union to reduce the financial cost of providing military assistance to [the two countries]." The document recommended that Soviet military assistance to Nicaragua be decided in conjunction with Cuba "in order to avoid precipitating an increase of tension in the region."[107]

With regard to Peru and Nigeria, both of which paid for Soviet weapons largely in hard currency, the Conception noted, with satisfaction, that "the leaders of those countries have a great interest in developing military cooperation with the USSR" and in ensuring that "we will maintain our positions there." Both Peru and Nigeria, the document added, should be "supplied with the latest weaponry, generally of a defensive nature."[108] Moving to lower-priority countries in Africa, the Conception indicated that

> in our military cooperation with smaller countries (Benin, Botswana, Burundi, Burkina Faso, Ghana, Guinea, Guinea-Bissau, Zambia, Zimbabwe, Congo, Cape Verde, Madagascar, Mali, the Seychelles, Sao Tome and Principe, Tanzania, Uganda), we ... must pursue a policy of reducing military assistance, offering it predominantly to countries that permit the USSR Armed Forces to use their air bases and port facilities.[109]

This approach was in accord with a resolution adopted by the CPSU Politburo in August 1987 conferring special status on Third World countries that had given Soviet troops broad access to their air fields and ports.[110] The preferential treatment of them remained in effect through the rest of the Soviet era.

Turning finally to "military-technical cooperation with Kuwait, Jordan, and the United Arab Emirates," the document said that "we should be guided by the economic benefits of cooperation [with these three countries], taking account of our policy in the region." All three countries were to be "supplied with the latest armaments, mostly of a defensive nature," which would be paid for in hard currency. The Conception also stated that "in each concrete instance when we provide military equipment to national liberation movements, we should do so only after taking account of the unfolding situation" in the Middle East.[111]

The document held out the possibility that the Soviet Union might "establish and develop military cooperation with foreign countries with which we do not currently have such cooperation." Of particular interest in this regard were "oil-producing countries and other states that are fully capable of paying" in hard currency.[112] Any decisions about supplying weapons to a new Third World country were to be "based on the USSR's political, economic, and military interests" and on "the specific features of the concrete international situation."[113] This point in the Conception soon became a reality with the Soviet authorities' decision in December 1989 to resume military exports to the People's Republic of China after a hiatus of some 30 years.[114] Subsequently, as discussed below, the Soviet Union approached several other Third World countries that until recently had been viewed with great hostility and suspicion by Moscow (e.g. South Korea), asking them about their possible interest in acquiring Soviet-made fighter aircraft and other weapons.

The Conception indicated that the Soviet Union's arms supply relationships with Third World countries must include a "strong emphasis on ensuring timely repairs, support, and spare parts for both weapons and production equipment." To promote this goal, the Soviet Union "should help [the recipient countries] set up their own repair facilities" as well as "sites for the basing, command, and combat application of armaments supplied to them."[115] The Conception called for the Soviet Union to "continue training military personnel from [Third World] countries" at Soviet institutions, but it suggested that these programs should focus mainly on senior officers and should "encourage lower-ranking officers to receive training directly in their own countries." The document also called for Soviet military-political officers to "expand and deepen their contacts and ties with military-political commanders [in LDCs] to strengthen our influence" with them and their governments. With regard to Soviet military advisers and specialists sent to Third World countries, the Conception said they should "come with at least some combat experience" and should focus on "bolstering the combat readiness of the [local] armies" by seeking "improvements in the training and command of troops and the maintenance of weapons systems and equipment in a combat-ready state."[116]

The Conception affirmed that the Soviet Union must hold recipient countries in the Third World accountable for the way they used Soviet weapons:

> We must consider reexamining agreements on military cooperation in cases when the recipient-countries fail to uphold their obligations or when they take the armaments we gave them and use them for purposes other than defense and with the aim of undermining international and regional security.

In particular, the Soviet Union "must strictly enforce the provision requiring the non-transfer of military items without our approval to third countries (including national liberation movements) or the creation of other offensive weapons systems on the basis of the military items we provided."[117] These passages in the document presumably applied first and foremost to countries like Ethiopia, Libya, Iraq, and Syria, all of which had violated the restrictions many times in the past. Indeed, the Conception stressed that "in relations with Ethiopia and Libya, we must ensure that our military cooperation with them in the future will be strictly in accordance with the criteria laid out in this Conception" – an admission that both Ethiopia and Libya had been using Soviet-made weapons for purposes contrary to Soviet interests (in Ethiopia's case for prolonging the ruinous war in Eritrea despite Soviet attempts to promote a diplomatic settlement, and in Libya's case for waging war against neighboring Chad).[118]

One of the most striking features of the Conception was its call for "the introduction of sweeping public disclosure and openness into the sphere of our military cooperation, taking account of the security interests of the USSR and its allies and friends." The document called for high-ranking Soviet officials to "provide a review of our military cooperation with foreign countries" in public testimony before committees of the Supreme Soviet, explaining how the military assistance "conformed to the Soviet Union's political, military, and economic interests." The document also recommended that "these matters be covered in the Soviet press" and that the Soviet government "endorse the establishment of a UN Register of all conventional arms transfers" – a register that was indeed officially set up in December 1991.[119] The Conception's proposals to bring a degree of transparency into an area of Soviet foreign policy that had previously been totally opaque were major departures from the policies and mindsets of all previous Soviet leaders. If the proposals on this matter had been fully carried out, they would have signaled a major advance in "new political thinking" and a reorientation of Soviet policy vis-à-vis the Third World.

Even though many provisions in the Conception (including the one about greater openness) were never really implemented, the document did serve as a rough framework for Soviet arms transfers to the Third World over the next two-and-a-half years. The seemingly contradictory proposals it embodied – seeking to reduce the total volume of weapons exports, on the one hand, while simultaneously striving to earn as much hard currency as possible from them, on the other – might eventually have come into conflict if the Soviet Union had lasted longer. But during the final two years of the Soviet Union, structural conditions in the global arms market ultimately determined the pattern of Soviet military supplies to the Third World.

Third phase: 1990–1991

The third and final phase of Soviet arms transfer policy during the Gorbachev era displayed a few areas of continuity with the second phase but also some major differences, as Soviet leaders abandoned their proposals to restrain military exports and instead embarked on a frantic (though largely unsuccessful) campaign to sell as many weapons as possible to any country that would pay in hard currency. The Soviet Union's efforts to expand arms exports proved abortive, but that was because of exogenous circumstances – the financial constraints facing many Third World countries, the embargos imposed in 1990 and 1991 against some erstwhile Soviet customers, and the success of other leading suppliers (especially the United States) in outflanking the Soviet Union – and had little to do with the "new political thinking." A slight residue of the "new political thinking" was still evident during this third phase, but its significance was greatly overshadowed by the impact of international conditions and changes that were beyond Gorbachev's control.

One area of continuity during this third phase was the Soviet Union's continued unwillingness to provide additional nuclear submarines to India or to help the Indian navy develop nuclear propulsion systems for its own submarines. After India received the *INS Chakra* in early February 1988, the Indian and Western news media featured many articles claiming that the Soviet Union had agreed to transfer at least five to six more nuclear submarines to India. Further such reports, apparently based on off-the-record comments by Indian officials, continued to appear in 1989 and 1990.[120] But it is now clear that all these reports were inaccurate or at least misleading. Even if some officials in the VPK or the Soviet General Staff or the MVES may have suggested to Indian envoys that the Soviet government had agreed to provide additional nuclear submarines or to help India build nuclear propulsion systems for its own vessels, declassified documents show that no such arrangement was ever approved by the CPSU Politburo or the Soviet Defense Council.

Although the June 1989 Conception of Military Assistance underscored the Soviet Union's determination to remain the dominant supplier of conventional arms to India, the Conception (like the March 1989 memorandum from Shevardnadze, Yazov, and Kamentsev) drew a sharp distinction between conventional arms and nuclear-powered submarines. On the grounds of realpolitik, Soviet leaders had long been ambivalent about the prospect of transferring nuclear submarines to India. Such transfers risked the compromise of sensitive data and equipment and threatened to spur

US retaliatory supplies to Pakistan. Neither before nor after February 1988 had any other arms-exporting country ever provided a nuclear submarine or nuclear propulsion technology to a Third World country. Hence, Soviet leaders had no reason to fear that if they refrained from leasing more nuclear submarines to India and from supplying nuclear-propulsion systems and expertise, another supplier would step in to fill the void. Instead, the issue could be decided on its own merits. Prime Minister Gandhi raised the topic several times with Gorbachev, notably during face-to-face discussions in July 1989 and in a personal letter to Gorbachev four months later.[121] But Gandhi's efforts to facilitate the transfers ultimately came to naught. Disappointing though this outcome must have been for officials in New Delhi, the Soviet government assured them – and demonstrated concretely – that the Soviet Union's broader commitment to supplying India with all the weapons it needed had not diminished at all.

One other area of continuity from 1989 to 1990–1991 was the Soviet government's willingness to accept greater transparency and openness regarding its arms exports and policymaking. Although a good deal of murkiness remained about Soviet weapons supplies, the degree of openness was much greater than at any time in the past. As recommended in the June 1989 Conception, Soviet leaders proved willing to devise a comprehensive register of arms transfers under UN auspices. Work on the matter proceeded in 1990 and 1991, culminating with the inception of the register in December 1991 as the Soviet Union was coming unraveled.

Moscow's endorsement of the UN Register of Conventional Arms was a notable departure from deeply engrained Soviet habits of secrecy, but one of the reasons Soviet officials supported it was that they were confident that "it will not hinder our arms trade."[122] This was accurate in the sense that the UN Register was never intended to be anything more than informational. Concrete limits on the global weapons trade, Soviet leaders believed, would be impossible without a formal multilateral convention. In the absence of such a convention, "the major suppliers will never agree to restrict [their own arms transfers] voluntarily."[123]

Nonetheless, the Soviet Politburo's deliberations in 1989 about the desirability of a multilateral convention to reduce the flow of weapons to the Third World did not engender follow-up action on the matter in 1990–1991. Work on setting up the UN Register substituted for efforts to forge a broader convention that would have specified concrete multilateral limits. The Soviet government's decision to focus on the former rather than the latter stemmed in part from a sense that proceeding with both simultaneously would be unfeasible and would probably doom the whole enterprise, but it also stemmed from a growing wariness in Moscow of any steps that would necessitate the sacrifice of much-needed hard currency.

By 1990, the turbulence and bureaucratic disarray in the Soviet Union, including within the foreign trade and energy sectors, meant that weapons exports were one of the few things the Soviet government could still rely on. The policymaking process for this key activity was restructured in the first half of 1990 to conform to the evolving political institutions in the Soviet Union. An Interdepartmental Commission on Military-Technical Cooperation (MKVTS) was set up to consider and coordinate proposals and recommendations submitted by ministries, military-industrial enterprises, the General Staff, and other bodies. The MKVTS, working with the MVES directorates, was then supposed to transmit its own recommendations to Gorbachev in his numerous capacities – as Soviet President (a post created in March 1990), as head of the Defense Council, and as CPSU General Secretary.[124] This reconfigured process was ostensibly highly centralized, but in reality it was less coherent than it appeared on the surface. The actual trend was toward greater leeway for agencies and defense enterprises to pursue transfers of weapons that would bring in hard currency. Even if some government officials and aides to Gorbachev had misgivings about the de facto decentralization of the process, the push for hard currency was fully in line with the Soviet President's own objectives.

The growing salience of financial considerations in Soviet weapons exports, reflected in the free-wheeling campaign to earn hard currency, was reinforced by mounting concern about the state of the Soviet military-industrial base. Gorbachev and his advisers realized early on that the fate of his ambitious plans for economic revitalization would depend in part on his ability to limit the amount of resources allocated to the Soviet armed forces for at least a decade or two. During his first few years in office, Gorbachev had some room to coast by relying on the sunk costs and huge investments made in the Soviet weapons industry when Leonid Brezhnev was CPSU General Secretary (1964–1982). But by the end of the 1980s this buffer was no longer available. Gorbachev's advisers feared that if all the best resources, both human and material, were still being channeled to the military sector at the expense of civilian industries, Soviet economic restructuring and technological prowess would be imperiled. Gorbachev's introduction of "new political thinking" was designed to achieve a stable and relaxed international environment that would permit him to cut military spending and convert military factories to civilian output. Although defense expenditures continued to grow at a brisk pace of roughly 3–4 percent per year during Gorbachev's first three years in office (thanks to the cushion left from the Brezhnev era), he eventually reversed the momentum of the 25-year Soviet military buildup and achieved sharp annual reductions in the defense budget starting in 1989.[125]

Gorbachev's success in reducing military spending was marred, however, by his inability to follow through with the proposed conversion of defense plants. Indeed, soon after Gorbachev announced his intention to transfer resources from military activities to the civilian sector, complaints began surfacing in the Soviet press about the slow pace of conversion and the lack of any tangible economic improvements. In some respects, of course, the meager results of the conversion program were not at all surprising. The continued deterioration of the Soviet economy was due mainly to systemic weaknesses that conversion alone could not have redressed, including the lack of market incentives and competition, the chaotic state of the country's supply network, and the bureaucratic confusion accompanying perestroika. Yet, even if these ailments had not been so acute, the initial expectations surrounding conversion might have been impossible to achieve because of the disorganized and limited nature of the official conversion program, and because of resistance on the part of senior military commanders, Communist Party officials, and military-industrial elites.[126]

Even if reductions in military spending had been carried out as originally projected, many of the factories under the auspices of the VPK intended to preserve a healthy level of weapons production by exporting more armaments to the Third World. When conversion proved chaotic and disruptive in its early stages (in part because it was so poorly implemented), enterprise managers began insisting that the future existence of their plants would be endangered and mass unemployment would ensue unless they continued producing military goods for new markets in the Third World.[127] The resulting pressure to boost weapons exports posed a dilemma for even the most ardent Soviet proponents of "new thinking" in foreign policy. The Soviet Union's economic problems had grown so acute by the start of the 1990s that Soviet leaders naturally were hesitant about taking any steps (such as banning or restricting arms transfers) that could undermine what was clearly a vital part of the Soviet economy. One of the leading proponents of "new thinking," Eduard Shevardnadze, acknowledged this point shortly before the abortive August 1991 coup in Moscow:

> The military-industrial complex is, whether we like it or not, the basis of our existing industry; and if we were simply to destroy it rather than intelligently place it on a new footing, we would be destroying the one thing that will help the country survive economically. It represents millions of the most highly skilled workers, engineers, and designers, and is a golden asset for our economy, which would be very easy to fritter away and impossible to re-create quickly.[128]

Thus, so long as military-industrial elites continued to warn that arms exports were necessary to keep their factories solvent and to avoid mass layoffs of defense workers, Soviet leaders were hard-pressed to turn them down.

This goal of using arms transfers to the Third World to preserve a sound industrial base in the Soviet Union, as well as the desire to earn hard currency from military sales, gave rise to elaborate Soviet efforts in the early 1990s to export greater quantities of weapons. Although Soviet military deliveries and new arms agreements declined in both 1989 and 1990, that was purely because of a general downturn in the global arms trade, stemming mainly from the saturation of the market in the mid-1980s and the severe financial problems confronting heavily indebted Third World countries.[129] Despite those adverse circumstances, Soviet military and industrial representatives did everything they could to drum up new business and find new Third World customers for Soviet-made weaponry. The most advanced Soviet aircraft and missiles were featured prominently at international defense exhibitions in the hope of attracting buyers.

Unlike in the past, when Soviet military-industrial officials and political leaders were reluctant to transfer top-of-the-line equipment to even their most reliable Third World clients, the Soviet Union by the early 1990s was offering its latest models of aircraft, tanks, surface-to-air missiles, radars, and other weapons to any country that was willing to pay in hard currency. The Soviet government avidly sought customers in the Third World (and among the newly democratizing countries of Eastern Europe) and resumed arms shipments to China, including top-of-the-line MiG-31 fighter aircraft. Soviet officials also approached countries that had never bought arms from the Soviet Union before and, in most cases, had long been seen in Moscow as "enemies" aligned with the United States. Among those courted as potential customers were South Korea, the Philippines, Malaysia, Pakistan, South Africa, Brazil, Sweden, Switzerland, Saudi Arabia, and even a few member-states of the North Atlantic Treaty Organization.[130] The Soviet government would probably have sought to increase its weapons exports (to earn hard currency) even if military conversion had not been under way, but there is little doubt that the intensity of the sales campaign was due mainly to the efforts of defense-industrial managers to make up for lost domestic orders through increased arms sales abroad.

The Soviet Union's all-out drive to boost weapons exports to the Third World proved unsuccessful in the end. For every new sale racked up, Soviet military factories lost others. The inauspicious situation facing the leading international arms suppliers at the end of the 1980s, with a paucity of Third World customers willing to make major purchases, had become even more unfavorable for the Soviet Union by 1991. After Iraq invaded Kuwait in August 1990, the UN Security Council imposed an arms embargo on Iraq, depriving the Soviet Union of one of its prime customers. Soviet leaders had hoped that the embargo would be lifted in due course, but far from being lifted, its restrictions were actually tightened in the aftermath of the 1991 Gulf War, with no near-term prospect of being lifted. Arms restrictions of various sorts were also imposed against a few other countries that had been key Soviet customers, notably Libya (in connection with charges brought against Libyan agents for the Pan Am bombing over Lockerbie) and Yugoslavia as it dissolved into civil war.

Even if all these developments had not militated against an expansion of arms transfers to the Third World, the spiraling turmoil in the Soviet Union would have severely complicated Soviet attempts to promote military exports. The plunge in Soviet weapons sales during the final phase of the Gorbachev era mirrored the steady enervation and eventual dissolution of the Soviet Union itself.

Conclusions

The role of arms transfers in Soviet policy toward the Third World expanded enormously from the mid-1970s through the mid-1980s, including the initial year of Gorbachev's tenure as CPSU General Secretary. During this period, the Soviet Union was by far the largest supplier of military goods and services to the developing countries. Soviet weapons exports were disproportionately concentrated in the Middle East and South Asia, but at least some weapons from the Soviet Union flowed to almost all other parts of the globe as well. The growth in the value of Soviet military assistance to the Third World was attributable not only to the increased number of items sold but also to the improved quality of the arms that the Soviet Union was willing to supply.

By the late 1980s however, the conditions for Soviet military sales were much less propitious. The surge of arms transfers to the Third World from the mid-1970s through the mid-1980s (transfers not only from the Soviet Union but also from other major suppliers) had saturated global markets and created problems of financing and absorption for many LDC customers. As a result, the number of selling opportunities decreased and the international weapons trade turned into a buyers' market. The impact of this trend on the Soviet Union was exacerbated in the late 1980s by the cuts that almost all Western countries were making in their defense outlays as the Cold War was winding down. Without as much potential to sell to their home armed forces, Western arms manufacturers did their best to expand sales to the Third World. The Western companies pursued new military transfer agreements so avidly throughout the developing world at a time of shrinking purchases that they created even more of a buyers' market. Of particular concern to Moscow were the efforts by Western firms to supply advanced armaments to Third World countries that had previously bought all (or almost all) of their weaponry from the Soviet Union. For these sundry reasons, attempts to increase Soviet military exports ran into daunting obstacles in the late 1980s.

By the end of the 1980s, Gorbachev urgently needed more revenue from arms transfers to fund his domestic reform program and to keep the Soviet military-industrial complex from collapsing. Despite the prolonged Iran–Iraq War, the world price of oil had plunged in the first half of the 1980s, depriving the Soviet Union of what could have been its most lucrative source of hard currency earnings. As the Soviet macroeconomic situation rapidly deteriorated in the late 1980s against the backdrop of Gorbachev's incoherent economic policies, the Soviet government began taking out large foreign loans. But to avoid being saddled with crippling levels of debt, the Soviet authorities desperately searched for other sources of hard currency revenue. Arms exports, which had soared to record levels in the early to mid-1980s, were the most obvious option. Soviet officials hoped that in addition to bringing in hard currency, expanded weapons sales would enable Soviet military industries to weather the painful transition to a less militarized economy. As the Soviet government's efforts to encourage conversion of defense plants to civilian output encountered ever greater obstacles, military-industrial managers eagerly pushed for expanded arms sales to Third World countries to make up for cuts in the Soviet Union's own procurement orders and to offset the costs of conversion.

For a brief while, in the first half of 1989, Soviet leaders seemed inclined to make the best of an adverse situation. During this heady time for "new political thinking," in the months before Soviet-backed Communist regimes collapsed in Eastern Europe, the Soviet Politburo considered (at least implicitly) the implications of "new political thinking" for Soviet arms transfers to the Third World. Top-secret reports adopted by the Politburo in March 1989 and June 1989 pointed the way toward a long-term reduction of Soviet military assistance to the Third World. The Politburo documents, however, were not always consistent in their arguments, and they included important qualifications, particularly regarding the need to augment the economic profitability of weapons sales and to retain all major LDC customers. In one respect this emphasis on improving economic gains from arms exports to the Third World was compatible with the proclaimed goal of reducing military assistance – both objectives were conducive to phasing out grants and highly concessionary loans – but in other respects these two policy strands were incompatible. To the extent that Soviet leaders were committed to maximizing hard-currency earnings from weapons sales, they had to sell more arms, not fewer, to Third World countries that were able to pay. They also had to sell higher-quality weapons, especially the latest fighter aircraft, bombers, air defense missiles, naval vessels, main battle tanks, self-propelled artillery, and armored combat vehicles, all of which drew higher prices.

These combined pressures led to a vigorous Soviet campaign in 1990–1991 to sell more armaments abroad, including the very latest Soviet conventional weapons that had only recently entered service with the Soviet Union's own armed forces. Despite the "new thinking" in Soviet foreign policy that favored diplomacy over military force, Soviet officials and defense factory managers (acting with high-level approval) went to great lengths to promote arms sales to Third World countries, regardless of whether such sales would increase the bloodshed in ongoing wars or precipitate new conflicts elsewhere. The Soviet Union's bid for expanded military exports was so aggressive that defense manufacturers in other supplying countries began to suspect that Gorbachev's government was trying to corner the market for Soviet firms. Nonetheless, despite the no-holds-barred campaign by the Soviet authorities and Soviet weapons producers to boost military sales abroad, the results were notably lacking. Soviet arms exports plummeted in the late 1980s and early 1990s, falling to levels unseen in many years – a striking reversal of the pattern through the mid-1980s.

The sharp decline in Soviet weapons sales to the Third World after 1986 has prompted numerous Western analysts to link this trend with the "new thinking" in Soviet foreign policy. The precipitous drop in Soviet arms transfers to LDCs after more than a decade of surging exports, the argument goes, stemmed from Gorbachev's embrace of a less militarized foreign policy and his desire to be a catalyst for peaceful settlements of regional conflicts. Plausible though this interpretation might seem, it is not borne out by the evidence.

Even though the CPSU Politburo in 1989 did accept the desirability of curbing weapons exports to the Third World, the Politburo did not want to carry out significant reductions of its own unless other major suppliers (especially the United States) did the same on a sustained and equal basis. Moreover, by 1990, the Soviet Union's frantic quest for hard currency overrode any inclination to refrain from trying to sell more weapons abroad. Far from deliberately seeking to reduce military exports to the Third World, the Soviet government by 1990 was doing everything it could to achieve precisely the opposite – a major increase in arms sales.

Despite the far-reaching impact of "new political thinking" on many Soviet actions in the Third World, the "new thinking" was not what led to the precipitous decline in Soviet arms transfers to the Third World. Analyses of Gorbachev's foreign policy that have drawn a causal link between "new thinking" and the curtailment of weapons supplies to developing countries give a misleading picture. The "new thinking" had wide-ranging, concrete effects on Soviet foreign policy and for a brief while seemed to be generating changes in the Soviet Union's approach to military exports, but proposals for restraint on this vital issue ultimately fell foul of domestic economic and political exigencies. Conditions in the global arms trade that favored buyers over sellers and that foreclosed certain channels of potential sales in the late 1980s and early 1990s, not any drastic change of Soviet policy, accounted for the steep drop in Soviet weapons exports to the Third World.

Notes

1 The term "Third World" (or "developing world" or "less-developed countries"), as used in this chapter, refers to all countries in Africa except South Africa, all countries in Asia except Japan, all countries in Latin America, and all countries in the Middle East. The term "arms transfers" refers to the

provision of military goods and services through direct sale, credit, or grants. The military goods and services supplied by the Soviet Union included weapons, spare parts, support equipment, advisers, training, and information. Arms transfers normally occur in two phases: agreements and deliveries. Agreements are contractual promises to provide military equipment and services, whereas deliveries are the actual shipment of goods or the performance of services.

2 "Voenno-tekhnicheskoe sotrudnichestvo (VTS)," Aide-mémoire by Vitalii Kataev, former deputy head of the CPSU Defense Industry Department, n.d. (mid 1992), in Hoover Archives (Stanford University), Papers of Vitalii Leonidovich Kataev (henceforth cited as Kataev Papers), Box 12, Folder 30, p. 1.

3 Constantin Katsakioris, "Soviet Lessons for Arab Modernization: Soviet Educational Aid Towards Arab Countries after 1956," *Journal of Modern European History*, Vol. 8, No. 1 (March 2010), pp. 85–106.

4 U.S. Arms Control and Disarmament Agency, *World Military Expenditures and Arms Transfers, 1990* (Washington, DC: U.S. Government Printing Office, 1992), p. 14.

5 The data here are taken from ibid., and are fully compatible with figures provided in "Voenno-tekhnicheskoe sotrudnichestvo," p. 1.

6 Richard Grimmett, *Trends in Conventional Arms Transfers to the Third World, 1985–1992*, Report No. 92–914-F (Washington, DC: U.S. Congressional Research Service, Library of Congress, September 1993), pp. 49, 61.

7 Ibid., p. 61.

8 U.S. Central Intelligence Agency (CIA), *Handbook of Economic Statistics, 1992*, CPAS-92–0001 (Springfield, VA: National Technical Information Service, September 1992), p. 158. Figures have been converted here to constant 1991 dollars using an inflation index based on the US Department of Defense's price deflator.

9 For early indicators of this trend, see, for example, CIA, Directorate of Intelligence, "Soviet Interest in Bilateral Discussion of Regional Conflicts," Intelligence Memorandum (Secret/Sensitive), 14 August 1986, pp. 1–9. Scanned images of his document and of other declassified CIA materials cited here can be found in the CIA Records Search Tool (CREST) at the National Archives and Records Administration, College Park, MD, or in the CIA Electronic Reading Room (www.foia.cia.gov).

10 Andrei Kozyrev, "Doverie i balans interesov," *Mezhdunarodnaya zhizn'* (Moscow), No. 10 (October 1988), pp. 5, 9–10.

11 "Vypiska iz protokola No. 147 zasedaniya Politbyuro," Extract from CPSU Politburo Resolutions P. No. 84 and P. No. 100 (Top Secret), 7–8 February 1989, in Rossiiskiii Gosudarstvennyi Arkhiv Noveishei Istorii (RGANI), F. 89, Op. 10, D. 20, Ll. 1–3, and F. 89, Op. 10, D. 21, Ll. 1.

12 CIA, Directorate of Intelligence, "USSR-East Asia: Moscow Realigning Its Policy," Intelligence Assessment, SOV 90–10025X (Secret), May 1990, pp. 14–15; "Vypiska iz protokola No. 179/4 zasedaniya Politbyuro TsK KPSS 14 fevralya 1990 goda: Ob utverzhdenii teksta Zayavleniya Sovetskogo pravitel'stva v svyazi s vozobnovleniem voennykh deistvii v Eritree (Efiopiya)," Extract from CPSU Politburo Resolution (Top Secret), in RGANI, F. 89, Op. 9, D. 78, Ll. 1–3; and "TsK KPSS," Memorandum (Top Secret) from D. T. Yazov (defense minister), I. S. Belousov (head of CPSU Defense-Industry Department), and K. F. Katushev (minister of foreign economic relations) to the CPSU Politburo, 18 April 1990, in RGANI, F. 89, Op. 10, D. 59, Ll. 1–3.

13 US Director of Central Intelligence (DCI), "Soviet Naval Strategy and Programs toward the 21st Century: National Intelligence Estimate," NIE 11–15–89/SC 03335–89 (Top Secret), June 1989, Vol. 1. This trend was a striking change from 1984–1985, when far-flung Soviet naval activities in Third

World waters reached an all-time high. See CIA, Directorate of Intelligence, "Soviet Naval Activities Outside Home Waters in 1985: A Research Paper," SOV 86–10041C (Secret), October 1986.

14 Among those who have taken this view are Melvin A. Goodman, *Gorbachev's Retreat: The Third World* (New York: Praeger, 1991); W. Raymond Duncan and Carolyn McGiffert Ekedahl, *Moscow and the Third World under Gorbachev* (Boulder, CO: Westview Press, 1990); and Jiří Valenta and Frank Cibulka (eds.), *Gorbachev's New Thinking and Third World Conflicts* (New Brunswick, NJ: Transaction Publishers, 1990).

15 Fifteen of the boxes have been accessible since 2002. The remaining five boxes were not accessible as of late 2010. Finding aids for the collection are available at the archive.

16 CIA, "Communist Aid Activities in Non-Communist Less Developed Countries, 1979 and 1954–79," Intelligence Report (Top Secret), ER 80–10318U, October 1980, pp. 5, 11.

17 Ragna Boden, "Cold War Economics: Soviet Aid to Indonesia," *Journal of Cold War Studies*, Vol. 10, No. 3 (Summer 2008), pp. 110–28; CIA, "Communist Aid Activities in Non-Communist Less Developed Countries, 1979 and 1954–79," Intelligence Report (Top Secret), ER 80–10318U, October 1980, pp. 6–7; C. W. Larson, "Soviet Economic Aid: Volume, Function, and Importance," *Development Policy Review*, Vol. 5, No. 3 (September 1987), pp. 257–76; C. R. Dannehl, *Politics, Trade, and Development: Soviet Economic Aid to the Non-Communist Third World, 1955–89* (Brookfield, VT: Dartmouth Publishing, 1995); and O. Cooper and C. Fogarty, "Soviet Economic and Military Aid to the Less Developed Countries, 1954–78," in US Congress, Joint Economic Committee, *Soviet Economy in a Time of Change*, 2 vols. 96th Congress, 1st Session, 10 October 1979, Vol. 2, p. 651.

18 CIA, Directorate of Intelligence, Office of Regional and Political Analysis, "Soviet and Cuban Intervention in the Angolan Civil War," Intelligence Memorandum (Top Secret UMBRA), March 1977.

19 CIA, "Soviet Military Capabilities to Project Power and Influence in Distant Areas: National Intelligence Estimate," NIE 10–11–79 (Top Secret), October 1979, pp. 21–3.

20 Interview with Anatolii Dobrynin, in Moscow, 14 June 1999.

21 Anatolii Dobrynin, *Sugubo doveritel'no: Posol v Vashingtone pri shesti prezidentakh SShA, 1962–1986* (Moscow: Avtor, 1996), pp. 311, 327.

22 CIA "Communist Aid Activities in Non-Communist Less Developed Countries, 1979 and 1954–79," p. 5.

23 Yong-Chool Ha, "Soviet Perceptions of Soviet–North Korean Relations," *Asian Survey*, Vol. 26, No. 5 (May 1986), pp. 573–90.

24 CIA, "Soviet Military Capabilities to Project Power and Influence to Distant Areas," pp. 21–3.

25 For examples of direct supplies to guerrillas and terrorists, see "Postanovlenie Sekretariata TsK Kommunisticheskoi Partii Sovetskogo Soyuza: Vopros Mezhdunarodnogo otdela TsK KPSS," No. ST-224/71gs (Top Secret/Special Dossier), 18 August 1980, in RGANI, F. 89, Op. 39, D. 28, Ll. 1–4; "Postanovlenie Sekretariata TsK Kommunisticheskoi Partii Sovetskogo Soyuza: Vopros Mezhdunarodnogo otdela TsK KPSS," No. ST-205/55gs (Top Secret/Special Dossier), 4 April 1980, in RGANI, F. 89, Op. 32, D. 24, Ll. 1–4; "Postanovlenie Sekretariata TsK Kommunisticheskoi Partii Sovetskogo Soyuza: Vopros Mezhdunarodnogo otdela TsK KPSS," No. ST-199/53gs (Top Secret/Special Dossier), 25 February 1980, in RGANI, F. 89, Op. 32, D. 23, Ll. 1–8; "Postanovlenie Sekretariata TsK Kommunisticheskoi Partii Sovetskogo Soyuza: Vopros Mezhdunarodnogo otdela TsK KPSS," No. ST-174/44gs (Top Secret/Special

Dossier), 30 August 1979, in RGANI, F. 89, Op. 32, D. 9, Ll. 1–4; "Postanovlenie Sekretariata TsK Kommunisticheskoi Partii Sovetskogo Soyuza: Vopros Mezhdunarodnogo otdela TsK KPSS," No. ST-38/36gs (Top Secret/Special Dossier), 30 December 1976, in RGANI, F. 89, Op. 27, D. 31, Ll. 9–12; "Postanovlenie Sekretariata TsK Kommunisticheskoi Partii Sovetskogo Soyuza: Vopros Mezhdunarodnogo otdela TsK KPSS," No. ST-37/37gs (Top Secret/Special Dossier), 27 December 1976, in RGANI, F. 89, Op. 27, d. 30, Ll. 54–64; "Postanovlenie Sekretariata TsK Kommunisticheskoi Partii Sovetskogo Soyuza: Vopros Mezhdunarodnogo otdela TsK KPSS," No. ST-9/25gs (Top Secret/Special Dossier), 17 May 1976, in RGANI, F. 89, Op. 27, D. 12, Ll. 32–5; "Postanovlenie Sekretariata TsK Kommunisticheskoi Partii Sovetskogo Soyuza: Vopros Mezhdunarodnogo otdela TsK KPSS," No. ST-10/4gs (Top Secret/Special Dossier), 24 May 1976, in RGANI, F. 89, Op. D. 13, Ll. 1–14; and "Postanovlenie Sekretariata TsK Kommunisticheskoi Partii Sovetskogo Soyuza: Vopros Mezhdunarodnogo otdela TsK KPSS," No. ST-112/28gs (Top Secret/Special Dossier), 31 January 1974, in RGANI, F. 89, Op. 89, D. 25, Ll. 1–2. See also "TsK KPSS," Memorandum No. 11/ss (Top Secret/Special Dossier) from Yurii Andropov, chairman of the KGB, to the CPSU Politburo, 8 July 1974, in RGANI, F. 89, Op. 51, D. 30, L. 1, which calls for the "clandestine acquisition and transfer, in the utmost secrecy, of firearms and explosives" to Cypriot terrorists. Soviet arms transfer contracts normally included a provision allowing the USSR to veto retransfers to third parties. This provision was honored more in the breach than in the observance. For samples of such contracts, see the series of top-secret Soviet military aid agreements with Grenada, in US Department of State and Department of Defense, *Grenada Documents: An Overview and Selection*, September 1984, Docs. 13, 14, and 15. The relevant articles are Article 6 in the 1980 agreement and Article 7 in the 1982 agreement. For other important transcribed Soviet State Security (KGB) documents on Soviet support for terrorist groups in the Third World, see Christopher M. Andrew and Vasili Mitrokhin, *The World Was Going Our Way: The KGB and the Struggle for the Third World* (New York: Basic Books, 1995), pp. 246–62.

26 James P. Nichol, "The Soviet Union," in James Everett Katz (ed.), *The Implications of Third World Military Industrialization: Sowing the Serpents' Teeth* (Lexington, MA: Lexington Books, 1986), pp. 71–89.

27 For evidence from the former Soviet KGB archive, see Vasili Mitrokhin, *The KGB in Afghanistan*, CWIHP Working Paper No. 40 (Washington, DC: Cold War International History Project, July 2002), esp. pp. 25–45.

28 Andrew and Mitrokhin, *The World Was Going Our Way*, pp. 214–21. For background, see David Pollock, "Moscow and Aden: Coping with a Coup," *Problems of Communism*, Vol. 35, No. 3 (May-June 1986), pp. 56–60.

29 DCI, "Soviet Foreign Military Assistance: Interagency Intelligence Memorandum," NI IIM 87–10004C (Top Secret), May 1987, pp. 14–19.

30 See the essentially identical figures in "Voenno-tekhnicheskoe sotrudnichestvo (VTS)," p. 1; and DCI, "Soviet Foreign Military Assistance," p. 13.

31 Calculated from data in DCI, "Soviet Foreign Military Assistance," pp. 11–14.

32 CIA, "The Soviet Weapons Industry: An Overview," DI 86–10016, September 1986, p. 8.

33 William Lewis, "Emerging Choices for the Soviets in Third World Arms Transfer Policy," in US Arms Control and Disarmament Agency, *World Military Expenditures and Arms Transfers 1985*, ACDA Publication 123 (Washington, DC: US Government Printing Office, August 1985), p. 31.

34 Percentages calculated from data in US Central Intelligence Agency and US Defense Intelligence Agency, "The Soviet Economy Under a New Leader," 19 March 1986, p. 25, reproduced in US Congress, Joint Economic Committee,

Allocation of Resources in the Soviet Union and China – 1985, 99th Congress, 1st Session, March 1986, pp. 163–5. Because weapons shipped abroad can come from stockpiles rather than from production lines, the percentages given here are only a rough indicator.

35 Andrew and Mitrokhin, *The World Was Going Our Way*, pp. 58–65; and DCI, "Soviet Foreign Military Assistance," p. 22.

36 "TsK KPSS: O voennom sotrudnichestve s Respublikoi Zambiei," Memorandum (Top Secret) from O. Belyakov, head of the CPSU Defense Industry Department, and A. Urnov, deputy head of the CPSU International Department, to the CPSU Politburo, December 1986, with cover note from L. Zaikov to S. F. Akhromeev, Yu.M. Vorontsov, K. F. Katushev, B. I. Aristov, and G. M. Kornienko, in Hoover Archives, Kataev Papers, Box 13, Folder 19, pp. 1–2.

37 Richard Grimmett, *Trends in Conventional Arms Transfers to the Third World, 1979–1986*, Report No. 87–418F (Washington, DC: CRS, May 1987), pp. 57–60.

38 US Department of Defense, *Soviet Military Power, 1987* (Washington, DC: US Government Printing Office, 1987), pp. 125–6. See also CIA, "Soviet Foreign Military Assistance," p. 13.

39 All percentages are calculated from data in ACDA, *World Military Expenditures and Arms Transfers 1991*, pp. 151–4.

40 Ibid., p. 153. See also DCI, "Soviet Foreign Military Assistance," pp. 11, 49.

41 Pedro Ramet, *The Soviet–Syrian Relationship Since 1955: A Troubled Alliance* (Boulder, CO: Westview Press, 1990), pp. 199–211. See also David Kinsella, "Conflict in Context: Arms Transfers and Third World Rivalries during the Cold War," *American Journal of Political Science*, Vol. 38, No. 3 (August 1994), pp. 557–81, esp. pp. 567, 571.

42 DCI, "Soviet Foreign Military Assistance," pp. 30–1; and CIA, "Soviet Policy in the Middle East and South Asia under Andropov: Special National Intelligence Estimate," SNIE 11/30–83 (Top Secret), 8 February 1983, pp. 8–9.

43 DCI, "Soviet Foreign Military Assistance," pp. 36–7.

44 Not surprisingly, this is what Soviet officials claimed publicly at the time. See, in particular, Colonel F. Kazanchuk, "Vstrechi na Siriiskoi zemle," *Krasnaya zvezda*, 29 January 1983 and Colonel G. Kashuba, "V doline Bekaa," *Krasnaya zvezda*, 31 August 1982. For further comments, see Craig Oliphant, "The Performance of Soviet Weapons in Lebanon," *Radio Liberty Research*, RL 68/83, 7 February 1983. Documents in the Kataev archive, however, indicate that Soviet officials privately worried that the conflicts and their aftermath had exposed serious deficiencies in Soviet weapons. See, for example, "O voennom sotrudnichestve v dvenadtsatoi pyatiletke s sotsialisticheskimi i razvivayushchimisya stranami: Iz reshenii Soveta Oborony SSSR ot 15 avgusta 1986 g.," Extract from Decision of the USSR Defense Council (Top Secret/Special Dossier), 15 August 1986, in Hoover Archives, Kataev Papers, Box 12, Folder 26, pp. 1–3, esp. p. 1.

45 DCI, "Soviet Foreign Military Assistance," pp. 19–44.

46 DCI, "Soviet Foreign Military Assistance," pp. 30–2.

47 Ibid., pp. 18–19.

48 See, for example, "O voennom sotrudnichestve v dvenadtsatoi pyatiletke s sotsialisticheskimi i razvivayushchimisya stranami," pp. 1–3.

49 See Walter F. Kitchenman, *Arms Transfers and the Indebtedness of Less Developed Countries*, N-2020-FF (Santa Monica, Ca.: RAND Corporation, December 1983).

50 See, for example, "Tezisy po problemam konversii voennogo proizvodstva," Memorandum for CPSU Politburo (Top Secret), 19 March 1989, in Hoover Archives, Kataev Papers, Box 14, Folder 10, pp. 1–18; and "VTS," handwritten

notes compiled for CPSU Defense Industry Department, n.d. (early 1990), in Hoover Archives, Kataev Papers, Box 12, Folder 30, pp. 1–6, esp. p. 6.

51 On the question of offsets in the international arms trade, see Peter Hall and Stefan Markowski, "On Normality and Abnormality of Offset Obligations," *Defence and Peace Economics*, Vol. 5, No. 3 (July 1994), pp. 173–88; Lloyd J. Dumas, "Do Offsets Mitigate or Magnify the Military Burden?" in Jürgen Brauer and J. Paul Dunne (eds.), *Arms Trade and Economic Development* (New York: Routledge, 2004), pp. 17–38; Stephen Martin (ed.), *The Economics of Offsets: Defence Procurement and Countertrade* (Amsterdam: Harwood Publishers, 1996); Grant T. Hammond, "Offset, Arms, and Innovation," *The Washington Quarterly*, Vol. 10, No. 1 (Winter 1987), pp. 173–85; Thomas Friedman, "Defense Sales Offsets," *National Defense*, Vol. 71, No. 426 (March 1987), pp. 28–33; and Stephanie G. Neuman, "Offsets in the International Arms Market," in ACDA, *World Military Expenditures and Arms Transfers 1985* (Washington, DC: US Government Printing Office, 1986), pp. 35–40. On the role of offsets in Soviet arms transfer policy, see Nichol, "The Soviet Union," pp. 71–89; and William H. Lewis, "Emerging Choices for the Soviets in Third World Arms Transfer Policy," in ACDA, *World Military Expenditures and Arms Transfers 1985*, esp. pp. 32–3.

52 "Spravka o poryadke osushchestvleniya voenno-tekhnicheskogo sotrudnichestva SSSR s zarubezhnymi stranami," Memorandum for CPSU Politburo (Top Secret), March 1989, in Hoover Archives, Kataev Papers, Box 12, Folder 30, pp. 1–3, esp. 2; and "VTS," Handwritten Notes for CPSU Defense Industry Department, n.d. (early 1989), in Hoover Archives, Kataev Papers, Box 12, Folder 30, pp. 3, 5.

53 See, for example, "Kontseptsiya voennogo sotrudnichestva s zarubezhnymi stranami (krome sotsialisticheskikh) na period 1990–1995 gg.," Conceptual Report for CPSU Politburo (Top Secret), 23 June 1990, in Hoover Archives, Kataev Papers, Box 12, Folder 25, pp. 1–11, esp. p. 3.

54 See, for example, "Polozhenie o Mezhpravitel'stvennoi komissii po koordinatsii na mnogostoronnei osnove rabot NRB, VNR, GDR, PNR, SSSR i ChSSR po eksportnomu kontrolyu," Supplement to CPSU Decision P35/VII (Top Secret/Special Dossier), 16 October 1986, pp. 1–5, in Hoover Archives, Kataev Papers, Box 12, Folder 26.

55 "O voennom sotrudnichestve v dvenadtsatoi pyatiletke s sotsialisticheskimi i razvivayushchimisya stranami: Iz reshenii Soveta Oborony SSSR ot 15 avgusta 1986 g.," Extract from Decision of the USSR Defense Council (Top Secret/Special Dossier), 15 August 1986, in Hoover Archives, Kataev Papers, Box 12, Folder 26, pp. 1–3.

56 Ibid., pp. 1–2.

57 "TsK KPSS: O voennom sotrudnichestve s Respublikoi Zambiei," Memorandum to the CPSU Politburo (Top Secret) from O. Belyakov, head of the CPSU Defense Industry Department, and A. Urnov, deputy head of the CPSU International Department, December 1986, with cover note from CPSU Politburo member and CPSU Secretary L. Zaikov to S. F. Akhromeev, Yu.M. Vorontsov, K. F. Katushev, B. I. Aristov, O. S. Belyakov, and G. M. Kornienko, in Hoover Archives, Kataev Papers, Box 13, Folder 19.

58 "Voenno-tekhnicheskoe sotrudnichestvo (VTS)," p. 1; DCI, "Soviet Foreign Military Assistance," p. 13; and CIA, Office of Global Affairs, "Soviet Military Assistance to the Third World: Major Cuts Unlikely in the Next Two Years," Memorandum No. GI M 89–20035 (Secret), 1 May 1989, p. 2.

59 "Spravka 'O polozhenii v Livane' (k No. 43–6)," Memorandum for CPSU Politburo, n.d. (late 1986-early 1987), in Hoover Archives, Kataev Papers, Box 13, Folder 15, pp. 1–3.

60 "VTS," handwritten notes (Secret) compiled by Vitalii Kataev, n.d. (1990), in Hoover Archives, Kataev Papers, Box 12, Folder 30, p. 2. For the Soviet High Command's preliminary contemporaneous assessment of the US raids and the Libyan response, see the report to the gathering of Warsaw Pact leaders and defense ministers by the commander-in-chief of Soviet Air Defense Forces, Marshal Aleksandr Koldunov, "Information des Hauptmarschalls der Flieger Koldunow zur Problematik 'Aggression der USA gegen LIBYEN,'" Transcript GVS-Nr. A 456 721 (Top Secret), 20 April 1986, in Bundesbeauftragte für die Unterlagen des Staatssicherheitsdienstes (BStU), Zentralarchiv (ZA), Arbeitsgruppe des Ministers (AGM), 533, Blatten 16–21 (my thanks to Bernd Schaefer for giving me a copy of the document).

61 CPSU Politburo Resolution No. P39/35, 31 October 1986, cited in "Spravka: K voprosu o peredache v arendu Indii sovetskoi atomnoi podvodnoi lodki," Memorandum for CPSU Politburo (Top Secret), n.d. (November 1986), in Hoover Archives, Kataev Papers, Box 13, Folder 14, pp. 1–3.

62 Ibid., p. 1.

63 "Spravka: K voprosu o peredache v arendu Indii sovetskoi atomnoi podvodnoi lodki," pp. 1–2.

64 Ibid. For Gorbachev's speech in Vladivostok, see "Rech' M. S. Gorbacheva vo Vladivostoke," *Pravda* (Moscow), 29 July 1986, pp. 1, 3–4.

65 "Spravka: K voprosu o peredache v arendu Indii sovetskoi atomnoi podvodnoi lodki," p. 3.

66 See Gorbachev's detailed report to the CPSU Politburo on the visit, "Ob itogakh vizita v Indiyu," in "Rabochaya zapis' zasedaniya Politbyuro TsK KPSS 4 dekabrya 1986 goda," Record of CPSU Politburo Meeting (Top Secret), 4 December 1986, in Arkhiv Gorbachev-Fonda (AGF), F. 10, Op. 2, Ll. 348–57. See also the various items from Gorbachev's visit in Mikhail Sergeevich Gorbachev, *Sobranie sochinenii*, 20 vols., Vol. 5: *Oktyabr' 1986 – fevral' 1987* (Moscow: Izdatel'stvo Ves' mir, 2009), pp. 222–56.

67 See, for example, "Soviet Nuclear Submarine Leased to Indian Navy," TASS, 5 January 1988; "India Leases A-Sub," *Washington Post*, 6 January 1988, p. A19; "N-Sub for India," *Financial Times* (London), 6 January 1988, p. 1; "India Gets Soviet A-Sub, with New Strategic Power," *The Christian Science Monitor*, 6 January 1988, p. 2; "Indians Now Have Soviet Nuclear Sub, Reports Say," *Sydney Morning Herald* (Australia), 7 January 1988, p. 4; Subhash Chakravarti, "India's Nuclear Submarine Lifts Local Arms Race," *The Sunday Times* (London), 10 January 1988, p. 7; "India's 1st Nuclear Submarine Sets Off Defence Alarm Bell," *The Courier Mail* (Canberra), 11 January 1988, p. 1; Brahma Chellaney, "India Bolsters Its Naval Defenses," *The Christian Science Monitor*, 22 January 1988, pp. 1, 10; "N-Submarine for India," *Financial Times* (London), 23 January 1988, p. 1; "Sub for India," *Herald Sun* (Melbourne), 4 February 1988, p. 1; R. Mahoney, "India Aims to Be World-Class Naval Power," *Herald Sun* (Melbourne), 23 February 1988, p. 7; and Brahma Chellaney, "India Shoots for Military Self-Sufficiency," *The Christian Science Monitor*, 21 March 1988, p. 9.

68 "Soviet Submarine Commissioned into Indian Navy," *Weekly Economic Report* (New Delhi), 16 March 1988, p. 3. See also "Quieter Soviet Subs Cost U.S. at Least $30 Billion," *Navy News & Undersea Technology*, 14 March 1988, p. 1.

69 Language to this effect was recommended in "Spravka: K voprosu o peredache v arendu Indii sovetskoi atomnoi podvodnoi lodki," p. 3.

70 "TsK KPSS: O voenno-tekhnicheskom sotrudnichestve s zarubezhnymi stranami," Memorandum Supplementing Op-2230 (Top Secret/Special Dossier), 11 October 1986, from O. Belyakov, head of the CPSU Defense Industry Department, and V. Mozhin, deputy head of the CPSU Economic

Department, to the CPSU Politburo, in Hoover Archives, Kataev Papers, Box 12, Folder 30, pp. 1–2.

71 See, for example, "TsK KPSS: O poryadke podgotovki dokumentov po voprosam voenno-tekhnicheskogo sotrudnichestva s zarubezhnymi stranami," Memorandum No 33s (Top Secret) to the CPSU Politburo from L. Zaikov, A. Lukyanov, and Yu. Maslyukov, 1 August 1987; with attached "Predlozheniya o poryadke oformleniya dokumentov po voprosam voenno-tekhnicheskogo sotrudnichestva s zarubezhnymi stranami," guidelines coordinated by the VPK, 1 August 1987, in Hoover Archives, Kataev Papers, Box 12, Folder 25, pp. 1–2, 3–7. See also "O sovershenstvovanii organizatsionnoi struktury vneshneekonomicheskikh organizatsii ministerstv i vedomstv SSSR," Extract from CPSU Politburo Resolution No. P112/VI (Top Secret), 24 March 1988, in Hoover Archives, Kataev Papers, Box 12, Folder 24.

72 "Tovarishchu Gorbachevu M. S.," Memorandum No. 242/OS (Top Secret) to M. S. Gorbachev from E. Shevardnadze, D. Yazov, and V. Kamentsev, 25 March 1989, in Hoover Archives, Kataev Papers, Box 13, Folder 14, p. 4.

73 Ibid., p. 5.

74 Ibid., pp. 7–8.

75 "Vystuplenie M. S. Gorbacheva v Organizatsii Ob"edinennykh Natsii," *Pravda* (Moscow), 8 December 1988, p. 2. On the concept of "reasonable sufficiency for defense," see Raymond L. Garthoff, *Deterrence and the Revolution in Soviet Military Doctrine* (Washington, DC: Brookings Institution Press, 1990), pp. 108–48; William E. Odom, *The Collapse of the Soviet Military* (New Haven, CT: Yale University Press, 1998), pp. 107–47; and John G. Hines and Donald Mahoney, *Defense and Counteroffensive Under the New Soviet Military Doctrine*, R-3982-USDP (Santa Monica, CA: RAND Corporation, 1991), pp. 17–42.

76 "Tovarishchu Gorbachevu M. S.," p. 8.

77 Ibid.

78 Ibid.

79 Joanna Spear, "Governmental Politics and the Conventional Arms Transfer Talks," *Review of International Studies*, Vol. 19, No. 4 (October 1993), pp. 369–84; and Raymond L. Garthoff, *Détente and Confrontation: American-Soviet Relations from Nixon to Reagan* (Washington, DC: Brookings Institution Press, 1994, rev. edn.), pp. 838–9; and Barry M. Blechman, Janne E. Nolan, and Alan Platt, "Pushing Arms," *Foreign Policy*, No. 46 (Spring 1982), pp. 138–54.

80 "Tovarishchu Gorbachevu M. S.," p. 6.

81 Ibid.

82 Ibid., p. 8.

83 "Postanovlenie Soveta Ministrov SSSR No. 203 ot 7 marta 1989 g.: O merakh gosudarstvennogo regulirovaniya vneshneekonomicheskoi deyatel'nosti," Resolution No. 203 (Top Secret), 7 March 1989, in Hoover Archives, Kataev Papers, Box 12, Folder 30, p. 3.

84 "Spravka o poryadke osushchestvleniya voenno-tekhnicheskogo sotrudnichestva SSSR s zarubezhnymi stranami," Memorandum compiled by CPSU Defense Industry Department (Top Secret), n.d. (early March 1989), in Hoover Archives, Kataev Papers, Box 12, Folder 30, pp. 1–3.

85 Ibid., p. 1.

86 Ibid.

87 Ibid., p. 2.

88 "TsK KPSS: O kontseptsii voennogo sotrudnichestva s zarubezhnymi stranami (krome sotsialisticheskikh," Memorandum (Top Secret) from L. Zaikov, V. Chebrikov, E. Shevardnadze, A. Yakovlev, D. Yazov, O. Baklanov, I. Belousov, V. Kamentsev, V. Kryuchkov to the CPSU Politburo, 23 June 1989, in Hoover Archives, Kataev Papers, Box 12, Folder 25.

89 Ibid., p. 1.
90 Ibid., pp. 1–2.
91 Ibid., p. 2.
92 Ibid., p. 3.
93 Ibid., pp. 3–4.
94 "Kontseptsiya voennogo sotrudnichestva s zarubezhnymi stranami (krome sotsialisticheskikh) na period 1990–1995 gg.," Memorandum (Top Secret), n.d. (May 1989), in Hoover Archives, Kataev Papers, Box 12, Folder 25, pp. 1–10.
95 Ibid., pp. 1–2.
96 Ibid., p. 7.
97 Ibid., p. 3.
98 Ibid., p. 9.
99 Ibid., p. 3.
100 "Voenno-tekhnicheskoe sotrudnichestvo (VTS)," p. 3. See also CIA, "Soviet Military Assistance to the Third World," pp. 3–5.
101 "Kontseptsiya voennogo sotrudnichestva s zarubezhnymi stranami (krome sotsialisticheskikh) na period 1990–1995 gg.," p. 5. The Conception lists Ethiopia here, but other passages in the document suggest that this should have been Iraq instead of Ethiopia.
102 Ibid., p. 6.
103 Ibid., p. 5.
104 See, for example, "Tovarishchu Zaikovu L. N.," Memorandum No. 318/2/0354 (Secret – Special Dossier) from Army-General M. Moiseev, chief of the Soviet General Staff, to Lev Zaikov of the CPSU Politburo and CPSU Secretariat, 21 March 1990, in RGANI, F. 89, Op. 2, D. 10, Ll. 1–2; "Postanovlenie TsK KPSS: O postavke Respublike Afganistan takticheskogo raketnogo kompleksa 9K52 ('Luna-M')," Memorandum No. 312/0069 (Top Secret) from L. Zaikov, E. Shevardnadze, D. Yazov, O. Baklanov, N. Belousov, V. Kryuchkov, and K. Katushev to the CPSU Politburo, transmitting a draft Politburo resolution and attached report, 10 July 1989, in RGANI, F. 89, Op. 18, D.123, Ll. 1–3; "Vypiska iz protokola No. 158 zasedaniya Politbyuro TsK KPSS ot 13 maya 1989 goda: O dopolnitel'nykh merakh vozdeistviya na afganskuyu situatsiyu," CPSU Politburo Resolution P. 158/13 (Top Secret – Special Dossier), with attached report from L. Zaikov, E. Shevardnadze, D. Yazov, and V. Kryuchkov, 13 May 1989, in RGANI, F. 89, Op. 10, D. 35, Ll. 1–3; "Ob okazanii dopolnitel'noi pomoshchi Respublike Afganistan v aprele-mae 1989 g.," No. P152/47 (Top Secret – Special Dossier), draft Politburo resolution with attached report from L. N. Zaikov, V. M. Chebrikov, E. A. Shevardnadze, A. N. Yakovlev, D. T. Yazov, and V. A. Kryuchkov, 10 April 1989, in RGANI, F. 89, Op. 10, D. 30, Ll. 1–6; and "Vypiska iz protokola No. 146 zasedaniya Politbyuro TsK KPSS ot 24 yanvarya 1989 goda," No.P146/31 (Top Secret – Special Dossier), with attached report from E. Shevardnadze, V. Chebrikov, A. Yakovlev, D. Yazov, V. Murakhovskii, and V. Kryuchkov, 24 January 1989, in RGANI, F. 89, Op. 10, D. 16, Ll. 1–9.
105 "Voenno-tekhnicheskoe sotrudnichestvo (VTS)," p. 2.
106 "Kontseptsiya voennogo sotrudnichestva s zarubezhnymi stranami (krome sotsialisticheskikh) na period 1990–1995 gg.," p. 5.
107 Ibid., p. 6.
108 Ibid., p. 7.
109 Ibid., pp. 5–6.
110 "Postanovlenie Politbyuro TsK KPSS No. P81/14 ot 25 avgusta 1987 goda," CPSU Politburo Resolution No. P81/14 (Top Secret) in Hoover Archives, Kataev Papers, Box 12, Folder 25.
111 "Kontseptsiya voennogo sotrudnichestva s zarubezhnymi stranami (krome sotsialisticheskikh) na period 1990–1995 gg.," p. 6.

112 Ibid., p. 9.
113 Ibid., p. 10.
114 "Voenno-tekhnicheskoe sotrudnichestvo (VTS)," p. 3.
115 "Kontseptsiya voennogo sotrudnichestva s zarubezhnymi stranami (krome sotsialisticheskikh) na period 1990–1995 gg.," p. 8.
116 Ibid., pp. 7–9.
117 Ibid., p. 4.
118 Ibid., p. 5. On the establishment of the UN Register of Conventional Arms, see Malcolm Chalmers and Owen Greene, "The Development of the United Nations Register of Conventional Arms: Prospects and Proposal," *The Nonproliferation Review*, Vol. 1, No. 3 (Spring-Summer 1994), pp. 1–17.
119 "Kontseptsiya voennogo sotrudnichestva s zarubezhnymi stranami (krome sotsialisticheskikh) na period 1990–1995 gg.," p. 4.
120 "India Moving to Obtain Second Nuclear Sub," *The Times* (London), 20 May 1990, p. 5; Rajiv Tiwari, "India: Moscow, Delhi Fit Ties to Post-Cold War Realities," *IPS-Inter Press Service*, 23 July 1990, Item 51; John Pomfret, "No Peace Dividend for South Asia," Associated Press, 13 April 1990, International News Item 13; "India Launches Its First Locally Manufactured Submarine," *The Washington Times*, 30 September 1989, p. 8; Richard M. Weintraub, "India Tests Mid-Range 'Agni' Missile; Weapon Proliferation Draws U.S. Criticism," *Washington Post*, 23 May 1989, pp. A1, A13; and Sheila Tefft, "Old Rivalries, New Worries Fuel Arms Race in Southeast Asia," *The Christian Science Monitor*, 2 January 1991, pp. 1, 8.
121 "Zapis' besedy M. S. Gorbacheva s Radzhivom Gandi, Moskva, 15 iyulya goda," Notes from Conversation (Secret), 15 July 1989, in Arkhiv Gorbachev-Fonda 1, Opis 1, Dok. 365, List 1–8; and two separate translations into Russian of a confidential letter in English from Rajiv Gandhi to Mikhail Gorbachev, 29 October 1989, in Hoover Archives, Kataev Papers, Box 13, Folder 14. Although the translations (at least one of which was done by a Soviet Foreign Ministry translator) differ somewhat in their specific wording, they were clearly done from the same English-language letter.
122 "VTS," handwritten notes (Secret) compiled by Vitalii Kataev, n.d. (1990), in Hoover Archives, Kataev Papers, Box 12, Folder 30, p. 3.
123 Ibid.
124 "Ob izmenenii poryadka prinyatiya reshenii po nekotorym voprosam oboronnogo stroitel'stva," Memorandum (Top Secret)to M. S. Gorbachev from O. Belyakov, head of CPSU Defense Department, and A. Pavlov, head of CPSU State and Legal Department, 26 July 1990, in Hoover Archives, Kataev Papers, Box 4, Folder 44, p. 1. See also "Voenno-tekhnicheskoe sotrudnichestvo (VTS)," p. 1.
125 US Department of Defense, *Military Forces in Transition, 1991*, Washington, DC, September 1991, pp. 18–21.
126 See the documents cited in note 50 *supra.*
127 Interview with M. P. Simonov, chief designer of the Sukhoi machine-building plant, in "Chelovek i ekonomika: Kuda rulit' konversii," *Soyuz*, No. 7, 12–18 February 1990, p. 14. See also "Rynochnaya ekonomika: Pervye shagi," *Tyl vooruzhenykh sil*, Nos. 11–12, November–December 1990, pp. 3–7; the interview with Vladimir Shimko, minister of radio industry, in "ne brosal pustykh obeshchanii," *Pravitel'stvennyi vestnik*, No. 19, May 1991, p. 8; and Oleg Mamalyga, "Tsena konversii," *Moskovskie novosti*, No. 6, 11 February 1990, p. 12. For a highly critical appraisal of this line of reasoning, see Aleksei Kuvshinnikov and Major-General Vadim Makarevskii, "Rol' sovetskogo VPK v postavkakh oruzhiya

stranam Yuga," *Mirovaya ekonomika i mezhdunarodnye otnosheniya*, No. 7, July 1991, pp. 147–8. See also Izyumov, "Konversiya i perekhod k rynku," pp. 34–5.

128 Interview in "Chtoby imet' vozmozhnost' khot' chto-to sdelat' po-svoemu, ya dovol'no dolgo dolzhen byl govorit', kak vse," *Komsomol'skaya pravda*, 3 August 1991, p. 3.

129 For figures on Soviet arms transfers, see CIA, *Handbook of Economic Statistics, 1991*, CPAS 91–10001, September 1991, p. 158.

130 "Voenno-tekhnicheskoe sotrudnichestvo (VTS)," pp. 1, 3; Steven Pearlstein, "Hard Sell for U.S. Arms: Weapons Makers Feel Same Competitive Pressures as Other Global Industries," *Washington Post*, 7 April 1991, pp. H1, H4; and "International Arms Business: The Binge Ends," Associated Press Newswire, 12 August 1991, Item 4.

3 China's changing policies toward the Third World and the end of the global Cold War

Chen Jian

In retrospect, the global Cold War experienced a profound transformation in the long 1970s.[1] China occupied a central position in the process of this transformation. Along with the escalation of the Sino–Soviet confrontation and the making of Sino–US rapprochement, the Cold War's basic feature was as a contest between Communism and liberal capitalism as two competing paths heading toward modernity became obscured. China's turning toward the "reform and opening" process in the late 1970s – characterized by the world's most populous country gradually embracing the west-capitalist-dominated "world market" as the central agent in its pursuit of modernization – virtually meant that China was departing the Cold War.

Against this background, Mao Zedong introduced in 1973–1974 a nuanced "three worlds" thesis. The Chinese Chairman contended that the first world was made up of the two superpowers, the US and the Soviet Union; the second world was composed of such relatively developed countries as those in Western Europe, Australia, Canada, and Japan; and the Third World was formed by the vast majority of developing countries in Asia, Africa and also Latin America. He announced that China, which remained "relatively poor," belonged to the Third World.[2]

An outstanding feature of the Maoist three-worlds thesis was that it took differences in levels of economic development, rather than contests and confrontations between different ideologies and political and social systems, as the basic criteria for defining the three worlds. Such a thesis nullified the boundaries between Communism and capitalism and had an enormous impact on the ongoing Cold War. In particular, it further reduced the influence and power of the international Communist movement that had already been in profound division, creating another important condition for the Cold War to end with the collapse of the Soviet camp.

This chapter discusses how the Maoist three-worlds thesis came into being; how the thesis and, related to it, Beijing's policies toward the Third World, evolved in the context of China's changing domestic situation and international perceptions in the long 1970s; and how China's Third World policies changed not only the balance of power between the US and the Soviet Union but also the orientation or even essence of the Cold War, contributing to the Cold War's eventual conclusion with the failure of International Communism and the collapse of the Soviet Union and the Soviet Bloc.

I

From a historical perspective, the Maoist conception of the three worlds had its roots in the Chinese Communist revolution's long course of development. Since its early years, the Chinese Communist Party (CCP) embraced such concepts as "world revolution" and "proletarian internationalism" while, at the same time, emphasizing that the Chinese revolution was also a "national revolution" and stood as an integral component of oppressed peoples' worldwide cause for national liberation. After the Second World War, when the Chinese Civil War erupted in the context of the rising Cold War, Mao introduced a series of new ideas about the postwar world situation, which the CCP would later characterize as Mao's intermediate-zone theory. Mao and his comrades argued that between the US and the Soviet Union there existed a vast "intermediate zone" in Asia, Africa and Europe, and that the US imperialists could not directly attack the Soviet Union until they had control of the zone. Accordingly, they contended that the principal contradiction in the world rested with the struggles between peoples in the intermediate zone and the reactionary US ruling class, as well as between China and the US.[3]

The Maoist intermediate-zone notion revealed the CCP's determination to challenge the US as a dominant imperialist power and to stand on the side of the Soviet Union. In the meantime, by highlighting the central role that China was to play in bridging world revolution and decolonization, the notion also presaged that the Cold War would have to become a phenomenon more complicated than if there had not been China's inputs.

After its establishment in 1949, the People's Republic of China (PRC) acted as a radical "revolutionary country" on the international scene, challenging the legitimacy of the existing international system controlled by Western powers. In October 1950, Beijing sent troops to Korea to support Kim Il-Sung's North Korean Communist regime, engaging in a direct military confrontation with the US that would last until July 1953.[4] Beijing also provided military and other support to the Vietnamese Communists in a war against the French colonialists.[5] PRC policies towards such non-Western countries as Malaya, Burma, Thailand, Indonesia, the Philippines and, on occasions, India were a mixture of harsh criticism (labeling them as "lackeys of Western imperialism") and attempts to neutralize them in the Cold War environment.[6]

A major turning point came in 1954–1955. At the Geneva Conference of 1954, the PRC delegation led by Premier Zhou Enlai took the initiative to meet with delegates from several non-Communist countries. In late June, Zhou visited India and Burma. Together with Indian Prime Minister Jawaharlal Nehru and Burmese prime minister U Nu, Zhou introduced the "Five Principles of Peaceful Coexistence."[7] On 18–24 April 1955, the Chinese participated in the Bandung Conference of leaders from 29 countries in Asia and Africa. Zhou made extensive efforts to have dialogs with leaders from other countries, emphasizing the common historical experience between China and other non-Western countries.[8]

Beijing's adoption of the five-principles-oriented Bandung Discourse had important normative meanings: this reflected the PRC's continuous challenge to the Western powers (and, potentially, also to the Soviet Union) by introducing a whole set of new norms and codes of behavior in international affairs. While doing so, Mao again went beyond the Cold War's bipolar framework and used the intermediate zone concept to illuminate and define the international structure.[9] In the meantime, Mao and his comrades repeatedly emphasized that China and such former colonies as India and Burma belonged to "Eastern countries," and they shared similar cultural and historical traditions as well as recent humiliation at the hands of Western powers.

Indeed, the Chinese experience at Geneva and Bandung revealed Beijing's strong desire to play a more central role in international affairs. Mao's intermediate-zone notion of the late 1940s tended to lean toward the side of the Soviet Union. In comparison, in the mid-1950s, within the context of the emerging leadership vacuum in the International Communist movement after Stalin's death, Mao increasingly believed that it was Beijing's overall capacity of revolutionizing the worldwide process of decolonization – a capacity that was not possessed by Moscow – that had enabled China's centrality in the world revolution.

In the wake of Bandung, the PRC established diplomatic relations with a dozen Asian and African countries. Beijing held positive attitudes toward the newly emerging non-alignment trend among Asian and African countries. When the Suez crisis erupted in 1956, Beijing adopted a high-profile approach to support Gamal Abdel Nasser's decision to nationalize the Suez Canal. In the meantime, Beijing strongly opposed Moscow's attempt to use Pancha Shila in dealing with Washington. During Mao's visit to Moscow in November 1957, he deliberately challenged the Soviet leader Nikita Khrushchev's emphasis on "peaceful coexistence" with Western imperialist countries.[10] When the relationship between Moscow and Beijing was in trouble, the bipolar structure of the Cold War became further shaken.

The PRC's foreign policy turned more radical in 1958 when the "Great Leap Forward" swept across China's cities and countryside. The trigger that Mao and his comrades used to justify the extraordinary mass mobilization during the Great Leap was the US–British intervention in response to the coup in Iraq led by Abdel Karim Kassim. Under the banner of "supporting the Arab people's anti-imperialist struggle," Mao ordered the

People's Liberation Army to shell the Nationalists-controlled Jinmen islands. When US President Dwight D. Eisenhower dispatched the US Seventh Fleet to help the Nationalists protect Jinmen's supply lines, a serious crisis erupted between Beijing and Washington. As Mao did not inform Moscow in advance of his decision to shell Jinmen, Chinese-Soviet relations worsened even more.[11]

The PRC's position and image in the non-Western world hit a major hurdle in 1959, when a series of conflicts erupted between China and India. In March 1959, Beijing used force to suppress an anti-Chinese Communist revolt in Tibet, and the Dalai Lama, Tibet's religious and political leader, took refuge in India, which led to serious tensions in Sino–Indian relations.[12] In the fall of 1959, two border clashes occurred between Chinese and Indian forces, further shattering any remaining trust between Chinese and Indian leaders. Underlying the deterioration of Chinese-Indian relations, though, was the potential conflict between Beijing and New Delhi concerning which country – China or India – should claim the leadership role in the larger non-Western world in the post-colonial age.

The early 1960s witnessed temporary relaxation of China's domestic and international policies following the Great Leap's disastrous failure. With Mao retreating to the "second line" after 1960–1961, his colleagues, such as Liu Shaoqi and Deng Xiaoping, adopted a series of more flexible domestic policies to pursue economic recovery and social stability. Along with this came the softening of China's radical international policies as well. Yet this period did not last long. When China's economy showed signs of recovery from the dark shadow of the Great Leap, Mao quickly pushed China toward another period of "revolutionary high tide." In order to legitimate the radicalization of China's domestic political and social life, Mao repeatedly stressed that China was facing an international environment full of crises, arguing that the international reactionary forces headed by US imperialists were preparing to wage a war against China.[13] Mao also openly criticized the Kremlin's strategy of "peaceful coexistence," claiming that it obscured the fundamental distinction between revolution and counterrevolution.

Against the above background Mao put forward his "two intermediate zones" thesis. He argued that between the US and the Soviet Union "there exist two intermediate zones." The first was composed of "the vast economically backward countries in Asia, Africa and Latin America," and the second included "imperialist and advanced capitalist countries in Europe." It was in the first intermediate zone, of which China was also a part, where both the US and the Soviet Union were "being rebuffed everywhere," and the US encountered challenges and difficulties in the second intermediate zone.[14] After 1962–1963, China's international discourse, while alleging that the center of the world revolution had moved to Beijing, increasingly highlighted the central role that the PRC had played in promoting revolutionary movements in Asia, Africa, and Latin America. In the wake of the

Gulf of Tonkin incident of August 1964, Beijing extended comprehensive security commitments and provided all kinds of support to North Vietnam.[15] When Indonesian President Sukarno, with the support of the Indonesian Communists, launched the New Emerging Force movement, Beijing supported it enthusiastically. Beijing also endeavored to expand China's influence in Africa, beginning by offering economic, technological and medical support to African countries that were most friendly to China, including Congo (Brazzaville), Guinea, Mali, Somalia, Tanzania, and Zambia. When the second Asian-Afro conference was scheduled to be convened in Algeria in June 1965, Beijing firmly opposed allowing the Soviet Union to participate in the conference, even as an observer. Beijing also argued that India, as a "lackey" of Western imperialists, should not play a major role in the conference.

When the "Great Proletarian Cultural Revolution" unfolded in the mid and late 1960s, Beijing's international behavior seemed to be running out of control. China's confrontations with the US and conflicts with the Soviet Union escalated, its hostility toward India continued, and even its relations with several friendly neighboring countries, such as Burma and Cambodia, deteriorated. In Sino–North Vietnamese relations, Beijing's leaders repeatedly urged Hanoi not to negotiate with Washington while, at the same time, rejecting any attempt by Moscow to use the theme of "supporting the Vietnamese people" to carry out any "united action" against the US within the International Communist movement.[16] Even Beijing's solidarity with North Korea suffered during the Cultural Revolution years as the Red Guards publicly attacked North Korean leader Kim Il-Sung as a "revisionist."[17]

By the late 1960s, the PRC had become one of the most isolated countries in the world, facing serious security threats from all directions. The US intervention in Vietnam put great pressure on China's southern borders. The hostility between China and the Soviet Union culminated in March 1969, when two bloody clashes erupted between Chinese and Soviet forces on Zhenbao island on the Ussuri River.[18] China also faced hostile enemies from the east (Taiwan, Japan and South Korea), and from the West (India).

II

The early 1970s witnessed sensational changes in China's external relations. The extreme tensions that had existed in Beijing's domestic and international policies during the Cultural Revolution years had made them unsustainable. The grave security situation that China was facing in the late 1960s, combined with the fading status of Mao's enterprise of "continuous revolution" (indeed, following the failure of the "Cultural Revolution," Mao's programs of transforming China's state and society were increasingly losing the "inner support" of China's ordinary people), created the larger context in which the Sino–US rapprochement occurred.[19] In February 1972, during "the week that changed the world," US President Richard Nixon made the historic trip to China and met with Mao in Beijing.[20]

The impact of the Sino–US rapprochement was far-reaching. As far as relations between Beijing and Washington were concerned, it ended the total confrontation between the PRC and the US that had lasted for almost a quarter of a century, opening a thoroughly new chapter in the development of relations between the world's most populous nation and its most powerful one. On the global scale, it dramatically shifted the balance of power between the two conflicting superpowers – the USA and the Soviet Union – in the Cold War. While policymakers in Washington found it possible to concentrate more US resources and strategic attention on dealing with the threats by the Soviet Union, Moscow's leaders, having to confront the West and China simultaneously, were more likely to seriously overextend Soviet strength and power.

In a deeper sense, though, Beijing's cooperation with Washington and confrontation with Moscow implied a changing essence of the global Cold War. Ever since its beginning in the late 1940s, the Cold War had been characterized by a fundamental confrontation between two contending ideologies – Communism and liberal capitalism. The Sino–US rapprochement obscured the distinctions between socialist and capitalist ways toward modernity. The Sino–Soviet split buried the shared belief among Communists in the world that Communism was a workable solution to the problems created by the worldwide process of modernization.

Against the above background, Mao introduced his three-worlds thesis in a series of talks with foreign leaders in 1973–1974. On 22 June 1973, he used the term "three worlds" to describe the world situation in a conversation with Moussa Traoré, Mali's head of state, then visiting China: "All of us have been called Third World (countries)," stated the chairman, "that is, we are all developing countries."[21] Several months later, Mao told Kenneth Kaunda, President of Zambia:

> The US and the Soviet Union belong to the First World. The middle elements, such as Japan, Europe, Australia and Canada, belong to the Second World. We are the Third World.... The US and the Soviet Union have a lot of atomic bombs, and they are richer. Europe, Japan, Australia and Canada, of the Second World, do not possess so many atomic bombs and are not so rich as the First World, but richer than the Third World.... All Asian countries, except Japan, and all of Africa and also Latin America belong to the Third World.[22]

Mao then said to Algerian leader Houari Boumediene that "China belongs to the Third World, as politically and economically China is not in the same group of the rich and powerful, and thus can only be with those countries that are relatively poor."[23]

Mao's new expressions immediately became the basic guideline of the PRC's international policies. On 10 April 1974, Chinese vice premier Deng Xiaoping brought Mao's three-worlds thesis to the General Assembly of the UN. Deng labeled the Soviet Union and the US, the two superpowers that formed the First World, as "the two largest international oppressors and exploitators" and the "main war originators in the contemporary era." The Second World, composed of other capitalist/developed countries, while facing the attempts by the two superpowers to control them, demonstrated in their policies the legacies of their own past as colonial powers. The Third World, formed by the vast majority of developing countries in Asia, Africa and Latin America, favored the "tendency of revolution" and opposed "the tendency of war," and they thus represented the "force playing a major role in promoting progress in the world."[24]

It is apparent that Mao's three-worlds thesis grew out of his intermediate-zone/two-intermediate-zones notions, and between them there existed striking similarities in perceptions of how the structure of the world should be defined and transformed. In particular, by highlighting the rising influences of non-Western countries in international affairs, they posed a fundamental challenge to the existing world order and envisioned China as a central actor in bringing about changes in the world. But there were also significant differences between the earlier intermediate zone/two intermediate zones notions and the three-worlds thesis. While the former was formulated around the discourse of "international class struggle" and revolution in its representation, what formed the foundation and the primary concern of the latter was the issue of economic development. In presenting the three-worlds thesis, Mao and his fellow Chinese leaders still used some "class struggle" language (such as describing the First World as international "oppressors" and "exploiters"). However, as far as the thesis's basic problematique is concerned, it already highlighted the importance of "development" as a question of fundamental importance that China and other Third World countries must encounter.

When the three-worlds thesis was made the dominant theme in China's international representation, with Mao's approval, a "four modernizations" discourse entered China's domestic affairs. At a speech to a National People's Congress assembly in January 1975, Chinese premier Zhou Enlai announced that China should aim to modernize its industry, agriculture, national defense, and science and technology by the end of the century.[25]

As is well known, Mao had championed transforming China and the world in revolutionary ways. Thus, his introduction of the development-oriented three-worlds theory and acceptance of the "Four Modernizations" representation toward the end of his life are worthy of some discussion. In the final analysis, this was Mao's way of dealing with the worsening legitimacy crisis that his "continuous revolution" had been facing. Ever since Mao proclaimed at the time of the PRC's formation that "we the Chinese people have stood up," he legitimated his "revolution after revolution" by repeatedly emphasizing how his revolutionary programs would change China into a country of "wealth and power." When the Chinese Communist state was encountering an ever-deepening legitimacy crisis as a result of the economic stagnation and political cruelty that Mao's revolutions had conferred on the Chinese people, the Chairman embraced the "three worlds" and "four modernizations" notions for emphasizing – first and foremost to the Chinese people – that his revolutions continuously played a central role in benefiting China and transforming the world.

China was then, still, in the middle of the Cultural Revolution, and Beijing's international representations were still replete with revolutionary phrases. Yet Mao's three-worlds thesis changed the discursive context in which China's patterns of development and, more generally, its path toward modernity would be defined, resulting in subtle changes in China's overall development strategies and policies. In 1973–1974, Beijing approved 26 major projects on importing new equipment and technology from Western countries and Japan, with a total budget of $4.3 billion.[26] Implementation of these projects strengthened China's ties with the "world market" dominated by Western capitalist countries. Even though until the last days of Mao's life, the Chairman never gave up his ideal and practice of "transforming" China in revolutionary ways, the insurmountable boundary between revolutionary China and the "outside world" was beginning to erode.

The Maoist three-worlds thesis also had a powerful impact in strategic terms, especially as, from the beginning, it had a strong pro-US and anti-Soviet tendency in its description and definition. Although Mao labeled the Soviet Union and the US as both belonging to the First World, he did not mean to treat them on equal terms. Informed by his previous experience in dealing with the Soviet threat, Mao had developed a strong conviction that of the two superpowers, the Soviet Union was the one that was on the offensive, and was thus more dangerous to China's security interests as well as to world peace than the US. In Deng's speech at the UN, which was approved by Mao, the Chinese vice premier pointed out that although both the US and the Soviet Union were the only powers capable of starting a nuclear war, the Soviet Union was more willing to do so.[27] With the introduction of the three-worlds thesis, Mao further developed the general ideas of forming an anti-Soviet "international united front." On 17 February 1973, in a conversation with US Secretary of State Henry Kissinger, Mao mentioned that, in order to cope with the Soviet threat, "we should draw a horizontal line – the US–Japan–China–Pakistan–Iran–Turkey–Europe."[28] He then repeated the idea on several other occasions, going so far as to emphasize that with the "horizontal line" as the axis, "a vast number of countries" should be mobilized to cope with the Soviet threat.[29]

The idea of building an "international united front against hegemony" became an important parameter in defining the orientation of Chinese policies towards the Third World in the early and mid-1970s. When

Beijing's leaders made policies toward a certain Third World country, they paid great attention to that country's attitudes toward the Soviet Union. Thus, we see that along with the introduction of Mao's three-worlds thesis, China's relations with a series of right-wing, anti-Soviet and anti-Communist Third World countries improved. A revealing case in this respect was Chile. Although Salvador Allende's left-wing, socialist government was the first among South American countries to recognize the PRC and establish diplomatic relations with it, Beijing was critical of Allende's pro-Soviet policies. When Allende's government was overthrown in a military coup in September 1973, Beijing's leaders refused to condemn the reactionary coup leaders, and attributed the main cause of Allende's downfall to "the mistaken economic policies" as well as pro-Soviet attitudes of his government. Despite the urges by many "progressive countries," including many in the Third World, for Beijing to cut off relations with Augusto Pinochet's military regime, Beijing, by citing the five principles, continuously maintained normal diplomatic, economic and even political relations with it.[30] In the meantime, the PRC's relations with Cuba, the only Communist country in the western hemisphere, were very bad, and this was largely because Beijing's leaders regarded Fidel Castro as an ally and agent of the Soviet Union, a perception that would become further enhanced in the late 1970s when Cuban "volunteers" actively intervened in Africa (more discussion on this later in this chapter).

In the Middle East, Beijing's policies were also conditioned by the "international united front against hegemony" parameter. Since the 1956 Suez Crisis, Beijing had persistently claimed that the PRC supported the Arab countries and opposed Israel's expansion and aggression. Yet, entering the 1970s, Beijing's attitudes toward various Arabic countries differed in accordance with a particular country's relations with the Soviet Union. For instance, the PRC's relationship with Egypt improved and expanded significantly after Egyptian President Anwar Sadat decided to expel Soviet advisors in July 1972. After the 1973 Arab–Israeli war, the PRC increased military aid to Egypt to "remedy the decrease of Soviet support" that Cairo had received, and Sino–Egyptian trade expanded by five times between 1971 and 1977, the year after Egypt abrogated its treaty of friendship and cooperation with the Soviet Union.[31] In comparison, Beijing's relationship with Syria was no better than lukewarm after the 1973 war, mainly because of Beijing's resentment of Damascus's pro-Soviet approach. Due to "the differences in attitudes toward the Soviet Union," Damascus did not send an ambassador to Beijing from the mid-1970s to the early 1980s.[32]

In Africa, Beijing had long claimed that the "new China" was a natural ally and firm supporter of the African people's causes of anti-Western imperialism/colonialism. Almost all of Beijing's friends in Africa until the early 1970s had been known as pro-socialist and anti-capitalist in their domestic and foreign policies. When, in the mid-1960s, Beijing's leaders made the decision to help with the construction of the Tanzanian–Zambian Railway, the largest and most ambitious project of foreign aid that Beijing had ever carried out, they justified it by contending that the project demonstrated the new China's willingness and capacity in supporting the African people's anti-imperialist and anti-colonialist struggles.[33] The basic tone of Beijing's African strategies changed subtly yet significantly in the late 1960s and early 1970s, when "anti-Soviet-social-imperialism" was added as a guiding principle. Accordingly, the PRC established or restored relations with several pro-US and right-wing regimes in Africa in the mid-1970s. For example, despite Beijing's previous condemnation of Zaire's reactionary dictator Mobutu Sésé Seko, Mao personally welcomed him to Beijing on 13 January 1973, and had a "very friendly conversation." The PRC and Zaire had then established "extensive cooperation and exchanges" on the common ground of anti-hegemonism.[34]

China and India had been mutually hostile and confrontational since the 1962 border war between them. Beijing had claimed that the Indian "reactionary ruling clique" fought the war against China for serving the interests of US imperialism and taking advantage of the legacies left over by British colonialism. In the 1965 and 1971 India–Pakistan wars, China stood firmly on the side of Pakistan. In the early stages of the process leading to the Sino–US rapprochement, Pakistan served as the most important channel of communication between top leaders in Beijing and Washington.[35] The hostility between China and India existed continuously throughout the 1970s. But the focal point of Beijing's criticism of New Delhi had changed, and the "reactionary Indian leaders" were now branded as the "accomplices of the Soviet social imperialists."

Beijing had long regarded Southeast Asia as the "cradle of revolutions," and, ever since the PRC's establishment, yet especially in the 1960s, Beijing had provided substantial support for Communist forces there. Chinese policies toward Southeast Asia experienced subtle changes with the introduction of Mao's three-worlds thesis. In 1974–1975, the PRC established diplomatic relations with Malaysia, Thailand and the Philippines, all of which had been labeled by Beijing as "lackeys of US imperialism" in the previous two decades. In the meantime, Beijing began to abandon the practice of supporting Communist insurgents in Southeast Asia, gradually reducing its military and other aid to the Communist parties in Burma, Malaya (Malaysia), and Thailand. In the Chinese media, reports about Communist revolutions in these countries gradually disappeared. Although Beijing's leaders repeatedly promised that they would not be reconciled with the US over Vietnam, in the last stages of the US–Vietnamese talks in Paris, to end the Vietnam War, Beijing's leaders urged their comrades in Hanoi to cut a deal with the US. After the signing of the Paris Accords, Beijing significantly reduced its military and other aid to Hanoi almost immediately.[36] Beijing's new policy tendency was also shown in the case of Korea. In April 1975, against the background of impending Communist victories in Indochina, North Korean leader Kim Il-Sung visited Beijing to try to gain China's backing for his renewed aspiration for using a "revolutionary war" to unify Korea. Beijing's leaders demonstrated little interest in, let alone support for, Kim's plans.[37] Even before Mao's death, China was no longer the same kind of country dominated by revolutionary zeal in its external behavior as it had been from the late 1940s to the early 1970s.

III

Mao died on 9 September 1976. After a short transitional period, during which Mao's hand-picked successor Hua Guofeng served as China's nominal Party leader and head of state, Deng Xiaoping emerged to become China's paramount leader. The most dramatic and far-reaching move that Deng made was to abandon Mao's class-struggle-centered discourse and revolutionary practice, placing the modernization of China's industry, agriculture, national defense, and science and technology at the top of his agenda.

Following his pragmatic "cat theory" – "black cat or white cat, so long as it catches mice, it is a good cat" – Deng allowed economics to take precedence over politics. Unleashed from these policies was the "reform and opening" process. Deng certainly sensed that the failure of Mao's "continuous revolution" had presented an ever-deepening legitimacy challenge to the Chinese Communist state, and he hoped that the improvement of living standards brought about by the "reform and opening" process would help bring legitimacy back to the Communist state.

In the shaping of the "reform and opening" process, there were major debates on many domestic issues between those who favored it and those who either opposed it or were suspicious of it. Yet, remarkably, there was little debate concerning foreign policies within the post-Mao Chinese leadership. From Hua to Deng, top Chinese leaders decided that they would follow the three-worlds framework that Mao had set up in the last years of his life. At the CCP's eleventh national congress, held in August 1977, the Party leadership used the three-worlds thesis to analyze the world situation, emphasizing that China would stand on the side of the majority of Third World countries, unite with second world countries, and form an "international united front against hegemony" (then a term exclusively used to point to the Soviet Union) that would also include the US.[38]

In assessing the two superpowers' relative positions in the world, following the thinking of Mao in his later years, Deng and his fellow Chinese leaders regarded the Soviet Union as more aggressive and, therefore, more dangerous than the US. After he climbed to the position of China's top leader, Deng repeatedly contended that the Soviet Union was on the offensive, whereas the US was on the defensive, although Moscow was yet to complete its global deployment of aggression and expansion (so he meant that there was still time to stop it).[39] Deng's judgment of the seriousness of the "Soviet threat" occupied a crucial position in the post-Mao Chinese leadership's definition of the goals and tasks of Chinese policies toward the US, the second world, and the Third World in the late 1970s.

Comparing Deng's grand strategic visions with those of Mao's, though, there were some important changes too. In Sino–US relations, out of considerations broader than strategic issues, Deng was more eager than Mao to pursue Beijing's formal diplomatic relationship with Washington. For Mao, the "tacit alliance" between China and the US was primarily a strategic issue that also had profound domestic implications – it helped enhance China's overall security position while, at the same time, allowing Mao to tell the Chinese people that, indeed, "we, the Chinese people, have stood up" in spite of the failure of his "continuous revolution" programs. For Deng, these of Mao's considerations remained valid. In particular, the development of China's relationship with the US, the strongest country in the world that had been hostile to the "new China" for over two decades, served the Chinese leadership's need of retaining the Chinese people's support of the "Communist" state (which was made increasingly anything but "Communist" with the unfolding of the "reform and opening" process).

In the meantime, Deng's vision of Sino–US relations was closely related to his perception of the missions and goals of the "reform and opening" process that, first and foremost, were based upon a transformed approach toward the capitalist-dominated world market. Throughout the Maoist era, markets and the pursuit of profits were treated as values and practices inimical to genuine socialism. With the introduction of the "reform and opening" policies, Deng and the post-Mao Chinese leadership began to perceive China's path toward modernity in a very different light, and they looked to the West for models to formulate China's own development strategy. This meant a drastic departure from the Chinese experience of building socialism from the early 1950s to the early 1970s, when China wholeheartedly embraced the Soviet model that was characterized by a rigid state-controlled command economy. For Deng, Beijing's partnership with Washington remained valuable in the geopolitical and strategic sense. Yet, more importantly for Deng, China's tacit alliance with the US was highly compatible with his new vision of looking to the West for models of modernizing China. Deng thus set great emphasis on the PRC gaining full diplomatic recognition from the US which happened on 1 January 1979.

Deng's "Soviet threat" perception and his "looking to the West" approach were of critical importance in shaping the post-Mao Chinese leadership's Third World strategies and policies. Reportedly, on his way to visit the US in late January 1979, Deng said to his assistants:

> If we look back, we find that all of those (Third World countries) that were on the side of the United States have been successful (in their

modernization drive), whereas all of those that were against the United States have not been successful. We shall be on the side of the United States.[40]

Within this context, Deng and his fellow Chinese leaders paid special attention to the successful experience of the "four little dragons" – Taiwan, South Korea, Singapore, and Hong Kong. When Deng justified, within the Chinese leadership, the necessity of China adopting the grand strategy of "reform and opening" to the outside world, he repeatedly quoted South Korea's and Taiwan's successful experiences in their modernization drives, emphasizing that China would have to learn from those experiences or, otherwise, it would lag further behind in economic development.

Against the above background, China's Third World policies in the late 1970s had three outstanding features: departing revolution, emphasizing development, and containing the "Soviet threat." The "reform and opening" process had already unleashed a de-revolutionizing process in China's domestic policies. Within this context, Beijing's leaders also decided to dramatically reduce and, then, completely stop China's material support for Communist insurgents abroad. Since the early 1950s, and especially during the Cultural Revolution years, China had provided military and other support to Communist rebels in such countries as Burma, Malaya (Malaysia), and Thailand. The trend began to change after Nixon's visit. With the inauguration of the "reform and opening" policies, Beijing's leaders determined that it was time for China to completely stop supporting Communist insurgents abroad. In 1980, Beijing informed the Burmese Communists that China would gradually reduce its aid to them over the next five years, and would then completely cut off the aid.[41] In December 1980, Deng told Chin Peng, the Secretary General of the Malayan Communist Party who had been in exile in China since 1960, to stop the operation of Suara Revolusi, the Party's radio station operating from Chinese territory since the early 1970s.[42]

Beijing's leaders also attached great emphasis to the economic aspects of China's foreign policies in general and its policies toward the Third World in particular. In order to concentrate China's limited resources on promoting the modernization drive at home and respond to the changing international situation, Beijing's leaders significantly reduced China's economic aid to quite a few Third World countries – and those with close relations with the Soviet Union (such as Vietnam) or hostile to China (such as Albania, which Beijing had regarded as the only Third World country in Europe) in particular. Beginning in the late 1970s, China was increasingly entering the "world market," and thus it also increasingly adopted the "normal methods" – that is, through the market – in handling trade relations with other countries, including many Third World countries. The barter method that China had previously used in trade relations with Third World countries had been gradually abandoned. All of this, as

Odd Arne Westad points out, "inevitably resulted in structural changes in the international market," and "made it more difficult for non-capitalist countries to obtain favorable prices in face of the diversification of the global economy" brought about, to a large extent, by China's "reform and opening" process.[43]

The overriding factor underlying Chinese policies toward the Third World in the late 1970s and early 1980s was the serious concern about containing the perceived global expansion of the Soviet Union. As discussed earlier, from Mao to Deng, the Chinese leadership believed that the Soviet Union was the one that was on the offensive among the two superpowers. Beijing's concerns about the seriousness of the Soviet threat had reached their most worrisome level by the late 1970s, as the Chinese leaders believed that they were seeing that the Soviets had been "gaining" in many different parts of the Third World. Those worries were most clearly spelt out by Deng himself in an interview with *Time Magazine*'s Hedley Donovan and Marsh Clark in early 1979:

> We see that last year South Yemen was taken over by the Soviet Union, and the Soviet Union gained influence in Ethiopia. If we go farther east there is Afghanistan, and now there is Iran, where there seems to be no end to the troubles. And Pakistan. And farther to the east, Viet Nam controls Laos by military means, and the Vietnamese made a major invasion into Cambodia with more than ten divisions. And then if we go even farther east, do we see that the Soviet military force has been strengthened or weakened in the Asian and Pacific region? At least its navy and air force have been strengthened. The Soviet fleet in the Far East is now equal in strength to the Soviet fleet in the Atlantic. So all this gives serious concern to the countries of the world, and they should deal with it seriously.[44]

Thus, in the late 1970s and early 1980s, Vietnam's invasion of Cambodia and Cuba's intervention in Africa became two central events in China's dealings with the Third World. In the case of Vietnam, Chinese and Vietnamese Communists were close allies during the First Indochina War and for most of the Second Indochina War. Beginning in the late 1960s, relations between the two Communist allies began to deteriorate. After the Vietnamese Communists unified the whole country in 1975, hostility quickly developed between Beijing and Hanoi. Yet it was not until Vietnamese troops invaded Cambodia in December 1978 that the breakdown of Sino–Vietnamese relations reached the point of no return. In addition to the memory of the historical conflicts between the two countries, Hanoi's discrimination against ethnic Chinese living in Vietnam, Beijing's long-existing suspicion of the Vietnamese intention to establish their own regional hegemony in Indochina (the Vietnamese invasion of Cambodia in December 1978 turned this Chinese suspicion into certainty), Beijing's leaders also firmly believed that Hanoi was acting as an agent of Moscow's hegemonic ambitions, leading Soviet expansion into the region south of China. Consequently, on 17 February 1979, Chinese troops started a large-scale invasion of Vietnam to "teach the Vietnamese a lesson." After fierce fighting and suffering heavy casualties, the Chinese troops seized Lang Son and Cai Bang, two strategically important Vietnamese border towns. Instead of pushing forward, Beijing announced that Chinese troops would begin to return to China. But the confrontation between China and Vietnam did not end with the withdrawal of Chinese troops. Throughout the 1980s, the borders between the two countries were turned into a front of protracted warfare.

In the case of Cuba, Beijing's leaders firmly opposed its intervention in Africa. They regarded Havana as another major agent of Moscow's hegemonic and expansionist ambition. Revolutionary Cuba was the first country in the western hemisphere to recognize the PRC. In the early 1960s, Beijing and Havana maintained a very close relationship. Yet, beginning in the mid-1960s, Sino–Cuban relations deteriorated in the context of the great Sino–Soviet polemic debate. When the Cultural Revolution occurred in China, Beijing openly attacked Fidel Castro and Cuba's domestic and international policies, causing hostility and conflicts to develop between the two Communist countries. In the early 1970s, Sino–Cuban relations experienced a short period of improvement. Yet, this episode quickly ended following Sino–US rapprochement, which Havana criticized fervently. In December 1974, Chinese vice premier Li Xiannian told the Cuban ambassador to China that "it is absolutely true that there exist differences in principles between China and Cuba."[45] After 1976, when Cuba dispatched "volunteers" to Africa, Beijing's relations with Havana worsened rapidly. Chinese leaders openly accused Cuba's intervention in Africa – and in Angola in particular – as part of Moscow's grand plan to dominate the world. In accordance with this perception, Chinese policies toward Africa were also formulated around what would be best for containing the Soviet threat. In Angola, Beijing firmly supported Jonas Savimbi's National Union for the Total Independence of Angola (UNITA) in the Angolan Civil War simply because its main enemy was the Moscow-backed People's Movement for the Liberation of Angola (MPLA). Beijing was also unfriendly toward Mengistu Haile Mariam's Socialist Ethiopia.

In late December 1979, Soviet troops invaded Afghanistan. For Beijing's leaders, this confirmed what they had believed during the previous decade: The Soviet threat was not only real but worsening. Immediately after the Soviet invasion of Afghanistan, Beijing's leaders decided to denounce it, as well as to prepare for possible consequences associated with it. Deng pointed out that the Soviet invasion, as "an important step toward pursuing worldwide hegemony," created threats of the most serious nature to peace and security in Asia as well as in the world.[46] On 10 January 1980, a Chinese Foreign Ministry spokesperson announced that the Soviet invasion of Afghanistan had created a new barrier to the improvement of relations between Beijing and Moscow.[47] Then, Beijing decided that China – which had just restored its membership in the International Olympic Committee – would join a group of others – mostly Western capitalist countries – in boycotting the Olympic Games in Moscow in the summer of 1980. Throughout the 1980s, even when tensions between Beijing and Moscow began to reduce after 1982–1983, Beijing provided substantial military and other support to Pakistan and, largely through Pakistan, to the resistance forces in Afghanistan. Beijing's close cooperation with Pakistan, in turn, made it more difficult for Sino–Indian relations to improve.

In the meantime, shared interests in containing Soviet expansion in Afghanistan allowed Beijing and Washington to develop a cooperative relationship (although on a limited scale) in military and security spheres. In January and May 1980, right after the Soviet invasion of Afghanistan, the US Secretary of Defense, Harold Brown, and the Chinese Defense Minister, Geng Biao, exchanged visits. By the end of 1980, Washington had approved "export licenses for some 400 items in the area of advanced technology in military support equipment."[48] When Ronald Reagan was elected US President in November 1980, despite his campaign promise that he would restore the "official relationship" with Taiwan and, after the election, and his decision to continue arms sales to Taiwan, he did not go so far as to undermine the foundation of Sino–US relations. While naming the Soviet Union as the "Evil Empire," Reagan continuously viewed China as a useful partner in the US mission to contain and defeat the Soviet Union in the Cold War competition.

By 1982–1983, Chinese foreign policy had reached another critical juncture. The most important factor in the background was that the "reform and opening" process, in political, social, economic, and ideological senses, had brought China past the point of no return. Indeed, it would have been next to impossible for any force to have brought China back to any of the following: The planning economy, the closed society, the Maoist ideology and Maoist mass mobilization phenomenon, the utopian-style justification of the legitimacy foundation of the state, or the isolated international status and the "revolutionary country" identity. In the meantime, the international conditions facing China were also changing. In Sino–US relations, the difficulties that Beijing encountered, especially on the Taiwan question, with the Reagan administration made Deng and his fellow Chinese leaders rethink how best to define the scope of Sino–US relations. In Beijing's dealings with Moscow, in March 1982, Soviet leader Leonid Brezhnev openly stated that the Soviet Union did not intend to threaten China, and that Moscow was willing to improve relations with Beijing.

These new domestic and international conditions combined together would lead to one of the most fundamental changes in the Chinese leadership's general perception of world affairs: They gradually abandoned the old estimate of the danger of a new world war. In the Maoist discourse, revolutions were always closely associated with wars. Throughout the history of the PRC, yet especially since the 1960s, Beijing persistently claimed that because of the existence of imperialism, a new world war could only be delayed but not averted. With the process in China's modernization drive and improvement in its security environment, Deng concluded that "it is possible that there will be no large-scale war for a fairly long time to come and that there is hope of maintaining world peace."[49]

At the CCP's twelfth national congress, convened in September 1982, Deng and the Party leadership announced that Chinese foreign policy would follow the basic principle of "independence and self-determination" (that is, keeping distance from both superpowers), would highlight the universality of the five principles of peaceful coexistence, and not enter any alliance with any country. The Third World remained important for China, according to the CCP leadership, especially because they believed that the overall influences of the Third World were increasing in international affairs. In the meantime, as China was also a part of the Third World and a developing county itself, it was crucial not to over-commit China's resources to supporting other Third World countries. In this respect, Deng's words were revealing:

> Our work toward the Third World should be strengthened in the future. As we ourselves are also facing difficult challenges, our support to other Third World countries cannot increase in volume. But we may increase friendly exchanges on all levels as well as enhance people-to-people relations.[50]

Deng also tried to introduce these ideas to leaders of other Third World countries. In meeting Samuel Kanyon Doe, Liberia's Head of State, on 5 May 1982, Deng made the following remarks:

> China has not given much help to its Third World friends. That is because our country, although vast in territory, is very poor and still faces many difficulties.... We are now devoting all our efforts to construction and the rather rapid development of our economy. When we have succeeded, we shall be able to do more for our friends in the Third World.[51]

After 1982, Beijing virtually stopped using Mao's three-worlds thesis in describing the structure of the world. Also disappearing from China's international discourse was the rhetoric of "the international united front against hegemony." China's partnership with the US, though weakened in the early years of the Reagan administration, was enhanced during the rest of the 1980s, especially in economic fields. In Sino–Soviet relations, Brezhnev's March 1982 speech mentioned earlier was welcomed by Deng, who made it clear that he was willing to reduce tensions between China and the Soviet Union. At the same time, Deng emphasized that unless Moscow used action to prove its intention, improved relations would not be achieved. Thus Beijing raised removal of "three big barriers" as the pre-condition for the improvement of Sino–Soviet relations: that Moscow should reduce its military forces deployed on Soviet–Sino and Mongolian–Sino borders, that Soviet troops should withdraw from Afghanistan, and that Vietnamese troops should withdraw from Cambodia.[52]

Thus it was two Third World issues – Afghanistan and Vietnam – that had blocked the prospect of quick improvement of Sino–Soviet relations. Of the two issues, Vietnam was the more difficult challenge for Beijing and Moscow: from the Soviet perspective, this was a question concerning a third country over which Moscow had no final control; but from Beijing's perspective, this was an issue of utmost importance as China's border war with Vietnam continued throughout most of the 1980s.

But the real issue involved in the Chinese leader's deliberation about the Vietnam question was not international but profoundly domestic. In the final analysis, China's continued confrontation with Vietnam would serve the needs on the part of Deng and his fellow Chinese leaders to identify useful resources for coping with the ever-deepening legitimacy crisis that the Chinese Communist state was facing in the age of "reform and opening." When Deng made the decision to "teach the Vietnamese a lesson," it provided him with a highly valuable opportunity to confirm his control of China's military and political power, as well as to crush any possible opposition to his position as China's paramount leader. Then, the confrontation with Vietnam created a sustained source – one that had the power to appeal to the Chinese people's patriotism and nationalistic feelings – of domestic mobilization. Throughout the 1980s, popular literature, movies, and music extolling People's Liberation Army soldiers' heroic fighting against the ungrateful Vietnamese in a "war of self-defense," formed an overwhelming theme in Beijing's campaigns for promoting "love of the socialist motherland." At a time when the "reform and opening" policies created profound economic inequality within Chinese society and, as a result, the legitimacy of the Chinese Communist regime was seriously called into question, the confrontation with Vietnam and Beijing's representation of it to the Chinese people served to retain the support of ordinary Chinese for the regime in Beijing. One of the most important results of this approach, however, was that the international Communist movement would remain deeply divided – at a time when the global Cold War was approaching its end.

Indeed, by the mid-1980s – that is, the end of the long 1970s – Beijing's leaders had probably realized that, in many key ways, the Soviet Union actually was a superpower in decline, but they would not acknowledge that they had almost certainly contributed to it. In addition to Beijing's partnership with Washington, which effectively altered the balance of power between the two superpowers, China's West-capitalist-market-oriented reforms undermined Moscow's claim that Communism remained a viable alternative to capitalism. Furthermore, Beijing's repudiation of the Soviet model discouraged other Third World countries from looking at Communism as a useful and competitive path toward modernity.[53] By doing so, China had virtually withdrawn from the Cold War. The Soviet Union and its Bloc persisted in the Cold War, but they found that this was a course increasingly more difficult for them to sustain. All of this, in one way or another, was the logical result of China's changing Third World policies, especially in the last two decades of the Cold War.

Notes

1 The term "long 1970s" was created by Professor Odd Arne Westad of the London School of Economics. He and I have used the term in our joint research project on "China's Great Transformation in the Long 1970s." We believe that China's Great Transformation was a process longer, broader, larger and deeper than the "reform and opening" process that began in the late 1970s. For us, the "long 1970s" covers the period from the late 1960s to the early and mid-1980s.

2 *Mao Zedong on Diplomacy* (Beijing: Foreign Languages Press, 1993), p. 454.

3 Mao, "Talks with Anna Louis Strong," *Mao Zedong xuanji*, Vol. 4 (Selected Works of Mao Zedong) (Beijing: Renmin, 1965), pp. 1191–2; *Renmin ribao* (People's Daily), 4 January 1947.

4 For discussions, see Chen Jian, *China's Road to the Korean War: The Making of the Sino–American Confrontation* (New York: Columbia University Press, 1994).

5 For China's involvement in the First Indochina War, see Zhai Qiang, *China and the Vietnam Wars* (Chapel Hill, NC: University of North Carolina Press, 2000), ch. 1–2.

6 See, for example, Liu Shaoqi to Stalin, "Report on Strategies of National Revolutionary Movements in East Asia," 14 August 1949, *Jianguo yilai Liu Shaoqi wengao*, Vol. 1 (Liu Shaoqi's Manuscripts since the Formation of the People's Republic) (Beijing: Zhongyang wenxian, 2005), pp. 50–3.

7 The Five Principles, also known as Pancha Shila, included (1) mutual respect for sovereignty and territorial integrity, (2) non-aggression, (3) non-interference in other countries' internal affairs, (4) equal and mutual benefit, and (5) peaceful coexistence.

8 Pei Jianzhang *et al.*, *Zhonghua renmin gongheguo waijiao shi, 1949–1956* (A Diplomatic History of the People's Republic of China, 1949–1956) (Beijing: Shijie zhishi, 1994), pp. 231–51.

9 See, for example, Mao's speech at a Politburo enlarged meeting, 7 July 1954. The Chinese chairman stated that "the biggest ambition of the United States at the moment is to castigate the intermediate zone, including the entire area from Japan to Britain, and to make all these countries cry while castigating them." *Mao Zedong wenji*, Vol. 6 (A Collection of Mao Zedong's Works) (Beijing: Renmin, 1999), p. 334.

10 Mao Zedong, "Speech at the Moscow Conference of Communist and Workers' Parties," *Jianguo yilai Mao Zedong wengao*, Vol. 6 (Mao Zedung's Manuscripts since the Formation of the People's Republic) (Beijing: Zhongyang wenxian, 1992), pp. 635–6.

11 Chen Jian, *Mao's China and the Cold War* (Chapel Hill, NC: University of North Carolina Press, 2001), ch. 7.

12 For a more detailed discussion, see Chen Jian, "The Tibetan Rebellion of 1959 and China's Changing Relations with India and the Soviet Union," *Journal of Cold War History*, Vol. 8, No. 3 (Summer 2006), pp. 54–101.
13 Zheng Qian, "The Nationwide War Preparations before and after the CCP's Ninth Congress," *Zhonggong dangshi ziliao* (CCP History Materials), 41 (April 1992), p. 205.
14 *Mao Zedong on Diplomacy*, p. 388.
15 Chen Jian, *Mao's China and the Cold War*, ch. 7.
16 Ibid., pp. 230–2.
17 Chen Jian, "Limits of the 'Lips and Teeth' Alliance: An Historical Review of Chinese-North Korean Relations," Woodrow Wilson Center *Asian Program Special Report*, No. 115 (September 2003), p. 7.
18 Yang Kuisong, "The Sino–Soviet Border Clash of 1969," *Cold War History*, Vol. 1, No. 1(August 2000), pp. 25–31.
19 For more substantial discussions about how the failure of Mao's "continuous revolution" shaped the larger context in which the Chinese-American rapprochement occurred, see Chen Jian, *Mao's China and the Cold War*, ch. 9.
20 Margaret Macmillan, *Nixon and Mao: The Week that Changed the World* (New York: Random House, 2007).
21 "Mao Zedong's conversation with Moussa Traoré," 22 June 1973, Song Yongyi (ed.), *Zhongguo wenhua dageming wenku* (Database of the Cultural Revolution, online database).
22 *Mao Zedong on Diplomacy*, p. 454.
23 "Mao Zedong's conversations with Houari Boumediene," 25 February 1974, CCP Central Committee Document, (1974), No. 10, Fujian Provincial Archive, 244–1-106, p. 4.
24 *Renmin ribao*, 11 April 1974, p. 1.
25 Li Ping *et al.*, *Zhou Enlai nianpu, 1949–1976* (A Chronological Record of Zhou Enlai, 1949–1976) (Beijing: Zhongyang wenxian, 1997), p. 691.
26 Chen Jinghua, *Guoshi yishu* (Recollections and Accounts on State Affairs) (Beijing: Zhonggong dangshi, 2005), ch. 1.
27 See, for example, Mao Zedong's talk with French Foreign Minister Maurice Schuman, 10 July 1972, *Mao Zedong on Diplomacy*, p. 452.
28 Mao Zedong's conversation with Kissinger, 17 February 1973, *Dangde wenxian* (Party History Documents), No. 2, 2002. The US record of the conversation, however, misses "China" in the sentence. See Memorandum of Conversation, Mao and Kissinger, 17–18 February 1973, Foreign Relations of the United States, 1973–1976, Vol. 18 (Washington, DC: U.S. Government Printing Office, 2007), p. 131.
29 Mao Zedong's talks with Wang Hongwen and Zhang Chunqiao, 4 July 1973, cited from *Dangde wenxian*, No. 2, 2002, pp. 70–1.
30 Wang Taiping (ed.), *Zhonghua renmin gongheguo waijiaoshi, 1970–1978* (A Diplomatic History of the People's Republic of China) (Beijing: Shijie zhishi, 1999) pp. 452–3.
31 Ibid., pp. 143–4, 151–2.
32 Ibid., p. 153.
33 Wang Taiping *et al.*, *Zhonghua renmin gongheguo waijiaoshi, 1957–1969* (A Diplomatic History of the People's Republic of China, 1957–1969) (Beijing: Shijie zhishi, 1998), pp. 174–5.
34 *Renmin ribao*, 14 January 1973, p. 1; see also *Renmin ribao*, 20 January 1974.
35 F. S. Aijazuddin, *From a Head, through a Head, to a Head: The Secret Channel between the US and China through Pakistan* (New York: Oxford University Press, 2000).

36 Chen Jian, "China, the Vietnam War, and the Sino–American Rapprochement, 1968–1973," Odd Arne Westad and Sophie Quinn-Judge (eds.), *The Third Indochina War: Conflict between China, Vietnam and Cambodia, 1972–79* (London: Routledge, 2006), pp. 53–9.
37 Mao's talks with Kim Il-sung, 18 April 1975, and Deng's talks with Kim, 20 April 1975, CCP Central Archive; see also Leng Rong and Wang Zuoling *et al.*, *Deng Xiaoping nianpu* (A Chronological Record of Deng Xiaoping) (Beijing: Zhongyang wenxian, 2004), Vol. 1: pp. 36–7.
38 Hua Guofeng's political report at the CCP's eleventh national Congress, 12 August 1977, *Renmin ribao*, 19 August 1977.
39 For example, in a speech at a CCP Central Military Commission plenary meeting on 28 December 1977, Deng made it clear that the CCP should "apply Comrade Mao Zedong's strategy of differentiating the three worlds and follow his line in foreign affairs." He pointed out that "the global strategy of the United States has shifted to the defensive after its defeat in Vietnam," and that the Soviet, while on the offensive, "has not yet finished its global strategic deployment." *Deng Xiaoping xuanji*, Vol. 2 (Selected Works of Deng Xiaoping) (Beijing Renmin, 1983), p. 74.
40 Information gained from an August 2008 interview with a leading Chinese party historian.
41 Yang Meihong, *Yingsu huagong: wo zai miangong shiwu nian* (Red Poppy: My Fifteen Years with the Burmese Communist Party) (Hong Kong: Tiandi, 2001), pp. 263–4.
42 Chin Peng, *My Side of History* (Singapore: Media Masters, 2003), pp. 457–8.
43 Odd Arne Westad, "China, the Third World, and the Last Years of the Cold War," *Lengzhan guoji shi yanjiu* (Cold War International History Studies), No. 4 (October 2007), pp. 132–3.
44 An interview with Teng Hsiao-ping (Deng Xiaoping) by Hedley Donovan and Marsh Clark, *Time*, 5 February 1979.
45 Wang Taiping *et al.*, *Zhonghua renmin gongheguo waijiaoshi, 1970–1978*, p. 456.
46 Leng and Wang *et al.*, *Deng Xiaoping nianpu*, Vol. 1, p. 589.
47 Tian Zengfei *et al.*, *Gaige kaifang yilai de zhongguo waijiao* (Chinese Diplomacy Since the Reform and Opening to the Outside World) (Beijing: Shijie zhishi, 1993), p. 291.
48 Zbigniew Brzezinski, *Power and Principle: Memoirs of the National Security Advisor, 1977–1981* (New York: Farrar, Straus and Giroux, 1983), p. 424.
49 *Selected Works of Deng Xiaoping*, Vol. 3 (Beijing: Foreign Languages Press, 1994), p. 132.
50 Leng and Wang *et al. Deng Xiaoping nianpu*, Vol. 2, p. 712.
51 Deng Xiaoping's conversation with the Liberian Head of State, Samuel Kanyon Doe, 6 May 1982, *Deng Xiaoping xuanji*, Vol. 2, p. 360.
52 Ibid., pp. 291–2.
53 Indeed, as Odd Arne Westad points out, the huge influence of China's adoption of a new path toward modernity, combined with greater pressures from the West in the late 1970s amd early 1980s, led to "disillusionment with Marxist-inspired planning in the Third World. By the mid-1980s, many Third World countries had embarked on "a gradual move toward market-based economies." Westad, "China, the Third World, and the Last Years of the Cold War," pp. 134–5.

4 The impact of the Cold War's end on the Arab–Israeli conflict

A view from Israel

Dima Adamsky

How did the end of the Cold War influence the approach of the Israeli strategic community towards the Arab–Israeli conflict? What were the ramifications of the war's end for Israeli bilateral relations with Lebanon, Syria, the Palestinian Authority, Jordan, Egypt, Iran, and Iraq and overall regional normalization? The nature of the Cold War significantly conditioned the dynamics of the conflict, and the end of the war had major implications for Middle Eastern confrontation. However, the conflict was not a direct function of the Cold War, it preceded it and extended beyond its termination. The Madrid conference of 1991 and the Oslo Accords of 1993, which brought together Israel and its foes in face-to-face talks, cannot be equated to the fall of the Berlin wall in Europe as a symbol of conflict resolution. Consequently, the meanings of "victory" and "defeat," in the global sense, were not identical to the meanings of "victory" and "defeat" on the "battlefields" of the Arab–Israeli confrontation.

How can one learn about national security decision making in Israel during the Cold War? The most relevant collection of documents, in Hebrew, would be the protocols of the governmental meetings from the Israeli National Archive. Today, researchers have partial access to the documents up to 1973. The situation is better with the Ministry of Foreign Affairs Archives, where partial access exists up to the late 1970s. The documents from the IDF, including annual national intelligence estimates and annual strategic planning overviews, are stored in the archives of the Ministry of Defense. Today, partial access is available to the collections dated from the mid-1960s and some files related to the 1967 war. Except for several signed treaties and international agreements, the end of the Cold War and the subsequent decade are hardly documented in the primary sources.[1]

To trace decision making processes in Israel during the Cold War one should take into account the characteristics of Israeli strategic culture. In contrast to other democratic countries, in Israel the center of decision making on foreign and security policy was not in the Ministry of Foreign

Affairs (MFA), Ministry of Defense (MoD) or National Security Council (NSC) (established only in the mid-1990s). The General Headquarters (GHQ) of the Israeli Defense Forces (IDF) served as the de facto main research and planning staff to systematically support the decision-making processes of the senior leadership in the MoD and Prime Minister's (PM) office.[2] This situation is explained by another anomaly. Military Intelligence (AMAN) had been primus inter pares in the Israeli intelligence community as far as national intelligence estimates were concerned. In other words, the Research and Analysis Directorate of Military Intelligence was responsible for producing systematic strategic political intelligence for the national leadership.[3] Similarly, the strategic planning department of the GHQ, in the IDF, had been functioning more like a national security council in other democratic countries and less like a planning function in the military staffs of other liberal democracies.[4] These characteristics of the Israeli civilian-military relations have direct implications for historians of the Cold War who try to reconstruct the decision making process in Israel. To put it simply, primary sources and the oral history of senior Israeli military officials can reveal more about Israel strategic and diplomatic history than one might expect.

Given that the most critical collections of documents from the period are still classified, there are three pools of primary sources which enable us to get an overview of Israeli strategic beliefs, perceptions and decision making processes towards the end of the Cold War.

The first pool of primary sources is Ma'arachot (Campaigns), a bi-monthly professional journal of the Israeli Defense Forces. It is the equivalent of the US *Joint Forces Quarterly* or the *Soviet Voennaia Mysl'*. Because of the central role that the military establishment plays in formulating Israeli security and foreign policy, reading Ma'arachot might be even more informative than reading *Voennaia Mysl'* during the Cold War. Senior and high ranking officers, including chiefs of GHQ, deputies, heads and seniors of Military Intelligence and of Strategic Planning at GHQ, and other relevant senior officers contribute to Ma'arachot on a regular basis.

The second pool of primary sources consists of memoirs published by political leaders, their assistants, chiefs of GHQ, heads of Military Intelligence, diplomats directly involved in policy making who played influential roles in the country's external and security policy, members of peace negotiation teams, and Israeli delegations, to talks with the Palestinian Authority, Jordan, Syria, and various international conferences. The nature of Israeli national security culture is such that often the same person serves throughout his career in high ranking military, intelligence, Ministry of Defense, Foreign Ministry, diplomatic and senior political posts. The memoirs of one person often encapsulate a wide spectrum of perspectives and information on strategic intelligence, military planning, and diplomatic relations with the Arab and non-Arab worlds.

The third pool of sources consists of serious investigative journalism and academic research on contemporary history. These works are based on the rich collections of oral history by relevant insiders and also, sometimes, on direct access to documents that cannot be published.

This chapter contributes to the Cold War historiography by overviewing the memoir literature in Hebrew that became available recently. During the last decade several dozen recently published books have explored how the Israeli political system perceived the end of the Cold War and its impact on the emergence of the post-Cold War security regime in the Middle East.

The chapter presents the Israeli view of how the end of the Cold War affected the Arab–Israeli conflict. In keeping with the research aims, the monograph deliberately reflects the biases of the Israeli sources, even if these observations sound contradictory to the conventional wisdom elsewhere. Based on available primary materials, this chapter presents three basic beliefs (i.e. perspectives and retrospectives) of the Israeli decision makers regarding the end of the Cold War.[5]

The first belief: the global superpower dynamic conditioned the development of the Arab–Israeli conflict, but did not determine its nature

Most Israeli sources argue that during the Cold War the two superpowers never introduced any revolutionary dynamics to the conflict, nor did they manage to change the existing fundamental regional tendencies. The superpowers only reinforced the existing trends or minimized their effects, and they often faced the undesirable consequences of the strategic behavior of their clients. That being said, Cold War logic, and the rules of the game that it imposed on the regional actors, shaped the history of the region for decades.

One can identify four epochs of the modern Arab–Israeli Conflict: the period when the conflict was relatively "local" (up to the beginning of the Cold War); "globalization" of the conflict (from the 1954 arms sales to Egypt to Gorbachev's new Middle Eastern policy); the relative "de-globalization" (from the late 1980s forward) and, finally, the "second globalization" (after the 2001).

Most of the Middle Eastern ethnic, religious, and territorial conflicts predated the superpower confrontation in the region. The Arab–Israeli conflict, in its essence, can be seen as a dispute between two national movements – Zionism and Arab (particularly Palestinian) nationalism – both of which relate to the same piece of land. Due to the different reasons specific to the region and not related to the Cold War, the conflict also acquired a religious connotation.[6] Thus, decades before the winds of the Cold War reached the Middle East, the nations and the ethnic groups of the region had reasons to fight and had actually been fighting.

Starting in the mid to late 1950s, particularly following the arms sales to Egypt and until the collapse of the Soviet Union, the conflict took on a global dimension. Although, originally, the Soviet–Egyptian alliance was more anti-Western than anti-Zionist, it was seen in Jerusalem as a potential anti-Israel pact. It eventually turned into such after the 1956 war, especially when Nasser, as the emerging leader of the Arab world, took responsibility for the Palestinian question.

Globalization of the conflict had a significant influence on the above dynamic. Questions of peace and war between Israel and its neighbors quickly became determined by the zero-sum logic of the superpower rivalry. Moscow pushed its Arab clients towards a peaceful solution, but opposed any US-moderated peace agreement because this, in the Soviet view, would enhance US power in the region and set back the Soviet position. This position intensified from 1967 onwards, when Moscow no longer had diplomatic relations with both sides and, thus, was not able to broker bilateral peace agreements. Consequently, throughout the whole Cold War, Moscow opted for the formula of the international conference. Given the logic of the Cold War, this was a nonstarter for the US, which sought to minimize the Soviet role in peacemaking and neutralize its influence in the region.[7] Thus, strategic reality, as constructed by the globalization of the Cold War, prevented the peace process from starting. The change in the superpowers' conduct from this Cold War pattern was a necessary condition for the peace process to start, but not a pledge for progress. The nature of the conflict was determined more by indigenous local factors, and had less to do with the global logic of the Cold War.

Even after its globalization, the Arab–Israeli conflict was never a mirror reflection of the East vs. West, socialism vs. capitalism, autocratic Communism vs. the democratic liberalism dynamics of the Cold War rivalry. The picture was always more complex. During the Cold War, Israeli experts and policymakers envisioned the Soviet–Arab and the US–Israeli patron–client relationship as a complex and nuanced mechanism which did not work precisely according to the logic of the global confrontation. Senior Israeli intelligence officers, prime-ministers, presidents, and senior Foreign and Defense Ministry officials, who were involved in Cold War policy making, were convinced that both superpowers often found themselves on a collision path with their regional clients who promoted their own strategic interests against the overall logic of the Cold War.[8] Egypt, Syria, and Iraq, although under the Soviet umbrella, constantly experienced tensions with Moscow because of their attempts to promote local national interests which frequently conflicted with Soviet global goals. Israel often experienced a very similar strategic dynamic with the US. As the available sources demonstrate, towards the Six Day War and afterwards, it became clear to the Israeli decision makers that they (and also the Arabs) often sought to exploit the vulnerabilities of their patrons and wag the dog according to their particular interests.[9]

Middle Eastern clients went to war and negotiation tables not necessarily according to the logic of the global Cold War and the wishes of their superpower patrons. The Arab clients initiated three wars (1967, 1969, and 1973) which ran counter to Soviet interests. Moscow tried, but did not succeed, in dissuading its Arab clients from their strategic choices.[10] The Kremlin played a key role mainly when it came to imposing a ceasefire according to the pledge of its clients. The Soviets did not succeed in guiding their clients (Egypt, Syria, and the PLO) towards the negotiation track and peaceful resolution of the conflict. Eventually, when Cairo opted for peace, its initiative went against Soviet interests and was not a direct result of Moscow's efforts. The same is true about Israel and the US. Israel made several dramatic decisions during the Cold War without fully coordinating them with its strategic ally. Israeli policy on the eve of and following the 1967 war, the management of the Israeli nuclear project, the 1981 raid on Osirak, and the 1982 Lebanon War, and other examples of Israeli strategic behavior, were counter to US interests, both global and regional.[11] Israelis saw the regional, strategic, earthquake of 1978 – the peace accord with Egypt and the fall of the Shah – less as a direct function of US policy in the region and more as a maturation of the indigenous strategic aspirations of the regional players.[12]

From the mid-1980s, Israeli decision makers started to realize the local implications of the global transformation in the nature of the Cold War. Jerusalem very quickly recognized the turn of the Soviet leadership, under Gorbachev, towards an evenhanded view of the Arab–Israeli conflict and noticed the Soviets distancing themselves from radical Arab positions. Israeli intelligence estimated that Moscow was signaling its readiness to accept Israel's existence within recognizable and secure borders and to resolve the territorial disputes through direct bilateral or multilateral talks. After two years in office Gorbachev made it crystal clear to Damascus that Moscow would no longer back the Syrian doctrine of "strategic parity" and urged the pursuit of a political solution with Jerusalem.[13] Israeli leaders closely monitored the curtailment of military aid and the withdrawal of Soviet advisers. Moscow stopped military support of the PLO, condemned terrorist attacks during the First Intifada, and advised the Palestinian leadership to opt for the diplomatic path aimed at reaching a two state solution.[14]

The de-globalization of the conflict and the moderation of the Soviet position, including the turn towards an evenhanded approach, made peace negotiations possible on the Palestinian, Jordanian, and Syrian negotiation tracks. As the subsequent decade showed, however, the success of these negotiations (or lack thereof) had nothing to do with the Soviet position, but with the approach to the conflict on the side of the Israeli, Jordanian, Palestinian, and Syrian leaderships.

Likewise, de-globalization affected the US attitude towards Israel. Although the special relationship between the two countries was preserved, the tendency of US policy towards a more "evenhanded" approach became obvious to the Israeli leadership leading up to and following the Madrid conference. The first tensions were already evident during Shamir's second tenure (1986–1992), and were associated with the decision of the Bush administration to withhold the loan guarantees to Israel.[15]

The first conflict of the emerging post-Cold War world order also supported pre-existing Israeli strategic beliefs. Israel and Syria coordinated their actions with the US-led coalition of Arab countries because of the collapse of Soviet Middle Eastern policy and lack of backing of Iraq. The convergence of interests occurred not because of the common antagonism towards Saddam's regime; in the view of Israeli sources, this antagonism had nothing to do directly with the Cold War or its end. According to the Israeli interpretation, the only superpower failed to impose its will on a regional actor. The US failed to prevent Iraq from invading Kuwait and then failed to coerce it, without the use of force, to leave the country.[16]

The second belief: the end of the Cold War had a limited impact on the essence of the conflict

Israeli sources argue that the Israeli and Palestinian leaderships did not become primed for the Oslo process because of the end of the Cold War. What disinclined them from fighting and predisposed them to talking was the experience of the first Lebanon War and the subsequent years of the first Intifada – the two longest wars of attrition that Israel had fought until then. The prolonged and intensive fighting, which turned fruitless for both sides, produced a feeling inside the Israeli decision making community that the conflict could not be resolved by military means or through the use of greater force. According to the Israeli view, this learning process was mutual – the decades of fighting brought the PLO leadership to a similar conclusion and predisposed it to try the political path. The end of the Cold War only enabled these emerging trends to materialize and be acted upon.[17]

Although Washington was enjoying the beginning of the "unipolar moment," the Israeli strategic community envisioned American mediation efforts on the Palestinian, Jordanian, and Syrian tracks more as pro-forma. According to Israeli beliefs, the end of the Cold War only enabled Israel to codify, de jure, the reality that was emerging de facto, or had existed for decades. As in the case of Jordan, where an objective potential for the breakthrough existed, the peace process went as smoothly as possible. Throughout the whole Cold War, Israel and Jordan had been the "best of enemies."[18] Since, in the case of Syria,[19] and (later on) in the case of the Palestinians,[20] the positions of the two sides were diametrically opposed, US involvement proved pointless and the end of the Cold War irrelevant.[21] Moderate authoritarian regimes, such as Egypt and Saudi Arabia, preserved their pro-US orientation and accepted the existence of Israel, de jure

(Egypt) and de facto (Saudi Arabia), regardless of Cold War dynamics or its end. The acceptance of Israel was conditioned by purely local considerations and the cumulative history of strategic interaction.[22] Following the total bankruptcy of the strategic logic advanced by Operation Peace for Galilee, the relationship with Lebanon, since the mid-1980s, has been conditioned by, if not determined by, the Israeli relationship with radical Muslim militias, primarily Amal and Hezbollah, and the strategic dynamic with Syria. The end of the Cold War has had little impact on that.[23]

The strategic regime which started to emerge in the Middle East during the final years of the Cold War (especially after the Soviet withdrawal from Afghanistan and the end of the Iran–Iraq War) predisposed the Israeli strategic community to think about trading territorial concessions for peace. However, the end of the Cold War did not terminate the threat perception which was deeply ingrained in the Israeli strategic mentality. During the Cold War one of the basic Israeli strategic beliefs was that military power was the foundation of peace. In other words, a military experience with Israel should teach an adversary that it would not be possible to defeat Israel and that, therefore, this would not be an option in the foreseeable future. Then, according to Israeli logic, a peace process would be feasible and a peace treaty would be stable. The end of the Cold War enlarged the group of Israeli politicians who wanted to introduce an alternative belief. They wanted to utilize the emerging climate of the "end of history" and envision peace treaties with neighbors as an ultimate substitute for military power and a genuine security guarantee. However, adaptations of this view always stayed in the minority and the Israeli strategic mentality preserved its indigenous orientation.[24]

The Israeli decision to opt for the peace process at the end of the Cold War rested on two basic assumptions. The first assumption was that the military balance in the foreseeable future would be in favor of Israel. When the Soviet Union withdrew its military assets and advisors from the region, the rejectionist states and radical elements started to lose political and military support. It became obvious to the Israelis that the Soviets would no longer rebuild Arab military potential following the military debacle – the constant assumption of Israeli strategic planning during the Cold War. Also, according to Israeli estimates, the Gulf War significantly enhanced the power of the moderates (Egypt, Saudi Arabia, and Jordan), weakened the potential of the radicals (Iraq, Syria, and Libya), and isolated radical groups such as the PLO and Hamas. Overall, Israeli intelligence estimates stated that Arab leaders had become convinced that Israeli military power could defeat any regional conventional coalition formed against it.[25]

The second assumption was that the regional hegemony in the foreseeable future would be controlled by the US. Although the Gulf War showed that the US was not an omnipotent power that could attain everything it wished for without resorting to force, at the same time it demonstrated that the US had the will and capability to do whatever it desired in the region. The war demonstrated to Israel that the US possessed both a political will and the military capability to intervene anywhere in the region to promote its interests and secure the interests of its allies. The assessment of Israeli military superiority, together with an estimate of the US hegemonic moment, created the belief within the Israeli strategic community that Israel could try risky political enterprises (i.e. a peace process). The hidden assumption was that if things went wrong Israel would have an effective strategic fallback position – potential political mistakes and wrong assumptions about Arab states would be corrected by military means.[26]

Thus, the end of the Cold War did not change fundamental Israeli strategic beliefs and has not solved the fundamental problems of the Arab–Israeli conflict. It just created the window of opportunity to start strategic probing.

The third belief: although the end of the Cold War did not change the fundamental trends of the conflict, it had a strong impact on the character of the Arab–Israeli warfare

It seems that the end of the Cold War had a stronger impact on the military-doctrinal realm than on the fundamental political-strategic trends or the nature of the relationship between Israel and its adversaries. Specifically, the end of the Cold War had a direct and immediate impact on the introduction of new tools of war and new theories of victory in the region.

Since its establishment, one of the pillars of the Israeli way of war has been the preservation of the Qualitative Military Edge (QME) over its numerically superior adversaries. Since the early mid 1980s, especially following the AWACS affair (the US sale of an Airborne Warning and Control system surveillance planes to Saudi Arabia), Israel had started to be concerned with US arms transfers to the "moderates" as much as it was concerned about Soviet arms transfers to "radicals."[27] This happened also because of the emerging information technology revolution in military affairs (IT-RMA), which downplayed the quantitative factor in conventional warfare and emphasized, instead, the qualitative components such as intelligence, command and control, and precision fire.[28]

The change in Soviet policy affected the strategic-military balance in Israel's favor on the Eastern front and almost nullified the military option to the Arab states (primarily Syria and Iraq). However, according to Israeli estimates at the end of the Cold War, the Eastern front was a diminishing concern anyway, because of potential benefits from the emerging IT-RMA, which, theoretically, enabled Israel to thwart this threat in a stand-off (without direct contact on the battlefield) manner. The Syrian and Iraqi military doctrines, and concepts of offensive and force structure, played precisely to the advantage of the IDF. Advanced intelligence sensors, linked through sophisticated command and control systems to advanced precision-guided stand-off munitions, were expected, in theory, to stop waves of advancing Arab armor formations and win a war without crossing the border with a ground maneuver. The mass of armed targets rolling toward its borders was seen by Israel as easy prey. Syrian and Iraqi numerical superiority were overplayed by the IDF's qualitative military edge.[29]

Thus, in Jerusalem's view, the sales of advanced US weaponry to the moderate Arab regimes eroded the Israel's QME more than the Soviet arms transfers. This trend intensified by the end of the Cold War, when potential risks from the moderate Arab regimes started to outweigh the actual threats from radicals.[30]

The end of the Cold War produced different operational constraints for Israel and its adversaries. However, for totally different reasons, both Israel and its adversaries shifted the preference for maneuver to the preference for fire. The lack of Soviet support coupled with the IDF's fire superiority forced Israel's adversaries to move away from the conventional realm [primarily based on maneuver capabilities] to the sub-conventional (terror) and non-conventional (WMD and SSMs) – [primarily based on fire capabilities]. This changed the main form of warfare, at least in the context of the Arab–Israeli confrontation. Missiles, terror, and WMD, which substitute for conventional superiority became the strategic arms of Israeli adversaries. Even before the withdrawal of Soviet support, Syria realized that achieving strategic balance with Israel might not be within its reach. Gorbachev's policies finally convinced it of the need to reorient its military build-up.[31]

While the end of the Cold War forced the radicals to change their military conduct and invest in fire capabilities (missiles and WMD) instead of maneuver, the IDF did not understand this development and continued in the same established direction (while also investing in fire capabilities). Available sources indicate that Israeli intelligence estimates of the late 1980s – early 1990s did not realize this new trend immediately. The IDF continued to invest in its fire capabilities, both as a response to the numerical superiority of the maneuvering enemy and as the most appropriate way of war for the peace process era. Only recently there has been a renaissance of military thought associated with maneuver warfare within the IDF.[32]

The end of the Cold War produced another transformation in the military regime. The non-state radical groups (for example the PLO, Hamas, and Hezbollah) started to seek state-like military capabilities, while the states (for example, Syria and Iran), in contrast, started to seek asymmetrical capabilities and to emulate the strategic behavior of non-state insurgencies practicing decentralized and asymmetrical warfare.[33]

As far as the new client-patron relationships were concerned, the emergence of strategic cooperation between radical Sunni and Shia elements was another interesting consequence of the Cold War's end. The vacuum produced by the withdrawal of Soviet support pushed the radical forces, of different kinds, to look for alternative strategic alliances. Thus, the Shia Lebanese Hezbollah and Shia Iran became strategic partners of the Sunni and Alawi Damascus. A similar strategic constellation could be observed in the case of the Sunni Hamas cooperating with the Shia Hezbollah.[34]

Conclusion

The de-globalization decade following the Cold War provided conditions and an opportunity for the long existing potential to mature into concrete political initiatives. However, this period demonstrated that the fundamental trends of the conflict are deeper and broader than the Cold War framework. When the "second globalization" of the conflict started, after 11 September 2001, the Arab–Israeli confrontation still showed more continuity than change, despite the chance that the "end of the Cold War" offered.

Similar argument can be made about the Israeli strategic mentality. The main trends of the global confrontation had a limited impact on shaping Israeli bureaucratic-organizational reflexes in the field of national security. Such fundamental traits of the Israeli strategic psyche as "siege mentality," "primacy of action and practice over theory and contemplating," "confidence in military power and distrust of diplomacy," and "primacy of improvisation and tactics over long term planning and strategy" originated prior to the globalization of the Arab–Israeli conflict in the late 1950s. These traits owe more to the Diaspora legacy, Zionist ideology and political-military experiences in Palestine during the first half of the twentieth century than to the Cold War. In other words, ideational factors independent of Cold War logic shaped, and sometimes determined, Israeli strategic behavior toward the outside world.[35]

It seems that the global, superpower dynamic (i.e. the Cold War) significantly conditioned the development of the Arab–Israeli conflict, but did not determine its nature. Consequently, the logic of the Cold War was often secondary to the primary indigenous trends of the conflict. If the superpower dynamic of the Cold War had only a secondary impact on the development of the Arab–Israeli conflict, then the end of the Cold War would have a limited impact as well. Although the end of the Cold War has not changed the fundamental trends of the conflict, it transformed the "theories of victory" and the main "tools of war" in the Middle East in a revolutionary manner and had an impact on the characteristics of subsequent Arab–Israeli wars.

Notes

1 For example, see: Gregory S. Mahler and Alden Mahler, *The Arab–Israeli Conflict: An Introduction and Documentary Reader* (London: Routledge, 2009).

2 Dima Adamsky, *The Culture of Military Innovation: The Impact of Cultural Factors*

2 Dima Adamsky, *The Culture of Military Innovation: The Impact of Cultural Factors on Revolution in Military Affairs in Russia, the US and Israel* (Stanford, CA: Stanford University Press, 2010), pp. 124–5.

3 Uri Bar-Joseph, "Military Intelligence as the National Intelligence Estimator: The Case of Israel," *Armed Forces and Society*, April 2010, No. 36, pp. 505–25.

4 For example, see: Yehuda Ben-Meir, *Civil Military Relations in Israel* (New York: Columbia University Press, 1995). Ben-Meir was a deputy foreign minister in the mid-1980s. Also see: Adamsky, *Culture of Military Innovation*, pp. 110–29.

5 Several arguments in this chapter are based on Efraim Karsh, "Cold War, post-Cold War: does it make a difference for the Middle East?" *Review of International Studies* (1997), No. 23, pp. 271–91.

6 Primarily due to the spread of the Salafi ideology. See for example: Assaf Moghadam, *Globalization of Martyrdom: Al Qaida, Salafi Jihad and Diffusion of Suicide Attacks* (Washington D.C.: Johns Hopkins University Press, 2008).

7 Itamar Rabinovich, *Hevlei shalom: Israel vehaaravim 1948–2003* (Or Ehuda: Dvir, 2004) Rabinovich was ambassador to the US, 1993–1996 and chief negotiator on the Syrian track.

8 Moshe Arens, *Milkhama veshalom be mizrah hatikhon 1988–1992* (Tel Aviv: Yediot Sfarim, 1995). Arens was Minister of Foreign Affairs, 1988–1990, Minister of Defense 1990–1992. Also see: Aharon Yariv, *Haarakha zahira* (Tel Aviv: JCSS, 1998). Yariv was head of Military Intelligence in the 1960s and the 1970s. Eli Zaira, *Mitus mul metziut* (Tel Aviv: Yedtio Akhronot, 1998). Zaira was head of Military Intelligence 1972–1974.

9 See introduction and conclusion in Yaacov R'oi and Boris Morozov, *The Soviet Union and the June 1967 War* (Stanford, CA: Stanford University Press, 2008).

10 R'oi and Morozov.

11 See: Shmuel Tzabag (ed.), *Ehudim, isrel ve astrategiia gariinit: asufat maamarim pri eto shel profesor Yval Neeman* (Ariel: Ehuda veshomron college, 2007). During the Arab–Israeli wars in the 1960s and the 1970s Yuval Ne'eman was the special assistant to the Minister of Defense responsible for the clandestine strategic dialogs with the US and other special missions. For many years he was a personal strategic advisor to Shimon Peres on strategic scientific issues. See ch. 2–3 for the Israeli perception of the superpowers during the Cold War and on the nuclear issues; pp. 77–175.

12 Gazit, Arens; Rabinovich; Halevi, Herzog. Shlomo Gazit, *Hamodiin vetahalih hashalom* (Jerusalem: Hebrew University in Jerusalem, 1994); Moshe Arens, *Milkhama veshalom be mizrah hatikhon 1988–1992* (Tel Aviv: Yediot Sfarim, 1995); Rabinovich, *Hevlei shalom*; Efraim Halevi, *Adam Betzel* (Tel Aviv: Matar, 2006); Chaim Herzog, *Derekh Khaim: Autobiografia* (Tel Aviv: Ma'ariv, 1997), *Derekh Khaim: Autobiografia* (Tel Aviv: Ma'ariv, 1997).

13 See Mark Kramer's chapter in this volume.

14 See: Sagi; Gazit, *Hamodiin vetahalih hashalom*. Gazit was head of Military Intelligence, 1974–1980. Shlomo Ben-Ami, *Hazit le lo oref: masa el gvulot tahalikh hashalom* (Tel Aviv: Yediot Akhronot, 2004) (Israeli Ambassador to Spain, 1987–1991; Foreign Minister during negotiations with the PA in the late 1990s).

15 Yitzhak Shamir, *Sikumo shel Davar* (Tel Aviv: Eidanim, 1994); Shamir was PM of Israel from 1986 to 1992. Also see: Yossi Ahimeir (ed.), *Yitzhak Shamir kesela eitan* (Tel Aviv: Yediot Sfarim, 2008). Also see: Zalman Shoval, *Lahatz Amerikani al reka tahalih hashalom: metziut o dimaion?* (Jerusalem: AJC, 1998). Shoval was the Israeli ambassador to the US in 1990–1993.

16 For analysis of these episodes see: Karsh, "Cold War, post-Cold War, pp. 271–91.

17 For example see: Yossi Beilin, *Lagaat beshalom* (Tel Aviv: Yediot Akhronot, 1995). Beilin was a Director General of the Foreign Ministry, 1986–1988 and Deputy Foreign Minister (1992–1995). Uri Savir, *Miakhorei haklaim shel hakraa historit* (Tel Aviv: Mishkal, 1998). Between 1993 and 1996 Savir served as director general of the Ministry of Foreign Affairs and was the Chief Negotiator of the Oslo Accords. Yair Hirschfield, *Oslo: Nusha le Shalom – masa umatan leheskemei Oslo astrategiia vemimusha* (Tel Aviv: Am Oved, 2000). Hirschfield was one of the key architects of the Oslo records.

18 The term is taken from Uri Bar-Joseph, *The Best of Enemies: Israel and Trans-Jordan in the War of 1948* (London: Routledge, 1978). Elyakim Rubinstein, *Derkei hashalom* (Tel Aviv: Misrad haBitahon, 2000). Rubinstein served in a variety of capacities in the Ministry of Foreign Affairs; was a member of an Israeli peace negotiating team at the Madrid Peace Conference, formulated the peace treaty with Jordan.

19 Itamar Rabinovich, *Sof hashalom: Israel vesuria 1992–1996* (Tel Aviv: Mishkal, 1998). Dore Gold (ed.), *Iahasei Israel-suria: la'an?* (Ramat Gan: Bar Ilan University, 1996) was advisor of the Israeli delegations to Madrid Peace Conference and on Syrian, Jordanian and Palestinian negotiation tracks. Israeli ambassador to the UN, 1997–1999.

20 Gilad Sher, *Tahalih hashalom: hazon mul matziut* (Tel Aviv: Tel Aviv University Press, 2001). Sher was the Chief of Staff and Policy Coordinator of Israel's PM and MoD Ehud Barak. Headed the negotiation project at the Planning Division of the IDF and served as delegate to the talks on the Interim Agreement during the Rabin tenure as PM. Dani Rubinstein, *Camp David 2000: ma beemet kara sham?* (Tel Aviv: Yediot Akhronot, 2003).

21 Kobi Michael, *Madua kashal hamodel shel shituf hapeula habitkhoni-tzvai bein Israel le Reshut hapalestinit?* (Jerusalem: David Institute for International Affairs, 2003).

22 The way the Cold War and the Gulf War ended enabled Cairo to become (maybe in part with Al-Riyadh) the leader of the moderate Arab camp. From the Israeli perspective this was definitely a preferable and positive development, especially in light of rising Iran. For overall regional normalization and a relationship with Egypt and the Saudis see: Halevi, *Adam Betzel.* Halevi served in the Mossad from 1961 and became its head in 1998. Ezer Weizman, *Rut, sof* (Tel Aviv: Yediot Akhronot, 2001). Weizman was Minister for Arab Affairs, 1984–1990 and the President of Israel, 1993–2000.

23 See for example: Barak; Netanyahu; Gold; Herzog, *Derekh Khaim: Autobiografia.* Herzog was President of Israel 1983–1993. Moshe Ya'alon, *Derekh Arukha ktzara* (Tel Aviv: Yediot Sfarim, 2008). Ya'alon was head of Military Intelligence, 1995–1998.

24 For example see: Shimon Peres, *Mizrah hatikhon hahadash* (Tel Aviv: Yediot Akhronot, 1993); *Im Herzel le aretz hahadasha* (Tel Aviv: Yediot Akhronot, 1999). Michael Bar-Zohar, *Shimon Peres: Biografia* (Tel Aviv: Sifrei Maskel, 2005). During the discussed period Shimon Peres was a Minister of Defense, Foreign Affairs, and Prime Minister. He introduced the umbrella term "the new Middle East." Also see: Yossi Beilin, *Madrikh leyona haptzuah* (Tel Aviv: Yediot Akhronot, 2001).

25 Ron Tira, "Shifting Tectonic Plates: Basic Assumptions on the Peace Process Revisited," *Strategic Assessment,* No. 91, Vol. 12, No. 1, June 2009.

26 Ron Tira, Uri Sagi, *Orot bearafel* (Tel Aviv: Yediot Akhronot, 1998). Sagi was head of Military Intelligence, 1991–1995. Also see: Benjamin Netanyahu, *Makom takhat shemesh* (Tel Aviv: Yediot Akhronot, 2005).

27 Aviad Sela, "Hashpaat artzot habrit al haitron haikhuti shel tzakhal," *Ma'arachot,*

May 2002, No. 383, pp. 42–9; Avi Kober and Zvi Ofer (eds.), *Ikhut ve Kamut bebenian hakoakh* (Tel Aviv: Ma'arachot, 1985). Dore Gold, *Haastrategiia hatzvait haamerikait bemizrah hatikhon* (Tel Aviv: Misrad haBitahon, 1993).

28 Adamsky, *Culture of Military Innovation*, pp. 93–131.

29 Ariel Levite, *Hadoktrina hatzvait shel Israel: hagana vehatkafa* (Tel Aviv: Hakibutz hameuhad, 1988). Levite was Deputy National Security Advisor and Head of the Bureau of International Security at the Israeli MoD. For more details see: Adamsky, *Culture of Military Innovation*, ch. 4. Ben Kaspit, *Ehud Barak: Biografia* (Tel Aviv: Alfa Tikshoret, 1998).

30 Later, although for pure opportunistic economic considerations, Moscow continued to stay the main supplier of the arms to the radicals of the region. As during the Cold War, the main arms transfers during the early 1990s consisted of SAMs, SSMs, and missile technology. Russian involvement in the nuclear projects is, of course, a new dimension. This would have been impossible during the Cold War. See: Ephraim Kam, *Iran mi terror le gar'in* (Tel Aviv: Misrad haBitahon, 2004), ch. 1–2, pp. 19–80. Ephraim Kam served in senior positions in the Research and Analysis Directorate of Military Intelligence in the late 1980s and early 1990s. Also see: Oded Eran, *Mediniut hutz shel brit hamoatzot mi lenin ad gorbachev* (Tel Aviv: Open University Press, 1993). Oded Eran served in senior positions in the Israeli intelligence community. The memoirs of the two ambassadors provide useful additional insights into the overall policy change. See: Arieh Levin, *Envoy to Moscow: Memoirs of an Israeli Ambassador 1988–1992* (London: Cass, 1996); for the memoirs of Haim Bar-Lev, an Israeli Ambassador to Russia 1992–1994 see: Carmit Gai, *Bar-Lev Biografia* (Tel Aviv: Am Oved, 1998).

31 Mustafa Tlaas (ed.), *Haplisha haisraelit lelevanon* (Tel Aviv: Misrad haBitahon, 1988). Mustafa Tlaas was the Syrian Minister of Defense, 1974–2004. Dore Gold, *Mirutz hatilim hahadash bemizrah hatikhon* (Jerusalem: Hamerkaz haerushalmi le inianei tzibur ve medina, 2000). Eitan Ben Eliyahu, *Haotzma haavirit shel Israel likrat shnot 2000* (Tel Aviv: JCSS, 1998). Ben Eliyahu served in senior positions, including Deputy and then Commander of the Israeli AF, 1988–1996. Also see Ron Tira, "Shifting Tectonic Plates: Basic Assumptions on the Peace Process Revisited."

32 During the Cold War, at first it was Israeli maneuver against Arab maneuver, then the situation turned into Israeli firepower against Arab maneuver, and then Arabs invested in firepower, but of a different kind. Brigadier General Itai Brun, "The Other RMA," in Dima Adamsky and Kejll Inge Bjerga (eds.), "The Information Technology Revolution in Military Affairs," *Journal of Strategic Studies*, Vol. 33, No. 4, 2010. Brigadier General Brun served in several senior positions in Military Intelligence. He published extensively on these topics in *Ma'arachot* in the mid-1990s. Yaacov Amidror, *Hirhurim al tzava ve bitahon* (Tel Aviv: Misrad haBitahon, 2002). Yaacov Amidror, was the head of the Research and Analysis Directorate of Military Intelligence and Military Secretary of the Minister of Defense. Amnon Lipkin Shahak, Introduction to Shmuel Gordon, *Keshet pireus* (Tel Aviv: Ramot, 1998.) Amnon Lipkin Shakhak was the head of Military Intelligence, 1986–1991.

33 David Ivry, *Ma'arachot shlita vepikud lemivtzaim* (Tel Aviv: Fisher Institute, 2003). Director General of the Ministry of Defense, 1986–1996 and ambassador to the US, 1998–2000. Also see Itai Brun, "The Other RMA," in Dima Adamsky and Kejll Inge Bjerga (eds.), *The Information Technology Revolution in Military Affairs.*

34 This resulted in what will be dubbed in, post-Cold War Israel, "a symbiotic strategic system of Iran–Hezbollah–Syria." Dore Gold, *Iran, Hizbullah,*

Hamas and Jihad globali: gishot iasod hadashot nohah tmurot astrategiot bemizrah hatikhon (Jerusalem: Hamerkaz haerushalmi le inianei tzibur ve medina, 2007). Benjamin Netanyahu, *Milkhama be Terror* (Tel Aviv: Yediot Akhronot, 2004).

35 Adamsky, *Culture of Military Innovation*, pp. 110–29.

5 The failure to resolve the Afghan conflict, 1989–1992

Artemy M. Kalinovsky

When Soviet troops left Afghanistan in February 1989, they left behind them nearly ten years of fighting in support of a Communist regime in Kabul. The regime was challenged by a heterogeneous armed insurgency that was united in its opposition to a Soviet presence, and, to a lesser extent, in wanting to oust the Kabul regime. The Afghan resistance was really a disparate assortment of armed groups, the most prominent of which coalesced among leaders like "Engineer" Gulbudin Hekmatyar or Professor Barhanuddin Rabanni. These leaders, in turn, received support from Pakistan through the Inter-Service-Intelligence (ISI). ISI efforts were supported by the CIA and funded by the US, Saudi Arabia, and some other donors. A number of Shiite groups also operated from bases in Iran.[1]

The Geneva Accords on Afghanistan, signed in April 1988, led to the start of the Soviet withdrawal from that country a month later and the departure of all Soviet troops by 15 February 1989. The Accords, signed by the Democratic Republic of Afghanistan and by Pakistan, with the US and the Soviet Union as guarantors, had taken six long years of UN mediated diplomacy. The final result left none of the signatories satisfied: not the government in Kabul, which would now have to fight for its survival without Soviet troops and not Pakistan, who had failed to set up a transition mechanism for its own clients and was worried about the possibility of chaos in a neighboring country.[2]

For Mikhail Gorbachev, who had wrestled with how to end the war since taking over as General Secretary in 1985, the Geneva Accords served a dual purpose: as a shield against conservatives as the withdrawal got underway and as proof of the Soviet Union's commitment to potential political solutions, for Western audiences. Despite the weakness of the document, Gorbachev had argued that it was the best way to get Soviet troops out. He put the issue in the wider context of his domestic and international challenges:

> It is hard to overestimate the political value of settling the Afghan problem. This will be a confirmation of our new approach to solving international problems. Our enemies and opponents will have their strongest arguments knocked out of their hands.[3]

The limited discussion of Afghanistan, in his memoir, stresses this aspect:

> The significance of this unprecedented settlement went far beyond its regional implications. It was the first time that the Soviet Union and the United States, together with the conflicting parties, had signed an agreement which paved the way for a political solution of the conflict.[4]

Yet, while Soviet troops did come home, the accords failed to bring peace to Afghanistan. The UN proved unable either to enforce the Accords or forge a lasting consensus among the parties involved; the Soviet leadership vacillated between positions, but generally opposed any settlement that did not include a leading role for its ally in Kabul. The resistance leaders preferred to wait for a collapse of the Kabul regime, meanwhile engaging in internal scuffles to secure dominance in a future government. Pakistan and the US indulged the fantasies of total victory primarily because both countries had constituencies that were themselves attached to the idea and believed it was possible. All of the actors involved spent the period dithering in expectation that time would resolve the issue; as a result, they missed an opportunity to bring peace to an unfortunate and war-ravaged land.

The Soviet Union

Soviet leaders had wrestled with the problem of how to end the war in Afghanistan almost from the moment they had invaded. They had hoped that, by building up their client's military capability, governing institutions, and providing economic aid, they could bestow enough legitimacy that Kabul could hold on without direct Soviet involvement. By 1987 Soviet leaders had largely given up on their nation-building program and the goal of defeating the resistance militarily. Rather, Mikhail Gorbachev and his allies hoped that the improved relationship with the US would translate into an international agreement on Afghanistan that would allow their clients to maintain a leading (but not necessarily dominant) role in government. They also believed that the UN could enforce the Accords and create a favorable international consensus under its auspices.[5]

At the same time, Moscow's approach to Afghan reconciliation in this period was dominated by three factors which limited the range of proposals that Soviet leaders could entertain and the leverage they could exercise in negotiations. The first was an almost unqualified support for Najibullah, the Afghan leader who replaced Babrak Karmal in 1986, especially on the part of KGB Chief Vladimir Kriuchkov and Foreign Minister Eduard Shevardnadze, in policymaking on Afghanistan.[6] The second was an unwillingness to jeopardize the US–Soviet relationship by taking a firmer position on Afghanistan. The third was the rapid economic and political decline of the Soviet Union in the period 1989–1991.

A number of reconciliation initiatives collapsed because of Soviet insistence that Najibullah stay on as head of any coalition government. The KGB believed that Najibullah was a strong Pushtun leader who could hold the country together, but that he needed to be able to demonstrate absolute support from the Soviet Union. KGB Chief Vladimir Kriuchkov vociferously opposed any initiatives that suggested a settlement not favored by Najibullah. This included sabotaging Soviet military efforts at negotiating with the Tajik leader Ahmad Shah Massoud and opposing any settlement that did not include Najibullah as head of state or that saw a cessation of Soviet military aid to his regime. It is not surprising, therefore, that the Soviet Union only agreed to a cut-off of supplies several weeks after Kriuchkov's arrest following the failed coup of August 1991.[7] Kriuchkov could largely count on the support of Eduard Shevardnadze, a close Gorbachev ally, who seems to have combined Kriuchkov's assessment of the Afghan situation with an emotional attachment to Najibullah.[8] Together Kriuchkov and Shevardnadze were usually able to win Gorbachev over to their point of view and dominate any debate on Afghan policy.[9]

Moscow's diplomatic strategy combined an effort to get the most out of the Geneva Accords and to capitalize on the improving relationship with the US. Moscow signed the Geneva Accords, accepting "negative symmetry," to end direct Soviet involvement in a long and bloody war.[10] Gorbachev and other Soviet leaders were also counting on the withdrawal helping Soviet–US relations. The new relationship might then pay dividends in the form of greater cooperation on the part of the US in enabling reconciliation in Afghanistan. The Accords did not oblige the US to stop supplying the opposition via Pakistan, although, technically, they did bind Pakistan to stop the flow of arms. They provided only for a weak enforcement mechanism: a small UN observation force that could take note of violations and pass them on to UN headquarters. For the Accords to be anything more than a face-saving exercise, the Soviets needed the strict cooperation of the signatories and strong enforcement on the part of the UN.[11] Throughout the withdrawal period (May 1988 to February 1989), Moscow sought to make the most of the Accords by continuing talks with the US, trying to press for enforcement of the Accords through the UN and continuing negotiations with opposition leaders and with Pakistan. At the same time, however, Soviet leaders largely subordinated the Afghan problem to the key goal of building on the Washington summit and improving US–Soviet relations.

Gorbachev's commitment to the Accords, at this stage, had several important implications. Using force now could result in the loss of Gorbachev's accumulated political capital. If, however, Najibullah fell too quickly, it could be ammunition for the conservatives and could harm the Soviet Union's relations with its allies. Afghanistan had been one of the major issues impeding improvement in Soviet–US relations since 1979; now the Geneva Accords offered an opportunity not only to remove that obstacle to a new *détente* but to provide a model for how the superpowers would settle similar difficult issues in the future.[12] The behavior of Soviet diplomats in the weeks around the Moscow Summit of May 1988 showed the US that Moscow was looking, first and foremost, for an improvement in bilateral relations.[13] Concerns about sustaining this momentum eclipsed concerns about what might happen in Afghanistan following a Soviet withdrawal. Further, despite the disappointing US attitude on arms supplies in the winter of 1988, Gorbachev still held out hope that, eventually, the Reagan administration might prove more cooperative, particularly if there were gains in other areas of the relationship.

The problem for Moscow was that, having committed itself to withdrawing Soviet troops from Afghanistan, it now had much less leverage in negotiations. When, in the fall of 1988, Soviet officials moved from simply filing complaints about violations with the UN to hinting that the Soviet Union would have to stop the withdrawal, their threat was not taken seriously. Since February, US officials had been convinced that the Soviet Union was determined to bring its troops home. It was this certainty that had allowed Shultz to maintain a tough line when negotiating with Shevardnadze in March and to brush off any hints that Moscow might halt the withdrawal.[14] When the Soviet Union hinted or threatened that the withdrawal might be reversed, or when they, in fact, halted it in mid-November, US diplomats saw through those tactics; they had little doubt that Soviet troops would be withdrawn by the deadline.[15]

Even as the possibility of threatening a continued Soviet presence faded, new opportunities presented themselves to solve the problem through diplomacy. Since the launch of National Reconciliation, Soviet diplomats, advisers, KGB officials, and the military had been engaged in an effort to negotiate with rebel leaders to bring them into a coalition government. With the start of the withdrawal these efforts intensified. One Soviet foreign ministry official even earned the nickname "mujahed" from his colleagues because he spent so much time working on negotiations with rebel commanders.[16] In the summer and fall of 1988 these efforts even began to show some success.

In trying to open channels to the mujahadeen during the withdrawal period, Soviet representatives were trying to achieve two goals. First, to provide for the safety of the 40th army during its return home,[17] and second, to do what they could to reconcile the regime and the resistance. By continuing talks with Pakistan, as well as individual commanders, Moscow tried to take advantage of Islamabad's earlier desire to create a coalition government in Kabul.[18] Parallel with talks to rebel leaders, Soviet officials continued talks with Pakistan about the possibility of a coalition government. In the summer of 1988, Pakistan's President, Zia ul Haq told Yuli Vorontsov, Moscow's ambassador to Kabul, that he would support a solution in which a third of the government would be PDPA (People's Democratic Party of Afghanistan), a third would be the "moderate" opposition, including royalists, and a third would be from the "Peshawar seven." Vorontsov passed the message back to Moscow and received a positive response.[19] Although such an arrangement might meet opposition from Najibullah or others in the PDPA, the opportunity to form a government that contained Moscow's allies but was also recognized by Pakistan was too good to pass up. Zia's death in a plane crash that summer put an end to that particular opening, but other opportunities appeared. In December, the UN Secretary General helped to arrange a meeting for Vorontsov and mujahadeen leaders, including Rabanni, in Saudi Arabia. That the meeting took place at all was a sign of how far the Soviet Union was willing to go try to find a settlement in Afghanistan, though it did not produce any concrete results.[20]

Negotiating with Pakistan and mujahadeen leaders was difficult enough, but perhaps equally challenging was the effort to push Najibullah and the PDPA toward an agreement.[21] Although they may have expressed great frustration in private, Soviet leaders could hardly dump him, particularly at a point when he seemed to be gaining support from within the country and seemed increasingly capable of standing on his own two feet. In a private letter to Bush and again at the Malta summit in December 1989, Gorbachev insisted that Najibullah could not be forced out prior to a settlement.[22] Still, by 1990 Moscow's support for Najibullah seemed to be as much a matter of decorum as a defense of interests, at least as far as Gorbachev and even Shevardnadze were concerned. At a meeting with US Secretary of State James Baker in February 1990, a frustrated Shevardnadze reportedly blurted out "Sometimes I wish all these people would just kill each other and end the whole thing." It was more an expression of frustration than a genuine wish, but it did seem to signal a slight shift in the Soviet position: Shevardnadze went on to say it would be better if Najibullah could stay at his post, but although the Soviet Union could not force him to step down "it might be acceptable if he decided to leave on his own."[23]

Najibullah's ability to survive without Soviet troops in some ways made the situation more complicated for the Soviet Union. At the time of the withdrawal a number of senior leaders had believed that he would not last long without Soviet troops.[24] During the attack on Jalalabad in March 1989, Gorbachev told his Politburo colleagues that they must come to terms with a regime without Najibullah: "For us the main thing is that a hostile government doesn't appear [in Kabul]. The rest ... let it be any governing combination – not our problem."[25] In practice, of course, he never quite made this policy, for the reasons discussed above. Moreover, as Najibullah's stature grew following the government's victory at Jalalabad, formulating a settlement that did not include him became much trickier for Soviet leaders.

Moscow's support for Najibullah, following the withdrawal, also stemmed from a sense that there was no viable alternative, no central figure around whom to build a government. In the fall of 1988 several senior Afghan military officials approached the chief Soviet military representative in Kabul to discuss a possible replacement of Najibullah and the formation of a government that included Ahmad Shah Massoud. This initiative, which met with some sympathy in the Soviet military, was effectively neutralized by the KGB.[26] An attempted coup in 1990 by the Minister of Defence, whose supporters were supposed to link up with the forces of Gulbudin Hekmatyar, was easily defeated by government troops.[27] Among the resistance leaders no one received much support from Moscow. Massoud was trusted by the Soviet military, but not by the KGB, Shevardnadze, or anyone else in the Soviet leadership. Gulbudin Hekmatyar, leader of the Hezb-i-Islami, was seen as too extremist. Nevertheless, the KGB did encourage Najibullah's efforts to reach out to him, perhaps in the hope that the two would form a stable "Pushtun" alliance.[28] Even if Soviet leaders were to seriously entertain the possibility of a government in Kabul that was not led by Najibullah, they had little reason to believe that this would be a stable government that would not cause trouble for the Soviet Union in Central Asia.[29]

Following the withdrawal of their troops from Afghanistan Soviet leaders learned that their new relationship with the US did not necessarily translate into ready cooperation on regional conflicts. In the case of Afghanistan, Soviet diplomats found that, without the leverage of a Soviet troop presence, it was very difficult to move the US closer to their own position on issues like an arms cut off and the role of Najibullah. Nor were Soviet leaders prepared to contemplate, in practice, the possibility of an Afghan government that did not include their client. Instead, they waited and hoped that Najibullah would acquire enough legitimacy that all parties involved would recognize the need for him to play a role in a settlement.

Najibullah and the PDPA

Moscow's client in Kabul was the government controlled by the People's Democratic Party of Afghanistan, renamed Hizb-i-Watan, or Homeland Party, in 1990. The party bore little resemblance to the relatively unified, disciplined Communist Party of the Soviet Union on which it modeled itself and on which its formal structures were based. In 1989 party members were still divided into supporters of two groups, Khalq and Parcham. Besides the Khalq and Parcham split, unity was compromised by the personal rivalries between various party leaders and their respective followers.[30] Party unity had been a goal of Soviet political advisers sent to Afghanistan since before the Saur revolution; ten years later it still appeared elusive.

For the Afghan leadership, the Geneva Accords were, at best, an unwelcome development and, at worst, they heralded doom. The Afghan Foreign Minister, Abdul Wakil, sought in vain to scuttle them at the eleventh hour. Najibullah himself tried to secure a Soviet commitment to keep some 10,000–15,000 troops to help guard vital roads. Not only did the

Accords fail to secure the end of US arms supplies, but they also suggested Soviet abandonment of the Communists in Afghanistan. For a fractious ruling class lacking confidence in its ability to survive, such perceptions could well have turned into a self-fulfilling prophecy.

Najibullah, the leader of the party and the state, was constantly fighting for survival not only of his regime but of his own position within it. He was selected by the Soviets because it had been hoped that he would play the role of a strong Pushtun leader, winning over enough of the population and opposition groups to hold out without Soviet troops and eventually form a government of reconciliation. Najibullah proved to be a more adept political survivor than perhaps even his sponsors had hoped; but they soon found that his vision of reconciliation could be quite different from their own, and that he would find a way to sideline any Soviet interlocutor who tried to impose a different approach. During the period in question he survived by using Soviet funds to pay off militias, moving the party away from Communist ideology, and making full use of the military hardware and advisors provided to him to fight off mujahadeen attacks and a coup attempt. The strategy helped his regime outlive the Soviet Union by four months, but did little to contribute to a more lasting settlement.

One of the reasons Soviet leaders replaced Babrak Karmal was that he was seen as moving too reluctantly on the reconciliation policies favored by Moscow and was unable to face down "radical" opponents within his party.[31] Najibullah, who had first gained the support of the KGB, quickly won over the rest of the Soviet leadership and senior officials working on Afghanistan, who saw him as a strong personality willing to push through radical reforms and help the Soviets withdraw.[32] With Soviet encouragement, Najibullah took a number of steps in 1987 and 1988 that seemed to demonstrate his commitment to the new Policy of National Reconciliation. He abandoned land reforms, which were widely seen as a failure, and allowed peasants to return land to expropriated landlords if they wished to do so.[33] Private traders were encouraged to take over from government monopolies in some crucial areas. The Democratic Republic of Afghanistan became simply the Republic of Afghanistan. Even in taking these steps, however, Najibullah faced opposition from "radicals" in the PDPA. Thus either as a result of his own caution or his limited freedom of action within the government, such measures were quite limited. While a number of senior government positions were opened to "opposition leaders," in practice most were occupied by former PDPA members or pro-government non-party figures. On a few occasions he seems to have used the opening of positions to remove unwanted figures from government.[34] Despite a law on parties passed in 1987, no major parties (aside from Watah) were operating between then and 1992.[35]

Najibullah's survival during this period rested on his ability to maintain support in the security services and government, pay militias and distribute patronage, and maintain Soviet support. He secured a personally loyal presidential guard, despite the opposition of Soviet military representatives.[36] Following a pause in arms deliveries after the withdrawal, he also won further deliveries of arms, fuel, and economic aid which lasted through 1991. With the help of loyal forces and friends in the Soviet Union he neutralized several challenges to his power, including an attempted coup by his Minister of Defense, in February 1990.

If Najibullah was successful in staying in power, he was less successful in neutralizing the major threats to his political survival – the resistance leaders in Peshawar and their field commanders. Soviet leaders hoped that National Reconciliation would bring a major defection that would split the ranks of the opposition and give the government greater legitimacy. This never happened. Najibullah refused to seriously entertain the notion of accommodation with Ahmad Shah Massoud. Massoud was the Soviet military's favorite candidate for reconciliation, and had won the respect of a number of diplomats, including Vorontsov. But Najibullah would not trust him, possibly because he feared that Massoud would emerge as an autonomous Tajik leader who would challenge his authority.[37] Najibullah sabotaged efforts by Soviet military representatives and diplomats to meet with Massoud, insisting, instead, on major military operations against the Tajik leader's forces. Because of his close relationship with Shevardnadze and Kriuchkov, he was usually successful in winning support for his point of view in Moscow.[38]

Najibullah seemed more interested in reaching out to Hekmatyar. It is difficult to establish the extent or seriousness of the clandestine discussions that took place. They seem to have been supported by the KGB. They were serious enough to worry some of Gorbachev's advisors, who saw in Hekmatyar a dangerous extremist who was unlikely to be friendly to the Soviet Union.[39] Nevertheless, these contacts also failed to provide any tangible benefits – no major rebel commanders ever joined Najibullah's government. And Hekmatyar himself plotted with Najibullah's Minister of Defense, Shahnawaz Tanai, to take power in 1990.

Najibullah did not play a completely obstructionist role. In January 1990 he announced, publicly, his support for UN-monitored elections and his willingness to step down if defeated, and even suggested that he might step down before the vote was held during the negotiation process.[40] When Pérez de Cuéllar met with him in September 1990, the Afghan leader reiterated his support for a transition period and elections and proposed that the UN supervise the process.[41] By August 1991, when his forces had begun to suffer serious military setbacks and the situation in the Soviet Union was unraveling, he dropped his insistence that he take part personally in any transition government.[42] Yet, when he felt that he was not getting support from Moscow he would write letters accusing Soviet leaders of betrayal. Parting with the last Russian advisors in April 1992, he again restated that the Soviets were traitors.[43] Clearly he hoped to preserve a central role for himself for as long as possible.

Najibullah's achievement was a zombie state. With Soviet support his regime may have survived indefinitely. It had fended off internal challenges and even grown in international stature. But, it had done little to further a lasting settlement in Afghanistan. The policy of paying off as many people as possible was bankrupting the state.[44] When Soviet funds began to run out, the effect was felt immediately – militias that had not been paid refused to fight. Like the other actors in this tragic story, he was mostly reactive to events rather than proactive. Najibullah had figured out how to maintain the status quo and hoped that he could continue doing so until enough of his enemies accepted it. This strategy was not completely farfetched – between 1989 and 1991 he impressed a number of people who had seen him as a mere Soviet puppet, including, as we will see, US President George H. W. Bush. It is not unforeseeable that in time his strategy might have paid off. But, in 1990 and 1991, events were moving far too fast for this strategy to hold out. The Soviet Union was disintegrating, and without its patronage Najibullah could not hope to sustain the status quo for long.

The United States, Pakistan and the Resistance

For the US, the Afghan problem diminished in importance after the signing of the Geneva Accords and the withdrawal of Soviet troops. The administration of George H. W. Bush was never as ideologically committed to the Afghan resistance as Ronald Reagan's had been. Nevertheless, it felt it could not support a settlement that allowed Najibullah to stay in power, nor could it cut off its aid to the resistance while the Soviet Union continued to support its client in Kabul. Even as US–Pakistani relations cooled, the Afghan effort continued to receive CIA support. Despite growing doubts, among some CIA and State Department officials, that the US policy of allowing the ISI to channel support to the more extremist elements in the resistance would hurt long-term US interests, the policy did not change substantially. In Pakistan, a tumultuous domestic situation, following the death of Zia ul Haq, helped make Afghan policy all the more amorphous. Benazir Bhutto, Prime Minister from 1988–1990, generally followed the lead of the ISI on Afghan questions, which in turn led to the disastrous attack on Jalalabad in March 1989. But the ISI itself would later try to use the mujahadeen, and an anti-Najibullah attempted coup in Kabul, to oust Bhutto.

Zia had a personal, ideological, commitment to the resistance and to Afghan policy in general. He also saw support for the resistance as a way to keep Soviet forces at bay. But in 1988, with a withdrawal imminent, he became seriously worried about the consequences of a power vacuum, unexpectedly insisting on the formation of a government *prior* to the signing of the Geneva Accords.[45] Yet, even Zia could not dictate a settlement: his proposal for a national reconciliation formula that would divide power equally between the government, the mujahadeen, and the monarchist groups, greatly impressed Vorontsov and, supposedly, even his superiors in Moscow, but not the mujahadeen.[46] As for the leaders who succeeded Zia, both Benazir Bhutto and Nawaz Sharif pledged "continuity" on Afghan policy, but they had virtually no clout with the resistance leaders, and were anyway too busy trying to stay in power to establish a coherent line, let alone dictate to the ISI or the resistance groups.[47]

The Peshawar-based alliance of seven was not a government in exile, but a motley group of charismatic warlords with varying motivations, personal and corporate ambitions, and networks of fighters. Early in the war Zia had decided not to encourage a true government in exile for fear that Soviet leaders might counter by setting up governments in exile to challenge Pakistani control in restless areas like the North West Frontier Province.[48] The alliance's disunity only contributed to the difficulty of forming a government; their Pakistani interlocutors found that they could only get the resistance leaders to agree to a united position after sustained pressure.[49] Even when the Alliance Interim Government was cobbled together, prior to the signing of the Geneva Accords, it never functioned as a proper government-in-exile, and the individual leaders who were its members continued pursuing strategies primarily for their personal advantage.

Moreover, with the withdrawal of Soviet troops, these leaders smelled blood. Having fought for their own visions of an Islamic government, in the case of some of the leaders since before the Communist coup, they were unwilling to settle for anything less than total victory. With ISI encouragement and CIA support, they launched a major attack on Jalalabad in March 1989, a month after the Soviet soldiers had gone home. Had the attack succeeded, it would have been the first loss of a major urban centre and a serious blow to the Kabul government.[50] Although Najibullah panicked and begged Moscow to send in its air force, his troops, with the help of Soviet advisers, held their own. Weeks later, as it became obvious that the attack had been a failure, Najibullah emerged stronger and more confident. The DRA recruits had proven that his regime could survive without Soviet troops, even if they were still reliant on equipment and material aid.[51] The attack proved a setback for the mujahadeen, but they did not give up on their goal of achieving power on their own terms.

Although, like the CIA and ISI officials who supported them, the resistance leaders may have felt that the Najibullah regime would be easily toppled, the prospect of victory did little to unite them. On the contrary, forces loyal to Hekmatyar and Massoud were engaged in sporadic fighting by mid-1990, foreshadowing the civil war that would erupt between their forces after the Kabul government fell.[52] The rivalry between the two commanders was made worse by the preference of the Pakistani ISI for Hekmatyar, to whom it directed a much larger share of funds. Hekmatyar showed that he was not above making separate deals with major defectors from the Communist government, as he did when he plotted with Shahnawaz Tanai to oust Najibullah in February 1990.[53]

Afghanistan continued to be on the agenda of bilateral US–Soviet meetings following the Soviet withdrawal. Soviet attempts to convince Washington to stop or at least reduce its support to the mujahadeen, however, generally proved fruitless. In May 1989, Shevardnadze made yet another in a series of private appeals to US leaders during a dinner at his apartment. Shevardnadze even went beyond earlier Soviet positions, de-coupling the cessation of Soviet arms supplies to the Sandinistas in Nicaragua and US aid to the mujahadeen. For the first time he even suggested that the Soviet Union would not insist on keeping Najibullah in a coalition government after the settlement.[54]

Over time, however, the attitude in Washington became more promising. US–Pakistani relations suffered a downturn in 1990 following revelations about Pakistan's nuclear program. Although this did not cause a rupture in CIA-ISI cooperation, it did signal a divergence of US and Pakistani interests.[55] There was a growing consensus that the US had reached its main objective (the Soviet withdrawal) and the realization was emerging that waiting for a military solution might not be in US interests. Whereas in late 1988 and early 1989 CIA analysts were confident of a quick military victory, the RA army's successful defense of Jalalabad in the spring of 1989 seemed to change the calculus.[56] In August UN officials had learned that both the US and Pakistan were "re-evaluating the desirability of a military solution in Afghanistan,"[57] and in October, the US Senate Foreign Relations Committee rebuked the Bush administration for holding out for a military victory. As a State Department analyst put it, two changes had taken place since February 1989:

> One, the congressional bipartisan consensus on Afghanistan is breaking up. And two, the perception that we are supporting a good cause is not there any more. We are no longer fighting the evil empire. They've gone. Now it's just Afghans fighting Afghans.[58]

For their part, US officials were moving closer to the Soviet position on Najibullah. Although the mujahadeen showed no sign of dropping their insistence that Najibullah resign before negotiations could take place, the policy review and the changing atmosphere in congress were moving the Bush administration towards dropping their insistence on such a scenario.[59] Moreover, Hekmatyar had shown his anti-US stripes, particularly when he spoke out against the Saudi-US alliance to oust Saddam Hussein's forces from Kuwait; at the same time, Massoud proved too untrustworthy and uncontrollable. Many Americans working on Afghanistan were, thus, increasingly pessimistic that a settlement could be put together around any of the Peshawar-based resistance leaders. Unlike their Soviet counterparts, however, they saw the solution not in Najibullah but in a more neutral figure, like the exiled king, Zahir Shah.[60]

Thus, in 1990 and 1991, Moscow and Washington seemed to be inching towards a mutually acceptable position. At the meeting with Shevardnadze cited above, Baker mentioned, for the first time, that the US might stop insisting that Najibullah leave the scene before negotiations could begin.[61] A week after his meeting with Baker in February, Shevardnadze published a new set of proposals calling for an international conference and also calling for a cease-fire, an end to both US and Soviet arms shipments ("negative symmetry"), and elections, to be monitored by the UN and the Islamic Conference Organization. Perhaps the biggest innovation was the idea that both government and opposition forces could hold on to the territory they controlled during the transition period.[62] The proposal was very similar to the UN plan being developed at the time.[63]

Following Shevardnadze's *Izvesti'ia* article, Moscow and Washington seemed to move more quickly towards an agreement. At a meeting in Helsinki in March, US and Soviet experts elaborated on the proposals that came out of the Baker-Shevardnadze meeting in February and the *Izvesti'ia* article. The failure of the Tanai coup confirmed that Najibullah still had enough support within the military and party to hold on to power, even if it also highlighted the challenges he faced from rivals at the top. In May, US officials said that they would agree to Najibullah participating in elections if he first stepped down. In testimony before the US congress in June, Baker confirmed that "a very, very narrow difference" separated the views of Moscow and Washington.[64] US President George H. W. Bush, meeting with Pérez de Cuéllar in June, noted: "I was dead wrong about Najibullah – I thought he would fall when the Soviet troops withdrew."[65] He went on to say that he could understand the Soviet insistence on keeping Najibullah through the election period, and their insistence on following the "Nicaraguan model."[66]

The Soviet leadership still found it hard to let go of Najibullah. The softening of the US position in the first half of 1990 and Najibullah's continuing hold on power, encouraged Moscow to believe that sooner or later the US (and Pakistan) would accept his involvement in a transitional government. In a meeting with Najibullah in August 1990, Gorbachev reaffirmed his belief that the US would, ultimately, recognize that they did not have someone better to offer as a national leader.[67] Moscow pointed out, with some justification, that even if the Soviet Union and the US both cut off arms supplies, the opposition would still be able to count on support from Pakistan, Saudi Arabia, and other minor donors. Therefore, Soviet officials insisted on a more comprehensive settlement, even offering "negative symmetry plus," i.e. the withdrawal of weapons, like the Scud missiles, from Afghanistan if a complete cut-off of supplies to the mujahadeen could be guaranteed.[68] Soviet diplomats held to this position until after the August coup.

Pérez de Cuéllar laid the blame for the failure of reconciliation at the feet of the mujahadeen, Pakistan, and the US, in that order.[69] Indeed, sensing that they were close to victory, the mujahadeen leaders never had much incentive to work with Najibullah; they preferred to attempt picking off his supporters instead. In Pakistan, Afghan policy was in the hands of the ISI, which sought to secure its influence in Afghanistan in the long term and thus favored mujahadeen leaders who seemed most likely to cooperate. Najibullah's efforts to build ties with India, Pakistan's traditional rival, no doubt contributed to the feeling among ISI officials that this time they must have someone reliable in Kabul. They may have overestimated the pliability of their clients; when the Najibullah regime fell and the mujahadeen turned to fighting each other, Pakistan turned to supporting a newcomer to the scene, the *Taliban*.

Conclusion

By March 1992, with the Soviet Union gone and the Russian government making it clear that it would not help him support the status quo of 1989–1991, Najibullah knew that his time was limited. Having sent his family abroad, he made clear his intention to resign and turn over power according to a UN plan, which foresaw an interim coalition to oversee elections before the transition to a more permanent government. Even at this stage, however, an orderly transfer of power proved elusive. The UN plan made sense on paper, but it could not compensate for the complex internal rivalries of the mujahadeen, on the one hand, and what was left of the Republic of Afghanistan on the other. Alliances were formed between Khalqists and Hekmatyar's party; Rashid Dostum, the Uzbek warlord whose support had been crucial to Najibullah over the preceding years, sided with Massoud. Najibullah's colleagues also looked for alliances with one or the other of the emerging victors – at the airport where Najibullah was to board a UN flight, it was Foreign Minister Abdul Wakil who pointed out his former boss to Dostum's men and encouraged them to arrest the recent RA President. Massoud did not trust the UN plan, fearing it would lead to a Pushtun dominated government, and tried to pre-empt Hekmatyar's arrival in Kabul. The fight against the Soviet invasion was years in the past; the fight against Najibullah's regime had ended. The civil war had begun.

Why did the Geneva Accords and the Soviet withdrawal fail to bring peace to Afghanistan? Why did the end of the Cold War not facilitate a settlement under the auspices of the Soviet Union and the US, as was the case, for example, in Angola? The explanation that the mujahadeen were ideologically opposed to a settlement that involved a serious Communist presence is not satisfactory and neither is one that places all the blame on Najibullah for not being willing to share power. In fact, resistance leaders proved more than happy to work with Communists before and after April

1992 and in some cases even to negotiate and make truces with the Soviets.

The sad truth may be that Afghanistan was one "hot spot" that did not benefit from the Cold War ending. The decreasing political importance of Afghanistan for both Soviet leaders (in light also of the other problems they faced) and US leaders meant that their countries' involvement devolved to mid-level intelligence agents and diplomats. The former may have been fighting their own battles, trying to see a war they supervised to an end that justified their role throughout. Thus, for most of the CIA officers involved, nothing short of a complete mujahadeen victory was satisfactory; even as US–Pakistani relations grew acrimonious CIA agents were allowed to continue cooperating with the ISI on Afghan matters. For the KGB, the idea of Najibullah falling was something not even to be mentioned out loud.[70]

More importantly, the "withdrawal" of both superpowers from the conflict after such a lengthy involvement left a vacuum that allowed the local actors to fight their own war of attrition. The Soviet Union no longer hoped or tried to give Najibullah some sort of overwhelming advantage against the opposition; it had subordinated its interests in Afghanistan to improving relations with the US. The Bush administration no longer believed in supporting a mujahadeen victory, but neither did it make the leap to advocating a settlement that included the PDPA, despite indications that the President himself was gaining an appreciation for Najibullah's staying power. Both US and Soviet leaders seem to have half expected and half hoped that the Afghans would find a solution among themselves. No wonder, then, that in such a situation the UN diplomats were powerless to achieve much. They had seen their job primarily as mediators helping to bring sides to an agreement; the UN could neither enforce the pre-existing agreement against blatant violations nor could it force an agreement when the support from key powers was lukewarm. UN officials could do little besides trying to work out the different positions and act as interlocutors. Most of the actors involved were expecting time to work to their advantage, and they did little to actively help. This was especially true of the mujahadeen and their ISI and CIA sponsors after February 1989.

Najibullah outlasted the Soviet Union by four months; the Afghan conflict, changing shape as it enters each new phase, has outlasted the Cold War by two decades and shows no signs of abating.

Notes

1 Iran was a much smaller player than Pakistan, and thus I have largely left it out of this story. Further, after the Soviet withdrawal Iran played a largely constructive role. Soviet relations with Iran had improved, evidenced by Shevardnadze's high profile visit to the country in February 1989, during which Ayatollah Khomeini hailed the Soviet withdrawal from Afghanistan. In August Kriuchkov and Shevardnadze noted that Iran was moving towards a more "constructive" position as a result of Soviet diplomatic efforts. In October, Iran cut off military

aid to Shiite insurgents, even encouraging them to work with the Kabul government. From that point Soviet officials began to see Iran as generally playing a constructive role in Afghanistan. Similarly, China, which had once been part of the coalition supporting the mujahadeen, was no longer playing a hostile role. "Regarding talk in Kabul and our potential further steps..." 11 August 1989 in *Sowjetische Geheimdokumente*, 686; See also "Iran's attitude to the settlement of the Afghan problem," GARF, F. 10026, op. 4, d. 2868.

2 On the end-game behind the Geneva Accords, see Artemy M. Kalinovsky "Politics, Diplomacy and the Soviet Withdrawal from Afghanistan: From National Reconciliation to the Geneva Accords," *Cold War History*, 8:3 (August 2008), pp. 381–404.

3 Politburo meeting, 1 April 1988, AGF.

4 M. S. Gorbachev, *Memoirs* (New York: Doubleday, 1996), p. 458.

5 Due to space constraints, I have left out a more detailed discussion of the UN's role in this period.

6 Karmal had come to power with Moscow's help in 1979, after the assassination of Amin by Soviet forces. By 1986, however, he had worn out the patience of his Soviet interlocutors and made a very poor impression on Gorbachev, who felt that Karmal expected Soviet troops to remain in Afghanistan indefinitely. See Gorbachev's report to the Politburo on his meeting with Karmal: Cherniaev Diary, 17 October 1985, National Security Archive.

7 Boris Pankin, *The Last Hundred Days of the Soviet Union* (New York: I. B. Tauris, 1996), pp. 117–18; Author's interview with Nikolai Kozyrev, 14 November 2008.

8 Shevardnadze seems to have developed an emotional bond with Najibullah which contributed to his sense that, in Afghanistan, Moscow had to remain true to its friends even as it withdrew its troops. See Kalinovsky, "Decision-Making and the Soviet War in Afghanistan: From Intervention to Withdrawal," *Journal of Cold War Studies* 11:4 (2009), pp. 46–73.

9 Ibid.

10 Negative symmetry meant that one side would decrease its support parallel to the other side; in other words, the US would not cut off aid to the mujahadeen unless the USSR did the same with the Kabul regime.

11 Author's interviews with Nikolai Kozyrev, Moscow, 14 November 2008, and Iulii Vorontsov, Moscow, 11 September 2007.

12 The presence of Soviet troops in Afghanistan had been a major obstacle to improving the US–Soviet relationship, and signaling the seriousness of Soviet intentions to withdraw, in September 1987, had helped the ultimate success of the Washington Summit that December. G. Shultz, *Turmoil and Triumph* (New York: Scribner, 1993), p. 987.

13 When the US Chargé d'Affaires in Kabul, Jon D. Glassman, met the Soviet Ambassador, Nikolai Egorychev, the latter avoided any discussion of violations of the Geneva Accords by either Pakistan or the US. When the US Chargé d'Affaires brought up Afghan allegations that the Accords were being violated, Egorychev replied that the "Soviet Union works with the Afghan government but is not responsible for its actions. Nor ... is the United States responsible for the acts of the mujahadeen." In his report back to the State Department, Glassman noted that "Yegorychev appeared to be dissociating the Soviet Union from RA allegations of Pakistani Geneva violations." US Embassy, Kabul to State Department, 21 May 1988, NSA End of the Cold War Collection, Box 3.

14 Author's interview with Ambassador Jack Matlock, 1 January 2008. Similarly, in June 1988 US Undersecretary of State Michael Armacost told Indian Prime Minister Rajiv Gandhi: "There was no evidence of Soviet suspension of withdrawal. It was hard to see how they could now do so. Forces impelling

continuing withdrawal were greater now than they were when the withdrawals had begun." Armacost to US Embassy, New Delhi, 9 June 1988, NSA End of the Cold War, Box 3.

15 Record of meeting between Mr. Benon Sevan and Mr. Michael Armacost, 14 November 1988, Yale University, SML, Pérez de Cuéllar Papers, Box 10, Folder 103.

16 Author's interview with Pavel Palazchenko, Moscow, 20 March 2008; Author's interview with Leonid Shebarshin, Moscow, 19 March 2008.

17 For this reason they were willing to accept cease-fires that did not necessarily extend to the Afghan army. See "Notes on a meeting between US Under-Secretary of State Michael Armacost and Benon Sevan," 14 November 1988, SML, Pérez de Cuéllar Papers, Box 10, Folder 103.

18 Pakistan had originally refused to discuss the issue, then demanded it be resuscitated when the Geneva Accords were about to be signed. Moscow, which had been trying to push a coalition government since the end of 1986, did not want to delay the start of the withdrawal any longer by agreeing to wait for one to be formed.

19 Author's interview with Iulii Vorontsov, Moscow, September 11, 2007.

20 Vorontsov interview. See also notes on Gorbachev and Pérez de Cuéllar Meeting, 7 December 1988, and Talking Points prepared for Pérez de Cuéllar, SML Pérez de Cuéllar Papers, Box 10, Folder 103.

21 Record of Conversation between Vladimir Petrovsky, Deputy Foreign Minister of the USSR, and Pérez de Cuéllar, 21 October 1988, SML, Pérez de Cuéllar Papers, Box 10, Folder 102.

22 "Soviets reassert policy on keeping Najibullah," *The Washington Times*, 2 November 1989, A7. "Soviet Support for Najibullah Blocked Political Headway at Malta Summit," *Associated Press*, 6 December 1989. In a letter to Pérez de Cuéllar, Gorbachev expressed his frustration that Bush refused to consider compromising on Najibullah:

> It is important to see the realities of today's Afghanistan. It is necessary to take into account the fact that following the withdrawal of Soviet troops the government of the Republic of Afghanistan has felt more confident. We think that the opposition is starting to become convinced of this as well. Gorbachev to Cuellar, 3 December 1989, AGF.

23 M. R. Beschloss and S. Talbott, *At the Highest Levels: The Inside Story of the End of the Cold War* (Boston, MA: Little, Brown, & Co, 1993), p. 180. See also "Moscow spells out Afghan plan," *The Independent*, 21 February 1990, p. 9. Moscow's position, as laid out to the UN Secretary General, was that the US insistence on removing Najibullah during the transition period was unacceptable. However, Moscow was ready to accept the results of elections, as were Afghan leaders. Untitled memorandum on Baker/Shevardnadze talks, 14 February 1990, SML, Pérez de Cuéllar Papers, Box 10, Folder 106.

24 See for example, M. A. Gareev, *Moia posledniaia voina: Afganistan bez sovetskikh voisk* (Moscow: INSAN, 1996), p. 127.

25 Cherniaev's notes of 23 March 1989 Politburo meeting in A. Cherniaev, *Afganskii Vopros* (Moscow: Mezhdunarodnye Otnosheniia, 2000), p. 50.

26 M. M. Sotskov, *Dolg i Sovest': Zakrytye Stranitsy Afganskoi Voiny* (St. Petersburg: Professional, 2007), pp. 113–20; Handwritten notes taken at Shevardnadze's meeting with Gulabzoi and Tanai, September 1988, provided to the author by Dr. Antonio Giustozzi, London School of Economics; Shebarshin interview.

27 S. Coll, *Ghost Wars The Secret History of the CIA, Afghanistan, and bin Laden, from the Soviet Invasion to September 10, 2001* (New York: Penguin, 2004), pp. 211–12;

B. Rubin, *The Fragmentation of Afghanistan: state formation and collapse in the international system* (New Haven, CT: Yale University Press, 1995), p. 253.

28 G. Shakhnazarov, Memorandum to MS Gorbachev Regarding Najibullah and Hekmatyar, 16 December 1988, AGF, Document 18188.

29 Earlier in the war Soviet leaders were not particularly concerned that an "Islamic insurgency" would break out in Central Asia as a result of the war in Afghanistan. However, the growing problems in the USSR in 1989, the emergence of nationalist groups throughout the country, and the first stirrings of Islamic radicalism in this period made this issue an increasing concern. "Regarding talks in Kabul and our potential further steps...," 11 August 1989, in *Sowjetische Geheimdokumente*, p. 692; Shebarshin interview; M. A. Gareev, *Moia posledniaia voina: Afganistan bez sovetskikh voisk*, pp. 107–8.

30 V. Plastun and V. Andrianov, *Nadzhibulla. Afganistan v Tiskakh Geopolitiki* (Moscow: Biograficheskii Institut, 1998), pp. 78–9; "Record of conversation with Colonel Mohammed Sarwari," 18 December 1987 in ibid., pp. 203–4.

31 Gorbachev's pressure did lead Karmal to announce "Ten Theses" in late 1985, a precursor to National Reconciliation which did lead to some expansion of non-party people in government. A. Giustozzi, *War, Politics and Society in Afghanistan* (London: Hurst, 2000), pp. 54–7.

32 "Regarding the talks with Comrade Najib," Politburo Protocol, 25 December 1986, Library of Congress, Washington, DC, Volkogonov Papers, Box 26, Reel 17.

33 Giustozzi, *War, Politics and Society in Afghanistan*, pp. 29–30.

34 Author's interview with Sultan Ali Keshtmand, 22 June 2009, London. Keshtmand was asked to step down as Prime Minister so that someone from the opposition could take his place; instead, the post went to Dr. Mohammed Hassan Sharq. While not formally a party member, Sharq had served the PDPA government as Deputy Prime Minister and Ambassador to India, and was thus not a true outside figure.

35 Giustozzi, *War, Politics and Society in Afghanistan*, pp. 154–85.

36 Varennikov argued that the guard was doing more harm than good, upsetting Afghan army officers who complained that guard officers were earning 5–10 times more than they did. Sotskov, *Dolg i Sovest'*, pp. 101–8.

37 In fact, the Soviet proposals did provide for some autonomy for Massoud and his forces, but such an arrangement would have hardly been a historical anomaly in Afghanistan. What probably worried Najibullah was that, unlike the local militia leaders on whose support he relied, Massoud was widely popular and seemed to be gaining Soviet support as well.

38 A. Liakhovskii, *Tragediia i doblest' Afgana* (Moscow: Nord, 2004), p.651; Valentin Varennikov, *Nepotovrimoe*, Vol. 5 (Moscow: Sovetskii Pisatel', 2002), pp. 369–76; Sotskov, *Dolg i Sovest'*, pp. 111–13, 548–50. Author's interviews with Aleksandr Liakhovskii, Moscow July 2006; and with Iulii Vorontsov and Sultan Ali Keshtmand.

39 G. Shakhnazarov, Memorandum to M. S. Gorbachev Regarding Najibullah and Hekmatyar, 16 December 1988, AGF, Document 18188.

40 "Afghan leader urges UN-monitored elections" *Washington Post*, 25 January 1990, p. A30.

41 Pérez de Cuéllar, *Pilgrimage for Peace: a Secretary General's memoir* (New York: St. Martin's Press, 1997), p. 205.

42 Ibid, pp. 206–7.

43 Liakhovskii, *Tragediia i doblest'*, p. 702.

44 Rubin, *The Fragmentation of Afghanistan*, pp. 161–5.

45 Hassan Abbas, *Pakistan's Drift into Extremism* (London: M. E. Sharpe, 2005), pp. 121–3.

46 Vorontsov interview; Riaz Khan interview.
47 Abbas, *Pakistan's Drift into Extremism*, pp. 135–45; Ahmed Rashid, *Descent into chaos: the United States and the failure of nation building in Pakistan, Afghanistan, and Central Asia* (New York: Viking, 2008), pp. 39–40. Author's interview with Riaz Khan, Washington, DC, 3 August 2009.
48 Author's interview with Riaz Khan, Washington, DC, 3 August 2009.
49 Riaz Khan, *Untying the Afghan Knot: Negotiating Soviet Withdrawal* (Durham, NC: Duke University Press, 1991), p. 214.
50 Coll, *Ghost Wars*, pp. 192–3; Liakhovskii and Nekrasov, *Grazhdanin, politik, voin: pamiati Akhmad Shakha Masuda* (Moscow: s.n., 2000), pp. 217–19; M. Yousaf and M. Adkin, *Afghanistan The Bear Trap: The Defeat of a Superpower* (New York: Casemate, 2001), pp. 226–8.
51 A. Cherniaev, *Afganskii Vopros*, pp. 49–50; Coll, *Ghost Wars*, pp. 193–4; M. Yousaf and M. Adkin, *Afghanistan The Bear Trap: The Defeat of a Superpower*, pp. 230–2; "After Jalalabad's Defense, Kabul Grows Confident," *New York Times*, 30 April 1989.
52 Shah M. Tarzi, "Politics of the Afghan Resistance Movement: Cleavages, Disunity, and Fragmentation," *Asian Survey*, 31(6), 1991, pp. 479–80.
53 Rizwan Hussain, *Pakistan and the Emergence of Islamic Militancy in Afghanistan* (London: Ashgate, 2005), pp. 148–51.
54 Carolyn McGiffert-Ekedahl and Melvin Goodman, *The Wars of Eduard Shevardnadze* (University Park, PA: Pennsylvania University Press, 2001), p. 193; M. R. Beschloss and S. Talbott, *At the Highest Levels: The Inside Story of the End of the Cold War*, p. 62; James A. Baker, *The Politics of Diplomacy: revolution, war, and peace, 1989–1992* (New York: G. P. Putnam & Sons, 1995), p. 74. Shevardnadze's hint that the Soviet Union might drop its insistence on keeping Najibullah in a coalition government was "off the record," and was not mentioned in a memorandum prepared by Soviet officials for the UN Secretary General, nor does Baker mention it in his memoirs. "USSR-USA Talks on Afghanistan," 17 May 1989, SML, Pérez de Cuéllar Papers, Box 10, Folder 104.
55 Rashid, *Descent into chaos*, p. 39; Hussain, *Pakistan and the Emergence of Islamic Militancy*, p. 150.
56 Indeed, mid-level and senior officials had begun re-evaluating their policies towards support for the mujahadeen. In the fall of 1989, Peter Tomsen, appointed ambassador to the Afghan resistance, led an inter-agency working group to re-evaluate US policy. They decided on a new approach: pressure on Najibullah would continue, but the US would work to form a moderate government to take his place. Coll, *Ghost Wars*, pp. 180–4, 205–7.
57 Pérez de Cuéllar, *Pilgrimage for Peace*, p. 203; Khan, *Untying the Afghan Knot*, pp. 306–7. This was also evident when Pakistani Prime Minister Benazir Bhutto, in a meeting with Pérez de Cuéllar in June, noted that "the situation around Jalalabad had made everybody think in a different perspective ... Pakistan was pursuing a search for a political settlement to the problem of Afghanistan." Notes on the meeting between the Secretary-General and the Prime Minister of Pakistan, 9 June 1989, SML, Pérez de Cuéllar, Box 10, Folder 105.
58 "Afghanistan: US goes cool on guerillas," *Guardian*, 6 October 1989. See also G. H. W. Bush and B. Scowcroft, *A World Transformed* (New York: Vintage Books, 1998), pp. 134–5.
59 "Najibullah 'can remain,'" *Guardian*, 6 February 1990.
60 Coll, *Ghost Wars*, pp. 189–221.
61 Beschloss and Talbott, *At the Highest Levels*, p.180.
62 "Soviets Offer Proposal for Afghan Settlement," *Washington Post*, 15 February 1990, p. A45; Beschloss and Talbott, *At the Highest Levels*, p. 243.
63 Pérez de Cuéllar, *Pilgrimage for Peace*, pp. 204–6.

64 "Superpowers plan Afghan arms freeze," *The Independent*, 5 April 1990, p. 14; "US and Soviets on New Tack in Effort to End Afghan War," *New York Times*, 3 May 1990, p. A1; "Baker Notes Gains on Afghan Accord," *Washington Post*, 14 June 1990, p. A34. Note on Afghanistan to the Secretary General (undated, but after 23 May 1990), SML Pérez de Cuéllar Papers, Box 10, Folder 106.

65 Note of the Secretary-General's luncheon with George H. W. Bush, 4 June 1990, SML, Pérez de Cuéllar Papers, Box 10, Folder 106.

66 Ibid. In Nicaragua, the Sandinistas remained in power while elections took place, then stepped down peacefully after the results were certified. Bush's growing doubts about the situation in Afghanistan were evident again later in the discussion, when he asked de Cuéllar "Is Hekmatyar a bad guy?" to which the latter responded "I don't like him at all, he is a fundamentalist."

67 "Record of conversation between Gorbachev and Najibullah," 23 August 1990, NSA, READ/RADD, Box 9.

68 Beschloss and Talbott, *At the Highest Levels*, p. 243; C. McGiffert-Ekedahl and M. Goodman, *The Wars of Eduard Shevardnadze*, p. 193; "Superpowers plan Afghan arms freeze" *The Independent*, 5 April 1990, p. 14.

69 Pérez de Cuéllar, *Pilgrimage for Peace*, p. 209.

70 Viacheslav Kevorkov, *Tainyi Kanal* (Moscow: Geia, 1997).

6 From battlefield into marketplace

The end of the Cold War in Indochina, 1985–1989

Balázs Szalontai

In 1988, recently appointed Thai Premier Chatichai Choonhavan declared his ambition to turn Indochina "from a battlefield into a marketplace." A retired general with a formidable business acumen, Chatichai was a real personification of this principle. To achieve his aim, Chatichai re-examined his country's Cold War allegiances with breathtaking pragmatism. The exiled Khmer Rouge guerrillas, who used to carry out raids into Cambodia from bases in Thailand, were among the first to be affected by Chatichai's adaptability. In mid-1989, they launched new attacks on the armed forces of the Vietnamese-backed Cambodian Communist regime, only to encounter devastating artillery fire that hit their troops with surprising accuracy. This accuracy reflected not so much the marksmanship of the Cambodian artillerymen but rather the diplomatic flexibility of the Thai leadership. That is, the Thai military, having generously assisted the exiled Khmer Rouge forces for a decade, decided to make a volte-face, and secretly radioed the coordinates of the guerrillas' positions to the Cambodian general staff.[1]

This episode aptly illustrates the dramatic nature of the diplomatic changes which occurred in the three Indochinese countries (Vietnam, Cambodia and Laos) in the final years of the Cold War. Due to its proximity to China, this region constituted a major battlefield of superpower competition from 1950 to 1989, considerably influencing the dynamics of Sino–US and Sino–Soviet relations. Its strategic importance may be gauged from the fact that the successful resolution of the so-called "Cambodian question" was not so much a consequence but rather a precondition of Sino–Soviet reconciliation.

For this reason, the diplomatic and military aspects of Soviet and Vietnamese disengagement from Indochina have received ample attention from historians and political scientists, including Ben Kiernan, Nayan Chanda, Grant Evans, Martin Stuart-Fox, Robert S. Ross, Gary Klintworth and others. Similarly, the post-1986 economic reforms implemented by the Indochinese governments have been carefully analyzed by economists, all the more so because the impressive achievements of Vietnam's *doi moi* (renovation) stood in sharp contrast to the country's previous misery.[2]

Nevertheless, the findings of the two research schools were only occasionally integrated into a synthesis. This chapter, therefore, seeks to link these two spheres of post-1985 Indochinese history; that is, to investigate the economic aspects of the diplomatic measures taken by the Southeast Asian Communist and non-Communist governments. Without going so far as to claim that economic factors played a paramount role in solving the Indochinese crisis, it intends to highlight the fact that economic issues were very frequently and extensively discussed during the post-1985 negotiations which the Soviet Union, the People's Republic of China (PRC) and the Association of Southeast Asian Nations (ASEAN) conducted with Indochinese Communist leaders and which led to a radical transformation of power relations in the region.

In Indochina, the post-1975 phase of the Cold War was not so much a Soviet–American confrontation but rather a Sino–Vietnamese/Sino–Soviet rivalry. After the Vietnam War, US military presence in the Southeast Asian mainland underwent a dramatic decline, but the Soviet Union was only partially able to fill the resulting power vacuum. By and large, Moscow had to rely on a single partner, the newly unified Socialist Republic of Vietnam (SRV), since in the Lao People's Democratic Republic (LPDR), the predominance of Vietnamese influence considerably limited Soviet contacts with the ruling Lao People's Revolutionary Party (LPRP), whereas the governments of Cambodia, Thailand and Burma were traditionally distrustful of Soviet intentions. Throughout the 1970s and 1980s, Chinese and Vietnamese Communist leaders competed intensely with each other for influence in the region. Both Hanoi and Beijing laid increasing emphasis on normalizing their relations with ASEAN, not least because neither side could afford a simultaneous conflict with its Communist rival and the local non-Communist governments. ASEAN initially maintained a position of equidistance from China and Vietnam, but when Vietnam, incensed by the border clashes provoked by the Khmer Rouge, invaded Cambodia and replaced Pol Pot's dictatorship with a pro-Hanoi regime, the ASEAN states – in alignment with China and the Western powers – refused to recognize the hastily proclaimed People's Republic of Kampuchea (PRK). During the 1980s, Vietnamese troops stationed in Cambodia waged a seemingly endless war against the exiled Khmer Rouge forces and other anti-PRK guerrillas who enjoyed the support of China and Thailand.

In the 1970s, the gradual deterioration of Sino–Vietnamese relations obviously pleased the Kremlin. In the Soviet strategy of containing and encircling China, special attention was paid to Vietnam and Mongolia, both of which had not only common borders but also disputes of their own with the PRC. After the Vietnam War, Soviet aid programs to these countries were motivated primarily by the diplomatic aim of making them capable of withstanding Chinese pressure and securing their loyalty to Moscow in the Sino–Soviet dispute. Due to the meager commercial potential of Vietnam and Mongolia, the Soviet Union's own economic interests rarely influenced Soviet decision-making to a great extent, and if they did, the results were not necessarily in accordance with the priorities and expectations of the aid-recipient countries.

From 1982–1983, however, Moscow became increasingly disinterested in relying on Hanoi and Ulaanbaatar against Beijing. Worried by the growing trilateral cooperation between the US, China and Japan, Soviet leaders concluded that this strategic challenge necessitated a selective rapprochement with China, which, they hoped, might dissuade Beijing from forming a long-term alliance with Washington. Emboldened by the signs of occasional Sino–US friction over Taiwan, Brezhnev and his successors made concentrated efforts to win over China, even if this required certain diplomatic concessions.

The Chinese leaders, for their part, showed readiness to improve their relations with the Kremlin, but only if the latter removed the so-called "three obstacles" to normalization: the stationing of Soviet troops in Mongolia, Soviet support for the Vietnamese occupation of Cambodia, and the Soviet occupation of Afghanistan. The Soviets, at first, refused to discuss these issues, but Chinese persistence finally compelled them to re-examine their standpoint.[3]

Moscow's initiatives to reach a modus vivendi with Beijing understandably aroused the suspicion of Vietnamese and Mongolian leaders, who feared that such a reconciliation might be made at their expense, not just in a diplomatic but also in an economic sense. In fact, they became aware of the limits of the Kremlin's financial commitment to their countries as early as 1978–1981 when Sino–Soviet relations were still extremely tense.[4] Thus, it was logical to assume that the more the Soviet Union improved its relations with China, the less it would be interested in making economic sacrifices for the sake of its Asian allies. As we will see, these anxieties were not fully justified, but, ultimately, they were proven right.

Signs of Vietnamese and Mongolian resistance to Moscow's new China policy started to appear as soon as 1982–1983, prompting the Soviet Union to put increasing pressure on its recalcitrant allies. In Mongolia, this conflict of interests culminated in the Soviet-engineered replacement of First Secretary Yumjaagiin Tsedenbal with Jambyn Batmünkh, who, to the chagrin of Hanoi, promptly made steps to reach a modus vivendi with Beijing. In Indochina, however, the Soviets were unable to interfere in the affairs of the local party leaderships as directly as they had in Mongolia, and, thus, the coercive measures they could potentially use to enforce Vietnamese compliance were mainly of an economic nature. After all, the Kremlin had considerable economic leverage over Hanoi. In the 1980s, the Soviet Union was Vietnam's largest commercial partner, as the Soviet share of Vietnamese exports of tea, coffee, natural rubber and timber ranged between 52 and 100 percent. By the end of the decade, over 300 economic projects had been completed with Soviet assistance. In electricity generation, cement production, coal mining and apatite production, the share of Soviet-equipped enterprises stood between 47 and 100 percent.[5]

The extent to which the Soviets used this economic leverage for achieving specific diplomatic purposes is still somewhat unclear, since the decline of Soviet support may have been as much a symptom of the Soviet Union's own economic crisis and its general reluctance to finance costly and unprofitable projects in a region of decreasing strategic importance as a purposeful policy designed to overcome Vietnamese resistance. Since Soviet–Indochinese economic relations continued to deteriorate, rather than improve, after Hanoi finally fulfilled Moscow's requests, the coercive aspects of Soviet aid policy should not be overestimated. After all, the Soviets had genuine reasons for dissatisfaction with the wasteful and inefficient practices of the Vietnamese state-owned enterprises (SOEs) to which they provided technical and financial assistance. Still, one cannot exclude the second explanation, either, because in the previous decades, the Soviet Union had frequently subjected noncompliant Communist regimes (Yugoslavia, Albania, China, North Korea and Cuba) to economic pressure. But even if there was no politically motivated pressure, the mere fact that Hanoi's largest aid donor was no longer as ready to adapt to the preferences of the Vietnamese leaders as before proved ultimately sufficient to compel the latter to re-examine their domestic economic policies and look for alternative economic partners.

As early as the brief rule of Yuri Andropov (1982–1984), Moscow's overtures toward China occasionally coincided with manifestations of Soviet unwillingness to fulfill Hanoi's requests for aid. Following the third unsuccessful round of Sino–Soviet talks, in October 1983, Deputy Premier Gaidar Aliev visited Vietnam, and managed to pressure his hosts to publish a joint communiqué in which the Vietnamese side, for the first time, grudgingly announced that it "fully supported the Soviet Union's principled line of normalizing relations with the PRC."[6] Worse still, Aliev harshly criticized Vietnamese leaders for their inefficient use of Soviet aid, and bluntly refused to assist them in the planned construction of a nuclear power plant and a new hydroelectric power station. As he explained, these projects would be too costly and ambitious, and Soviet financial resources were not unlimited.[7]

In 1985–1986, the Soviet leadership, headed now by Gorbachev, temporarily changed tack, and sought to combine its détente-oriented actions with a more generous attitude toward Moscow's aid-dependent Indochinese allies. In Gorbachev's global strategy, special attention was paid to the Asia-Pacific region whose growing economic importance he quickly realized. His original objective was to counter America's Far Eastern policies – which, in his opinion, were aimed at encircling the Soviet Union – by reaching reconciliation with China and ASEAN and, simultaneously, reinforcing Soviet influence in Indochina and North Korea. At first, he appeared ready to make additional financial sacrifices in order to achieve this goal. For instance, the Kremlin considerably increased its economic assistance to Indochina. The total value of the aid and credit which the Soviet Union intended to give to Vietnam and Laos during their next five-year plans (1986–1990) was planned to be 100 and 50 percent higher, respectively, than the amount provided during the previous FYPs.[8]

Gorbachev's new Far Eastern policy yielded only limited results as far as Indochina was concerned. In June 1985, General Secretary Le Duan visited Moscow, after which the Vietnamese press toned down its attacks on the PRC, and Hanoi proposed to start secret talks to normalize Sino–Vietnamese relations. In Laos, the LPRP leaders finally took two steps for which the Soviets had been waiting quite impatiently for a substantial time: they concluded an agreement on the construction of a new Soviet embassy compound, and in October, they held the first congress of the Laotian–Soviet Friendship Society. These gestures must have been, at least partly, inspired by Moscow's new aid practices.[9]

At the same time, there were various phenomena which indicated that the Vietnamese Communist Party (VCP) leaders, unnerved by Gorbachev's attempts at rapprochement with Beijing, decided to reinforce their grip over Indochina, even at the expense of their Soviet donors. In 1985, their diplomatic efforts were still focused at isolating China, for which purpose they even made overtures toward the US. As Foreign Minister Nguyen Co Thach pointedly remarked, Hanoi, unlike the Soviet Bloc, regarded China, rather than America, as its main enemy.[10] In May–June 1985, Truong Chinh, Vietnam's head of state, paid his first official visits to Laos and Cambodia, during which decisions were made to intensify economic cooperation between the three Indochinese countries. Laos drastically cut its imports from Thailand, and sought to further redirect its foreign trade toward the Vietnamese ports of Da Nang and Ho Chi Minh City.[11] At the end of the year, the Laotian government, without any plausible explanation and, most probably, due to Vietnamese pressure, asked the Kremlin to withdraw all Soviet civilian advisers from the LPDR, whereas the number of Vietnamese advisers underwent a simultaneous increase.[12] On 27 December, Thach and his Cambodian counterpart, Hun Sen, signed an agreement about the Vietnamese–Cambodian land border that settled the long-standing Vietnamese–Cambodian territorial dispute wholly in Hanoi's favor.[13]

Hanoi's inflexible Cambodia policy was actually detrimental to Vietnam's own economic interests. As a Hungarian diplomat reported in January 1986:

> It has become obvious that in [Southeast Asia], only Vietnam, and the Indochinese region in general, has failed to show any substantial economic achievement..., though its aspiration to actively influence the conditions in SEA cannot be effective without economic might. At present, Vietnam's Cambodia policy prevents it from concentrating its full strength on the development of its economy.[14]

Similar views were expressed by a Cambodian diplomat, who stated that the leaders of the ruling Kampuchean People's Revolutionary Party (KPRP) wanted to find an internationally acceptable solution for the political crisis, in the shortest possible time, because only under peaceful conditions could the Cambodian economy recover from its long stagnation.[15]

In 1986, Gorbachev still refrained from directly pressuring Vietnam to resolve the Cambodian question, but the increased aid he promised to Hanoi was not to be provided without strings. The Soviet Union suspended its assistance to certain unprofitable projects in heavy and chemical industry, and urged Vietnam to improve its export performance on the grounds that Soviet–Vietnamese economic relations should serve mutual interests, rather than solely Vietnamese ones.[16] By 1987, the Kremlin became increasingly unwilling to fulfill Hanoi's abrupt requests for emergency aid, and started to impose stricter conditions on the supply of technology. If the Vietnamese failed to construct the infrastructure needed for the Soviet-assisted projects, they could not expect any Soviet deliveries.[17]

On the other hand, the Indochinese governments also had reasons to complain about the practices of their Soviet aid donors. For instance, in January 1986, the planning delegations of the Soviet Union and Czechoslovakia, trying to prod Laos to use foreign aid more efficiently, informed their negotiating partners about their intention to impose interest rates on the loans to be granted to Indochinese countries. The Laotians, however, promptly remarked that the World Bank and the Asian Development Bank provided them with interest-free loans, and, eventually, persuaded Gorbachev to shelve the idea.[18] Both Laotian and Cambodian officials urged their COMECON partners to switch from ruble-based deals to dollar-based ones, because they knew very well that rubles, non-convertible as they were, could not be used in transactions with the non-Communist countries from which they wanted to obtain the goods that the Soviet Bloc was unable to provide. Such proposals, however, elicited very negative reactions from the Soviet side.[19]

Dissatisfied with COMECON's aid performance and pressured by the process of Sino–Soviet rapprochement, the Indochinese countries became increasingly interested in normalizing their relations with their neighbors. Among VCP leaders, a group headed by Nguyen Co Thach stressed, as early as 1986–1987, that Vietnam's economic crisis could not be solved without reaching a modus vivendi with China and the West. Nonetheless, they still wanted to settle the Cambodian question from a position of strength, that is, by withdrawing their troops without making any political concession to the anti-PRK guerrillas in general and to the Khmer Rouge in particular.[20]

This attitude led to further disagreements with Moscow, because the Kremlin, anxious to placate the Chinese leaders, who doggedly supported the Khmer Rouge, started to prod Hanoi to adopt a more flexible stance. During a visit to Vietnam in March 1987, Soviet Foreign Minister Eduard

Shevardnadze, having stressed the urgency of solving the Afghan and Cambodian questions, declared that the "masses of the Khmer Rouge," except Pol Pot and his high-ranking accomplices, should be involved in the peace process. He also encouraged the Cambodian leaders to learn from the example of the "national reconciliation" policy pursued by the Soviet-controlled Afghan Communist regime. Thereupon, the Vietnamese pointed out that the Afghan "counter-revolutionaries" were not genocidists like the Khmer Rouge, and the Soviet Union did not negotiate with them anyway.[21]

The KPRP leaders, on their part, were more interested in drawing lessons from the Laotian model of national reconciliation. In June 1987, Premier Hun Sen discussed this issue with Kaysone Phomvihane, the supreme leader of the LPDR, and concluded that "reconciliation" should mean bringing a few individual opposition leaders into the state apparatus, rather than sharing power with their organizations.[22]

Hun Sen's interest in Vientiane's experiences was quite natural, since détente arrived in Laos somewhat earlier than in the other Indochinese countries. In fact, the LPDR never suffered from such extensive diplomatic isolation as Vietnam and Cambodia, and, thus, it found it easier to initiate a dialog with its external opponents. Those Western governments which refused to recognize the PRK had no objections against maintaining official relations with Vientiane. In the mid-1980s, when Vietnam faced an international embargo, the LPDR continued to receive aid from Sweden, the Netherlands, Australia and Japan. Alone among the Indochinese states, Laos even hosted a US embassy. Only Thailand constituted a partial exception, since Thai rulers, who traditionally aspired to extend their influence to neighboring Laos, were more willing to use coercive measures in order to enforce Lao compliance than any other power.[23]

On the other hand, Laos, a landlocked, extremely underdeveloped and militarily weak country, sharing long common borders with Thailand and China, could ill afford a long-term conflict with Bangkok and Beijing, because if Lao–Thai and Sino–Lao trade was disrupted by political tension, neither Vietnam nor the European Communist countries would be able to fully fill the gap. In 1985, Thailand was still the LPDR's largest single commercial partner, with the volume of Lao-Thai trade constituting no less than 30 percent of Laotian external trade. In the northern provinces of Laos, border trade with China proved essential for providing local tribes with much-needed consumer goods. In fact, neither Bangkok nor Beijing hesitated to use its economic leverage for achieving diplomatic aims. The Thai authorities repeatedly imposed transport restrictions on Lao–Thai trade whenever they disagreed with LPRP policies, and Sino–Laotian border trade also underwent a marked decline after the Sino–Vietnamese war. In 1983–1984, Beijing changed tack, and offered to resuscitate border trade in exchange for a more cooperative Lao attitude. The Laotian leaders, at first, rejected these suggestions, but in October–November

1986, they decided to take the initiative. Anxious to broaden their country's external economic relations, they concluded agreements on aid and credit with a delegation from the European Economic Community (EEC), and proposed to start negotiations with Thailand and China.[24]

Nonetheless, the LPDR's unique situation could as much hinder as facilitate Vientiane's efforts to reach reconciliation with its neighbors, because the VCP leaders distrusted the idea of a bilateral Sino–Laotian rapprochement that would not be accompanied by a Cambodian settlement acceptable to Hanoi. They were of the opinion that China considered Laos the "weakest link" in the trilateral alliance of Indochinese countries, and its overtures toward Vientiane, combined as they were with an inflexible stance toward Hanoi, served only as a divide-and-rule policy. Vietnam's distrustful attitude created serious obstacles for the LPDR. In December 1986, the first high-level Sino–Laotian talks yielded few results, because the LPRP leaders, though their own principal objective was to revitalize Sino–Laotian trade, tried to act in accordance with Vietnam's preferences, and refused to discuss China's economic proposals unless Beijing ceased to assist the Khmer Rouge guerrillas.[25]

Probably, this is why the effective normalization of Sino-Laotian relations began only in November 1987, that is, the same month in which the VCP Politburo finally resolved to withdraw its troops from Cambodia. In contrast with the coercive measures China used against Vietnam, Sino–Laotian rapprochement was based on the principle of mutual concessions: Beijing ceased to support the Lao exiles residing in southern China, whereas the Laotian media discontinued its anti-Chinese propaganda. Reassured that China no longer posed a threat to the Laotian regime, in January-March 1988 Hanoi withdrew the bulk of its troops from the LPDR, after which ambassadorial-level relations were restored between Beijing and Vientiane, and the two countries signed a trade agreement for 1989–1990.[26]

Reconciliation with Thailand was soon to follow, albeit after a bumpy start. In November-December 1987, the Thai side – which may have wanted to force the LPRP leaders to the negotiating table by warning them that they should not try to make a deal with Beijing at the expense of Bangkok – provoked armed clashes in a disputed border area. The fighting continued until February 1988 when Laotian Chief of Staff Sisavat Keobounphan and Thai Commander-in-Chief Chaovalit Yongchaiyut signed a ceasefire agreement. During the subsequent negotiations, the Thai military officers, remarkably enough, showed far more interest in promoting economic cooperation than in discussing the border problem. Thanks to Chaovalit's extensive connections, in March a delegation of influential Thai businessmen visited Vientiane, and pledged to invest one billion baht in various projects related to tourism, forestry, agriculture and livestock farming. Characteristically, the first Thai firm to make a major deal with Laos was a military-affiliated company that undertook to supply much-needed consumer goods in exchange for timber. Anxious to stimulate the development of the local manufacturing sector, the Laotian government sought to encourage Thai entrepreneurs to establish joint ventures with Lao SOEs in the textile industry and wood processing.[27]

While Laos, understandably, focused its efforts on reaching reconciliation with its two powerful neighbors, China and Thailand, Vietnam's search for alternative diplomatic and economic partners was, at first, directed toward Indonesia, whose government considered China, rather than Vietnam, the most serious potential threat to Southeast Asia, and, hence, it was far more inclined to agree with Hanoi's anti-Chinese standpoint than any other ASEAN country.[28] As early as 1982–1983, the VCP leaders sought to divide ASEAN and isolate Thailand by making overtures toward Indonesia, but such tactics yielded few practical results until they decided to withdraw their troops from Cambodia. Once they had taken that step, Indonesia was also ready to shift from expressions of sympathy to concrete assistance. In November 1987, a Vietnamese economic delegation traveled to Indonesia, and, having received ample practical advice from President Suharto himself, gained useful experience for Hanoi's economic reform program. Moreover, numerous Indonesian companies expressed interest in importing various agricultural products and handicrafts from Vietnam, and investing in oil exploration.[29] In February 1988, Indonesian Foreign Minister Mochtar Kusumaatmadja went so far as to promise that once the Cambodian problem was solved, an international consortium would be established to provide economic assistance to Hanoi. As he put it, "Indonesia will not allow [others] to corner Vietnam."[30]

The spectacular progress of Vietnamese–Indonesian rapprochement hardly pleased the Thai leaders, who, unlike Indonesia, sought to rely on Beijing against Hanoi. This divergence of interests generated considerable tension between Bangkok and Jakarta. For instance, in February 1989, when the participants of the so-called Second Jakarta Informal Meeting failed to reach a satisfactory agreement on the Cambodian question, the Thai foreign ministry promptly blamed the Indonesian hosts – who, in Bangkok's opinion, made inappropriate concessions to Hanoi – for the fiasco.[31] Still, the gradual withdrawal of Vietnamese troops from Laos and Cambodia brought about a rapprochement in Thai–Vietnamese relations, too. As early as 1987, Thai entrepreneurs started to urge their government to relax its economic pressure on Hanoi, for they noticed that despite the still unsolved status of the Cambodian question, Japanese–Vietnamese and Vietnamese–Singaporean trade was already developing at a rapid pace. Premier Chatichai Choonhavan, appointed in July 1988, was more than ready to represent their interests. Following his talks with Thach in August, Thai companies were no longer prevented from establishing joint ventures with Vietnamese SOEs. Chatichai's "Golden Peninsula" plan, aimed at fostering multilateral economic cooperation between Thailand, Indochina and Burma, was considered attractive by VCP leaders, who were eager to learn from the experiences of Thailand's economic modernization. Since Vietnam's foreign investment law, passed in late 1987 and confirmed in September 1988, was one of the most attractive in Southeast Asia, Hanoi expected Thai firms to make substantial investments in tourism and food processing.[32]

Chatichai paid similar attention to the two other Indochinese countries, too. In November 1988, he traveled to Laos, and concluded agreements with the LPRP leadership on technical cooperation in agricultural production, energy generation, and road construction. In their joint communiqué, the two governments expressed their intention to play a constructive role in solving the Cambodian crisis. In January 1989, Chaovalit also visited Vientiane, during which he sent an invitation to Hun Sen for a visit to Bangkok.[33]

By that time, the Cambodian authorities, motivated by the necessity of obtaining additional economic assistance, had mostly overcome their distrust of the various international aid organizations. In the spring of 1989, the total number of aid officials already exceeded the combined number of all non-Soviet Communist diplomats. Moreover, the representatives of these organizations were allowed to visit even those areas from which the Soviet Bloc diplomats were barred "on security grounds." While the activity of the "fraternal" diplomats remained confined to Phnom Penh, the aid officials managed to establish contacts with the provincial and district authorities as well.[34]

Having realized that the withdrawal of Vietnamese troops from Cambodia was likely to stimulate Japanese, US, French and Chinese investments in the PRK, Chatichai concluded that he should act quickly if Thailand wanted to gain a substantial share of the Cambodian market. In fact, Singapore had already become Cambodia's largest non-Communist commercial partner, though its official diplomatic stance toward the PRK was more inflexible than that of the other ASEAN states. To overtake his competitors, the Thai premier decided to establish a "special relationship" with Hun Sen and earn his favors, even if this required certain unusual moves. As described before, in the summer of 1989 the Thai military went so far as to provide the Cambodian general staff with information about the operations of the Khmer Rouge guerrillas. By September, not only were the offices of the two premiers linked via direct satellite communication but their wives also forged a close personal relationship, not the least because the spouse of Hun Sen, nicknamed the "Iron Lady" of Cambodia's ethnic Chinese community, was deeply involved in the rapidly growing legal and illegal trade between Cambodia and Thailand.[35]

Anxious to isolate the Khmer Rouge and find new economic partners, Hun Sen was ready to cooperate with Thailand in general and Chatichai in particular, whereas his conservative rival, General Secretary Heng Samrin, still preferred to rely on Vietnam.[36] The conflict between the two KPRP factions became so embittered that in August 1989 two high-ranking pro-Heng Samrin military officers, who had attempted to stamp out the corruption fueled by the massive smuggling activity between Thailand, Cambodia and Vietnam, were assassinated on the orders of persons belonging to Hun Sen's inner circle whose financial interests seem to have been threatened by the officers' investigation.[37]

The Soviet Bloc also became involved in the competition between the two Cambodian factions. Soviet dislike for the Vietnamese-backed Heng Samrin clearly manifested itself during his visit to Moscow in 1989 when he repeatedly, but unsuccessfully, asked for a meeting with Gorbachev. Heng was received only by Anatolii Lukíanov, a candidate member of the CPSU Politburo, who concluded that his views sharply differed from the ones which Hun Sen expressed during his meeting with Shevardnadze.[38] Those Cambodian cadres who sought to restructure the economy along market-oriented lines often cited Hungary's recent economic reforms as a precedent. The inspiration of Hungarian models was clearly perceptible in the measures they took to attract FDI, encourage private entrepreneurship, increase the autonomy of SOEs, and decentralize the banking sector.[39]

Even after the introduction of a multiparty system in Poland and Hungary, Cambodian reformers continued to show great interest in these countries.[40] Their attitude stood in marked contrast to that of Vietnamese leaders, whose sympathy for the "Hungarian model" was confined to the economic sphere. At the 7th plenum of the VCP Central Committee (CC) (August 1989), General Secretary Nguyen Van Linh sharply condemned the process of East European democratization.[41] In Phnom Penh, many cadres were of the opinion that Linh's critical comments had been partly motivated by the desire to discourage the Cambodian government from implementing any "excessively" radical reforms.[42]

The political changes in Eastern Europe in 1989 had a negative effect on Soviet–Vietnamese relations, too. Following the 7th plenum, the VCP leadership prohibited high-ranking party cadres from undergoing ideological education in the Soviet Union, and sent a number of Soviet-trained generals into forced retirement. At the same time, however, Hanoi continued to request Soviet assistance with various massive projects, such as the construction of power transmission lines between Vietnam, Laos, Thailand and China. These pleas fell on deaf ears, because the Kremlin decided to "freeze" its economic cooperation with Vietnam until the two sides managed to find ways to make the Soviet-financed projects more profitable.[43] In fact, Soviet commitment to Indochina had been steadily decreasing since Gorbachev's Krasnoyarsk speech (September 1988). The number of Soviet civilian and military advisers in Vietnam – 10,000 and 15,000, respectively, in early 1989 – was to be halved by the end of that year, and then reduced to 10 percent within two years.[44] Similarly, in January 1989 there were only 600 Soviet civilian and military advisers in Cambodia (half as many as a few years before), and nearly all military advisers (about 80 persons) were to be recalled by the end of that year.[45]

Shocked by the successive dismantling of East European Communist regimes, the VCP leaders initially thought that the main error to be avoided was adopting a too "soft" position. In December, however, the unexpected downfall and execution of Romanian leader Nicolae Ceauşescu, the Warsaw Pact's most repressive dictator, revealed that excessively hard-line policies might lead to even worse consequences. In the light of the Romanian events, the Vietnamese leaders started to approve the peaceful and smooth nature of Hungary's transition, but remained committed to the preservation of one-party rule. As they put it, the introduction of a multiparty system would create a situation in which "we might be able to retain a hold over the North but the southern part of the country would be lost within two or three months."[46]

Facing the East European wave of democratization, the Laotian regime adopted a position that was neither as flexible as Cambodia's approach nor as hostile as Vietnam's. At the 8th plenum of the LPRP Central Committee (November 1989), the leadership concluded that the East European model of transition was not applicable to Laos. Enumerating the errors which cadres were to avoid, the plenum focused its criticism on such "negative phenomena" as "unrestrained freedom and democracy." Remarkably, the condemnation of bureaucratic and dictatorial methods was only the very last item on the list. Nonetheless, Lao leaders refrained from castigating Eastern Europe's transition in any explicit way.[47]

The growing rift between Indochina and the disintegrating Soviet Bloc was paralleled by the cracks which appeared in the trilateral Vietnamese–Laotian–Cambodian alliance. Once Vietnamese troops were withdrawn from Laos and Cambodia, there were insufficient grounds to justify either the continued presence of the ubiquitous Vietnamese advisers or Hanoi's economic domination over its satellites. Actually, conflicts over economic issues had constituted a major element of post-1979 Vietnamese–Cambodian and Lao–Vietnamese disputes.

For example, in 1985 a Cambodian diplomat told a Hungarian colleague that the new currency exchange rates, set by a recent Vietnamese monetary reform, were disadvantageous to both Cambodia and Laos. Unfortunately, he lamented, "it is more difficult to raise such problems to one's closest friend than to the more distant ones."[48] The Vietnamese government, anxious to partly recover the massive expenses of stationing troops in the PRK, obtained Cambodia's valuable raw materials at below-market prices, and re-exported them with a substantial profit. Such transactions deprived Cambodia of a revenue of $50 million per annum – half as much as Hanoi spent on occupying its small neighbor.[49] The Cambodian cadres resented that their Vietnamese advisers tried to prevent the PRK from establishing direct commercial relations with Thailand, Singapore and Hong Kong, and often retaliated by intentionally misinforming the advisers or simply refusing to carry out their instructions.[50]

Thanks to the end of the Cold War, Hanoi's satellites gradually increased their room for maneuver. For instance, in late 1987 – that is, when Vietnam decided to withdraw its troops from Cambodia – the Vietnamese and Laotian governments finally resolved a problem that had irritated the LPRP regime ever since it came to power in 1975. Due to the recurrent Lao–Thai disputes, COMECON aid shipments to Laos were usually transported via Da Nang, which enabled Vietnamese authorities to misappropriate a substantial part of the goods. For a long time, the Lao cadres received little more than evasive replies to their complaints, but now, under the changed circumstances, they managed to persuade Hanoi to assume responsibility for the transport of goods to the Laotian border.[51] As an additional guarantee, they sought to find alternative economic partners. In June 1989, a Lao diplomat told a Hungarian colleague that the LPRP leaders, anxious to lessen their dependence on Hanoi, decided to pursue a policy of equidistance between their three powerful neighbors: Vietnam, China and Thailand.[52]

In fact, the decline of Soviet–Vietnamese cooperation and the weakening of Vietnamese control over Laos and Cambodia were closely interrelated. On the one hand, the reduction of Soviet support undermined Hanoi's capacity to act as a regional hegemon; on the other hand, the dissolution of the Indochinese Bloc lessened Vietnam's interest in collaborating with Moscow. After all, the Soviet–Vietnamese alliance had been based not only on cooperation against China but also on the Kremlin's acquiescence in Vietnam's dominance over Laos and Cambodia. As early as during the Cambodian civil war (1970–1975), the Soviets made it clear that they did not intend to compete with Hanoi in Indochina. When the Cambodian guerrillas asked the Communist powers to provide them with direct assistance, Moscow insisted on sending its aid shipments through North Vietnam, whereas Beijing had no compunctions about bypassing Hanoi.[53]

This link between Soviet–Vietnamese cooperation and Moscow's acquiescence in Hanoi's regional ambitions also meant, however, that any Soviet attempt to criticize Vietnam's Indochina policy was bound to alienate the VCP leadership. Even at the zenith of Soviet–Vietnamese cooperation, Hanoi jealously guarded its Laotian and Cambodian fiefdoms against any unwanted Soviet interference, to the extent that a substantial part of the brand-new Soviet military equipment shipped to the Cambodian army failed to arrive, because the Vietnamese intercepted it, and sent used arms and vehicles instead.[54] As a consequence, Gorbachev's efforts to persuade (or force) Hanoi to withdraw its troops from Cambodia, coupled as they were with the reduction of Soviet economic aid, resulted in a rapid deterioration of Soviet–Vietnamese relations, and induced the VCP leaders to seek new economic and political partners.

The decrease of COMECON assistance compelled the Indochinese Communist regimes to improve their economic performance by introducing various market-oriented reforms, such as Vietnam's famous *doi moi* and the LPDR's New Economic Mechanism. These reforms, however, could not eliminate the long-standing aid-dependency of those countries overnight.[55] Continued access to external financial resources remained a vital necessity, and since neither aid nor FDI could be obtained without substantial diplomatic and economic adjustment to the expectations of the potential new partners (ASEAN, Japan, Western Europe and the US), the latter gained substantial leverage over the policies of the Indochinese regimes. Such adjustment was greatly facilitated by the fact that Vietnam did not regard the ASEAN countries, with the partial exception of Thailand, as a strategic threat. On the contrary, ASEAN, and particularly Indonesia, appeared to be a potential and much-needed counterweight to China. Moreover, Indochinese Communist leaders, impressed by the spectacular economic boom of the Newly Industrialized Countries (NIC) and anxious to find a formula that would enable them to develop their economies without dismantling their dictatorial political systems, concluded that the "NIC model," in which rapid modernization had been achieved under authoritarian or, at best, semi-democratic regimes, was certainly applicable to their own conditions.[56]

Fortunately for the Indochinese countries, their non-Communist neighbors were as much interested in economic cooperation as the leaders in Hanoi, Vientiane and Phnom Penh, and, thus, the latter's requests to gain accession to ASEAN did not fall on deaf ears. In fact, the idea of joining ASEAN in the future was discussed by the Vietnamese leaders as early as June 1978.[57] Nevertheless, these early initiatives were made in the context of Hanoi's anti-Chinese strategy, and ASEAN, unwilling to get involved in the Sino–Vietnamese conflict, was not yet ready for such a step. After the end of the Cold War, however, the withdrawal of Vietnamese troops from Cambodia and the normalization of Sino–Vietnamese relations opened new avenues for Vietnam, Laos and Cambodia, which eventually joined ASEAN in 1995, 1997 and 1999, respectively.[58]

All in all, economic factors seem to have played a major role in reshaping the balance of power in Indochina and enabling the local Communist leaders to overcome the legacy of the Cold War. This importance of the economic dimension was rooted partly in the extremely aid-dependent nature of the Indochinese economies – which made their governments quite susceptible to the pressures or inducements of their actual and potential aid donors – and partly in the attractive economic performance of their non-Communist neighbors.

To be sure, the role of economic factors was not equally decisive in every political change in Indochina. For instance, the gradual normalization of Sino–Vietnamese relations was hardly, if at all, motivated by economic considerations. While the resuscitation of border trade, initiated by the VCP Politburo in November 1988, did constitute an integral element of the reconciliation process, in the early 1990s the prospect of large-scale Chinese investments was still regarded in Vietnam as neither likely nor particularly desirable.[59] Nor could the rapid development of post-1988

Thai–Indochinese economic cooperation overcome the political obstacles created by China's commitment to the Khmer Rouge. As Ben Kiernan points out, the intervention of Washington and Beijing ultimately overruled regional initiatives to exclude the Khmer Rouge from the Cambodian peace settlement, for Thailand found it advisable to adapt to the preferences of its Chinese and US allies.[60]

Still, the economic aspects of Indochina's post-Cold War realignment should not be underestimated. The attractive prospects of mutually beneficial economic cooperation with ASEAN – a practice largely absent in the relationship between Indochina and the Soviet Bloc – greatly sweetened the pill which the VCP leaders had to swallow in 1987–1989, and served as a much-needed lubricant in the process of Thai–Vietnamese, Vietnamese–Indonesian, Lao–Thai, Sino–Laotian and Thai–Cambodian rapprochement. Committed to the ideas of economic cooperation and political non-interference ever since its establishment, ASEAN constituted a favorable external environment for the economic reforms launched by Indochinese Communist leaders, to whom the end of the Cold War was by no means a victory, but it was not an utter defeat, either.

Notes

1 Hungarian Embassy to Thailand [henceforth HE-TL], Report, 9 September 1988, Hungarian National Archives (MOL), XIX-J-1-j Vietnam, Top Secret Documents [henceforth VTS], 1988, 103. doboz, 10, 003852/1/1988; Hungarian Embassy to the PRK [henceforth HE-PRK], Ciphered Telegram, 2 August 1989, XIX-J-1-j Cambodia, Top Secret Documents [henceforth CATS], 1989, 47. doboz, 73–10, 00201/42/1989.

2 For a list of publications about *doi moi*, see Binh P. Le, "Doi Moi. A Selected Bibliography of Vietnam's Economic Transformation, 1986–2000." Available online at www.coombs.anu.edu.au/Biblio/biblio_doi_moi.html (accessed 10 May 2008).

3 Robert S. Ross, "China and the Cambodian Peace Process: The Value of Coercive Diplomacy," *Asian Survey* 31:12, 1991, pp. 1174–6; Gary Klintworth, "Forces of Change in Vietnam," in Dean Forbes *et al.* (eds.), *Doi Moi. Vietnam's Renovation: Policy and Performance*, Canberra: Department of Political and Social Change, Australian National University, 1991, pp. 230–1.

4 Hungarian Embassy to the SRV [henceforth HE-SRV], Telegram, 20 June 1978, VTS, 1978, 139. doboz, 162–1, 002556/26/1978.

5 HE-SRV, Report, 27 April 1988, VTS, 1988, 103. doboz, 54, 002243/1988.

6 Robert C. Horn, "Vietnam and Sino–Soviet Relations: What Price Rapprochement?," *Asian Survey* 27:7, 1987, pp. 733–4.

7 Balázs Szalontai, "The Diplomacy of Economic Reform in Vietnam: The Genesis of *Doi Moi*, 1986–1989," *Journal of Asiatic Studies* 51:2, (2008), p. 204.

8 HE-SRV, Report, 12 December 1985, VTS, 1985, 148. doboz, 162–10, 005807/1985; Hungarian Embassy to the LPDR [henceforth HE-LPDR], Report, 12 April 1986, XIX-J-1-j Laos, Top Secret Documents [henceforth LTS], 1986, 91. doboz, 86–10, 002621/1986. See also Michael C. Williams, "New Soviet Policy toward Southeast Asia: Reorientation and Change," *Asian Survey* 31:4, (1991), pp. 367–73.

9 HE-SRV, Report, 12 December 1985, VTS, 1985, 148. doboz, 162–10, 002562/3/1985; HE-LPDR, Report, 12 April 1986, LTS, 1986, 91. doboz, 86–10, 002621/1986.
10 HE-SRV, Report, 27 January 1986, VTS, 1986, 147. doboz, 10, 00765/1986.
11 HE-SRV, Ciphered Telegram, 11 June 1985, VTS, 1985, 148. doboz, 162–13, 003237/1/1985.
12 HE-LPDR, Report, 12 April 1986, LTS, 1986, 91. doboz, 86–10, 002621/1986.
13 HE-SRV, Report, 14 April 1986, VTS, 1986, 147. doboz, 331, 002609/1986.
14 HE-SRV, Report, 27 January 1986, VTS, 1986, 147. doboz, 10, 00765/1986.
15 HE-SRV, Ciphered Telegram, 22 October 1985, VTS, 1985, 148. doboz, 162–10, 004958/1985. See also Harish C. Mehta and Julie B. Mehta, *Hun Sen: Strongman of Cambodia* (Singapore: Graham Brash, 1999), pp. 99–101.
16 Szalontai, "The Diplomacy of Economic Reform in Vietnam", p. 207.
17 HE-SRV, Report, 27 April 1988, VTS, 1988, 103. doboz, 54, 002243/1988.
18 HE-LPDR, Report, 21 January 1986, LTS, 1986, 91. doboz, 86–513, 00761/1986; HE-LPDR, Report, 12 April 1986, LTS, 1986, 91. doboz, 86–10, 002621/1986.
19 HE-LPDR, Report, 16 April 1986, LTS, 1986, 91. doboz, 86–51, 002622/1986; HE-PRK, Report, 8 May 1989, CATS, 1989, 47. doboz, 73–50, 002388/1989.
20 Szalontai, "The Diplomacy of Economic Reform in Vietnam", pp. 214–28.
21 Hungarian Foreign Ministry [henceforth HFM], Memorandum, 22 April 1987, CATS, 1987, 74. doboz, 73–146, 002563/1/1987; HE-SRV, Report, 27 April 1988, CATS, 1988, 55. doboz, 73–10, 00685/5/1988; HE-SRV, Ciphered Telegram, 13 May 1988, VTS, 1988, 103. doboz, 162–135, 002621/1988, Gerald Segal, "The USSR and Asia in 1988: Achievements and Risks," *Asian Survey* 29:1, 1989, p. 102.
22 HFM, Memorandum, 2 July 1987, LTS, 1987, 83. doboz, 86–135, 003722/1987.
23 HFM, Memorandum, November 1986, LTS, 1986, 91. doboz, 86–14, 003933/1986.
24 Hungarian Embassy to the PRC [henceforth HE-PRC], Ciphered Telegram, 28 November 1986, LTS, 1986, 91. doboz, 86–25, 005576/1986; HE-LPDR, Report, 5 October 1987, LTS, 1987, 83. doboz, 86–4, 005341/1987.
25 HFM, Memorandum, 30 January 1987, LTS, 1987, 83. doboz, 86–10, 00685/1987.
26 HFM, Memorandum, June 1988, LTS, 1988, 62. doboz, 86–20, 003179/1988; HE-LPDR, Report, 20 September 1989, LTS, 1989, 54. doboz, 87–25, 003758/1989. See also Grant Evans, *A Short History of Laos. The Land in Between* (Crows Nest (NSW): Allen and Unwin, 2002), pp. 197–200; Martin Stuart-Fox, "Laos: The Chinese Connection," *Southeast Asian Affairs* 2009, pp. 141–69.
27 HE-LPDR, Report, 18 April 1988, LTS, 1988, 62. doboz, 86–34, 00678/1/1988; HE-LPDR, Report, 15 September 1988, LTS, 1988, 62. doboz, 86–50, 003896/1988.
28 Andrew J. MacIntyre, "Interpreting Indonesian Foreign Policy: The Case of Kampuchea, 1979–1986," *Asian Survey* 27:5, 1987, pp. 515–34.
29 Szalontai, "The Diplomacy of Economic Reform in Vietnam," pp. 235–6.
30 Hungarian Embassy to Indonesia, Ciphered Telegram, 26 February 1988, CATS, 1988, 55. doboz, 73–10, 20, 00685/3/1988.
31 HE-TL, Ciphered Telegram, 24 February 1989, CATS, 1989, 47. doboz, 73–10, 00201/16/1989.
32 HE-TL, Report, 9 September 1988, VTS, 1988, 103. doboz, 10, 003852/1/1988; HE-SRV, Report, 30 April 1989, VTS, 1989, 92. doboz, 10, 002238/1989.
33 HE-LPDR, Report, 26 January 1989, LTS, 1989, 54. doboz, 86–10, 00774/1989. See also Geoffrey C. Gunn, "Laos in 1989: Quiet Revolution in the Marketplace," *Asian Survey* 31:1, 1990, pp. 85–6; Larry A. Niksch, "Thailand in 1988: The Economic Surge," *Asian Survey* 29: 2, 1989, pp. 170–1.

34 HE-PRK, Report, 17 April 1989, CATS, 1989, 47. doboz, 73–14, 002234/1989. On Cambodia's efforts to attract FDI, see Mehta and Mehta, *Hun Sen*, pp. 139–41.

35 HE-PRK, Report, 25 April 1989, CATS, 1989, 47. doboz, 73–5, 002232/1989; HE-PRK, Ciphered Telegram, 4 September 1989, CATS, 1989, 47. doboz, 73–10, 003538/1989; HE-PRK, Report, 18 September 1989, CATS, 1989, 47. doboz, 73–10, 003538/1/1989. See also Scott R. Christensen, "Thailand in 1989: Consensus at Bay," *Asian Survey* 30:2, 1990, pp. 181–3; Puangthong Rungswasdisab, "Thailand's Response to the Cambodian Genocide," in Susan E. Cook (ed.), *Genocide in Rwanda and Cambodia: New Perspectives* (New Haven, CT: Yale Center for International and Area Studies, 2005), pp. 99–103.

36 HE-PRK, Ciphered Telegram, 25 August 1989, CATS, 1989, 47. doboz, 73–10, 003466/1989.

37 HE-PRK, Ciphered Telegram, 28 August 1989, CATS, 1989, 47. doboz, 73–4, 003477/1989.

38 HE-PRK, Ciphered Telegram, 25 August 1989, CATS, 1989, 47. doboz, 73–10, 003466/1989.

39 HE-PRK, Report, 25 April 1989, CATS, 1989, 47. doboz, 73–10, 002231/1989. On Cambodia's economic reforms, see also Margaret Slocomb, *The People's Republic of Kampuchea, 1979–1989. The Revolution After Pol Pot* (Chiang Mai: Silkworm Books, 2003), pp. 206–26.

40 HE-PRK, Report, 15 November 1989, CATS, 1989, 47. doboz, 73–10, 002231/2/1989.

41 HE-SRV, Report, 26 April 1989, VTS, 1989, 92. doboz, 1, 001696/1/1989; HE-SRV, Ciphered Telegram, 6 September 1989, VTS, 1989, 92. doboz, 162–2, 001697/4/1989. See also Williams, "New Soviet Policy toward Southeast Asia," p. 375.

42 HE-PRK, Ciphered Telegram, 25 August 1989, CATS, 1989, 47. doboz, 73–10, 003466/1989.

43 HE-SRV, Ciphered Telegram, 13 October 1989, VTS, 1989, 92. doboz, 162–10, 003760/1/1989.

44 HE-SRV, Report, 18 September 1989, VTS, 1989, 92. doboz, 10, 003760/1989.

45 HE-PRK, Report, 20 January 1989, CATS, 1989, 47. doboz, 73–10, 00771/1989. See also Justus M. van der Kroef, "Cambodia in 1990: The Elusive Peace," *Asian Survey* 31:1, 1991, p. 99.

46 HE-SRV, Ciphered Telegram, 6 September 1989, VTS, 1989, 92. doboz, 162–2, 001697/4/1989; HE-SRV, Ciphered Telegram, 28 December 1989, VTS, 1989, 92. doboz, 162–10, 004726/1989.

47 HE-LPDR, Ciphered Telegram, 15 November 1989, LTS, 1989, 54. doboz, 86–24, 004569/1989; HE-LPDR, Ciphered Telegram, 19 December 1989, LTS, 1989, 54. doboz, 86–2, 004605/1989.

48 HE-SRV, Ciphered Telegram, 22 October 1985, VTS, 1985, 148. doboz, 162–10, 004958/1985.

49 HE-PRK, Report, 21 September 1989, CATS, 1989, 47. doboz, 73–10, 003761/1989.

50 HE-PRK, Report, 20 January 1989, CATS, 1989, 47. doboz, 73–10, 00771/1989.

51 HE-LPDR, Report, 19 January 1988, LTS, 1988, 62. doboz, 86–50, 00677/1988.

52 HE-PRC, Ciphered Telegram, 2 June 1989, LTS, 1989, 54. doboz, 86–10, 002630/1989.

53 Hungarian Embassy to the USSR, Telegram, 11 February 1971, CATS, 1971, 62. doboz, 73–10, 00471/2/1971.

54 HE-SRV, Ciphered Telegram, 23 March 1987, XIX-J-1-j Soviet Union, Top Secret Documents, 1987, 126. doboz, 145–135, 002103/1/1987. See also Gerald Segal, "The USSR and Asia in 1987: Signs of a Major Effort," *Asian Survey* 28:1, 1988, p. 4.

55 Francois Guégan, *Historical perspectives on development assistance to the Lao PDR.* Available online at www.sono.ens-cachan.fr/IMG/pdf/article_guegan.pdf (accessed 10 April 2010); Tooch Van, *International Aid and Democracy Building Process: Cambodia.* Available online at www.fletcher.tufts.edu/research/2004/Van-Tooch.pdf (accessed 10 April 2010).

56 HE-SRV, Report, 24 April 1989, VTS, 1989, 92. doboz, 162–25, 001697/2/1989.

57 HE-LPDR, Telegram, 13 June 1978, VTS, 1978, 139. doboz, 162–1, 003954/1978.

58 Allan E. Goodman, "Vietnam and ASEAN: Who Would Have Thought It Possible?," *Asian Survey* 36:6, 1996, pp. 592–600; Martin Stuart-Fox, "Laos in 1997: Into ASEAN," *Asian Survey* 38:1, 1998, pp. 75–9.

59 Brantly Womack, "Sino–Vietnamese Border Trade: The Edge of Normalization," *Asian Survey* 34:6, 1994, pp. 495–512. See also Ramses Amer, "Sino–Vietnamese Normalization in the Light of the Crisis of the Late 1970s," *Pacific Affairs* 67:3, 1994, pp. 357–83.

60 Ben Kiernan, "The Inclusion of the Khmer Rouge in the Cambodian Peace Process: Causes and Consequences," in Ben Kiernan (ed.), *Genocide and Democracy in Cambodia: The Khmer Rouge, the United Nations, and the International Community* New Haven: Yale Council on Southeast Asia Studies/Orville H. Schell, Jr. Center for International Human Rights, 1993, pp. 191–272.

7 India and the end of the Cold War

Sergey Radchenko

India's emergence as an independent state coincided with the onset of the Cold War; and India's foreign policy, born of the Cold War, was, from the outset, defined more by what it was not than by what it was. India became a sponsor of the Non-Aligned Movement (NAM), a poorly defined association of mostly Asian and African, and mostly postcolonial, countries in search of a role in the increasingly rigid bipolar framework of the postwar world. But truly, although Yugoslavia and Egypt, alongside India, claimed prominent positions at the pinnacle of the NAM ideological hierarchy, India became the soul of non-alignment. No other country lived non-alignment to quite the same degree as India; the first Indian Prime Minister, Jawaharlal Nehru, pursued this idea with passion and determination indicative of a deeply held belief that in a world where so many great powers, not least India's former colonial overlord, had failed to find a role, India had a role to play – the role of a broker between the East and West, the role of the peace-maker in the Gandhian tradition of non-violence, the role of the third pole of attraction for all those unwilling to be thrown about like pieces on the chessboard of the superpower confrontation.

This chapter shows how the end of the Cold War rendered India's grand strategy obsolete. This was, in part, inevitable; the very concept of non-alignment entailed an element of fence-sitting, and that does not work when fences – or walls – begin to come down. But there was more to the debacle of India's foreign policy than met the eye. Prime Minister Rajiv Gandhi overplayed his hand. In the mid-1980s, as he set out to improve relations with both Moscow and Washington, India briefly punched above its weight; in the end, neither the Soviet Union nor, especially, the US, valued their relationship with India above their respective regional and global priorities. As the policy-makers in the Kremlin and the White House worked to accomplish their respective agendas in South Asia (which in effect boiled down to the settlement in Afghanistan), India's interests were, by and large, neglected. New Delhi's renewed assertiveness as a regional power broker (and the tensions that this assertiveness created in relations with neighbors, not least Pakistan and Sri

Lanka), were met with increasing impatience and frustration by the two superpowers.

India's balancing act

For the better part of the Cold War, India had a close, even intimate, relationship with the Soviet Union. By extension, New Delhi was often on strained terms with the US. That the world's two largest democracies would be at odds, even as Washington managed to get along (although, at times, not without difficulties) with the likes of Pakistan and China, suggests that Indo-US relations were shaped less by intrinsic incompatibilities than by the tides of the global Cold War. For US policy makers, India mattered less than the imperative of containing the Communist threat. Political and military backing of Pakistan seemed like a *sine qua non* of checking Soviet encroachment in South Asia; that such policy strengthened India's principal foe was something that successive US administrations could live with. The same logic worked for the US rapprochement with the People's Republic of China in 1971–1972, an uncomfortable development for the Indians who were weighed down by their own viciously adversarial relationship with Beijing. US support for India's enemies was a consequence of Washington's Cold War strategy. This support itself had the unintended consequence of forcing India to rely more on the Soviet Union, which, in turn, reinforced US apprehension of the growing Soviet menace on the subcontinent.

More by coincidence than design India was caught up between the hammer of US strategic interests and the sickle of Soviet efforts to "save India from the arms of the imperialists." The latter cliché was a favorite of the self-proclaimed pioneer of Soviet–Indian friendship, Nikita Khrushchev. Khrushchev berated his predecessor Joseph Stalin for neglecting India's vast potential. (It is true that Stalin was, basically, ill-informed about India and did not really look that far in his expansionist manipulations in the border areas). But, from the mid-1950s, the Soviet Union offered both economic and military assistance to India; in the course of the 30 years between 1954 and 1983 Soviet credits to India (according to CIA estimates) exceeded $3.2 billion, much of it spent on industrial construction, in particular steel mills and oil refineries.[1] In addition, Moscow offered extensive military aid, helping India maintain a large margin of military superiority over Pakistan. Soviet arms deliveries to India (once again, according to CIA estimates) topped $10 billion dollars by 1987.[2]

Soviet–Indian relations were raised to a new level of trust with the conclusion of the 1971 Treaty of Friendship and Cooperation between Moscow and New Delhi. A falling out between India and the US in the wake of the 1971 Indo-Pakistan War (which ended with the partition of Pakistan), aggravated by a difficult personal relationship between Prime

Minister Indira Gandhi and the Nixon/Kissinger duo, convinced the Soviet leadership that India, for all intents and purposes, and despite continued disagreements on issues like collective security in Asia and nuclear non-proliferation, was a dependable Soviet ally, and a vehicle of Soviet influence within the ranks of the non-aligned movement. Indira Gandhi's fall from power in 1977, a brief rein of the opposition under Morarji Desai and an interregnum under Charan Singh did not occasion any monumental shifts in India's foreign policy, although Desai's (and his foreign minister's Vajpayee's) relatively pro-Western views initially encouraged speculations of a foreseeable improvement in Indo-US relations. It also helped that under President Jimmy Carter, Washington suspended aid to Pakistan because of Islamabad's covert efforts to develop nuclear weapons.[3]

The Soviet invasion of Afghanistan in December 1979 upset the delicate balance of power in the subcontinent. President Reagan's extensive – $2.5 billion – military aid program to Pakistan (including provision of advanced F-16 fighter aircraft) triggered strong protests in New Delhi, which were, characteristically, brushed aside by the Undersecretary of State, James Buckley: "I am not an international psychologist. I honestly do not understand the Indian reaction."[4] This reaction was confidentially elaborated by the one-time head of the Indian Foreign Ministry's Policy Planning Division M. L. Trivedi: China and the US, he said, are supplying Pakistan with weapons including F-16s that can strike India's oil producing regions, the bombing of which could send India back by 100 years.[5] On top of this, New Delhi was increasingly concerned by the developments in Pakistan's nuclear program; the Indian military reportedly considered a strike against Pakistani nuclear facilities patterned after Israel's pre-emptive bombing of an Iraqi reactor in June 1981.[6]

The Indians were worried not only by the prospect of a rearmed Pakistan but also by the symbolism that US weapons transfers represented for the balance of US priorities in South Asia. Indira Gandhi, returned to power in 1980, was no doubt unhappy about the Soviet invasion of Afghanistan (she voiced her reservations repeatedly to Soviet chagrin), for all her supposedly pro-Soviet inclinations. Yet Gandhi's public, even if qualified, acceptance of the Soviet occupation raised the ire of Washington, adding new grievances to a difficult relationship. An Indo-US conflict following India's refusal to permit implementation of IAEA safeguards at its nuclear facilities, and a row over two US companies – Coca-Cola and IBM – quitting the country in protest of government regulations, added to tensions between Washington and New Delhi at the turn of the decade.[7]

However, Indira Gandhi made a conscious effort to steer India towards a more balanced relationship between the Soviet Union and the US. Her July 1982 visit to Washington proved to be a public relations success; Mrs. Gandhi established a personal rapport with Reagan who – contrary to expectations – found her "shy," "warm" and "generous."[8] Gandhi assured

Reagan that "Indians as a whole are neither communist nor pro-communist" and that "friendship with one country [the USSR] does not preclude friendship with any other." The Prime Minister received the promise of US support for India's "independent foreign policy."[9] Substantively, the Indian Prime Minister walked away with an agreement to resolve the long-standing deadlock over US supplies of fuel for the Tarapur nuclear power plant, and to develop science and technology cooperation between India and the US. In May 1984, the US Vice President, George H. W. Bush, visited New Delhi in a bid to take the relationship forward despite continued disagreements over the arming of Pakistan. Bush's visit helped to make progress with the memorandum of understanding on technological cooperation, despite strong resistance to this prospect in certain quarters of the US government (mainly, the Defense Department, which feared leakage of sensitive technologies to the Soviets).[10]

A lot of what transpired between New Delhi and Washington in 1982–1984 was atmospherics, but that was enough to cause serious apprehension in the Soviet Union. Lamenting India's increasing interest in developing ties with the West and especially gaining access to Western technology, the Soviet Ambassador in New Delhi, Vasilii Rykov, complained in May 1982 that "India is not actively supporting our [Soviet] proposals; they only express regret over the severance of links between the USSR and the USA, without saying who is at fault."[11] Some of this was panicky nonsense; a US State Department study concluded in 1983 that in the UN "India sided with the USSR 80 percent of the time, and only 20 percent – with the US."[12] But the Soviets worked hard to prevent what in their imagination was already a rapprochement in the making. In view of India's increasing disillusionment with the prospect for Soviet–Indian economic cooperation, Moscow did not have that much leverage with the Indians, save for oil shipments and the good old instrument of military aid. Indeed, oil and oil products constituted over a half of all Soviet exports to India after 1977 (peaking at 78 percent in 1982), while the bill for Soviet arms transfers to India just for 1982–1987 reached an estimated $6.8 billion.[13]

But, of course, there was no shortage of harebrained schemes in the Kremlin, not when the war in Afghanistan assumed an ominously protracted character. In 1982, for example, the Soviet Ambassador in Kabul, Firkit Tabeev, reportedly proposed to his Indian colleague that India should take advantage of the Soviet Union's presence in Afghanistan to assert control over all of Jammu and Kashmir at Pakistan's expense. Whoever stood behind this probe – the Foreign Ministry, the military or the KGB – it was immensely provocative and exceptionally dangerous for regional stability. It was probably inspired by the Soviet belief that India was on a collision course with Pakistan, and that it would strike as soon as international conditions so permitted.[14] However, Indira Gandhi's foreign policy confidant, G. Parthasarathi, thought that Tabeev had made an "adventurous" proposal, which, if implemented, would not only heighten Indo-Pakistani tensions and cause wide-spread condemnation of India in the West but possibly trigger China's military intervention in Kashmir. Unsurprisingly, the civilian Indian leadership vetoed the idea.[15] Other Soviet probes had better luck: the KGB, for example, was relatively successful in feeding Mrs. Gandhi disinformation about CIA and ISI (Pakistani intelligence) plots against her and her government.[16]

In the early 1980s India's relations with both superpowers effectively stagnated. Divergence of US and Indian strategic interests precluded New Delhi from moving towards qualitatively better relations with Washington. Indian and Soviet regional interests were, by contrast, relatively compatible but Indo-Soviet relations had lost momentum, certainly in large part because Soviet party leaders died one after another at embarrassingly short intervals, leaving no scope for long-term policy planning. In the meantime, India's domestic problems – especially unrest in the Punjab – increasingly commanded Mrs. Gandhi's attention at the expense of foreign policy, which had, basically, succumbed to inertia. It was under these circumstances that Rajiv Gandhi assumed power in November 1984, upon his mother's death at the hands of her Sikh bodyguards.

Soviet–US competition for India

Rajiv Gandhi's emergence as India's leader coincided with Mikhail Gorbachev's assumption of power in the Soviet Union, following the death of the feeble Konstantin Chernenko in March 1985. On March 13 Gorbachev had his first encounter with Rajiv Gandhi at Chernenko's funeral in Moscow. In a gesture full of unmistakable symbolism, Rajiv's delegation was whisked to the front of the line to shake hands even as Gorbachev snubbed the star of the previous Soviet funeral, Margaret Thatcher (the Chinese were also brought forward). Indeed, in foreign relations Gorbachev looked East before he looked West; he looked to India before he looked anywhere else. Closer Soviet–Indian relations were central to Gorbachev's efforts to imbue Soviet foreign policy with a new sense of dynamism and vitality. India would be a part of a new, international, order he had set out to create at the expense of the US. It was, therefore, exceptionally important to maintain and expand the Soviet foothold in India now that Rajiv had taken the reins of power.

The key question for Gorbachev was whether Gandhi was a reliable partner, and how close a partnership he could count upon. The subject came up at a Politburo meeting on 20 March 1986, after the Soviet leader received an invitation from Gandhi to make an official visit to India. "A trip to India," Gorbachev said, "is a good thing ... but a very careful analysis of the situation is needed. So that we don't leave something out or simplify anything." Gorbachev spoke of Rajiv Gandhi's efforts to determine the direction of India's foreign policy. In just over a year since Indira

Gandhi's assassination, it was too early to tell where Rajiv was heading. But, Gorbachev believed, "Rajiv will not begin to dismantle what had been built by his mother unless we, of course, do something stupid." In Gorbachev's view, the new Prime Minister realized very well that he was being courted by the US and the Soviet Union at the same time and he will "use both us and the West in the country's interest." But there was no room for complacency: "there will be a big misbalance if India turned to the West." The bottom line for Soviet policy was, therefore, to act "without imposing ourselves" [nenaviazchivo] because "relations with India cannot depend on anyone's disposition. They have a strategic character." But Gorbachev resolved that he had to visit India before the year was out to keep up the momentum of Soviet–Indian relations.[17]

The element of Soviet competition for Gandhi's loyalty was, thus, most clearly present in Gorbachev's early approaches to India. In fact, this element came out all the more clearly at the first Indo-Soviet summit in Moscow in May 1985, for which detailed transcripts are, unfortunately, lacking. However, we do have Gorbachev's talking points for his meeting with Rajiv on 21 May, which narrow down to a nasty anti-US tirade with a few jabs in the Chinese direction. Washington was condemned for its efforts to control Asia, not so much to oppose socialism, but to secure the region's enormous resources. "The American ruling circles," Gorbachev was expected to say,[18] "would like to turn history backwards, to take 'social revenge.' Therefore, they bid on the arms race, on the military machine, on imposing their will on those countries, which do not want that."[19] Gandhi won Soviet appreciation by criticizing Washington on a wide number of questions, including the deployment of Pershing missiles in Europe and, unsurprisingly, US military aid to Pakistan. Reportedly, he told Gorbachev that while the Indians were no doubt interested in Western technology, they would "never sacrifice their principles for this end."[20]

But there was more to Rajiv's thinking than his assurances would have revealed. The new Prime Minister, like his Soviet counterpart, did not so much have a strategy for what he wanted to accomplish as enthusiasm for what seemed like endless possibilities for rebuilding India's foreign relations. In global terms, this meant a qualitative improvement in relations with both the Soviet Union and the US. Evident willingness of both superpowers to compete for India's loyalty created a positive environment for raising India's international profile and extending its foreign influence and winning the best terms from all contenders. During the banquet at the end of Gandhi's visit, Gorbachev said that "in all spheres of cooperation with India, we, as a friend, share the best of what we have with it."[21] Rajiv's talks in Moscow proved that much. The General Secretary of the Congress Party Shrikant Verma commented, in the wake of the Prime Minister's visit, that India "got practically everything from the USSR it asked for."[22]

It is interesting to compare these statements to what Rajiv Gandhi heard from US President Ronald Reagan, whom he saw only a few days after that meeting with Gorbachev. The President went into great detail about Soviet savagery in Afghanistan, recounting the story of an arrested doctor who was "subjected to numerous tortures, including being made to watch as the eyes of a captured Afghan freedom-fighter were plucked out and set on the table in front of her." Gandhi responded that he was appalled by the report and Reagan pressed on, telling how Soviet soldiers were being told "to kill women and children." The President went on to discuss Soviet resistance to disarmament, how they have been "deeply suspicious throughout their history. They have had an abiding fear of foreign domination, and yet it's the Soviets who dominate in so many places." Then, responding to Gandhi's complaints about Pakistan, Reagan promised to do everything possible "to ease those strains."[23] For his part, Gandhi, reportedly, assured Reagan that "India does not want the Soviet U[nion] to have a foothold anywhere in S[outh] Asia" (of course, he could well have said the same thing about the US – in both cases, with complete sincerity).[24]

Nevertheless, Indo-US relations were clearly on an upward curve. Reagan wanted to capitalize on Rajiv's obvious interest in expanding economic and military cooperation with the US. In May 1985, the US indicated willingness to work with India in the production of light combat aircraft. Up to that point, military cooperation between India and the US had been virtually non-existent (since the US suspended military aid to India in 1965), in part because Washington felt uneasy about arming a potential Soviet ally, and in part because the Indians themselves felt uncomfortable about US weaponry because "sooner or later it would end in blackmail."[25] This was one of the reasons for India's backing out of discussions with the US, in the early 1980s, on the procurement of 155mm howitzers and anti-tank missiles.[26] This time, New Delhi thought differently. Despite Rajiv Gandhi's reservations – "We'll have to see exactly what the small print is" – India and the US concluded an agreement in January 1987 on the provision of 11 General Electric jet engines for the aircraft-in-the-making, an agreement widely heralded as a breakthrough for Indo-US military relations.[27]

Also, in May 1985, Washington and New Delhi had agreed on the implementation of a "memorandum of understanding" on technical cooperation, opening a way to US computer exports to India. The highlight of this arrangement was the proposed US sale of a Cray XMP-24 supercomputer to India for weather-related research. That such a sale was discussed at all was a sign of hitherto unseen US eagerness to woo India from the Soviets who were not in a position to provide anything remotely as powerful. In fact, XMP-24 was so powerful that, apart from being used for weather-related research, it could help the Indians with nuclear and ballistic missile research, and with cryptography. Concerned that US confidence in India had exceeded comfortable levels, thanks to the enthusiasm of the

State and the Commerce Departments, Reagan backed out of the XMP-24 sale, proposing, instead, to sell a less powerful supercomputer, an XMP-14 model. The Indians were, predictably, outraged. On the whole, Indo-US relations, after seemingly gaining momentum 1984 onwards, began to run out of steam towards 1987, although it is fair to say that economic relations widened and prospered.

India and its neighbors

Reagan's unease about the depth of Indo-US cooperation gave an opening to Gorbachev. Between 1985 and 1987 he made a major effort to upgrade the Soviet relationship with India by supporting Rajiv's regional policies. The circumstances were favorable for Soviet posturing as the true friend of India, especially with regard to the intractable problem of Sri Lanka. Moscow had a problem-free record in Sri Lanka, unlike its archrival Washington, whom the Indians suspected of duplicity and subversion on the Tamil question. In the early 1980s New Delhi, which viewed Sri Lanka as lying squarely within its sphere of influence, watched Colombo's foreign policy with increasing unease as Sri Lankan President J. R. Jayewardene extended friendly feelers to the US, China, Pakistan, and even Israel. Indian-Sri Lankan tensions came to a head after the July 1983 ethnic riots in Sri Lanka, which set in motion the island's rapid decline into a brutal civil war. New Delhi, under pressure from Tamil constituencies in the southeast, looked the other way when the Tamil Tigers sought shelter and support in India's province of Tamil Nadu. Nevertheless, India tried to mediate in the conflict, no doubt with an eye to excluding any other potential mediators or foreign supporters to whom Colombo may have turned. In fact, the Indians exaggerated Jayewardene's chances of finding reliable friends in faraway quarters.[28]

Yet the Soviet leader, predictably, blamed the problems in Sri Lanka on the US. "Look at the conglomerate of countries which has been pulled into Sri Lanka's problems," he told Indian Foreign Minister Shiv Shankar, on 14 June 1986:

> And the spring here is the United States. Neither Pakistan, nor Israel, nor South Africa could do anything without encouragement on the part of the United States. The political conductor here is the United States, and the helper to the conductor is Great Britain.

The conflagration in Sri Lanka, Gorbachev reasoned, was a US ploy intended to "put India under political pressure, create tension in the Indian society, undermine the Prime Minister's personal authority." By contrast, the Soviet Union had a great respect for India's independence:

> Such a huge and ancient country as India, which has a huge experience of struggle for independence, which enjoys universal recognition

as an influential force in world politics, [cannot] become someone's satellite. This is reality and this is the point of departure for us.[29]

These views had a ring of truth to Rajiv Gandhi's ear, especially as the Sri Lankan situation went from bad to worse in early 1987, and the government launched a new offensive against the Tamil rebels in the north. By June 1987 the Tamils seemed to be on the verge of annihilation. Faced with the prospect of the collapse of the insurgency, Rajiv Gandhi, unwisely, authorized an airdrop of supplies from India to the Jaffna peninsula. Colombo protested bitterly – but so did all of India's neighbors who, far from appreciating Rajiv's proclaimed humanitarian motives (the Sri Lankan offensive had left the population of Jaffna in desperate straits), claimed that India's action was a blatant act of gunboat diplomacy. Gandhi's standing in the eyes of US policy makers slipped considerably. The *New York Times* lamented: "Where is the calm, good-humored and conciliatory Rajiv Gandhi who so impressed the world a year ago?"[30]

Under these circumstances, Soviet support was essential to the Indian Prime Minister. On 2 July 1987 Gandhi and Gorbachev had a most telling exchange:

RAJIV GANDHI: [...] [Sri Lanka] has long been friends with the Americans. I have in mind calls by the American Navy, visits by highly placed American military officials. Sri Lankans have relations of military character with Pakistan. We suppose that the Americans want to obtain a base in Trinkomali. So far we have been able to apply sufficient pressure so that Sri Lanka does not agree to this. But in recent months, the leadership of Sri Lanka has come closer and closer to Pakistan and the USA. They may even sign treaties with these two countries. I have an impression that the United States will not want to act in too obvious a manner there. Perhaps, under some exceptional circumstances they will send ships from the 6th or the 7th fleet. But if they see that the conflict gets worse, the United States will not want to be pulled into military action.

M. S. GORBACHEV: Yes, the Americans are afraid of this.

RAJIV GANDHI: The US does not like it when Americans get killed.[31]

For the time being, Rajiv thought that his gamble had paid off. In July 1987 Sri Lanka and India reached an agreement to pave way for a peaceful settlement of the ethnic conflict on the island. This agreement resulted in the deployment of an Indian Peace-Keeping Force in Sri Lanka, which, before long, found itself embroiled in counter-insurgency warfare against the Tamils. Rajiv, who was increasingly bogged down by domestic unrest and corruption allegations, now found himself stuck in a quagmire in a neighboring nation, which would last for more than two years. Reflecting upon his woes in Sri Lanka, in March 1989, Gandhi criticized the US,

Pakistan, Israel and South Africa for supposed meddling in the island's affairs but defended his decision to send troops:

> It was an expensive measure on our part to send troops to Sri Lanka. Even so, if we think about the danger from the gathering of the evil forces, which had threatened our security [in Sri Lanka?], the decision to send troops was a correct one.[32]

There was a tinge of paranoia in Rajiv's words about the evil forces. In any case, India's military intervention in Sri Lanka was one of the worst foreign policy blunders of his administration. It also cost Rajiv his life – in May 1991 he was killed by a Tamil Tiger suicide bomber for his role in the intervention.

If, in relations with Sri Lanka, Gandhi could count on unequivocal Soviet support, with regard to Pakistan he found himself outpaced by events and practically abandoned by the Soviets by 1988–1989. Commonality of Indian and Soviet interests with regard to Pakistan had been one of the strategic pillars of their relationship, especially after the Soviet invasion of Afghanistan. As Gorbachev put it, "In our actions, we will take as our point of departure our common interests, common striving towards ruining Pakistan's plans, directed against the Soviet Union and India." This was a far stronger message to the Indians than Reagan's vague promise to "ease strains" in Indo-Pakistani relations. For as long as tensions plagued Soviet relations with Pakistan (and no improvement could be expected in this respect for as long as Soviet troops remained in Afghanistan), Gandhi could count on Gorbachev's unwavering support – something he could never expect to get from the US.[33]

The big question was whether a quasi-alliance with India, envisioned by Gorbachev, could put undesirable constraints on the foreign policy of the Soviet Union or possibly commit it to support India to the detriment of Soviet interests in the region. Anatolii Dobrynin, former Soviet Ambassador to the US who had taken over the International Department in the Central Committee in 1986, cautioned Gorbachev to keep an eye on Indo-Pakistani relations: "India is preparing its own nuclear bomb ... Some circles do not rule out a preventive strike against Pakistan." Gorbachev responded that Gandhi "understands the consequences."[34] Yet, what would the Soviet Union do about another Indo-Pakistani conflict, especially at a time when Gorbachev tried hard to project a peace-loving image in foreign affairs in the context of "new thinking"? The contradiction between a Soviet–Indian alliance and the broader goals of Gorbachev's foreign policy were already present if not yet fully evident to all, including the Soviet leader. Indeed, his hope for closer relations with India was premised on the understanding that Rajiv Gandhi would opt for compromise and negotiations with his neighbors, first and foremost Pakistan.

It did not take long before this theoretical dilemma created complications for day-to-day Soviet policy. The occasion was a new flare-up along the India-Pakistan border in January 1987. Tensions had been growing since November 1986, when the Indian Army carried out exercises along the border. In December Islamabad responded with a build-up of its own, and on 23 January Rajiv Gandhi placed the Indian army on highest alert and closed the border with Pakistan as the Indian press prophesied an inevitable war. Observers disagreed about the causes of the latest crisis, with some speculating that Gandhi meant to put pressure on Pakistan to dissuade it from procuring the latest military technology from the US, and others suggesting that Rajiv was responding to mounting domestic pressures over unrest in the province of Punjab.[35]

Gandhi later explained his actions with reference to Pakistan's intentions in the Punjab. "It is quite possible that if we did not deploy our forces, the Pakistanis would be able to quickly grab a piece of our territory, proclaim 'Khalistan' there, and hand it over to the Sikhs," he said, pointing out that the Indian army was "itching" to turn the situation to its advantage and "cut Sindh from Punjab." According to Rajiv, only New Delhi's peace-loving attitude prevented this lamentable (for Pakistan) scenario.[36] In any case, the state of Soviet–Indian relations left Moscow with few options but to support India's cause in cautiously phrased TASS reports.

But there was much more to the Soviet reaction than TASS reports could tell. On 24 January Anatolii Cherniaev addressed the problem in a memorandum to Gorbachev. He had an impression that

> R. Gandhi (or his circle) want to "make a little war" or something like this in order to "unite the nation" and fix [their] domestic problems. Willingly or unwillingly on his part, but it turns out that India is exploiting its friendship with us for this purpose. We can end up in an awkward situation because the whole world will see that it was not Pakistan that unleashed a military clash.

Cherniaev added that sending a protest to Pakistan – this had been decided at a recent Politburo meeting – was a "necessary measure." However, he felt that it was also necessary to send an intelligence report to New Delhi to the effect that "our information on the military activities and intentions in the ruling circles of Pakistan do not lead to a conclusion that [they are] preparing an invasion of India's territory."[37] One-sided condemnation of Pakistan, Cherniaev argued, was "not profitable" to the Soviet Union from the perspective of achieving a settlement in Afghanistan, where, as Gorbachev well recognized, Pakistan was bound to play a major role.[38] Such, then, was the "interconnection" of things, to use Gorbachev's favorite word: Soviet regional priorities – in particular, pull-out from Afghanistan, which was really the key priority – required careful maneuvering to win over Pakistan, the US, even the Chinese.

Unequivocal support for India in its long-running feud with Pakistan did nothing to help the Soviet situation. Gorbachev saw the contradiction and urged, at a Politburo meeting on 26 February, to "remove Rajiv Gandhi's concern about Pakistan," admittedly something easier said than done.[39] In his own meeting with the Indian leader in July 1987 (it was Rajiv's third visit to Moscow in just over two years), Gorbachev dwelled on the prospect of peace talks between India and Pakistan a la Tashkent in 1966:

> At one moment, in a concrete historical situation [in 1966] such a trilateral meeting of the leaders of the Soviet Union, India and Pakistan was held. Perhaps, time will come when it will be appropriate to repeat such a meeting, keeping in mind, of course, other, new tasks. I think we should not discount this idea.

Gandhi said he tried to improve relations with Pakistan "but the problem is that they talk a lot and when it comes to doing something, [they] don't do anything good."[40]

But, in the following months, the Soviet Union moved a long way towards a better relationship with Pakistan. The main reason was, of course, the urgency of the Afghan settlement. Soviet withdrawal from Afghanistan (and the Geneva Accords with a timetable for the pull-out were signed in April 1988) left the war-torn country at the mercy of the mujahadeen who, even if they were not controlled by Islamabad, could at least be influenced by Islamabad. So Pakistani cooperation was essential if the Soviets were not to suffer a complete defeat in Afghanistan. Indications from Islamabad, in turn, suggested Pakistani interest in improving relations with the Soviet Union. As Gorbachev's close ally Aleksandr Iakovlev commented at the Politburo in February 1988,

> there are forces in Pakistan who understand that they cannot live under the American wing forever, especially that there is India here on one side, and the Soviet Union on the other, and they [the Pakistanis] need a buffer state, well disposed towards them, and they do not want a regime hostile to them.[41]

Time proved Iakovlev right: by February 1989, when the Soviet Foreign Minister, Eduard Shevardnadze, visited Islamabad, "Pakistani leaders at all levels insistently emphasized their country's interest in intensifying relations with the USSR, widening and deepening Soviet–Pakistani cooperation in all spheres."[42] In other words, by the late 1980s, there was no longer much scope for Indo-Soviet cooperation at Pakistan's expense or even for tolerating any hints of a regional anti-Pakistan combination involving the Soviet Union. Reflective of this change was Gorbachev's reaction to the Afghan leader Najibullah's proposal, in June 1988, "to organize a joint war: USSR-India-Afghanistan against Pakistan." "M. S. [Gorbachev] rebuffed him pretty bluntly," recorded Cherniaev.[43] Given that only a few years earlier a similar proposal came from the Soviet Ambassador in Afghanistan, the dramatic turn-about in the Soviet Union's South Asia policy had to be obvious to Najibullah. Rajiv Gandhi had noticed, too.

Rajiv's own efforts to match Soviet achievements with Pakistan by and large failed. After the 1987 war-scare, Indo-Pakistani relations appeared to change for better in 1988, in large part because of the visible democratic advance in Pakistan occasioned by the death of President Zia ul-Haq and the election of Benazir Bhutto as Prime Minister. In July 1989 Rajiv went to Islamabad amid high expectations in both countries that Gandhi and Bhutto, a new generation of leaders who had no direct experience of the partition, could somehow close the page on decades of rivalry. In particular, Bhutto expected Indian concessions on Jammu and Kashmir, but to no avail – Rajiv took a hard line. As Indian diplomat J. N. Dixit argues, "Benazir was bitterly disappointed and took great umbrage at being thwarted in her expectations which, in any case, were unrealistic."[44]

Rajiv was equally disappointed. Although she may have been well-intentioned, Rajiv noted in March 1989, "in order to become the Prime Minister she made a lot of concessions to the Americans, the Pakistan military and the President, and to the intelligence. All of this limits her ability to work freely."[45] In a meeting with Gorbachev a few months later, Rajiv illustrated his views about Bhutto with a specific example:

> By the way, when in December [1988] I talked to her in Islamabad, and the conversation touched on sensitive subjects, she did not speak but wrote notes and handed them to me. I answered her in a similar manner. And all of this was in her office.[46]

Soon after his return from the July 1989 summit with Bhutto, Rajiv Gandhi was swept up in the electoral frenzy, which took the wind out of his Pakistan policy. In the meantime, the situation in Kashmir seriously deteriorated, marked by an increase in secessionist activities and terrorism, mostly – the Indians claimed – inspired by the ISI with Bhutto's quiet agreement. Rajiv's appraisal of the situation, in December 1989, was that India had not done enough to crush separatism in Kashmir and Punjab – it was a fitting, if ironic, postscript to five years of Gandhi's futile efforts to arrive at a settlement with Pakistan.[47]

Nothing shows better Rajiv's loss of touch in foreign policy than his approach to the settlement in Afghanistan in 1988–1989. Although New Delhi disliked the Soviet invasion, Gorbachev's resolve in seeking a political settlement left the Indians with a dilemma. The biggest problem was that India was not a part of a major international settlement within its sphere of interest, while Pakistan was. The exclusive nature of the April

1988 Geneva Accords dealt a serious blow to Rajiv Gandhi's efforts to project the image of India's regional and global indispensability as a great power and a broker between the East and the West. The other major problem with the Soviet military withdrawal, from New Delhi's perspective, was that its most likely result would be the creation of a fundamentalist Afghanistan, courtesy of the ISI. This was also unacceptable to Rajiv.

In a conversation with Gorbachev in July 1987 Rajiv argued that "if Afghanistan becomes a fundamentalist country or if the Americans have a strong influence there, like in Pakistan, Afghanistan will not be a truly independent country, and this will create problems for us."[48] Reflecting on these comments days later, Gorbachev told the Afghan leader, Najibullah, that, in his view, Indians do not truly want a Soviet withdrawal from Afghanistan.

> The Indians are concerned that a normalization of the situation in Afghanistan will result in Pakistan directing its subversive activities against India. [...] But this [Rajiv's] position takes only India's interest into account 100 percent while the interests of Afghanistan and the Soviet Union are a mere 20 percent.[49]

Seeing that a political settlement was inevitable, New Delhi lobbied the Soviets to, at least, include provisions for constraining Pakistan, for example, by forcing Islamabad to scrap the stockpiles of weapons intended for the mujahadeen (but certainly usable against India). India's Defense Minister, K. Ch. Pant, worried that if terrorists got their hands on the US-supplied "stingers" and used them against civilian (presumably Indian) aircraft, "there would be chaos."[50] But the Soviet leader turned down this linkage, because he feared that Soviet insistence on the disarmament of Pakistan would come back to haunt the Soviets in the form of US demands that they do the same with respect to Najibullah's government in Kabul. By early 1989 Rajiv, having been sidelined in the Afghanistan settlement, was at pains to come up with a way to seize the initiative in the solution to outstanding problems in the subcontinent. Yet he did not appear to have an overall strategy, save for fantasizing about the prospects of a joint Afghan-Indian war on Pakistan, which would be unleashed in case Islamabad dared to use force to topple the Najibullah regime. Mongolia's President, Jambyn Batmünkh, with whom Rajiv shared his views, was so taken aback that he even asked the Prime Minister to repeat himself, for fear that something had been lost in translation. Rajiv Gandhi reiterated his readiness to intervene to save Najibullah from Pakistani aggression.[51]

Conclusion

Rajiv Gandhi's defeat in the November 1989 elections brought an end to his five-year effort to reshape India's foreign relations. He was deeply dissatisfied with where India was heading:

the new government [headed by Rajiv's fierce critic V. P. Singh] has not put forward a clear concept to develop the country. [...] Most importantly, it is necessary to give an answer to the question of whether India can keep pace with the changes that are now happening in the world.[52]

Rajiv had thought he had an answer. Five years earlier he had taken the reins of power to lead India towards a greater role in a refashioned world order. It was not very clear to him what this new world order would look like but Rajiv felt that the US was an obstacle one way or another. "One can feel a feudal, colonial approach on their part – they cannot depart from it," he cautioned Gorbachev in 1989:

> There will be a very difficult period when they see that everything is changing in the world, and they are unable to prevent it. And if they do not understand that it is necessary to change their patterns of behavior, we will all suffer.[53]

In Rajiv's view, the Soviet–Indian relationship could become the cornerstone of this new world order. For this reason, he was keen to develop relations with Gorbachev early in his tenure. "Not everyone likes the Soviet–Indian friendship," he reasoned, "because it shows that so called international rules of the game can be changed."[54] Early on, Gorbachev concurred. His equal enthusiasm for a new world order found expression in a declaration, signed in the wake of his visit to New Delhi in November 1986, which called for nuclear disarmament, one imperative he and Gandhi could easily agree upon. But it did not take long for the Soviet leader to see that Rajiv was not interested in playing second fiddle to Gorbachev's in his grand schemes, not least his sweeping initiatives for collective security in Asia. Gorbachev came to realize that

> in India, we are faced with a great power policy. At the same time, [they] understand that they cannot implement it without us and that we do not want "to give them the leading role." There is a nuance here, and we sense it. India wants for everyone to "rotate" around it: Burma, Bangladesh, Sri Lanka, Maldives etc. In other words, it wants to have a "patrimony" with vassals in this region. That's why it is not reacting well to our initiatives about naval disarmament in the Indian Ocean.[55]

For once, the General Secretary's assessment was basically on target.

By 1990 Soviet–Indian relations were limping along, rapidly losing momentum. Anatolii Cherniaev captured the spirit of the times in a thoughtful observation in his diary (July 1990):

> How many solemn words were uttered! And M. S. [Gorbachev] sincerely believed that things will go forward with "great India." Nothing

> happened. In economic relations – everything is as it was, and we are cutting back military [ties] ... This was not the main direction.[56]

Much worse was to come. By 1991 trade relations between the Soviet Union and India had shrunk from $5 billion to $3.4 billion, and that was reduced to $1.2 billion by 1992. Military cooperation had reached a dismal level. Political relations were plagued by a series of scandals – from the Russian leadership implicitly endorsing Pakistan's territorial claims against India to bitter disagreements over exchange rates and who owed what to whom.[57]

For all the momentum in Soviet–Indian relations in 1986–1987, Moscow and New Delhi pursued increasingly different agendas. Gandhi was interested in developing India's regional hegemony, primarily at Pakistan's expense. He needed Soviet political endorsement in this task, as well as Soviet weapons. But Moscow's key interest was in ending hostilities in Afghanistan, and that, in turn, required improvement in Soviet–Pakistani relations. Provided that Rajiv Gandhi was also moving towards rapprochement with Islamabad, Soviet policy towards Pakistan need not have caused any friction for Soviet–Indian relations. However, in practice, policy trajectories in Moscow and in New Delhi frequently diverged. At a more fundamental level, shifts in Soviet foreign policy since Reykjavik – Gorbachev's peace offensive and his increasing engagement with the West – soon began to contradict the logic of closer Soviet–Indian relations. After all, these relations were originally premised, basically, on anti-US assumptions.

When Rajiv Gandhi formed his government in 1984, improvement of relations with the US was quite high on his agenda. Access to US technology was an important consideration underpinning his policy but the bigger idea was to increase India's international leverage by projecting an image of true non-alignment. This effort appeared to bear fruit but New Delhi and Washington failed to achieve a genuine rapprochement. This was not Rajiv's fault even though Gorbachev, for his part, tried hard to fuel Gandhi's resentment of the US by means of occasional disinformation about CIA plots against him. The key obstacle to better relations was in Washington, where strategic imperatives of an anti-Soviet nature and deeply felt, if misplaced, suspicions that India was merely a Soviet pawn, continued to influence policy making in ways highly unfavorable to India. By the late 1980s, however, far from failing to realize the changes unfolding in the world, the White House was riding those changes. With the Afghanistan problem out of the way, India lost relevance for Washington; its sights were upon events in Europe and, to a lesser degree, in China.

Rajiv Gandhi set out to change India's foreign policy course: to improve its battered standing in the eyes of other regional players; to reshape India's relations with the superpowers; to recast the international order itself – a moral imperative to which, in his view, India had much to contribute. Unfortunately, Rajiv's great hopes were not realized. As he stood down from power in late 1989, India's relations with its neighbors (with the important exception of

China) were as bad as ever and, in the global setting, India was sidelined and marginalized as the two superpowers were coming to terms, as their bitter competition died away at last. The international order changed, for sure, but it changed in spite of, rather than because of, India's efforts, and these changes were not at all what Rajiv Gandhi had had in mind. Much of India's familiar world crumbled around it as the Cold War came to an end. Two decades later, India has still to find a role comparable to what it once had as the soul of non-alignment and the broker between East and West.

Notes

1 "Communist military transfers and economic aid to non-communist less developed countries,1984," 1 May 1985, p. 89. CIA FOIA online reading room.
2 DCI, "Soviet Foreign Military Assistance," Interagency Intelligence Memorandum, 1 May 1987, p. 42. CIA FOIA online reading room.
3 Dennis Kux, *India and the United States: Estranged Democracies* (Washington, DC: National Defense University Press, 1993), pp. 347–62.
4 Ibid., p. 383.
5 "The Hungarian Embassy in Ulan Bator to the Foreign Ministry: Indian Diplomat on Indo-Soviet relations," 17 August 1983. Hungarian National Archives (MOL), XIX-J-1-j, India, Top Secret Documents, 1983 60. doboz, 004736/1983. Obtained, translated and kindly provided to the author by László Borhi. Courtesy of the Parallel History Project.
6 "Report by the Hungarian Embassy in New Delhi – Confidential Soviet Information on India's Plan to Attack Pakistan's Nuclear Facilities," 19 January 1982. MOL, XIX-J-1-j, India, Top Secret Documents, 1982 60. doboz, 00599/1982. Obtained, translated and kindly provided to the author by László Borhi. Courtesy of the Parallel History Project.
7 Dennis Kux, *India and the United States: Estranged Democracies*, pp. 363–74.
8 Douglas Brinkley (ed.), *The Reagan Diaries* (New York: Harper Collins, 2007), p. 97.
9 "Visit of Indian Prime Minister Indira Gandhi," Cable from Secretary of State to select US embassies overseas, 2 August 1982 (?). National Security Archive, Washington, DC.
10 Dennis Kux, *India and the United States: Estranged Democracies*, pp. 391–8.
11 "Sotsialist orny elchin said naryn zuvlulguunii tukhai" [About a meeting of ambassadors of socialist countries], 13 June 1984. Mongolian Foreign Ministry Archive: F. 13, kh/n 197, khuu 85.
12 Dennis Kux, *India and the United States: Estranged Democracies*, p. 397.
13 Peter J. S. Duncan, *The Soviet Union and India* (London: Routledge, 1989), p. 74. DCI, "Soviet Foreign Military Assistance," Interagency Intelligence Memorandum, 1 May 1987, p. 42. CIA FOIA online reading room.
14 "Report by the Hungarian Embassy in New Delhi – Confidential Soviet Information on India's Plan to Attack Pakistan's Nuclear Facilities," 19 January 1982. MOL: Küm, India tük 1982 60. doboz, 00599. Obtained, translated and kindly provided to the author by László Borhi. Courtesy of the Parallel History Project.
15 J. N. Dixit, *Across Borders: 50 Years of India's Foreign Policy* (New Delhi: Picus Books, 1998), pp. 156–7. According to Soviet information, the idea of going to war with Pakistan appealed in particular to the Indian military; the Foreign Ministry had a different opinion. "Report by the Hungarian Embassy in New Delhi – Confidential Soviet Information on India's Plan to Attack Pakistan's Nuclear Facilities," 19 January 1982.

16 Christopher Andrew and Vasili Mitrokhin, *The World Was Going Our Way*, pp. 336–9.
17 Mikhail Gorbachev, *Sobranie Sochinenii*, Vol. 3 (Moscow: Ves' Mir, 2008), p. 463.
18 In fact, there are very strong indications that these "talking points" (called thus for convenience in this chapter) were a part of Gorbachev's verbatim statement to Rajiv Gandhi; on later occasions, Gorbachev referred to specific phrases, which appear on the talking points, as to what he had actually told Gandhi.
19 "Sovetsko-Indiiskie otnosheniia," 21 May 1985, Archive of the Gorbachev Foundation (AGF), F. 3, Document 4766.
20 "The Hungarian Embassy in New Delhi to the Foreign Ministry: Soviet Appraisal of Gandhi's Visit to Moscow," 18 June 1985. MOL, XIX-J-1-j India, Top Secret Documents, 1985, 67. doboz, 003197/1985. Obtained, translated and kindly provided to the author by László Borhi. Courtesy of the Parallel History Project.
21 Mikhail Gorbachev, *Sobranie Sochinenii*, Vol. 2 (Moscow: Ves' Mir, 2008), p. 278.
22 "The Hungarian Embassy in New Delhi to the Foreign Ministry: The General Secretary of the Congress Party (Srikan Verma) on Indo-Soviet Relations," 28 June 1985. MOL XIX-J-1-j India, Top Secret Documents. doboz, 001411/2. Obtained, translated and kindly provided to the author by László Borhi. Courtesy of the Parallel History Project.
23 Conversation between Ronald Reagan and Rajiv Gandhi, 12 June 1985. National Security Archive, Washington DC.
24 Rajiv Gandhi's comments in the conversation with Gandhi were heavily redacted from the available transcript. Reagan made the latter observation in his diary following his meeting with Gandhi. D. Brinkley (ed.), *The Reagan Diaries*, p. 334.
25 "The Hungarian Embassy in New Delhi to the Foreign Ministry: The General Secretary of the Congress Party (Shrikant Verma) on Indo-Soviet Relations," 28 June 1985.
26 Dennis Kux, *India and the United States: Estranged Democracies*, p. 394.
27 Stuart Auerbach, "Gandhi hits US 'Soft Line' on Pakistan," *Washington Post*, 5 June 1985, p. A25; Stuart Auerbach, "India Signs Agreement For US Jet Engines," *Washington Post*, 7 January 1987, p. A16.
28 For a useful overview, see J. Gooneratne, *A Decade of Confrontation: Sri Lanka and India in the 1980s* (Pannipitiya: Stamford Lake, 2000) and A. J. Bullion, *India, Sri Lanka & the Tamil Crisis, 1976–1994: an International Perspective* (London: Pinter, 1995).
29 Mikhail Gorbachev, *Sobranie Sochinenii*, Vol. 4 (Moscow: Ves' Mir, 2008), pp. 167–8.
30 "Mr. Gandhi, on Four Fronts," *New York Times*, 7 June 1987, p. 28.
31 Conversation between Mikhail Gorbachev and Rajiv Gandhi, 3 July 1987. National Security Archive, Washington, DC, Russian and Eastern European Archival Database (REEAD), Box 15.
32 Conversation between Rajiv Gandhi and Jambyn Batmünkh, 7 March 1989. Mongolian Foreign Ministry Archive, F. 13, kh/n 219, khuu 48.
33 Mikhail Gorbachev, *Sobranie Sochinenii*, Vol. 4 (Moscow: Ves' Mir, 2008), pp. 169–70.
34 Anatolii Cherniaev *et al.* (eds.), *V Politbiuro TsK KPSS*, (Moscow: Al'pina Biznes Buks, 2006) pp. 114–16.
35 Sanjoy Hazarika, "India puts military on full alert, citing a Pakistani troop buildup," *New York Times*, 24 January 1987, p. 4; Gordon Barthos, "India, Pakistan troop buildup climaxes months of hostility," *The Toronto Star*, 27 January 1987, p. A13.
36 Conversation between Mikhail Gorbachev and Rajiv Gandhi, 3 July 1987, National Security Archive, REEAD, Box 15.
37 Memorandum from Anatolii Cherniaev to Mikhail Gorbachev, 24 January 1987, AGF, F. 2, Document 503.

38 Anatolii Cherniaev *et al.* (eds.), *V Politbiuro TsK KPSS*, p. 138.
39 Ibid., p. 152.
40 Conversation between Mikhail Gorbachev and Rajiv Gandhi, 2–3 July 1987, National Security Archive, REEAD, Box 15.
41 Aleksandr Iakovlev (ed.), *Perestroika: 1985–1991* (Moscow: Mezhdunarodnyi Fond Demokratiia, 2008), p. 180.
42 "Ob itogakh ofitsial'nogo vizita v Kitai i rabochego vizita v Pakistan E. A. Shevardnadze," (undated, 1989), MOL: XIX-J-1-j-Soviet Union, Top Secret Documents, 1989, 146. doboz, 0037/1/1989. The author is grateful to Peter Vamos for providing a copy of this document.
43 Entry for 19 June 1988, Anatolii Cherniaev's diary, National Security Archive. Translated by Svetlana Savranskaya.
44 J. N. Dixit, *Across Borders: 50 Years of India's Foreign Policy*, p. 199.
45 Conversation between Rajiv Gandhi and Jambyn Batmünkh, 7 March 1989. Mongolian Foreign Ministry Archive, F. 13, kh/n 219, khuu 48.
46 Conversation between Mikhail Gorbachev and Rajiv Gandhi, 15 July 1989. National Security Archive, REEAD, Box 16.
47 Conversation between D. Chuluundorj and Rajiv Gandhi, 19 December 1989. Mongolian Foreign Ministry Archive, F. 13, kh/n 223, khuu 48.
48 Conversation between Mikhail Gorbachev and Rajiv Gandhi, 3 July 1987. National Security Archive, REEAD, Box 15.
49 Conversation between Mikhail Gorbachev and Najibullah, 20 July 1987. National Security Archive, REEAD, Box 15.
50 Conversation between Mikhail Gorbachev and K. Ch. Pant, 11 February 1988. National Security Archive, REEAD, Box 15.
51 Conversation between Rajiv Gandhi and Jambyn Batmünkh, 7 March 1989. Mongolian Foreign Ministry Archive, F. 13, kh/n 219, khuu 48.
52 Conversation between D. Chuluundorj and Rajiv Gandhi, 19 December 1989. Mongolian Foreign Ministry Archive, F. 13, kh/n 223, khuu 48.
53 Conversation between Mikhail Gorbachev and Rajiv Gandhi, 15 July 1989. National Security Archive, REEAD, Box 16.
54 Conversation between Mikhail Gorbachev and Rajiv Gandhi, 3 July 1987. National Security Archive, REEAD, Box 15.
55 Anatolii Cherniaev *et al.* (eds.), *V Politbiuro TsK KPSS*, pp. 420–2.
56 Anatolii Cherniaev, *Sovmestnyi Iskhod: Dnevnik Dvukh Epokh, 1972–1991 gody* (Moscow: Rosspen, 2008), p. 865.
57 S. Lunev, "Rossiisko-Indiiskie otnosheniia v 90-e gody" in A. Kutsenkov & F. Iurlov (eds.), *Rossi'ia i Indi'ia na Poroge Tret'ego Tysiacheleti'ia* (Moscow: IDV RAN, 1998), pp. 30–2.

8 Nicaragua, Chile and the end of the Cold War in Latin America

Victor Figueroa Clark

In March 1988 Alfonso Castro was part of a column of Sandinista troops ambushed by Contras in the north of Nicaragua. For what seemed like an eternity he lay behind a small tree stump as a Contra sniper repeatedly tried to hit him. In an interview in July 2009 Alfonso confessed that this was the most terrifying experience of his life. Alfonso is Chilean, born and bred in Santiago; he had reached adulthood under the Pinochet dictatorship, taking part in demonstrations and participating in the activities of the Chilean Communist Party Youth. He had left Chile in 1983, was recruited to the Communist Party's "military task" which led him to the Antonio Maceo infantry officers academy in Cuba, and then, upon graduation in 1987, to Nicaragua, where he joined the Juan Pablo Umanzor Battalion of the Sandinista Popular Army (EPS by its Spanish acronym). It was as part of this battalion that Alfonso took part in some of the heaviest fighting of the Contra war in Nicaragua.[1] How did Alfonso, and many others like him, come to fight for the Sandinistas in Nicaragua? What, if anything, linked the processes in Chile and Nicaragua? What do they reveal about the nature of the final years of the Cold War in Latin America?

Geopolitical, economic and political factors made the Cold War in Latin America different from elsewhere, although it did contain some obvious similarities, with elite concerns over "internal" subversion and US support for "stability" and authoritarian, and US-friendly governments. There was no Soviet military presence in the region, with the exception of Cuba, and this meant that for the rest of Latin America the Cold War was, in essence, a regional phenomenon, and Soviet influence was fundamentally ideological. Marxist ideas had arrived in Latin America during the nineteenth century, and provided a framework for understanding and critiquing the region's place in the hemispheric system, and the justification for changing it.[2] During the twentieth century these ideas and their practical application in the Soviet Union, and by national liberation struggles around the world, influenced many and, in some countries, resulted in strong Left-wing movements which took the ideological message of socialism and made it their own. These ideas threatened both the pre-eminent position of local elites and, through their anti-imperialist message, the dominance of the US which had always regarded Latin America as an ideological, economic and political "backyard."

The Latin American Cold War was characterized by internal class conflicts that occurred within the framework of a global confrontation between capitalism and socialism. These class conflicts matched elites tied to the regional and hemispheric socio-economic order against societies that were undergoing structural changes as a result of gradual economic modernization which was creating ever-greater inequalities that exacerbated class, ethnic and cultural conflicts.[3] Superimposed upon this were the geopolitical and ideological interests of the US, as sponsor, guarantor and dependant of this international system and the history of relations between the US and Latin America. This history, marked by US occupations and interventions in Mexico, Central America and the Caribbean, was one of the causes of both nationalism and of Latin Americanism, both of which played an important role in the region throughout the Cold War, often in combination with socialist ideas. The role of US business interests and their close relations with local elite sectors and the US government made them part of the political scenario and also promoted Latin American nationalism. It was the interplay of these factors that made the Cold War in the region unique – a "protracted revolution" in search of a second independence.[4]

The struggle in Chile from 1973–1990 between right-wing authoritarianism and democratic forces, and the struggle for sovereignty of the Nicaraguan revolutionary process of 1979–1990 were important manifestations of the regional struggle described above during the last two decades of the Cold War. Looking at how they developed during the 1980s helps to show how Latin America was shaped by the policies that the Reagan administration adopted on the one hand, towards authoritarian regimes such as Pinochet's, and on the other, towards nationalistic and revolutionary governments such as that represented by the Sandinistas. It also illustrates the minor role played in the region by the Soviet Union, as well as underlining the way that US-supported coups and dictatorships helped foster links and solidarity between Latin American leftist movements that had vastly different histories and political approaches.

The history of the Popular Unity government and the 1973 coup against it is well known, and merits no more than a brief recount here. The Allende government sought a "Chilean road to socialism" within the bounds of the existing institutional and political framework. Their economic program meant to take control of Chile's natural resources, while also providing a fairer distribution of land and income. The social program involved heavy State investment, reform of the education system, the construction of social housing, and the rectification of long-standing abuses against the peasant and indigenous population. In the political arena the governing coalition was following a path of gradual institutional reform that would lead Chile through a "bourgeois-democratic" revolution towards a socialist system in the unspecified future, while carrying out a non-aligned foreign policy. The US had long feared Allende's coming to power at the head of a Communist-Socialist coalition, and as soon as he had been elected it began a concerted campaign to overthrow it.[5] In this Washington could take advantage of the openness of the Chilean media, and the ownership of large parts of it by elite sectors ideologically and culturally allied to the US. Furthermore, the Chilean economy depended on mineral exports to the US, and its mining and transport sectors depended heavily on spare parts from the US. This made Chile vulnerable to destabilization. Chilean elites were outraged at having lost their control of the country's political destiny, and frightened of what the future held. As the US-sponsored, hostile, media campaign advanced, sectors of the middle classes and, of the military, increasingly began to oppose the government. A sense of chaos and fear was created by the media amid the severe economic disruption promoted by the US government and corporations. Eventually Chilean armed forces carried out the coup as if occupying a conquered country; with hundreds of thousands were arrested and tortured, and thousands killed and "disappeared."

The defeat of the Chilean Left's political project was extremely traumatic for the Chilean Left, for it had been the result of a sustained political effort. Through the rest of the 1970s the Left, dispersed in exile, prison camps and, clandestinely, in Chile, tried to evaluate what had happened and develop strategies for resisting the dictatorship and returning Chile to democracy. This process occurred in consultation with "fraternal" parties from around the world, but in particular with those of the Soviet Union, Cuba, Bulgaria and the GDR. All the organizations of the Left agreed on one thing – they had made serious mistakes, one of which was to undervalue the importance of the military element in politics.[6] This led them to accept Cuban offers to train cadres in Cuban military academies, with the idea that they could be included in future, democratic, Chilean armed forces, although there was no coordination between them.[7] They also sought similar help from other friendly governments and by the end of the decade had military cadets studying in Cuba, the GDR and Bulgaria. However, none of the Europeans encouraged this activity, with the Bulgarians reminding the Socialists that it was extremely complicated, and that there were still debates in their Party over their own experiences of armed struggle against the authoritarian Tsankov regime in the early 1920s and against the pro-Nazi regime of the war years, the Soviets trying "not to inflame attitudes favorable to armed struggle" and the Cubans emphasizing the need to create a broad democratic front.[8] Thus, the stimulus for the inclusion of a strong military element within the Chilean Left came from within, motivated by the violence with which their non-violent political process had been met by the Chilean elite and the US.

The history of the Nicaraguan process is also well known. Resistance to the Somoza dictatorship had a long pedigree in Nicaragua, and the FSLN (*Frente Sandinista de Liberacion Nacional*, Sandinista National Liberation Front) was one of many that took up arms against "*somocismo*" during the 1960s. The Somoza regime was an expression of what Edelberto Torres-Rivas calls "façade democracy" where the oligarchy ruled through the military, and access to political power was severely restricted and which ultimately survived because its power derived from its relationship with the US.[9] This eventually resulted in the creation of a cross-class, political-military, alliance against *somocismo*, which was able to lead a mass uprising against the dictatorship and the old political system in July 1979. In an interesting linkage between the Chilean and Nicaraguan processes, nearly 100 Chileans, mostly military cadres trained after the 1973 coup, fought for the Sandinistas on their Southern Front, beginning a relationship between the Chilean Left and the Sandinistas that was to continue through the 1980s.

The Sandinistas had studied previous revolutionary experiences in Latin America, and knew that, precisely because the dynamic of the Cold War in the region went beyond mere superpower competition, they would have to confront the US if they wanted to make the socio-economic changes that they thought would lead towards Nicaraguan development. However, they hoped that, by maintaining a non-aligned foreign policy and a mixed economy, they might be able to keep this conflict with the US within controllable limits. Just in case, they ensured that the armed forces would be technically and ideologically prepared to confront a US invasion, in order not to repeat the Chilean experience. At the same time the Carter administration was aware that the Sandinista leadership contained both Social Democrats and Marxists, and it worked to ensure that the former group came out on top in the post-revolutionary confusion, pouring money into opposition political groups, and maintaining contact with Social Democrat leaders with links to the military, such as Eden Pastora.[10] In case this policy failed, the CIA began to establish support and supply networks, and to bring together former members of the National Guard as the basis of the Contras who would later terrorize Nicaragua.

The election of Ronald Reagan in November 1980 sealed the direction of US relations with the Sandinista Revolution. The Reagan administration's policy towards Latin America was guided by the ideas of the "Committee of Santa Fe," which saw the hand of Soviet subversion everywhere, and placed loyalty to friendly regimes above all other considerations.[11] The prescribed solution to the losses incurred under Carter was to rollback these perceived Soviet advances, and Nicaragua was first in line. This meant maintaining a constant threat of direct military intervention alongside a counter-revolutionary army that would provide the basis for intervention, and at the same time help bleed and weaken the revolution, as Daniel Ortega had predicted shortly after the Sandinistas overthrew Somoza in 1979:

> Today the enemy is not Somoza, the enemy is present in all those parts of the continent beginning with the US, which have always carried out an interventionist policy towards the peoples of Latin America. [...] The enemy is he who when he has noticed nationalist, reformist airs in Latin America – not to mention revolutionary ones – has come with his guerrillas, has come with his class groups, has come with his putschists to repress these expressions. [...] The danger is latent, the gringo senators, the gringo millionaires, the politicians and the military gringos who backed Somoza until the last possible moment are there, mindful of this situation [Nicaragua]. And they are the enemies of this process, and will try to liquidate this process.[12]

The Reagan administration's hostility to Nicaragua would ensure that the military arena would become crucially important for the survival of the revolution and its socio-economic program. In this area the Sandinistas at first attempted to keep a diverse range of military suppliers but were eventually obliged to turn towards Cuba and the Socialist Bloc countries by US pressure. Western sources of arms and advice were unreliable, given their close relationship with the US, as was proved by the block placed on the sale of boats and helicopters by France to Nicaragua after 1981.[13] At the same time the Sandinistas were facing an increasingly well-equipped enemy in the Contras, and they needed arms and equipment to confront them. Cuba provided the conduit for relations with the Soviet Union, which began providing some military equipment with which to equip the Sandinista Popular Army (Ejercito Popular Sandinista, EPS) after negotiations in Moscow in 1980. However, Soviet equipment only began to arrive in bulk after the war had begun in earnest, and other sources had been blocked off. Thus, US hostility, in effect, forced the Sandinistas to depend on the Socialist countries for the survival of their revolutionary process. This dependency was then used by the Reagan administration as a justification for their counter-revolutionary intervention.

While the Reagan administration was trying to subvert and overthrow the Sandinista Revolution, it had also learned valuable lessons from the Sandinista revolutionary victory in 1979. These lessons were understood within the context of the renewed effort to cast the US as defender of "liberty" and "democracy" throughout the world in the wake of the Vietnam War. These lessons indicated that it was difficult to muster domestic public support for authoritarian regimes abroad, especially when trying to sell itself as the world's beacon of freedom – and yet it was vital to continue this support when such regimes were under threat. What was needed were examples of what US Secretary of State George Schultz called "economic freedom coupled with political freedom."[14] The US also ensured that other regimes understood another lesson from the fall of Somoza – that elite disunity had resulted in revolution. The result was the initiation of political transition processes in friendly authoritarian countries that would move them from being unsophisticated and embarrassing military regimes to controllable and limited democracies that kept US-friendly elites in power. These "protected democracies" would maintain the military and security forces of the dictatorships intact, create institutional barriers to full democracy, exclude the Left from politics and, therefore, continue the economic legacy of the dictatorial regimes. The political opposition and Left-wing movements had generally been severely weakened by years of dictatorship, and, therefore, it was relatively easy to maintain their exclusion from political power.[15] The resulting political systems have been termed "restricted," "militarized" or "protected democracies" and were the model that the Chilean transition followed during the 1980s.[16]

Thus US policy towards Chile during the 1980s was framed by the desire to avoid another Nicaragua, and at the same time cement the economic and social "achievements," as US leaders saw them, of the Pinochet regime. As the Sandinistas had said of the Carter administration's efforts to mediate a transition in Nicaragua in 1979, the Reagan administration in the 1980s wanted "*Pinochetismo* without Pinochet." The main obstacle to this was Pinochet himself, who was "corrupted" by the fear of what would happen to him and his family after 1989, the date when Chilean elections were due, according to the 1980 Constitution written by the regime.[17] Therefore the Reagan administration tried to ensure a transition that would allow for complete immunity for human rights abuses for Pinochet and the Chilean armed forces, as well as maintain a political, economic and social order that was acceptable to the US. Ensuring an effective transition acquired more urgency as Chile plunged further into economic crisis in 1982 and was rocked by mass demonstrations that continued until 1984. What worried the regime and proponents of a transition was encouraging to the Chilean Left, which saw the opportunity and popular will to overthrow the dictatorship. The eruption of popular discontent led the Communist Party, by now the largest and most coherent organization after the division of the Socialist Party, to begin implementing its "Policy of Mass Popular Rebellion" which called for the introduction of "all forms of struggle" including "acute violence."[18] This violence was, in essence, defensive, designed to raise the morale of a population that had already lost its fear of the regime and taken to the streets, and it took the form of occasional spectacular propaganda actions such as creating electricity blackouts and, more frequently, actions in support of mass demonstrations. These were mostly defined by home-made weaponry, the digging of trenches and the construction of barricades in *poblaciones* (shantytowns) to prevent incursion by the military and the police. The perceived success of this policy encouraged the Communists and their allies to consider even more daring actions.

The mass demonstrations and general unrest forced Pinochet to appoint a civilian interior minister, in August 1984, as a fop to the centrist opposition. However, the continued popular protests led him to re-instate a state of siege later that year. This was lifted under US pressure in early 1985, which allowed the moderate opposition to reach a National Accord that agreed to make some concessions in return for the armed forces guaranteeing a return to democracy. Pinochet refused to negotiate with the Accord parties at the end of the year, and this caused renewed public protest and negotiations between some of the Accord parties and the Communists. The prospect of a united opposition led to the military lining up behind Pinochet, a position that increased the potential for polarization and confirmed Communist accusations that Pinochet's talk of transition was false. The danger of polarization was acute and made the US step up efforts to pressure Pinochet to negotiate and accept a transition, while at the same time using their influence, and that of key allies like West Germany and the UK, to "strengthen the democratic [non-communist] centre."[19] The US also increased military-to-military contacts to encourage support for a transition among military officers. No doubt they pointed to recent examples of successful transitions in Central America (El Salvador, Honduras, Guatemala), as well as to the rather less successful example of Nicaragua.

At the same time, the Communist Party was envisioning a possible overthrow of the dictatorship through "broad unity and intense social mobilization" which "threatened to undermine the US goal of encouraging an orderly transition."[20] To back this mobilization the Party's military apparatus, many of them veterans of Nicaragua, began planning for two spectacular and linked actions. The first was the assassination of Pinochet; the second was the caching of 90 tons of arms and ammunition with which to arm the National Uprising (*Sublevacion Nacional*) that would "paralyze the country with the decisive and permanent mobilization of the masses."[21] While preparations for these actions were underway the Party also worked hard at building its political links with other political parties and organizations that were broadly opposed to the Pinochet regime, in an effort to build opposition consensus around the rejection of Pinochet's transition ground rules.

The Communist Party's plans were disrupted by the August 1986 discovery, by Chilean *Carabineros* (a militarized police force), of several arms caches in Northern Chile. The scale of the caches shocked the regime, and also some of the moderate opposition, making both realize that the Communists had been utterly serious about 1986 being the "decisive year." Despite the discovery, the go ahead was given by the Communist Party leadership for the assassination of Pinochet, and on 6 September 1986 his convoy was ambushed on a mountain road near Santiago.[22] The attempt narrowly failed; Pinochet escaped, although 5 of his bodyguards were killed. The assassination attempt led to a severe crackdown on the opposition, and a renewed state of siege, but at the same time facilitated building links between the regime and the "moderate opposition" who both shared concerns that if the transition were not agreed, then the Communists would be best placed as the staunchest opponents of the regime. This could lead to a polarization of the situation that would only benefit the Communists and could lead to revolution, as it had done in Nicaragua in 1979.

The arms caches and the attempt on Pinochet's life gave the US push for talks renewed urgency, and undoubtedly contributed to the rapprochement between the regime and the centrist opposition which eventually led the latter to accept the legitimacy of the 1980 constitution and the transition towards a protected democracy that conserved the fundamental socio-economic aspects of the military regime. At the same time US National Endowment for Democracy (NED) funds poured into the conservative wing of the Christian Democrat opposition and into social organizations controlled by them, rewarding them for accepting the dictatorship's constitution.[23] Resources were also put into training Christian Democrats and other moderate opposition leaders, organizing conferences and schools for them and local community leaders to try to undermine the social organizations of the Left.[24] However, despite these efforts it was far from clear that Pinochet would accept the transition, and the possibility of his remaining in power could not be discounted despite his promise to abide by the results of the scheduled 1988 plebiscite. This entailed risks for both sides, but the US government felt that "the Chilean government must recognize that there can be no transition to democracy without risks. There is no ironclad guarantee of success, but the current political paralysis is a definite prescription for disaster."[25] For the Communists the risks were also high. Repressed at home, and increasingly marginalized from political processes they had to prepare for different outcomes. Therefore, the Communist Party continued to send its military cadres to train, and gain combat experience abroad, while still concentrating on its political efforts. In this way the Communists hoped to be in a position to take advantage of any problems during the transition, while avoiding being caught out by what they thought was a probable continuation of authoritarian rule after 1989.

Throughout this period the Reagan administration was using far more interventionist methods in Nicaragua. During the early 1980s the Contras were pushed to seize Nicaraguan territory, which would allow the establishment of a provisional government that could then call for US assistance, thereby justifying an intervention. This possibility preoccupied the Sandinistas for the entire war, and was the basis of their military doctrine.[26] The Contras themselves were not consulted on the political and military methods to achieve the overthrow of the Sandinista revolution, they were simply expected to provide the blood while the US provided the rest. The Contra leadership was appointed by the CIA, and by the late 1980s the CIA was planning and commanding many of the Contras larger operations.[27] The reason for this more direct involvement was the military defeat of the Contras during 1985–1986, a period which saw the Contras' ability to militarily challenge the revolution destroyed. Despite millions of dollars of investment, and the best intelligence and training that the US could provide, the Contras were unable to seize the strategic initiative after 1984. The reason for this failure was largely the Contras' lack of support among the Nicaraguan population. Still, the Reagan administration continued to provide the money and equipment needed to keep the war going. In the wake of the Iran–Contra scandal the political costs of doing so were becoming increasingly high, and by the end of the decade the US and its regional allies were persuaded that political efforts would serve them more effectively, as they were doing in the "democratic" transitions from authoritarian regimes.

However, the Contras continued to be a useful tool to pressure the Sandinistas, and, therefore, at no point was assistance to them halted. Although they were unable to mount large operations after late 1987, they continued their attacks on civilian and economic targets, which obliged the Sandinistas to continue dedicating huge resources to the war effort. At the same time economic pressures were becoming unbearable, with international credit drying up, and natural disaster completing the work of the Contras, resulting in a dire economic situation. These factors formed the context for continuing US efforts to reverse the Sandinista process. As in Chile, US money poured into opposition hands; the effects of this were multiplied by the ongoing economic crisis. US efforts to unify the opposition eventually resulted in the forming of the *Union Nacional Opositora* or UNO (National Opposition Union) which then narrowly won the 1990 election. This result was the culmination of nearly 10 years of political and military aggression, that had succeeded in wearing down enough of the Nicaraguan population to ensure the victory of the candidates that sought to take Nicaragua back into the US fold.

The Soviet Union featured little in both these processes. Soviet support for the Chilean opposition was unconditional and based upon requests made by the Chileans themselves.[28] Through the 1970s the Soviet military intelligence (GRU) provided political-military training to cadres selected by the Communist and Socialist Party leaderships. This training consisted of some military elements but mostly of courses on operating political organizations in clandestine conditions. During the 1980s, after the Communists and one faction of the Socialists adopted policies that included military elements, the Soviets began to provide specialist military training to small numbers of Chilean cadres. Apart from this, Soviet assistance was mostly financial and political, providing the Chilean Left with a presence in international forums and, notably, providing them with radio stations that broadcast into Chile, for many years providing the only opposition news. Soviet solidarity went beyond the technical and included humanitarian assistance such as educational grants, medical care and psychological assistance to Chileans coming from Pinochet's concentration camps. Other Socialist countries provided similar assistance. At no point did the Soviets or their allies push the Chileans to adopt particular policies, or strategies with which to confront their political reality. Furthermore, by the second half of the decade much of the Communist leadership was no longer permanently based in Moscow and had moved clandestinely to Chile. Therefore, the changes that began to affect the Soviet Union in the late 1980s had little direct effect on the politics of the Chilean Left. For the Soviets the commitment to supporting the Chileans was not a large financial drain, and remained unaffected by the changes in the Soviet Union. The Soviets also played a very secondary role in the Nicaraguan conflict, a role that was conditioned by US hostility to Nicaragua in that their support increased in times of heavier US aggression.[29] Socialist economic support provided the Sandinista economy with its basic necessities after 1985, and its military support kept the EPS fighting as part of its commitment to the independent economic development of Nicaragua. The Soviet Union refused to bow to US pressure to use this support as a lever against them. The Soviets consistently supported the Sandinista position for a multilateral and regional solution to the Central American conflict, even during the last months of the decade, stating that they would end arms supplies to the Sandinistas when the US withdrew aid from its Central American allies.[30] However, the Soviet desire to bring regional conflicts to an end, as part of Gorbachev's policy of new thinking, did mean that from 1989 onwards they placed an emphasis on talks with the Sandinistas with a view to finding a political solution to the conflict, limiting direct military supplies.

In fact, both the Sandinistas and the Chileans had much deeper relationships with the Cubans than with the Soviets and the other Socialist countries. This was partly for geographic and linguistic reasons but also as a result of Cuban assistance in training the majority of their military cadres. While guerrilla training for the Sandinistas prior to the revolution had been largely limited to the GPP (*Guerra Popular Prolongada*, Prolonged Popular War) faction of the FSLN, after the revolution thousands of Sandinistas received technical education and military training in Cuba. Thousands of Cubans also worked in Sandinistan Nicaragua as teachers, doctors, construction workers and technical advisers. This assistance provided cultural and practical reasons for the good relationship between the Sandinista Nicaragua and the Cuban revolution on top of the political similarities of their confrontation with the US. This confrontation also bound them to the Chilean Left, which had been defeated by a coup that was largely the result of US interference. Thousands of Chileans had spent years of exile in Cuba following the coup, where the solidarity received from Cuban institutions and people in general caused a profound and lasting impression on them. Cuba provided medical care for victims of torture and imprisonment, and also allowed Chileans to work and study. When the Chilean Left requested military and undercover training the Cubans provided it, allowing the military cadres to work within the Cuban armed forces. Dozens of Chilean officers taught in Cuban military academies, and many more worked in the units of the Cuban FAR (*Fuerzas Armadas Revolucionarias*, Revolutionary Armed Forces), in an unprecedented demonstration of Cuban trust in them.

In fact the Chilean officers of the FAR went on to fight for the FSLN in 1979, and established the first structures of the Sandinista Armed Forces. Once these were established, Cuban officers arrived, and the Chileans went on to help with training individual units of the EPS, as part of the Cuban military mission. It was this rapid training that allowed the Sandinistas to withstand the sustained Contra attacks during late 1982. Once the Contra war was underway in earnest, the Chileans began sending officers, trained in Cuba and other socialist countries, to Nicaragua to fight in the specialized units established to tackle this threat. This helped the Sandinistas make up for their shortage of trained officers, and helped the Chileans gain combat experience and broaden their political horizons. The Chileans continued to fight in these irregular warfare battalions until 1988, gaining combat experience in preparation for a possible future military struggle in Chile.

In all three cases the relationships were not defined by power. Neither the Soviet Union, Cuba nor any other socialist country ever imposed a policy on their "fraternal" partners in Latin America. Both the Soviets and the Bulgarians urged the Chileans to think thoroughly before including elements of armed struggle in their fight against Pinochet. Igor Rybalkin, then member of CPSU International Department, responsible for relations with Chilean organizations, recalled that the CPSU "never tried to inflame attitudes favorable to armed struggle" and Konstantin Tellalov Member of the Bulgarian Communist Party (BCP) Secretariat, emphasized that work with the army and military training was "very complicated" and that the Bulgarian Communist Party had never, in 50 years, "exaggerated the role of armed resistance." Instead, the BCP stressed that their success had been the result of the correct calculation of all forms of struggle, both legal and illegal, with the weight falling on mass organizations with armed resistance being included "at the moment when the conditions exist."[31]

Nor did the Cuban leadership push the Chileans to adopt the Policy of Mass Popular Rebellion, emphasizing the importance of a broad political alliance instead.[32] Furthermore, interviews indicate that the relationship between these groups was respectful, and characterized by an appreciation that the various parties understood their own political environments and the best methods to adopt.[33] The role of the Soviets and others was largely to provide whatever assistance they could, based upon what the Chileans and Sandinistas requested. This completely refutes the assumptions made by the Reagan administration about the nature of relations between Moscow, Havana, Managua and the Chilean Left. Official Soviet policy naturally reflected Soviet interests, but these were understood through an ideological lens. Soviet support for Nicaragua and the Chilean Left was responsive, and had more to do with ideological considerations linked to the concepts of internationalism and solidarity than to strict considerations of the balance of power, which did, however, influence military thinking to an extent. No doubt, it was easier for the Soviet Union to adopt this approach in a region as distant as Latin America, but this does not detract from its merits despite the fact that by the end of 1989 a far more "pragmatic" and less ideological foreign policy was being implemented by Mikhail Gorbachev and Eduard Shevardnadze.[34]

By contrast, the US relationship with the Contras was characterized by hierarchical power relations, as appropriate for an organization that was largely artificially created from abroad. The Contras could not have been established without the support of the US, and it was US money, equipment and training that turned it into a force capable of challenging the Sandinista Revolution.[35] Most importantly, the CIA and the Pentagon provided detailed satellite intelligence as well as operational planning for the Contras. However, the Contras were never allowed to develop an independent political-military strategy, having leaders imposed by the CIA, often in response to what would play well in Congress. Eventually, even military leaders at tactical level were being appointed by the US, and CIA advisers and mercenaries worked throughout the Contra army.[36] Together, these factors made the Contras a tool of US policy, and not a genuinely Nicaraguan resistance army, as confirmed by the testimony of Edgar Chamorro at the International Court of Justice in 1985:

> When I agreed to join the FDN (Fuerza Democratica Nicaragüense-Nicaraguan Democratic Force) in 1981, I had hoped that it would be an organization of Nicaraguans, controlled by Nicaraguans, and dedicated to our own objectives which we ourselves would determine [...] I turned out to be mistaken. The FDN turned out to be an instrument of the United States Government and, specifically of the CIA.[37]

Frustrations with this situation built up among the Contras and several leaders either handed themselves in during government amnesties, or simply left the Contras, disillusioned by the way they had been manipulated in the interests of the US. This reliance on external support proved to be the Contras' fundamental weakness. Once they had been militarily defeated they were replaced, in US policy, by civilian actors, leaving them abandoned and without a voice.

The Chilean and Nicaraguan processes show how the ideological concerns of the US, always present in its policy towards Latin America, became even more pronounced during the Reagan administration. Reagan thought that Pinochet had "saved his country" from Communism, and, therefore, he ought to be recognized for this "achievement."[38] They also admired the economic policies that the Chicago Boys (Chilean Chicago-trained neo-liberal economists) had put into place in Chile, which had resulted in an immense transfer of wealth to the elite and gave foreign companies a free hand, but they saw that "in order for the economic situation to continue as positively as it can, there has to be a transition to democracy." Unfortunately, Pinochet did not share this appreciation, and was willing to remain in power as long as he could, potentially until 1997.[39] This endangered the situation because it could lead to increased polarization, a scenario which would benefit those seeking a rupture with dictatorial institutionality and not transition. In Chile, then, US intervention was aimed at preserving and sustaining a profoundly unjust economic system, while simultaneously making efforts to gently push Pinochet out of power, while maintaining his political and institutional legacy. By doing so the Reagan administration was aiming to keep Chile within the sphere of US hegemony in all its senses.

The Sandinista Revolution had been greeted with dismay in the US. The Carter administration had done what it could to keep alive "*Somocismo* without Somoza" and it was well aware of the Left-wing inclinations of the Sandinista leadership. What wasn't immediately clear was the direction the revolution would take. If moderates were able to come to power, they would maintain a dependent economic structure that would guarantee that Nicaragua would have to remain firmly within the sphere of US-dominated nations. Once Reagan took power, in January 1981, the process of waiting to see which faction would dominate in Nicaragua ended. The FMLN (Frente Farabundo Martí para la Liberación Nacional, Farabundo Marti National Liberation Front) offensive in El Salvador that same month nearly succeeded in overthrowing the dictatorship there, and the Reagan administration found it convenient to blame this on Nicaraguan and Cuban support for the FMLN. Thereafter, the US tied the two conflicts together, trying to equate its aggression against Nicaragua with supposed Nicaraguan–Cuban–Soviet aggression in El Salvador. The Central American situation, with wars in Guatemala, El Salvador and Nicaragua, provided the US with "justification for everything we do" as National Security Adviser Richard Allen commented in an early NSC meeting on 6 February 1981.[40] The Reagan administration conjured up a phantom Soviet menace in Central America and used it to justify propping up genocidal regimes, while forcing a brutal and unnecessary war upon Nicaragua in order to destroy a political process that challenged the emerging orthodoxy of unfettered free market capitalism and representative and restricted democracy.

Therefore, to a large extent, US support of the war in Nicaragua and the dictatorship in Chile represented different fronts in the same Cold War against the danger posed by the ideas of socialism, because these ideas threatened the economic and political supremacy of the US in the hemisphere and in the long run that of capitalism itself. It was this threat to the material and ideological foundations of the US and its supremacy that caused successive administrations to fall victim to what Jorge Dominguez has called the US "ideological demons" which led it to pursue irrational and politically costly policy avenues.[41] The history of the 1980s in Chile and Nicaragua also clearly shows the internal factors within the Cold War struggle in the region. Elites that were economically, culturally and ideologically dependent on the US conflicted with majority populations that suffered from huge inequities caused by the regional economic structure. In this scenario the existence of a socialist alternative strengthened Left-wing forces, and this, in combination with the east–west mentality, of both US foreign policy and the Latin American elites, sharpened social conflict. In this conflict the US took the side of those who represented continuity over change, both from an exaggerated fear of the Soviet threat, and from an understanding that their own position depended upon the subordination of Latin America to its interests.

Perhaps the best argument for this analysis is that it explains the continuation of the "irrational" Cold War against Cuba, and hostility towards other Left-leaning governments in the region, notably in Venezuela, Bolivia and Nicaragua. Throughout the Cold War, and still today, the threat to US interests in Latin America was that governments would be able to carry out modernization together with broad socio-economic development that would encourage country after country to abandon the inter-American system that formed the basis of US global economic and political power.

Notes

1 Interview with Alfonso Castro, 23 July 2009, Managua, Nicaragua.

2 R. M. Bakhitov and S. A. Kazakov, "Rasprostranenie Marksizma v Latinskoi Amerike. Vliyanie Velikogo Oktyabrya na Obrazovanie Kommunisticheskikh Partii," in M. F. Kudachkin (ed.), *Velikii Oktyabr i Kommunisticheskie Partii Latinskoi Ameriki* (Moscow: Nauka, 1978), p. 9.

3 I use the term modernization in the way Paolo Freire understands it, in that all development is modernization, but not all modernization is development. Thus, modernization is a purely mechanistic process occurring outside a society, while development occurs when a society is a subject of its own transformation. See Paolo Freire, *Education for a Critical Consciousness* (London: Continuum, 2008), p. 115.

4 Greg Grandin, *The Last Colonial Massacre: Latin America in the Cold War* (London: Chicago University Press, 2004), p. 174.

5 Church Committee Report "Covert Action in Chile 1963–1973," pp. 148–9.

6 Report of the August 1977 Plenum of the Central Committee of the Chilean Communist Party; "March Document" of the Socialist Party of Chile, 1974.

7 Interviews with Jacinto, 9 February 2009, Santiago, Chile; Carlos Altamirano, 20 March 2009, Santiago, Chile; Eduardo Contreras, 28 January 2009, Santiago, Chile.

8 Bulgarian State Archives, Sofia, Archive of the Bulgarian Communist Party, F. 1, Op. 60, ae. 164, "Stenographic Protocol of the Meeting Between Konstantin Tellalov and Hernan del Canto," 4 February 1975, pp. 4–7; Interviews with Igor Rybalkin; Carlos Altamirano.

9 Edelberto Torres-Rivas, "Crisis and conflict, 1930 to the present," in Leslie

Bethell (ed.), *Central America Since Independence* (Cambridge: Cambridge University Press, 1991), p. 112.

10 Robert A. Pastor, *Not Condemned to Repetition: The United States and Nicaragua* (New York: Westview Press, 2002), p. 162.

11 Henry Raymont, *Troubled Neighbors: The Story of US–Latin American Relations from FDR to the Present* (Cambridge MA: Westview Press, 2005), p. 234.

12 Barricada, 27 July 1979, "To Fortify the Sandinista Popular Army!" Speech by Daniel Ortega.

13 Danuta Paszyn, *The Soviet Attitude to Political and Social Change in Central America, 1979–1990: Case Studies on Nicaragua, El Salvador and Guatemala* (New York: St. Martin's Press, 2000), p. 48.

14 Minutes of NSC, "Meeting on Chile," 18 November 1986, Folder NSC 139 18 November 1986 [1], Box 91304, Executive Secretariat NSC, NSC Meeting Files, Ronald Reagan Library [hereafter RRL].

15 Brian Loveman, "'Protected Democracies' and Military Guardianship: Political Transitions in Latin America 1978–1993," *Journal of Interamerican Studies and World Affairs*, Vol 36, No. 2 (Summer 1994), p. 123.

16 For a detailed description of this process in US policy-making and the manner in which it was applied in Latin America, see William Robinson, *Promoting Polyarchy: Globalization, US Intervention and Hegemony* (Cambridge: Cambridge University Press, 1998); Loveman, "'Protected Democracies,'"; Pamela Constable and Arturo Valenzuela "Is Chile Next?" in *Foreign Policy*, No. 63 (Summer 1986); Patrice McSherry "Military Power, Impunity and State Society Change in Latin America," *Canadian Journal of Political Science*, Vol. 25, No. 3 (September 1992).

17 Memorandum from Senator Laxhalt to President Reagan, re Chile, 26 March 1986, Folder CO33 (400000–400999), Country File CO33, RRL.

18 Luis Corvalan Speech, "The People's Right to Rebel is Indisputable," 3 September 1980.

19 Background Paper on "US Policy Goals in Chile," 14 November 1986, Folder NSC 139 18 November 1986 [2], Box 91304 Chile, Exec Sec NSC, NSC Meeting Files, RRL.

20 Chilean Communist Party declaration, 28 January 1986; CIA Research Paper "The Chilean Communist Party and its Allies," May 1986, Folder "The Chilean Communist Party and its Allies: Intentions Capabilities and Prospects," Box 91703, Flower, Ludlow "Kim" Files, RRL.

21 *Boletin de Informacion del FPMR*, January 1984.

22 Interview with Salvador, 11 December 2007, Buenos Aires, Argentina.

23 Robinson, *Promoting Polyarchy*, p. 176.

24 Ibid., p. 180.

25 Paper, "US Policy Towards Chile" Folder Chile 1987 [02/15/1985–02/21/1985], Box 91172, Latin American Affairs Directorate, NSC Records, RRL.

26 Centro de Historia Militar, Managua, EPS Collection, Box 2, Comandante en Jefe Humberto Ortega, Top Secret Document, "Disposicion de Combate" 25 1982 and Box 44, iDOP, State Secret Report "Caracter probable de las acciones del enemigo en una operacion de invasion contra el territorio de Nicaragua," Document number 008900, 8 January 1980.

27 Enrique Bermudez (Former Contra leader) quoted in Jaime Morales Carazo, *La Contra* (Mexico D. F.: Planeta, 1989), p. 53.

28 Interviews with Igor Rybalkin, 3 September 2007, Moscow, Russia; Luis Corvalan, 11 February 2007, Santiago, Chile; and Oscar de la Fuente, 20 March 2009, Santiago, Chile.

29 Paszyn, *Soviet Attitude*, p. 51.

30 Robert Kagan, *A Twilight Struggle: American Power and Nicaragua, 1977–1990* (New York: The Free Press, 1996), p. 645.

31 Bulgarian State Archives, Sofia, Archive of the Bulgarian Communist Party, F. 1, Op. 60, ae 164 "Stenographic Protocol of the meeting between Konstantin Tellalov and Hernan del Canto," 4 February 1975, pp. 6–7.
32 Interview: Altamirano and unrecorded conversation with Jacinto.
33 Interviews with Rybalkin, De la Fuente, Altamirano.
34 Paszyn, *Soviet Attitude*, p. 83.
35 Affidavit of Edgar Chamorro, Washington DC., 5 September 1985, for the International Court of Justice, Case Concerning Military and Paramilitary Activities In and Against Nicaragua.
36 Enrique Bermudez (Former Contra leader) quoted in Jaime Morales Carazo, *La Contra*, p. 53.
37 Affidavit of Edgar Chamorro.
38 Minutes of NSC "Meeting on Chile," 18 November 1986, Folder NSC 139 18 November 1986 [1], Box 91304, Executive Secretariat NSC, NSC Meeting Files, RRL.
39 Ibid.
40 Minutes to NSC Meeting, 6 February 1981, Folder NSC 00001 6 February 1981 [Caribbean Basin and Poland], Box 91282, Executive Secretariat NSC, NSC Meeting Files, RRL.
41 Jorge I. Dominguez, "US–Latin American Relations During the Cold War and its Aftermath," in Victor Bulmer-Thomas and James Dunkerley (eds.), *The United States and Latin America: The New Agenda* (London: Institute of Latin American Studies and David Rockefeller Center for Latin American Studies, 1999).

9 The "missing Cold War"

Reflections on the Latin American debt crisis, 1979–1989

Duccio Basosi

In the early 1980s, when Latin America fell into a dramatic economic crisis, typical "Cold War" concerns grew stronger in the US. John Milius' widely seen film *Red Dawn* (1984) took Mexico's woes as the starting point of a chain of events culminating in a Soviet, Cuban and Nicaraguan invasion of the US. In one of the first interviews following his inauguration as President, and in many other public appearances, Ronald Reagan (himself endowed with a strong Hollywood background) relentlessly repeated that Latin America was subject to a Soviet-orchestrated destabilization plan.[1] The President's main obsession, then and in the following years, was the Caribbean basin, where revolutionary governments and movements were taking hold.[2] However, even in his memoirs Reagan repeated that the entire continent was at stake.[3] Not all observers agreed with such a reading, and some even refused to consider the support Moscow was giving to the revolutionary forces in Nicaragua, Grenada, Guatemala and El Salvador as a real threat to the US.[4] Several commentators, however, did believe that, just as pitiful socio-economic conditions had helped the rise of revolutionary movements in the Caribbean, the economic crisis might offer the Soviet Union a comfortable opportunity to shore up its influence in the whole region to the detriment of US traditional interests.[5] As it turned out, during the 1980s the Caribbean area remained the exception in a context of virtually unchallenged US dominance. As far as the great majority of Latin America is concerned, the historian is thus confronted with two possible explanations for what was, in a sense, a "missing cold war." Either Reagan's tough approach, in the Caribbean and elsewhere, prevented the further spreading to major Latin American countries of what had so far seemed an unstoppable Soviet advance in the Third World, or Reagan's alarmed cries were much ado about nothing.[6]

While recognizing that Reagan's military pressure against the revolutionary left in the Caribbean might have contributed to raising the perceived costs to the Soviet Union of supporting pro-socialist movements throughout the continent, the conclusions of this chapter come closer to the latter alternative. In fact, the study of the epochal economic and political phenomena that came to be known globally as the Latin American debt crisis – and as the "lost decade" throughout Latin America – confirms that the Soviet Union did not only face constraints in the Latin American context, but also opportunities that it simply did not exploit. While the explanation of the motives behind Soviet restraint must await more research in Soviet archives, declassified records from the Ronald Reagan Presidential Library, the Digital National Security Archive, the Declassified Documents Reference System, the CIA Freedom of Information Act website, and the Intelligence Resource Program of the Federation of American Scientists, show that, despite all its rhetoric about Soviet machinations, the Reagan administration was largely conscious, at least after its early months in power, of the condition of virtually unchallenged leadership it enjoyed on the continent.[7] The momentous change in hemispheric economic relations that occurred as a consequence of the debt crisis, this chapter argues, was to an extent the product of such (well based) self-confidence.

The first section of the chapter briefly discusses the origins of the Latin American debt crisis, analyzes its real and potential interactions with the US–Soviet confrontation, and describes the making of US policies during Reagan's first year in power. The second section shows that, following a period of relative uncertainty, from late 1982, the US administration, as reflected in its internal documents, showed a greater tendency to downplay the "Soviet threat" that it kept denouncing publicly. The third section describes the growing challenges posed to the US by the ongoing debt crisis during 1983–1985, but also the absence of significant Soviet moves on the issue. In this context, the US government could promote bolder policies aimed at bringing Latin American economies more strongly within US-dominated international markets. While briefly considering the events of the second half of the decade, and highlighting a set of points that need further clarification, the final section summarizes the main conclusions that can be drawn from an analysis of the Latin American debt crisis conducted through the lenses of the US–Soviet bipolar confrontation.

The Latin American debt crisis and the bipolar confrontation

The 1970s had been a decade of easy borrowing for most Latin American governments. At least until 1976, in the context of a shift toward right-wing authoritarian rule that spared only a few countries, Latin American rulers were deemed both trustworthy partners and reliable borrowers by influential players such as the Nixon and Ford administrations in the US and the main international financial institutions. As for the following years, when the Carter administration in the US submitted loans and aid to deeper scrutiny in the name of "human rights," the big – mainly US-based – commercial banks continued to lend money enthusiastically to the regimes in question, making up for the diminished public funding.[8]

Most Latin American governments began to face serious economic problems in late 1979, when the US turned to high interest rates to counter domestic inflation. With international loans indexed in dollars (as a result of the US currency's controversial role as the international monetary pivot), repaying outstanding loans became a difficult exercise. To cope, new loans were activated. Total Latin American debts jumped from $240 billion to $331 billion between 1980 and 1982 (they were only $30 billion in 1970). To make the situation more critical, most governments, after advice from the US Treasury and the International Monetary Fund (IMF), reacted to the incipient crisis by adopting austerity policies. Facilitated by the authoritarian nature of the regimes in power, these were supposed to create sufficient trade surpluses. In practice, however, they only led to economic stagnation without solving the foreign accounts problem and actually made it worse.[9]

As Ronald Reagan entered the White House in January 1981, most Latin American countries were experiencing grave social crises domestically and potential default internationally. The debt issue involved both a sensitive area for US security concerns and the financial interests of hundreds of US-based banks. As a presidential candidate, Reagan had criticized Carter's "human rights" conditions on international loans. A deep-rooted conviction in Washington was that if "Usonia" did not help, Third World governments might turn to "Russonia" as an alternative lender of financial, technical and military resources.[10] Reagan's conservative economic views were well known, but with the Soviet Union already gaining friends in the Caribbean basin, even the conservative Republican seemed willing to stick to the traditional largess of US "Cold War" economic diplomacy in the hemisphere.[11]

It is not easy to assess the Soviet Union's actual expectations from Latin America at the turn of the decade. During the 1970s, sympathetic governments, namely Peru and Chile, had been toppled by right-wing coups. In the southern cone, leftist militancy had been literally drowned in blood.[12] The Kremlin could count on a sound relationship with Cuba, welcomed revolution in Nicaragua and Grenada (1979), and declared its sympathetic feelings for the guerrillas operating in Guatemala and El Salvador. But, while supportive, Moscow had not promoted revolutionary developments in Central America.[13] In the wider region, besides keeping ties with the (often outlawed) Communist parties, the Soviet Union had pragmatic relations with odd partners: following Carter's embargo on US grain sales to the Soviet Union (1980), it had arranged for Argentina to become its principal grain supplier; the Soviet Union supplied the army of the then anti-Communist Peru; and there is evidence of Soviet interest in tighter cooperation in the nuclear sector with Brazil's right-wing military regime in 1980–1981.[14] While it might be difficult to interpret Soviet designs on the basis of the scant available Soviet primary sources, assuming that an objective growth in its influence would be the likely consequence of an economic crisis in the area does not seem unreasonable. This was, to be sure, the US view as expressed in the 1982 *US National Security Strategy*, or National Security Decision Directive (NSDD) 32, which recognized that in Mexico and South America there existed "few direct threats" to US national security, but also expressed the fear that "political and economic instability would offer the Soviets [new opportunities]."[15] Some US documents did advance the hypothesis that (after the 1979 Soviet invasion of Afghanistan) the Third World was now less receptive to Soviet appeals,[16] but US analysts generally kept claiming that "when the countries of the western block [did] not show interest to offer [economic] support, the chances [grew] that developing countries would turn to Moscow."[17]

Early in his presidency, Reagan seemed to follow the traditional approach: while raising the military pressure on the revolutionaries in Central America, one of his earliest decisions was to reactivate the credit lines to the South American dictatorships. During 1981, the administration "promoted" Chile, Argentina, Uruguay and Paraguay as "non-violators of human rights," and facilitated the approval of World Bank loans to them for a total $484 million (an economically small, but politically significant, sum).[18]

In the following months, however, the administration did not prioritize the debt issue as a political issue, reconciling itself with its economically conservative beliefs. The main US decisions in the financial field seemed indifferent to the ongoing (and potentially worsening) Latin American difficulties: beginning with the President, US officials seemed concerned mainly with recommending that the indebted countries adopt policies of market opening and privatization, accompanied by the ever-present promise that the social costs paid in the short run would be offset in the future by the expected liberation of new productive energies.[19]

There appears to have been some disagreement within the administration between the officials of the Treasury and those from agencies concerned with national security and foreign policy. In any event, during 1981, the Treasury aroused the contempt of NSC officials by successfully boycotting all attempts at having the administration evaluate the security questions that were raised by the growing Latin American indebtedness.[20] In September, the Treasury successfully opposed the deployment of several tools that would have injected liquidity into the thirsty economies of Latin America: the US delegation at the IMF turned down a Latin American request for a new issuance of Special Drawing Rights (the Fund's virtual currency), while the administration also managed to reduce the US contribution to the World Bank.[21] The message was clear: indebted governments had to raise capital through cuts in social programs, austerity policies and privatizations.

The attitude of the US government can be explained on the basis of the advantages that large US-based companies expected to obtain from tariff reductions and privatization of public assets in the indebted countries. In

October 1981, when Reagan announced the guidelines of his approach to North-South issues (not specifically targeted at, but obviously inclusive of, Latin American countries), his pro-business mentality was clearly discernible: trade and foreign private investment, not public international aid or changes in the structure of the monetary system, would lead to the South's development (and in the Latin American case, to the solution of the debt problem).[22] Ironically, however, Reagan's recipes received the same critiques of exposing Latin America to Soviet influence that he had once reserved for Carter.[23] To take Reagan's reasoning at face value, austerity measures today would produce not only the necessary surplus for loan repayment, but also the conditions for greater economic dynamism tomorrow, through greater integration in core capitalist markets. The problem with this approach was that there was simply no economic reason for which private investments should keep flowing to countries that were on the brink of collapse. This was an economic dilemma. But to the extent that Reagan eluded the question, he also seemed to imply that the "red threat" was not as serious as he initially expected (and was still publicly denouncing).

Managing the debt crisis

During 1982, Reagan's optimism came under heavy fire. In spring, partially trying to conceal the economic crisis, Argentina's military regime (with which Reagan had established a good working relationship) tried to seize control of the British-held Falkland Islands (Islas Malvinas), an archipelago in the southern Atlantic, which had been the subject of a long-standing territorial dispute. After some hesitation, Reagan sided with Britain, which quickly came out victorious from the ensuing war. This allowed the Soviet Union to denounce US imperialism and to consolidate its own relationship with the Argentine junta.[24] Thus, the crisis in the southern Atlantic seemed to confirm the permanent validity of the usual paradigm of the bipolar confrontation. Considering the numerous negative reactions created by the US stance, in the wake of the conflict the White House ordered a review of its Latin American policies, admitting that a number of steps were needed in the whole region "to repair the damage" and "to prevent further communist inroads in [the western] hemisphere." An inter-agency working group was formed to evaluate what were "the major threats to [US] interests in the region from whatever quarter."[25]

In this framework, a Special National Intelligence Estimate entitled "Soviet policies and activities in Latin America and the Caribbean," seemed to be in no doubt that "Soviet activity and interest in Latin America ha[d] grown significantly in recent years" and that "in the wake of the Falklands war, the Soviets and their Cuban allies [would] look for new opportunities."[26] The deep-seated belief that Cuba was only a Soviet puppet possibly led to an overestimation of Soviet capabilities, but the study also expressed the conviction that the Soviet Union could count on a "growing network of good bilateral relations" with the main countries of the continent, and in particular with Argentina, Mexico and Brazil.[27] Indeed, the study commented, numerous constraints (geographic distance, traditional US economic, political and military presence, the deep anti-Communism of most governments and regimes in power) imposed restraint on Soviet diplomacy, so as not to irritate the US in what was still judged "a peripheral area for Soviet security concerns." According to the authors of the study, however, these obstacles would not prevent the Soviet Union from trying to push its influence further in the following years, in an attempt to exploit "the persistent anti-US sentiment in the region" and to emphasize "the expansion of commercial exchanges and, in some cases, the possibility to sell military equipment" (the Argentine regime, although in deep difficulty, was seen as the main candidate).[28]

In the following months the Latin American economic situation worsened. On 13 August, the Mexican authorities declared a unilateral moratorium on debt repayment. After one week of tough negotiations, the US Treasury and Federal Reserve agreed to issue a new $2 billion loan, conditional upon Mexico's commitment to repay the entire debt at market rates and to supply the US with oil below the market price. Other western central banks and the IMF added some $6 billion in the following months. Only then did the 115 commercial creditor banks agree to reschedule the Mexican debt.[29] Meanwhile, however, Brazil had declared its own moratorium, while Bolivia and Argentina threatened to follow more or less the same path. The Chilean regime, the one that had opened up the most to "neoliberal" ideas in the previous decade, re-nationalized the entire banking sector within a few days, leading critics to speak sadly of a "new Chilean road to socialism."[30]

Everywhere, the financial crisis destabilized the anti-Communist regimes. Following the threats of default, the negotiations on debt rescheduling, undertaken by Latin American governments with the US Treasury, the private banks and the multilateral financial institutions, did not serve to alleviate the social consequences of the large capital outflows from the region. In some ways, the results of such negotiations, with their emphasis on austerity, helped push Latin American economies further into stagnation: at the beginning of 1987, Latin American GDP was 6 percent below the 1980 level, while the region's total debt had gone up to $450 billion. In the same period, real consumption fell by 8 percent in Brazil and Mexico, 14 percent in Bolivia and 17 percent in Argentina and Chile.[31] In several countries, popular protests and Communist activism revived, directed both against the national governments and the international actors that contributed to dictate their policies.

In this context, in May 1983, Secretary of State George Shultz showed some interest in working on a plan to alleviate the social consequences of the economic shock, arguing that the Soviet Union fed on political instability "like a virus on a host."[32] One year later, such a view was echoed in the report to the President of the National Bipartisan Commission on Central America chaired by former Secretary of State Henry Kissinger (whose indications actually went beyond Central America to include the entire southern half of the hemisphere).[33] However, Shultz's was probably the only expression of such sentiment on the part of a high official of the Reagan Administration, which instead, implicitly turning upside down the consolidated practices of the preceding decades, never substantially changed its purely economic approach to the debt crisis. In the same spring of 1983, Donald Regan, Reagan's First Secretary of the Treasury, bluntly stated that Latin American debtors "should be made to pay as much as they can without breaking them," although he did accede to give the IMF, in this field, greater resources and responsibilities than he had originally expected and hoped for.[34]

The administration's rigidity in demanding the repayment of existing loans, at "market rates" which largely depended on the US Treasury's and Federal Reserve's choices, often led to a humiliating treatment of the governments of the region. Further, the conditions attached to the renewal of existing loans implied processes of privatization and deregulation which, at least in the short term, promised to produce an exponential growth of unemployment, inequality, and penetration of foreign (mainly US) capital: all factors which, admittedly, could bolster the left, the economic nationalists, and Soviet influence.[35] Nevertheless, the review of US policy undertaken in the wake of the Falklands-Malvinas war, whose results were discussed by the NSC on 30 November 1982, probably scored a crucial point for the consolidation of the administration's purely economic approach. In fact, although readable only in part, NSDD 71, the result of the review process, seemed to leave the Soviet Union with a rather marginal role. While Moscow was still considered a relevant actor in the Caribbean basin, the wider Latin American region did not seem prone to the spreading of Soviet influence. US objectives in the region, according to the directive, should be the renewal of ties with the local elites (Reagan embarked on a diplomatic tour in Latin American capitals on the same 30 November), "the promotion of free enterprise economies" and "the advance of US trade and investment."[36] All in all, these did not sound like defensive positions.

For several months, monitoring the international financial situation was the task of a mid-level interdepartmental group. Only in March 1983 did the Latin American crisis find its way into the administration's agenda as a question of national security, with the decision to begin a study on the topic. The results of that study, presented in NSDD 96 of 9 June, are still classified. However it is difficult to believe that "Cold War" concerns received any particular attention: the memorandum that ordered the preparation of NSDD 96 did recognize, for the first time, that the financial situation was related to "other areas of critical interest for the United States and for the other industrial democracies," but it only made a vague reference to issues such as "international political stability" at the very end of a list of worries for world trade, domestic employment in the US and world growth.[37] Some months later, NSDD 131, dated 12 March 1984, spelled out US objectives for a forthcoming summit of western industrialized countries. As regards the debt issue, the US should simply seek "a review of the continuing requirements of the debt strategy, emphasizing the importance in the years ahead of investment and further trade liberalization."[38]

The Reagan administration limited itself to resisting all pressures aimed at achieving lower US interest rates, and to controlling multiple negotiations between the indebted countries and creditor banks. The latter were allowed to form a cartel to deal with the debtors and to avoid the standard controls of the Federal Reserve (although they were also invited to keep on lending beyond their own desires).[39] The US Treasury placed more and more stringent conditions on new loans bilaterally, and exerted growing pressure on multilateral financial institutions to follow the same line. Reagan's approach was to incentivize so-called "structural reforms" through what came to be known as "tight conditionality."[40] While the growth of poverty and social disparities registered in the continent after such shock therapy were subject to multiple critiques, what is relevant here is the fact that the debt crisis (and the US recipes to confront it) did not engender a new cycle of North-South confrontation, nor did it become a field of competition for the superpowers. On the contrary, it was precisely the ease with which US authorities managed the debt crisis that demonstrated that the US now enjoyed a condition of virtual dominance with no challengers in Latin America, to the point that those policies were later called the policies of the "Washington consensus."[41]

Multiplying challenges to "structural reforms" and continuing Soviet restraint

The story of the Latin American debt crisis could be told entirely without ever mentioning the Soviet Union. At least until 1986, the Soviet leadership failed to put in place any significant campaign on the subject, even a purely rhetorical one.[42] It is hard, however, to believe that there could be more propitious conditions to castigate the US. Not only was the economic crisis, after all, a quintessential capitalist crisis, but the events themselves exposed the US to external critiques, both for the harsh conditions attached to its rescue packages, and for the failure of those same conditions, once turned into (socially painful) policies, to spark economic growth.

On the contrary, the Soviet Union refrained from interfering, except for very minor moves. It kept developing modest economic and trade relations with various countries, and consolidated Argentina's role as a grain supplier.[43] As a creditor of Peru, it negotiated, in 1983, a "friendly" debt restructuring plan that demanded far less than did the US in the same period.[44] Moscow also negotiated a set of agreements with Mexico and Venezuela to rationalize respective oil sales, while negotiations continued for a Soviet contribution to the development of the Brazilian nuclear sector. Soviet international aid and credit in the area, however, remained negligible and, in general, there was never a broad political and diplomatic initiative to capitalize on the difficulties and resistance met by the US-backed "structural reforms."[45]

What seems to have been largely self-imposed restraint, on the part of the Soviet Union, still needs to be analyzed in detail. Soviet economic aid to the Third World did not diminish substantially in the 1980s, although it was being absorbed to a growing degree by Afghanistan and the Middle East.[46] Trade, particularly in weapons, grew in 1980–1985 but, again, Latin America was a tail-ender.[47] Soviet diplomacy in Latin America might have been affected to a certain extent by that sort of conservative approach that, according to Vladislav Zubok, was the main characteristic and legacy of Leonid Brezhnev's years in power (although western perceptions might have been different at the time).[48] Or, possibly, the long leadership transition which took place in Moscow from 1982 to 1985, from Brezhnev to Mikhail Gorbachev, through the ageing Yuri Andropov and Konstantin Chernenko, might have prevented the appreciation of the opportunities that were opening in Latin America.[49] Whatever the interpretation of Soviet behavior, its restraint probably gave the US a degree of freedom in its dealings with Latin American countries that was probably not (or not considered) available elsewhere in the early 1980s: in fact, in the Congo and the Middle East, but also in the Central American area, the US Treasury kept following State's indications to finance local clients with the "usual" largess.[50] Neither in 1983 nor in 1984 did the Reagan administration heed the World Bank's request for more funds (still judging the Bank's policies too strongly inspired by Keynesianism or, in the words of one Reagan advisor, "too socialist").[51] Further, tough negotiations such as those with Brazil and Argentina dragged on for months without provoking the US government to take any significant direct steps with interest rates (nor pressure on the commercial banks) to alleviate the debt burden.[52] On the contrary, Reagan openly preached "tight conditionality" during his meetings with Latin American leaders.[53]

Reagan's approach perplexed officials in some branches of the administration.[54] However, even the critics soon abandoned the argument that the Soviet Union might take advantage of the situation. While such preoccupations may have remained somewhere in the background, the critics now more often expressed concern for political stability in indebted countries, and fear that excessive austerity might completely block Latin American debt repayments to private banks and, thus, drag the entire Western financial system into bankruptcy.[55]

The challenges to the US approach multiplied in 1984 and, particularly, during 1985. As parliamentary democracy took hold in a growing number of countries, it became more and more difficult to impose the social costs of budget cuts through pure repression, more so as most of the debt burden had been accumulated by the dictatorships.[56] In most cases, the new governments' objections to their Western public and private counterparts consisted of very timid moves, coherent with the "controlled" form of the democratic transitions, that were often very keen not to reverse the policies of the military regimes.[57] Besides some not-so-effective positions taken by individual Finance Ministers and central bankers, however, there were also attempts at greater regional convergence, namely the so-called "Cartagena consensus," a consultation group of 11 Latin American governments that threatened to respond with a cartel of debtors to the existing cartel of creditor banks.[58] Alan Garçia, the (then) new social-democrat President of Peru, forcefully denounced his country's dependence on foreign capital before the UN, and refused to commit more than 10 percent of his country's export earnings to repay foreign debt, every year until after the crisis was solved.[59]

The Catholic church, an influential voice in Latin America, questioned the morality of the US administration's approach to debt negotiations.[60] More radically, in March 1985, in an interview with the Mexican newspaper *Excelsior*, Fidel Castro began what would soon become a relentless campaign for Latin American unity against "orthodox" foreign debt management.[61] While denouncing the "economic, political and moral" implications of the packages recommended by the US Treasury and the international institutions, the Cuban leader directly challenged the Reagan administration by advancing a provocative suggestion: in order to avoid a global financial collapse, the *líder máximo* suggested that, rather than having the new Latin American democracies pay for the debts incurred by their authoritarian predecessors, the US federal government should cut its defense budget (by 12 percent, to be precise) and devote the amount saved to repaying the creditor banks.

The Cuban government also complemented the diplomatic offensive by hosting in Havana, in August 1985, a large continental meeting "against the debt." Although only a few governments sent ministerial delegations, the success in terms of public opinion was huge, involving more than 1,000 delegates from NGOs, workers unions, religious groups, political parties and even some businessmen, who reached the Cuban capital from all over the continent at the expense of the Cuban government.[62] Debt relief found its way into the slogans of large swathes of Latin American public opinion, and the Cuban campaign did have some "soft power" consequence: in an article entitled "Cuba's emergence, America's Myopia," the *New York Times* columnist Tad Szulc wrote that the widespread perception in Latin America was that President Ronald Reagan, at best, "did not care about their awesome economic crisis, [while] Fidel Castro did."[63] As for the leaders, in public they often showed annoyance at Castro's campaign, but the international press reported that most of them were "privately delighted" to see the Cuban leader strengthening their bargaining position vis-à-vis the creditors (although no government was interested in repealing the debt, but rather in having better conditions for rescheduling).[64]

Castro's success with Latin American audiences, and the diplomatic rapprochement between the socialist island and the rest of the continent, did not go unnoticed in Washington. NSDD 235, dated 18 August 1986, further hardened US policy toward the island, blaming Cuba for "obsessively promoting a moratorium on payment of foreign debt by Latin American countries, seeking thereby to enhance its own influence in the region and to exacerbate political and economic problems."[65] Coming from an administration that saw Soviet puppets everywhere, however, it is worth noting that NSDD 235 never mentioned the Soviet Union. In fact, the Soviet Union remained conspicuous by its absence, to the point that even in Peru's case, US intelligence reports excluded the likelihood of "a massive [Soviet] commitment to aid the Garçia government, or Soviet over-exposure to influence the negotiations between Garçia and the western creditor banks."[66]

It was relatively easy for the Reagan administration to maintain its approach, with only minor changes. The US successfully kept refusing to "politicize" the debt issue, that is to treat it as a part of broader North-South negotiations or of comprehensive plans to reform the international monetary system. It responded to Latin American initiatives through intense diplomatic pressures, which were not too costly, however, in either economic or political terms.[67] The most significant step by the US government was the announcement of the *Program for Sustained Growth* at the joint meeting of the IMF and the World Bank in September 1985, by the new Secretary of the Treasury, James Baker. Also known as the "Baker plan," the program recognized, for the first time, that the Latin American crisis was not simply a liquidity crisis and it did make more US public funding available for the World Bank. The access to such funds remained conditional, however, upon the repayment of the entire debt at market rates, the undertaking of "structural reforms," and the abandonment of a "global" solution to the debt crisis: the negotiations should be kept strictly on bilateral terms with each indebted country.[68] Further, of the announced $29 billion that made up the package, $20 billion was supposed to come from the private banks that were "invited" to keep their flows active. In the following months, the Baker plan was subject to deep criticism even in the US: as it lacked any public guarantee to private banks, it did not activate a substantial return of investment into Latin America and was thus judged insufficient to restart the region's economic growth. To many observers, it seemed basically to have been conceived only as an operation to take time and divide the debtors, when not simply as a way to bail out private banks with public money.[69] However, as the very nature of such critiques demonstrated, the debate on the debt crisis now had little to do with the US–Soviet competition in the Third World.

Toward a unipolar world

The year 1986 marked a set of important changes in the Soviet Union: the worsening domestic economic situation implied a de facto limitation of the possibilities of its global reach, while the affirmation, at the 27th Congress of the Soviet Communist Party, of the "new thinking" promoted by the new General Secretary Mikhail Gorbachev, officially downplayed the importance of competition with the west in Soviet foreign policy, while opening up to expanded cooperation.[70] Paradoxically, it was only at this time that the Soviet Union began to play an active diplomatic role in Latin America: between the end of 1986 and the end of 1988, Gorbachev gave "royal receptions" and "red carpet welcomes" to several Latin American leaders, including Argentina's and Brazil's Presidents, Raúl Alfonsin and José Sarney, and Mexico's Foreign Minister Bernardo Sepúlveda Amor.[71] In September 1987, Eduard Shevardnadze was the first Soviet Foreign Minister ever to make a diplomatic tour of Latin America south of Mexico, when he visited Brazil, Argentina and Uruguay.[72] In this context, Latin American foreign debt problems naturally showed up in meeting agendas, and the Soviet Union repeatedly expressed its support for the rescheduling of international debt.[73] However, to support debt rescheduling was very different to supporting debt relief: the Soviet Union was very keen on avoiding a militant tone (the language of "global interdependence" was by then clearly prevailing over that of "international class struggle").[74] Indeed, Gorbachev's interest in expanding cooperation seemed reciprocated by Latin American governments and some observers saw, for a brief period, a "slipping" of US influence in the Gorbachev era.[75] But, as some anonymous Latin American diplomats already noted at the time, with the Soviet economy itself contracting considerably in the second half of the decade, increased Soviet activism also reflected its own growing need for good trade deals and, above all, it was deeply undermined by its own inability to substantiate words with facts, that is to provide Latin American economies with either aid or viable export markets.[76]

By the eventful year 1989, as superpower tensions subsided and commentators began to speak of the "end of the Cold War," Gorbachev attempted to make the debt issue a field of East-West global cooperation (by then several African countries had joined the Latin American ones as big debtors), with an open appeal to the yearly summit of the western industrialized powers.[77] By that time, however, the political and economic situation in the Soviet Union was so precarious that the General Secretary's move could easily be regarded as a de facto acceptance of Soviet subordination to western economic institutions and practices.[78] In any case, in

1989 Gorbachev assured the new US President, George H. W. Bush, that the Soviet Union was not seeking a sphere of influence in Latin America.[79]

In short, for the years after 1986, it is neither difficult to explain Soviet choices, nor to understand the scarce interest exerted by a decadent power with Latin American countries and the degree of self-confidence shown by US economic diplomats in proposing "tight conditionality" on a truly global scale.[80] With regard to the first half of the decade, however, the interpretation of some political aspects of the debt crisis seems more problematic. Even with all the threats of a moratorium on repayment, Latin American governments never really questioned the mechanisms of structural adjustment, often accepting conditions that were very harsh socially, humiliating in terms of their international prestige and, often, quite useless in macro economic terms (with the exception of inflation control).[81] Attempts at regional coordination had little more than symbolic value, while the search for help from the "other" superpower was undertaken only by a very small number of governments and to a very limited extent.[82]

Obviously, regardless of what the superpowers did or didn't do, these dynamics depended essentially on the choices of the governments in charge in Latin America: from this standpoint, there is no doubt that, both in the years of the dictatorships and in the early years of the fragile democracies, conservatism was the main characteristic of most governments in power in the region. In the years in question, the model of deregulated capitalism promoted by the Reagan administration clearly exerted attraction among Latin American elites, not only because of the economic boom then in place in the US, but also because of the widespread interpretation of the success of the "Asian tigers" as a result of those same policies.[83] Considering the low rates of growth delivered by the Soviet economy in the early 1980s, it is also likely that the Soviet centrally planned economic model had lost all of its attractiveness to Latin American leaders even before its ultimate crisis in the second half of the decade. Finally, well documented cases of corruption, Reagan's tough policies in Central America and the consolidated relationship between Latin American and US military apparatuses plausibly contributed to bring the message home to those leaders that were not enthusiastic fans of "market reforms."[84]

At the same time, all those elements were emphasized by the weakness of the Soviet stance, which was such as not to encourage any government to try, even in a purely instrumental way, the road of a tighter cooperation with the Soviet Union. From a US standpoint, the observation of the passivity of the global antagonist in the Latin American context paved the way for pursuing, with a very favorable balance of strength, economic objectives that were not easy to reach, such as the continued repayment of loans at high rates, and the greater integration of the indebted countries into US-dominated markets. It is difficult to tell, on the basis of the available sources, whether there was a precise moment in which the US reconsidered its own initial analysis of Soviet potentialities in Latin America. Possibly, the change in US perceptions was the result of a progressive acquisition of elements, although the late months of 1982 seem to have marked a watershed. Similarly, it is difficult to tell when the US acquired enough confidence to push the "structural reforms" in other areas of the world.[85] In general, however, with the limited exceptions of Fidel Castro and the Catholic church, the Reagan administration was the only real political interlocutor of the Latin American governments throughout the decade. While Reagan publicly campaigned against Soviet machinations in the Western hemisphere until the very end of his second term in office,[86] US policy-makers had largely acquired, after a relatively short time in power, the consciousness of the extremely favorable conditions they enjoyed in Latin America, and acted consequentially in shaping their economic diplomacy. In short, a vast region of the Third World presented a US-centered unipolar order almost one decade before the "official" end of the "Cold War."

Notes

1 R. Reagan, "Excerpts From an Interview With Walter Cronkite of CBS News," 3 March 1981, in University of California at Santa Barbara, *The American Presidency Project* (henceforth APP). Available online at www.presidency.ucsb.edu (accessed 12 June 2010).

2 Reagan attributed important tasks in the White House and State Department to a group of neoconservative intellectuals (Lewis Tambs, Roger Fontaine, David Jordan, Gordon Sumner and Lynn Francis Bouchey) who had authored, in 1980, a controversial pamphlet describing the Caribbean as a "red lake." See: Committee of Santa Fe, *A New Inter-American Policy for the Eighties* (Washington, DC: Council for Inter-American Security, 1980).

3 R. Reagan, *An American Life* (New York: Simon & Schuster, 1990), p. 239.

4 A "skeptical" view was expressed, for example, by W. LaFeber, "The Reagan Administration and Revolutions in Central America," *Political Science Quarterly* 1, 1984, pp. 1–25.

5 R. Leiken, "Eastern Winds in Latin America," *Foreign Policy* 42, 1981, pp. 94–113: 96; "New Latin Focus Urged," *The Chicago Tribune*, 3 January 1984, p. B1.

6 From the very beginning of his presidency, in order to "take back the Caribbean," Reagan escalated the military, psychological and economic pressure on the Cuban, Nicaraguan and Grenadian socialist governments, and actively supported counterinsurgency in El Salvador and Guatemala: R. Reagan, *The Reagan Diaries* (New York: Harper Collins, 2007), p. 1 (entry of 28 January 1981). Several obituaries for the ex-president in 2004, and some lengthier pieces of work, identify in such decisions the root cause of the halt of Soviet advances in the Third World: L. Aron, "How Reagan Made Soviet Society Face Its Failures," *USA Today*, 10 June 2004, p. 15; P. Schweizer, *Reagan's War. The Epic Story of His Forty-Year Struggle and Final Triumph over Communism* (Westminster, MD: Doubleday, 2003). Besides noting that, technically, the Caribbean was not a part of the US "to take back," several scholars have downplayed instead the relevance of Soviet activism in the Latin American context in the 1980s, stressing primarily the indigenous roots of the revolutionary movements: W. LeoGrande, *Our Own Backyard: The United States in Central America, 1977–1992* (Chapel Hill, NC: University of North Carolina Press, 1998); G. Grandin, *The*

W. LeoGrande, *Our Own Backyard: The United States in Central America, 1977–1992* (Chapel Hill, NC: University of North Carolina Press, 1998); G. Grandin, *The Last Colonial Massacre. Latin America in the Cold War* (Chicago, IL: Chicago University Press, 2004).

7 These issues can be considered the "local" version of broader questions concerning the "end of the Cold War": see J. Suri, "Explaining the End of the Cold War: A New Historical Consensus?," *Journal of Cold War Studies* 4, 2002, pp. 60–92; C. Wallander, "Western Policy and the Demise of the Soviet Union," *Journal of Cold War Studies* 4, 2003, pp. 137–77. They also intercept the debate on the interpretation of the "Cold War" itself, stimulated by A. Stephanson, "Liberty or Death: The Cold War as US Ideology," in O. A. Westad (ed.), *Reviewing the Cold War. Approaches, Interpretations, Theory* (London: Cass, 2000), pp. 81–98.

8 On these issues (and in general on the debt crisis): C. Marichal, "The Finances of Hegemony in Latin America: Debt Negotiations and the Role of the US Government, 1945–2005," in F. Rosen (ed.), *Empire and Dissent. The United States and Latin America* (Durham, NC: Duke University Press, 2008), pp. 90–117; P. Gowan, *The Global Gamble. Washington's Faustian Bid for World Dominance* (London: Verso, 1999); J. Ward, *Latin America: Conflict and Development since 1945* (London: Routledge, 1997); T. Biersteker (ed.) *Dealing with Debt. International Financial Negotiations and Adjustment Bargaining* (Boulder, CO: Westview, 1993); A. Colosimo, *Il debito estero dei Paesi in via di sviluppo* (Padova: CEDAM, 1991); B. Stallings and R. Kaufman (eds.), *Debt and Democracy in Latin America* (Boulder, CO: Westview, 1989).

9 B. Crossette, "Latin America's Economies Lose Steam," *New York Times*, 19 October 1981, p. A6.

10 See, in particular: A. Hirschman, "The Stability of Neutralism: A Geometrical Note," *The American Economic Review* 2, 1964, pp. 94–100. On Latin American governments' attempts to play the triangular game with the two superpowers between the late 1960s and the mid-1970s (when the wave of right-wing military coups realigned the region more firmly with the US): H. Brands, "Third World Politics in an Age of Global Turmoil: The Latin American Challenge to U.S. and Western Hegemony, 1965–1975," *Diplomatic History* 1, 2008, pp. 105–39. In general on "Cold War" economic diplomacy: L. Tosi and L. Tosone (eds.), *Gli aiuti allo sviluppo nelle relazioni internazionali del secondo dopoguerra* (Padova: Cedam, 2006); M. Alacevich, *Le origini della Banca Mondiale. Una deriva conservatrice* (Milano: Bruno Mondatori, 2006); M. Del Pero, *Libertà e impero. Gli Stati Uniti e il mondo 1776–2006* (Roma-Bari: Laterza, 2008), pp. 330–3. On US–Soviet competition in the Third World in general: Westad, *Global Cold War*.

11 On US–Latin American relations: M. Cricco, M. E. Guasconi and M. L. Napoletano (eds.), *L'America Latina tra Guerra fredda e globalizzazione* (Firenze: Polistampa, 2010); J. Smith, *The United States and Latin America A History of American Diplomacy, 1776–2000* (London: Routledge, 2006); A. McPherson, *Intimate Ties, Bitter Struggles: The United States and Latin America since 1945* (Washington, DC: Potomac Books, 2006); R. Nocera, *Stati Uniti e America Latina dal 1945 a oggi* (Roma: Carocci, 2005); G. Grandin, *Empire's Workshop. Latin America, the United States, and the Rise of the New Imperialism* (New York: Owl Books, 2007). See, also, the chapters on Latin America in G. C. Herring, *From Colony to Superpower. US Foreign relations since 1776* (New York: Oxford University Press, 2008). Soviet–Latin American relations have received less attention in scholarly monographs: C. Blasier, *The Giant's Rival: The USSR and Latin America* (Pittsburgh, PA: Pittsburgh University Press, 1983). Also see the relevant chapters in V. Zubok, *A Failed Empire. The Soviet Union in the Cold War from Stalin to Gorbachev* (Chapel Hill, NC: University of North Carolina Press, 2007).

12 P. Kornbluh, *The Pinochet File: A Declassified Dossier on Atrocity and Accountability* (New York: New Press, 2003).

13 D. Paszyn, *The Soviet Attitude to Political and Social Change in Central America, 1979–1990: Case Studies on Nicaragua, El Salvador and Guatemala* (New York: St. Martin's Press, 2000).

14 C. Andrew, V. Mitrokhin, *The World Was Going Our Way* (New York: Basic, 2006), pp. 104–7.

15 NSDD 32, "US National Security Strategy 1982," 15 April 1982, top secret, in National Security Archive, *Digital National Security Archive* (henceforth DNSA). Online. Available online at www.gwu.edu/~nsarchiv (accessed 12 June 2010).

16 See National Security Adviser R. Allen to White House counsellors E. Meese, J. Baker and M. Deaver, "Policy Action Requirements for President's Participation in Cancun," 20 August 1981, confidential, in *Declassified Documents Reference System* (henceforth DDRS). Online. Available online at www.galegroup.com (accessed 12 June 2010); Department of State Bureau of Intelligence and Research, "The Mexico Summit: Sign of a New Era in North-South Negotiations?," 22 June 1981, secret, DDRS.

17 National Intelligence Council Memorandum, "US–Soviet Competition for Influence in the Third World: How the LDCs Play It," 1 April 1982, secret, in CIA, *Freedom of Information Act* (henceforth CIA-FOIA). Available online at www.foia.cia.gov (accessed 12 June 2010).

18 L. Schoultz, "Politics, Economics, and US Participation in Multilateral Development Banks," *International Organization* 3, 1982, pp. 537–74: 566. The request to re-examine Carter's policies is discussed in Secretary of the Treasury D. Regan to Secretary of State A. Haig, "Human rights and the Multilateral Development Banks," 23 February 1981, confidential, Ronald Reagan Presidential Library, Simi Valley, USA (henceforth RRL), Executive Secretariat NSC (henceforth ES), Subject File (henceforth SF), box 39, Human Rights. This controversial choice was defended in J. Kirkpatrick, *Dictatorships and Double Standards. Rationalism and Reason in Politics* (New York: Simon & Schuster, 1982).

19 B. Nossiter, "Haig Aide Says U.S. Opposes Sharing the Wealth," *New York Times*, 7 August 1981, p. A6.

20 See NSC staff member N. Bailey to R. Allen, "International Debt, Eurocurrency Movements and the IMF," 3 June 1981, RRL, ES, Meeting files, box 91282, NSC00013.

21 Council of Economic Advisers chairman M. Weidenbaum to R. Reagan, "IMF/WB Meetings," 17 September 1981, RRL, White House Office of Records Management (henceforth WHORM), SF, IT 044; "Executive Summary," 21 September 1981, RRL, Meese Files, Multilateral Development Banks, box OA9946. Budget director David Stockman had actually requested even larger cuts to US contributions to the World Bank: C. Gwin, *US Relations with the World Bank 1945–92* (Washington, DC: Brookings Institution Press, 1994), pp. 37–45.

22 R. Reagan, "Remarks at a Luncheon of the World Affairs Council of Philadelphia in Philadelphia, Pennsylvania," 15 October 1981, APP.

23 S. Karnow, "Pluck won't do it," *The Chicago Tribune*, 17 October 1981, p. S9; A. Pine, "Reagan Will Confront Some Political Risk At 22-Nation Summit in Mexico This Week," *The Wall Street Journal*, 20 October 1981, p. 5.

24 NSDD 34, "US Actions in the South Atlantic Crisis," 14 May 1982, top secret, DNSA. In general: A. Cèsar Vacs, "Soviet Policy toward Argentina and the Southern Cone," *Annals of the American Academy of Political and Social Science* 494, 1985, pp. 159–71: 164.

25 NSSD 10–82, "US Policy toward the Americas as a Result of the Falkland Crisis," 23 June 1982, secret, DNSA.
26 Special National Intelligence Estimate, "Soviet Policies and Activities in Latin America and the Caribbean," 25 June 1982, secret, p. 1.
27 Ibid., p. 2. On the complexity of Cuba's relationship to the USSR: P. Gleijeses, "Moscow's Proxy? Cuba and Africa 1975–1988," *Journal of Cold War Studies* 4, 2006, pp. 98–146.
28 Special National Intelligence Estimate, "Soviet Policies," p. 2.
29 C. Urzua, "Five Decades of Relations between the World Bank and Mexico," in D. Kapur, J. Lewis and R. Webb (eds.), *The World Bank. Its First Half Century*, Vol. 2, *Perspectives* (Washington, DC: Brookings Institution Press, 1997), pp. 49–108: 69.
30 J. Demetrius, E. Tregurtha, S. MacDonald, "A Brave New World: Debt, Default and Democracy in Latin America," *Journal of Interamerican Studies and World Affairs* 2, 1986, pp. 17–38; D. Kapur, J. Lewis and R. Webb (eds.), *The World Bank. Its First Half Century*, Vol. 1, *History* (Washington, DC: Brookings Institution Press, 1997), pp. 597–629; S. Brooks, "Explaining Capital Account Liberalization in Latin America: A Transitional Cost Approach," *World Politics* 1, 2004, pp. 389–430.
31 H. Handelman, W. Baer, "Introduction," in H. Handelman and W. Baer (eds.), *Paying the Costs of Austerity in Latin America* (Boulder, CO.: Westview, 1989), pp. 2–15.
32 Cited in S. Livingston, "The Limits of High Politics: When National Security and International Economic Goals Conflict in American Foreign Policymaking," *Polity* 3, 1994, pp. 417–394: 435.
33 See "Without Large Scale-Assistance ... [Progress] Will Be Set Back," *Washington Post*, 12 January 1984, p. A13.
34 Cited in S. Livingston, "The Limits of High Politics," p. 434. Donald Regan was the former president of the New York Stock Exchange and chief executive of Merrill Lynch financial company. In general, for four consecutive years in 1981–1984, Latin America transferred abroad more money than it was receiving: D. Kunz, *Butter and Guns: America's Cold War Economic Diplomacy* (New York: Free Press, 1997), p. 278.
35 On the "neoliberal" policies recommended by Washington: J. Frieden, *Global Capitalism. Its Fall and Rise in the Twentieth Century* (New York: Norton, 2006), pp. 364–90; D. Harvey, *A Brief History of Neoliberalism* (New York: Oxford University Press, 2005), pp. 5–31.
36 NSDD 71, "US Policy toward Latin America in the Wake of the Falklands Crisis," 30 November 1982, top secret, DNSA.
37 NSSD 3–83, "US Approach to the International Debt Problem," 14 March 1983, secret, DNSA.
38 NSDD 131, "United States Goals and Objectives for the 1984 Economic Summit," 12 March 1984, secret, in Federation of American Scientists, *Intelligence Resource Program* (FAS). Available online at www.fas.org/irp/offdocs/nsdd/index.html (accessed 12 June 2010).
39 B. C. Lee, *The Economics of International Debt Renegotiation* (Boulder, CO: Westview, 1993), pp. 14–26.
40 M. Weidenbaum to R. Reagan, "IMF/WB Meetings," 17 September 1981, RRL, WHORM, SF, IT 044.
41 J. Williamson, "What Washington Means by Policy Reform," in J. Williamson (ed.), *Latin American Adjustment: How Much Has Happened* (Washington, DC: Institute for International Economics, 1990), pp. 7–20.
42 Keyword search on the combined databases of the *New York Times*, the *Los Angeles Times*, the *Washington Post*, the *Wall Street Journal*, and the *Chicago Tribune*, between 1979 and 1989.

43 R. Evanson, "Soviet Political Uses of Trade with Latin America," *Journal of Inter-american Studies and World Affairs* 2, 1985, pp. 99–126: 113.
44 R. Berrios, C. Blasier, "Peru and the Soviet Union (1969–1989): Distant Partners," *Journal of Latin American Studies* 2, 1991, pp. 365–84: 370.
45 W. R. Duncan, "Soviet Interests in Latin America: New Opportunities and Old Constraints," *Journal of Interamerican Studies and World Affairs* 2, 1984, pp. 163–98.
46 Zubok, *Failed Empire*, p. 297. US intelligence reached similar conclusions at the time: CIA Directorate of Intelligence, "Communist Military Transfers and Economic Aid to Non-Communist LDCs, 1983," 1 May 1984, secret; and CIA Directorate of Intelligence, "Communist Military Transfers and Economic Aid to Non-Communist LDCs, 1984," 1 May 1985, secret, CIA-FOIA.
47 A. Nove, *An Economic History of the USSR* (London: Penguin, 1989), p. 376.
48 Zubok, *Failed Empire*, pp. 223–46. A similar conclusion can be inferred also from a large set of considerations in A. Graziosi, *Storia dell'Unione Sovietica*, Vol. 2, *L'URSS dal trionfo al degrado* (Bologna: Il Mulino, 2008), pp. 460–501.
49 The story of the "jockeying invalids" at the top of the Soviet echelon of power is told in S. Kotkin, *Armageddon Averted. The Soviet Collapse 1970–2000* (New York: Oxford University Press, 2001), pp. 49–57.
50 State Department Executive Secretary P. Bremer to R. Allen, "Visit of President Mobutu to the US," 16 November 1981, secret, RRL, ES, Country File, Africa, box 5, Zaire; NSC staff member R. Robinson to National Security Adviser R. McFarlane, "Honduran Economic Requests," 6 January 1984, confidential, RRL, ES, SF, box 42, IMF.
51 White House aide C. Fuller to R. Reagan, "Meeting with Tom Clausen," 8 July 1983, RRL, WHORM, SF, box 44408–73399, IT 044.
52 D. Regan to R. Reagan, "Brazilian financial negotiations," 2 September 1983, secret; D. Regan to National Security Adviser W. Clark, "Brazil's financial situation," 15 September 1983, confidential; White House counsellor C. Hicks to various recipients, "Interagency group on international economic policy (IG-IEP)," 19 September 1984, unclassified with confidential attachment, RRL, ES, SF, box 42, IMF.
53 See for example: R. Reagan, "Responses to Questions Submitted by Latin American Newspapers," 30 November 1982, APP; R. Reagan, *Diaries*, p. 105 (entry of 9 August 1983, about a meeting with Mexican President Miguel de la Madrid); R. Reagan, "Remarks at the Welcoming Ceremony for President Raúl Alfonsin of Argentina," 19 March 1985, APP.
54 During 1983, NSC officials confidentially referred to Treasury as the "ostrich brigade" for its perceived inaction on the debt crisis: N. Bailey to W. Clark, "CIA Reports on the IMF and the International Debt Crisis," 5 May 1983, unclassified with confidential attachment; note by unidentified NSC staffer, 13 October 1983, commenting the attached Regan to Reagan, "Results of the 1983 World Bank/International Monetary Fund Annual Meetings," 6 October 1983, confidential, RRL, ES, SF, box 42, IMF.
55 The 1983 *Regional Strategic Plan* of the State Department's Agency for International Development (AID) made only one brief reference, in more than 100 pages, to unspecified "hostile forces" that "actively sought to exploit the region's economic difficulties to their advantage": AID, "Regional Strategic Plan for Latin America and the Caribbean," 1 December 1983, p. 2, DNSA. Fears of Soviet gains from the debt crisis would surface instead, from time to time, in the public debate: see, for example, Democrat Senator B. Bradley, "A Venice Lifeboat for Drowning Debtors," *Washington Post*, 9 June 1987, p. A35.

56 Bolivia went back to parliamentary democracy in 1982, Argentina in 1983, Uruguay in 1985. Brazil completed in 1988 a long transition. In Paraguay, Alfredo Stroessner's long dictatorship ended in 1989, while Chilean dictator Augusto Pinochet left power (but not control of the armed forces) in 1990. In Mexico, the formally democratic political system built on the centrality of the *Partido Revolucionario Institucional,* was shaken in 1989 by the creation of the left-leaning *Partido de la Revolución Democrática.*

57 This aspect of the democratic transitions (and, more generally, the lingering power of the military) affected Latin American societies and politics more than just through economic policy continuity: laws such as the Argentine *Ley de Punto Final* (abolished only in 2003) guaranteed the former military rulers exemption from criminal prosecution.

58 The Cartagena consensus, created in July 1984, was formed by Brazil, Mexico, Argentina, Venezuela, Chile, Colombia, Peru. Ecuador, Uruguay, Bolivia and the Dominican Republic.

59 E. Ferrero Costa, "Peruvian Foreign Policy: Current Trends, Constraints and Opportunities," *Journal of Interamerican Studies and World Affairs* 2, 1987, pp. 55–78.

60 Pontifical Justice and Peace Commission, "An Ethical Approach to the International Debt Question," *Origins* 34, 1987.

61 See in particular: "La Deuda Debe Cancelarse: Fidel Castro," interview in *Excelsior,* 27 March 1985, p. 1; J. Treaster, "Castro's Modest Proposal," *New York Times,* 25 August 1985, p. E3. Also see: P. O'Brien, " 'The Debt cannot Be Paid': Castro and the Latin American Debt," *Bulletin of Latin American Research* 1, 1986, pp. 41–63; D. Basosi, "In the Shadow of the Washington Consensus: Cuba's Rapprochement with Latin America in a World Going Unipolar," in A. Lorini and D. Basosi (eds.), *Cuba in the World, the World in Cuba. Essays in Cuban History, Politics, and Culture* (Firenze: Firenze University Press, 2009), pp. 279–90.

62 J. Treaster, "Cuban Meeting Stokes Emotions on Latin Debt," *New York Times,* 1 August 1985, p. D1.

63 T. Szulc, "Cuba's Emergence, America's Myopia," *New York Times,* 5 May 1985, p. E25.

64 J. Treaster, "Castro Builds relations with South America," *New York Times,* 19 May 1985, p. 1.

65 NSDD 235, "Strengthening Policy Toward Cuba," 18 August 1986, secret, FAS.

66 Special National Intelligence Estimate, "Peru: Prospects for Increased Soviet Bloc Influence," 1 November 1985, secret, CIA-FOIA.

67 Garçia's activism, in particular, was defined "disturbing" in confidential White House exchanges. But traditional bilateral and multilateral diplomatic channels were believed sufficient to convince him and the other Latin American leaders that the US-sponsored "debt strategy [was] still valid and sufficiently flexible" and that "radical 'political' approaches [were] counterproductive": memorandum for the Vice-President, "Peruvian Debt Situation," 25 July 1985, secret, DDRS. Also: Treasury paper, "Second Cartagena Follow-Up Meeting," 18 September 1984, confidential, RRL, ES, SF, box 42, IMF.

68 C. Farnsworth, "US May Back Higher Lending by World Bank," *New York Times,* 7 October 1985, p. 50.

69 See: R. Broad, "How About a Real Solution to Third World Debt?," *New York Times,* 28 September 1987, p. A25; C. Bogdanowicz-Bindert, "The Debt Crisis: The Baker Plan Revisited," *Journal of Interamerican Studies and World Affairs* 3, 1986, pp. 33–45; K. Lissakers, *Banks Borrowers and the Establishment* (New York: Basic, 1991). Those interpretations according to which the "Baker plan" was only a public relations operation, seem to be confirmed by a set of NSC memos

from the days preceding the announcement, expressing almost complete ignorance of what the secretary of the Treasury would actually announce: NSC staff members S. Danzansky and H. Soos to R. McFarlane, "African Economic Initiative," 4 October 1985, unclassified with confidential attachment, RRL, Danzansky Files, International Trade VIII (A), box 90971, IMF.

70 S. Brooks, W. Wolhforth, "Power, Globalization, and the End of the Cold War," *International Security* 3, 2000–2001, pp. 5–53; R. English, "The Sociology of New Thinking. Elites, Identity Change, and the End of the Cold War," *Journal of Cold War Studies* 2, 2005, pp. 43–80.

71 B. Graham, "Argentina Leads Latin America toward Closer Ties with Soviets," *Washington Post,* 4 November 1986, p. A12; B. Keller, "Soviet, in a Shift, Expands Contact with Third World," *New York Times,* 25 May 1987, p. 1; M. Dobbs, "Brazilian Gets Red Carpet Welcome," *Washington Post,* 19 October 1988, p. A26.

72 G. Lee, "Moscow Seeks Closer Latin Relations," *Washington Post,* 27 September 1987, p. A28.

73 M. Dobbs, "Brazilian." Also see Svetlana Savranskaya's chapter in this volume.

74 In general: H. Zadeh, "Perestroika and the Third World," *Review of Radical Political Economics* 2–3, 1990, pp. 252–75; Westad, *Global Cold War,* p. 385.

75 G. Lee, "US World Influence Seen Slipping in Gorbachev Era," *Washington Post,* 29 May 1987, p. A27.

76 G. Lee, "Moscow." Also: F. Bustamante, "Soviet Policy toward Latin America: Time for Renewal," *Journal of Interamerican Studies and World Affairs* 4, 1987, pp. 35–65.

77 See: S. Greenhouse, "Gorbachev Urges Economic Accords," *New York Times,* 16 July 1989, p. 17.

78 By September 1986, the US government recognized "the recent Soviet interest in global economic institutions" and did not rule out a possible Soviet demand to join the IMF and World Bank: NSSD 2–86, "Soviet Initiatives in International Economic Affairs," 16 September 1986, secret, DNSA.

79 Zubok, *Failed Empire,* p. 328.

80 In 1986, Shultz and Baker openly emphasized the "winds of freedom that [were] sweeping the world" to indicate the two processes (which they presented as inseparable) of economic deregulation and political democratization that seemed to be taking hold in large portions of the Third World: G. Shultz and J. Baker to R. Reagan, "Tokyo Economic Summit: Scope Paper," 1 May 1986, confidential, DNSA.

81 Mexico underwent a new major financial crisis in 1994, Brazil in 1998 and Argentina in 2001.

82 S. Tussie, "The Coordination of Latin American Debtors: Is There a Logic behind the Story?," in S. Griffith-Jones (ed.), *Managing World Debt* (New York: St. Martin's Press, 1988), pp. 282–307.

83 This interpretation has been recently questioned. See: D. Rodrik (ed.), *In Search of Prosperity: Analytic Narratives on Economic Growth* (Princeton, NJ: Princeton University Press, 2003).

84 Consolidating (the already good) military-to-military relations was a constant goal expressed in US strategic directives on Latin America: NSDD 71, "US Policy toward Latin America"; NSSD, "8–85. US–South American Relations," 19 November 1985, top secret, DNSA. Corruption involved many Latin American leaders of the time, whose personal fortune grew inversely to those of their countries.

85 In early 1985, NSDD 156 launched the *Food for Progress* initiative for Africa, claiming that "the socialist economic systems, prevalent in LDCs, [had not succeeded] in promoting economic growth," and that "as a result, and because of

insufficient economic aid from the Soviet Union, a growing number of Third World countries once dominated by the socialist model [were] experiencing with market approaches": NSDD 156, "US Third World Food Aid: A 'Food for Progress' Program," 3 January 1985, confidential, FAS.

86 R. Reagan, "Interview With Soviet Television Journalists Valentin Zorin and Boris Kalyagin," 20 May 1988, in APP.

10 Brazilian assessments of the end of the Cold War

Matias Spektor

This chapter deals with the reception in Brazil, of the end of the Cold War. It shows that Brazilian estimates of international relations in and around 1989 mixed some gloom and much expectation about the future, but betrayed very little of the triumphalism that was common in other quarters of Latin America. It also argues that Brazilian readings of change in the international system at that time help explain why and how the global Cold War shaped modern Brazil and it suggests that the terms of the debate in Brazil about the end of the Cold War sit at the heart of the strategic concepts governing the country's behavior in the era of unipolarity that followed the fall of the Berlin Wall.[1]

Brazil was never a major hot spot in the global narrative of the Cold War. The Soviet Union and the Soviet worldview never represented a feasible alternative for Brazil's development, and the relationship between the Brazilian Communist Party and Moscow had been strained since the mid-1930s. Unlike other parts of the Western hemisphere – most noticeably Cuba and Central America – Brazil's world was never truly bipolar. Strategic debates inside the country, throughout the period that coincides with the Cold War, evolved around how close or how distant to be, politically and diplomatically, from the US. But, whenever local leaders chose strategies of distancing, their move did not imply a swing towards the Soviet camp. For all the drama that marked the historical clashes between the Right and the Left inside the country, the argument sometimes prevalent in Washington that "If Brazil were to be lost it would not be another Cuba. It would be another China" was always unwarranted.[2]

Yet, the global Cold War mattered enormously to Brazil. Part of the story was political: global ideological confrontation limited policy space at home, skewing the balance of power among local elites towards the military and the ideological Right. Under the banner of anti-Communism, successive governing regimes chased, imprisoned, exiled and killed opponents representing indigenous forms of socialism or Communism – both before the Second World War and after. And, while no Brazilian leader truly feared Soviet intervention or foreign-sponsored guerrilla activity in the country, concern for national security against perceived threats from the indigenous

Left, and its manifold transnational ties, underpinned a powerful system of state-led repression and authoritarianism from the mid-1930s to the mid-1940s and then, again, from the mid-1960s to the mid-1980s. By the same token, those in opposition to successive administrations oftentimes framed their own vision in terms of the global struggle between capitalism and socialism. The Brazilian Left saw itself as part and parcel of a wider international network of activists bound together by the common experience of repression and exile. For those Brazilian university professors fleeing to Salvador Allende's Chile for asylum; for students imprisoned in the aftermath of major protests in Rio de Janeiro in 1968; and for those who lost their loved ones as a result of political polarization and violence, the Cold War was not only real, but one of the single, most powerful, international constraints shaping political life in Brazil.

But politics was only part of the story. Equally powerful was the connection between the Cold War and Brazil's political economy. The global struggle set the international parameters under which successive Brazilian generations built their own model of conservative, state-led, modernization. The institutional pillars for global economic management in the West – free trade and private sources of investment, the Bretton Woods agencies, the power of the US dollar and the authority of the US Treasury, the financial regulations emanating from private bodies originated in the leading economies – set the framework within which Brazil transitioned from backward, rural, economy in the 1940s to fast-industrializing, urbanized, top ten, economy in the world at the end of the Cold War.

For all of its inequalities and perversities, Brazil's economic development throughout this period was simply remarkable. Surely the country did not achieve this by adhering fully to the rules emanating from Washington. On the contrary, to a large extent the policy mix it adopted did not fit in neatly with US priorities. In this period Brazil built up tariff walls and subsidies to protect and foster indigenous capitalist enterprise; it conditioned international investment to rules that propped up local capitalists; it focused its industrial policies not for export, but for the internal market; its officials picked up "strategic" sectors for massive investment with only partial care for merit and competitiveness; its state-owned enterprises proliferated and dominated the national economy; and successive administrations tried hard to secure technology transfers to develop indigenous technological capacity in nuclear power, weapons and the space and aircraft sectors. But successive Brazilian leaders could get away with violating and adapting so many of the rules of the game because the environment of the Cold War was permissive enough to allow such experimentation. As declassified documents show, political/security considerations in the US secured support in Washington's acceptance for Brazil's economic management. Also, "embedded liberalism" – the practice of highly regulated capitalism that was common from the mid-1940s to the mid-1970s – helped legitimize Brazil's strategy at home and abroad.[3]

To some extent, however, the tight constraints and divisions typical of the Cold War began to recede in Brazil years before 1989. At least in the eyes of many Brazilians, the Cold War had come to an end sometime in the 1970s. This was a period when the tiny revolutionary Left lost momentum and greater social participation in public life pushed the ruling military out of power, slowly but surely. Also, as Brazil began to clash with the US over human rights abuses and nuclear proliferation in the mid-1970s, the domestic impact was national cohesion rather than division along ideological lines. When those purged and exiled in the 1960s returned, under a new amnesty law in 1979, nobody feared the reopening of previous ideological wounds. Increasingly, as the 1980s progressed, most Brazilians worried about rampant inflation and the pace of democracy's restoration rather than the Left/Right divide. The hardening of the global Cold War in the 1980s remained distant for most Brazilians, even if Latin America remained one of the major theatres for the international struggle. The rise of a workers party and a social democratic party in the 1980s brought back onto the scene notions of social justice and fairness, coupled with a staunch critique of Brazilian-style capitalism. But, for all the waves that these arguments did generate, fears of radicalization, typical of the early 1960s, were on the wane.

One month after the fall of the Berlin Wall, Brazilians elected their first president for over two decades in what was the first election, ever, by universal suffrage (prior to that election only literate citizens could vote). Yes, the presidential race pitting Fernando Collor de Mello against Luiz Inácio Lula da Silva was reminiscent of the old battles between the Right and the Left. But the two candidates had come of age in the late 1970s and embodied a post-Cold War attitude to the world. In seeking a mandate, they emphasized their commitment to curbing social inequality, modernizing government practices and taming inflation. For those attending campaign rallies, on either side, the dominant dynamics were domestic, and the connections between what was going on at home and major transformation abroad were both vague and unobvious.

The fall of the Berlin wall was heralded in much of Latin America with an enormous sense of optimism. As the major regional countries began to move towards greater political liberalization or even democracy, the general tenor was one of positive expectation about the future. The most cursory glance at the commentary in the Brazilian press at the time will show that the feeling of liberation reverberated there too. But at least among strategists there was none of the triumphalism that set the tone elsewhere.

Brazilian leaders reacted to the events of 1989 with a good dose of apprehension. Going through the existing evidence it is possible to identify at least two recurring themes: Brazilian concern that US vindication in the global struggle would push Washington into ever more forceful, intrusive, policies worldwide; and fear that the neoliberal agenda, that so challenged Brazil's traditional development model, would now further limit policy options. Even if many in Brazil welcomed the end of the Soviet empire, the ruling elites felt ill at ease with the notion of a global order marked by the overwhelming power of an unrivalled US.

There is no doubt that the global Cold War "closed down" Latin America. By integrating the region into the US-alliance system more strongly than it had been before, the Cold War caused the rewriting of the rules of the game in the region and the imposition of stricter limits on what Latin Americans could do. This was a hegemonic system formalized through military alliance, military training and transfers, trade and investment, aid, and a network of regional institutions. But coexisting with these elements were other forces pushing in the opposite direction. The Cold War diverted US attention from the region – or from parts of the region – and, by and large, US preoccupations with the region remained both intermittent and selective. Brazilian leaders, for long periods during the Cold War, never felt that anyone in Washington was watching too closely or seeking to control too tightly. On the contrary, from a Brazilian perspective, the trajectory had been one of growing voice and power in dealings with the US because there were massive cracks in the US alliance system, because Washington had too many pressing concerns in other parts of the world, and because Brazil had become too big economically and demographically to be pushed around.

While fear of US dominance had been very real in the 1940s and early 1950, by the mid-1960s the pattern of US hegemony in the region could not be characterized by a tight imperial system in any detectable way. This is not to say that the US was indifferent to developments in Brazil – after all, the country was the single largest beneficiary of "Alliance for Progress" funding. It is also useful to remember the various counterinsurgency activities and the genuine concerns in Washington about the rise of the Left and student protest in the country under Presidents Lyndon Johnson and Richard Nixon. Nor is it true to say that the US was not powerful or influential in Brazil. Rather, it suggests that, for all the problems inherent to the international system of the Cold War, over time Brazil enjoyed ample room for maneuver.

Starting in the early 1960s, Brazil went into Third-Worldist mode – albeit partially and never forcefully. Brazilians sought to establish contacts with states in the Communist Bloc and began to support the loosening of Portuguese control over African colonies. Brazil also launched mildly revisionist initiatives that were far more assertive than previous practice, although not radical at all when compared to that of other large, developing, countries at that time, such as Egypt, India or Indonesia. The general orientation was not necessarily anti-US, but was, surely, one geared towards greater de-alignment from Washington. In this period Brazilian diplomats co-founded UNCTAD and pushed for the notion of collective economic security; Brazil refused to sign the Non-Proliferation Treaty; it began to support the decolonization movement, loudly, for the first time; it argued at the UN for a transference of 1 percent of global military expenditure to the promotion of global economic development; it kept observer status at the Non-Aligned Movement (although it never joined it, making its support conditional and fluctuating); it canvassed for UN Charter reform to increase its say on key committees; it joined Third-World pledges for a New International Economic Order; it abandoned its support for Israel and South Africa; it extended its territorial waters from 3 to 200 miles against US protest; it fought against international norms for environmental protection; and it rejected population control measures advocated by the IMF, the World Bank and the UN.

Within this, the international system of the 1960s and 1970s was relatively flexible for Brazil. There is ample evidence from this period showing that many in the country believed the Cold War had actually come to an end. By the time we get to détente, there were several contradictions in Brazilian readings. Negative views of détente coexisted with the more positive ones. Some saw détente as a superpower coalition to "freeze up" the structures of the international system and prevent rising states from the postcolonial world from emerging. According to this view, détente was a neocolonial project. But others thought that Brazil could efficiently exploit the "cracks in the grand Western alliance," namely the new foreign policy interests of Western Europe and Japan, to its own advantage. In their eyes, greater contact with these "new centers of power" would help Brazil "diversify its existing dependence on the US." Viewed from this standpoint, détente had great, and largely positive, strategic significance because it reduced the ability of the US to push and shove Brazil on a range of issues. Even if Brazil had no choice but to live in a US-led world, the rules and norms governing that world would have to be negotiated rather than imposed. The expectation here was that détente should provide a key to blunt and hedge US power, while also making it legitimate to clash with Washington's preferences more overtly.

The point here is that in the 1970s Brazilian leaders saw and portrayed the international system as a place of limited but real opportunities rather than one of insurmountable constraints. Within such a system, the argument went, countries like Brazil differed from, and had better prospects than, weak, backward, Third World states:

> Those uncharacteristic states will possibly never transcend their condition as objects of History. Some, however, have the conditions, due to their territorial extension, their demographic importance and their historic vocation, to progress towards higher grounds of autonomy and self-determination. Such countries will be able to reach the condition of subjects and escape the fatality of being mere passive spectators, manipulated in accordance to the conveniences of the Grand

> Alliance [between the United States and the industrialised world]. The existing cleavages among and within the countries of the alliance can be used by the key-countries of the developing world, with great margin of autonomy, to conduct foreign policies based on the national interest. Brazil is typical of the category of countries that cannot be turned into satellites.[4]

In this view the distinctive mark of détente was the flexibility that stemmed from the fact that the interests and goals of those at the top of the US-led world diverged. Now it was the emerging states, like Brazil, that, in their dealings with the industrialized West, could play a dividing game, with the attendant consequence of reinforcing their own room for maneuver on their way up the ladder of international stratification. Their "margin of autonomy" had increased. From a Brazilian standpoint, then, if great-power concert in the early 1960s had signaled with the tightening up of controls over what emerging states could aspire to achieve, *détente* and its many contradictions ten years later opened up a window of opportunity. A position paper prepared for a presidential inauguration in Brasilia in 1974 reads:

> The fundamental interests of the alliance [in fighting Communism] will impose certain limits on Brazilian diplomacy: but the great mobility and fluidity inside the alliance will allow for a foreign policy that is sovereign, authentic and imaginative.[5]

Increasingly, then, Brazil learned to live with the Cold War in ways its leaders thought served their own interests well. While fervently anti-Communist, the Brazilian leadership emphasized notions of autonomy and the utility of Third World coalitions, while critiquing the dominant norms emanating from the West. Brazil systematically turned down US proposals to act as a regional sheriff in South America even when Brazilian generals were fighting their own regional Cold War. Adherence to liberal norms and principles was conditional and partial – the triad of representative democracy, Anglo-Saxon capitalism, and free markets never took root, with the country moving towards limited democracy (or outright authoritarianism), state-led capitalism, and protectionism instead.

Autonomy became such an important force for shaping Brazilian policy that, at the height of right-wing military domination in Brasilia, there were generals supporting the Marxist-inspired MPLA in Angola against clear US preferences. The choice there was to remain very much on the fringes of – but not totally outside – the US-led Western formation.

So, part of Brazil's answer to the problems of living under the shadow of a hegemonic US, during the Cold War, was to carefully select fights and areas of attrition, while also signaling that it was not prepared to accept and embrace all US preferences. The key was to negotiate Brazil's adherence to the US-led order, which leaders in the country never saw as a creation of their own. The Brazilian foreign minister in 1976 expressed this view thus:

> With no other country in the world are our relations so close as they are with the United States ... Paradoxically, however, it is our relations with the US that is the source of some of the most constant concerns of our government. The issue is that ... ideological coincidence does not suffice to solve specific bilateral problems or even to make good friends and allies to assess international problems in the same fashion. The disparities of political and economic power between the US and Brazil are sources of constant reciprocal incomprehension, aggravated by the sentiment, somewhat immature, of moral superiority that is still very present in the American behaviour.[6]

But by the late 1970s Brazil's relatively positive views of the Cold War had begun to sour. Seeking to reverse the public mood, post-Vietnam and post-Watergate, President Carter launched intensive diplomatic campaigns for non-proliferation and human rights, and, half-way through the presidential campaign, Brazil was singled out as a target state for change. In a speech in Chicago, Carter called Kissinger's policy of engagement with Brazil a "slap on the face of the American people." Carter's revisionist drive, for all its inconsistencies, was unusually strong. For those at the receiving end, be they Soviets or Brazilians, the unnegotiated push was both baffling and offensive. Upon taking office, it was clear that the Carter administration had not thought through a policy for Brazil. But the White House was fast to pressurize Brazil to fall into line. The new administration's goal was to arrest Brazilian capacity to obtain weapons-grade nuclear materials and to speed up the collapse of the dictatorial regime.

Seen from Brazil, if the relationship with Carter's US was bad, the arrival of President Reagan on the scene made things worse. Reagan's arrival in power marked a move towards US resurgence in the Third World that had begun to occur in the latter part of the Carter administration. Essential in the US equation was the decision to increase the pace and range of containment, while also tackling the emergence of radical nationalist movements across the periphery. Effecting change in the Third World was not to be achieved through direct involvement or through key countries, although proxy wars remained on the scene. But a characteristic tool in this period was the channeling of US support for guerrilla fighters and counterrevolutionaries, non-state actors that could fight the Cold War without necessitating a direct US presence on the ground. Outside of the equation was concern for the North-South agenda and its ramifications.

As far as strategic concepts went, the time for engagement with regional powers was over. Such shifts in US priorities made it more difficult for the

White House to sustain any form of engagement with Brazil. In turn, Brazilian leaders saw events abroad as fundamentally threatening to the relatively benign external environment which they had grown used to. Furthermore, while a severe economic crisis inside Brazil curtailed its ability to pursue an activist policy abroad, the progress of political liberalization made for an increasingly divided polity at home. These factors made the leadership increasingly risk-averse, and led to introversion and distancing as the dominant strategies to deal with the US.

Brazilian estimates in the early days of the first Reagan administration were, therefore, full of gloom. The leadership expected difficulties with the North-South agenda and with Africa (but also with the Middle East and Eastern Europe, where Brazilian trade was beginning to gather momentum). In the Americas, the Brazilians predicted that the new administration would push for hegemonic reassertion "compress[ing] certain spaces ... previously opened up by Brazil."[7] The hemisphere was closing under an hegemonic grip once again. As the commander of the Brazilian School of Naval War put it a few years later, Reagan would seek to "facilitate the exercise of US hegemony ... not necessarily stop Soviet expansionism."[8]

The gloom, however, did not necessarily translate into fear. Predictions in Brazil foresaw that South America would remain largely tangential to Reagan's grand strategy. Furthermore, the turbulent Carter years had proven that toughness paid off and the most relevant documents pertaining to that period suggest that the expectation in Brasilia was that it would be possible to escape future US pressures once again if Brazil toughened its own stance.[9]

The problem, of course, was that Washington did not simply put pressure on Brazilian preferences. It also had expectations about what Brazil might contribute. While the Reagan administration did not seek to turn Brazil into a regional policeman, or a partner in managing order in the hemisphere, it used the services of Vernon Walters, the early proponent of bilateral rapprochement in the late 1960s, to ask for Brazilian support against the Sandinistas in Nicaragua, an operation that also included El Salvador, Guatemala and, in South America, Argentina.[10] President Figueiredo rebuffed the overtures.[11] Brazil also rejected a Pentagon plan for a South Atlantic Treaty Organisation bringing together Brazil, Argentina and South Africa. Officials in Brasilia feared that the US would try to dominate the new arrangement and turn it into a launching pad for hegemony in the South.

In turn, the US rejected Brazilian attempts at brokering a meeting, in 1981, between the Angolan foreign minister and US Assistant Secretary of State for Africa Chester Crocker.[12] In 1982, Reagan and General Figueiredo saw each other for quick, protocol, visits and failed to reach any agreement on the Malvinas/Falkland islands dispute between Argentina and the United Kingdom.[13] By late 1982, Washington had come to grips with the limits of what was achievable through diplomacy with Brazil.

Although key documents telling this part of the story are still unavailable for research, there are indications that relevant figures in the US administration had run out of patience. Assistant Secretary of State for Inter-American Affairs, Thomas Enders, told the Brazilians that he would no longer ask Brazil for assistance in Latin America, that he would not again bring up the issue of the Falklands, nor deal with trade and economic matters. Perhaps, he suggested, the two sides should limit their discussion to trying to set up military-industrial joint ventures, the "most viable [area for cooperation] in the present circumstances."[14] Indeed, it was in the field of military cooperation that Washington and Brasilia saw some progress. In 1980 the post of Brazilian military attaché to Washington (which had been suspended in 1977) was restored. A year later the two countries announced a joint program of seminars and bilateral visits with a view to exchanging information on their respective military doctrines.[15] In 1984 they signed a memorandum for high-tech military transfers.[16] In October 1981, Vice President Bush was instrumental in suspending a multimillion-dollar fine that Brazil was in danger of facing for purchasing enriched uranium elsewhere.[17] And Bush also played a role in having the US government accept new Brazilian export subsidies, in violation of the 1978 agreement to scrap them.[18] But, as an article in *Foreign Affairs* put it in 1982, this was "the case of the missing relationship."[19]

As the diplomatic relationship decayed, a deeper set of structural changes transformed the environment inhabited by the two countries. Globalization, technology and the revival of the liberal creed in places as disparate as London, Beijing, Santiago de Chile, and Washington added up to the most serious challenge to face contemporary Brazil. The Brazilian leadership's perception of the world was one where national sovereignty and autonomy worked as the best filters against pressures originating in the external environment. From the early days of the Reagan administration the Brazilians thought they were being forced on the defensive – by the mid-1980s they were sure about it.[20] Change now threatened the very survival of the world in which Brazil, as a modern nation, had come of age.

For many in Brazil, at least at first, the transformation was not obviously structural. Early assessments by strategists suggested this was less a shift in the logic of capitalism and more a program carried out by the US with a view to expanding US power, influence and prestige worldwide. The problem was that, if the Cold War period had witnessed enormous economic transformation in Brazil, now Washington's requirements for neoliberal reform challenged Brazil's ability to remain "autonomous" all the more. During the Cold War Brazil had not bought the US economic model at face value, but it had exploited it in its own favor instead. The developmental model successive administrations embraced in the second half of the twentieth century, rested on an international setting that, for all its problems, was relatively benign and open to some degree of experimentation. Neoliberalism threatened to bring that setting to an end. "The disparity of relative power between the two countries ... makes the relationship essentially unbalanced, risking to turn any form of inter-dependence, even if by accident, into dependence." Interdependence with the US would only make the relationship, already "failing and frustrating," worse. If the two societies were to interact without the shield of autonomy, then the way would be paved for an "incalculable array of emotional reactions" on both sides.[21] Foreign minister Ramiro Saraiva Guerreiro put it thus:

> The American strategy seems to be one that creates ties in various sensitive areas in ways that, if the exercise succeeds, such intimacy would end up influencing Brazilian foreign policy in the direction of alignment with the United States.[22]

Notions of complex interdependence were anathema to Brazil's conception of international relations and nowhere to be seen in official discourse. Instead, this was a US plan to:

> Confront the Brazilian government with such volume of proposals and initiatives ... that it is very difficult for us to process them in an ordered fashion and in accordance with our own priorities; exploit the possibilities of dividing the Brazilian negotiating front ... [But] Brazil's most important bargaining chip is to ... stimulate the use of diplomatic channels as a way to maintain the indispensable coordination and the discipline necessary to the good management of relations with the United States ... Preventing the exaggerated intensity of contacts from distorting in the execution of [our] foreign policy by associating it excessively to American goals.[23]

Without a model to adopt, the Brazilian choice was one that emphasized greater distancing from the US. The problem was, of course, that in the 1980s the US became all the more important to Brazil. The management of foreign debt – perhaps Brazil's greatest foreign-policy challenge in the 1980s – depended heavily on the US Treasury, Washington-based agencies, or US-dominated private committees. Between 1980 and 1987, the American share of Brazilian exports increased from 17.4 percent to 29.2 percent. Between 1985 and 1987, the US accounted for 40 percent of Brazil's trade surplus. That Brazilians saw this as dependency was only reinforced by the fact that their exports to the US market were now dominated by manufactured goods (72 percent in 1985 as against 29 percent in 1972), where difficult negotiations over protectionism were bound to be toughest and most frustrating. Soon conflict surfaced over Brazil's computer industry too. And even if Reagan's military attention in the hemisphere was largely confined to Central America (from Nicaragua to

Grenada to Panama), it was clear that US grip on the region now was tighter than it had been in previous administrations.[24]

As a result, when the Cold War came to an end many in Brasilia worried. Soon the debate became polarized between two alternative positions. One argued that the international system had become a place of mounting pressures and constraints, where space for Brazil was limited but secure if the country learned to adapt to its new surrounding realities. The other saw that unipolarity and US hegemony were unsustainable in the long run, and that Brazil should, therefore, stick to the strategic concepts of autonomy that had proven successful in the past.

After his election in late 1989, President Collor de Mello framed much of his foreign policy priorities in terms of adapting to unipolarity, complying with the new rules of the game and trying to resist those elements in the new order that were anathema to Brazilian strategic concepts. The transformation here was enormous: massive privatizations, the end of state-led industrialization, the redrawing of monetary policy to fight hyperinflation, the return of the military to the barracks, the end of the secret nuclear program, the abandonment of protectionism, and the most significant attempt made by Brazil to mend its relationship with the US. But in the face of events in Europe in 1989 Brazilians did not take to the streets. High officials from all shades of the political spectrum were suspicious of the emerging world order and kept clear of any triumphalism.

To some extent at least the foreign policy debate in Brazil at the end of the Cold War can be seen as a conversation between two Celsos: foreign ministers Celso Lafer (1992; 2001–2002) and Celso Amorim (1993–1995; 2003–2011). For Lafer, the Cold War had been problematic but not necessarily pernicious. "In the interstices opened by the Cold War, underdeveloped countries (...) had the opportunity to search for their own paths with the view to affirm their international presence."[25] In his view, global deterrence had opened up room for economic development issues to climb up to the very top of the international agenda, creating space for countries like Brazil to push for their own preferences in international forums. Suddenly, the very terms of the agenda were being transformed. In and around 1989, the sense was one of deeper, more disturbing, new threats. Transnational problems like narcotics, migration, and the environment, or the new trade agenda, based on intellectual property, energy, informatics, telecommunication and biotechnology, caught Brazil unguarded and were seen as major challenges to traditional ways of conducting international relations.[26] The question driving Brazilian foreign policy would, therefore, cease to be "how to obtain greater degrees of autonomy" and would become "how best to secure some degree of autonomy in the face of unrivalled US power and liberal hegemony in the marketplace of ideas." The task, in Lafer's words, was "not ... to passively accept and accommodate to the new international order ... but find new opportunity niches" within a more constraining system. So, there was no capitulation or subservience to the new system. But the sense was clear that "the power resources of the Third World to alter the current international stratification seem to be far smaller than we previously thought."[27]

In turn, Amorim took a stance that was more critical of the direction of change. "American hegemony has reached such a high point that not only does the US reach its foreign policy objectives, but these sometimes become the dominant concepts of order and justice in international relations."[28] Such a state of things, he concluded, was unsustainable. A new order was bound to emerge, and the 1990s should be seen as "a ritual of passage between two structures." He never said exactly what the second structure would be, but there is a sense, recurrent in his writing, that resisting and securing autonomy will in the end pay off: "liberal capitalism is far from having answers to the numerous problems that make up the global agenda today."[29] Coupled with this there was a more optimistic reading of what could be achieved. "The conservative utopia that dominated after the collapse of the Soviet Union proved to be fragile (...) political and military unipolarity (...) has been unable to solve conflicts in various parts of the world." On this view the problem lay in the fact that unipolarity in the field of hardcore power had to coexist with growing multipolarity in the global economy.

> It is intrinsically contradictory to speak about unipolarity when new economic great powers pop up on the scene with uncontested vigour ... The simultaneous existence of political unipolarity with economic multipolarity does not seem logical or historically accurate, nor is it a realist hypothesis upon which the organization of the international system can rest.[30]

The logical conclusion here was that Brazil should not follow the way of other countries in Latin America that jumped on the US bandwagon (like Chile, Mexico and Argentina), but, rather, seek inspiration from the likes of Russia and China, which had adopted an "independent line." To achieve this, Amorim concluded, it was paramount to strengthen the Brazilian state and to keep pursuing "autonomy" from the wider capitalist system and from US pressure. Much later, as he returned as foreign minister under President Lula in 2003, Amorim would go on to work on the assumption that coalitions of large developing countries could provide an answer to the problems of unipolarity. What is important to highlight here is how much of the rationale driving Brazil in the more recent period flows from the dilemmas the Brazilian leadership confronted at the end of the Cold War.

One other crucial dimension of the end of the Cold War in Brazil is the country's move to the South American region. This is an area where conceptual change had been taking place since the late 1970s but had gathered dramatic momentum in the aftermath of 1989. By the end of the Cold War, Brazil was undertaking a major reassessment of its policies towards its neighbors. The old-time acrimony and rivalry with Argentina had come to an end, and, for the first time, grand strategy was now rooted in notions of regional integration. The new, unprecedented, goal here was an ambitious project to build a South American alliance centered around increased security and mutual trust between Brazil and Argentina. The move was, to a large extent, triggered less by ideas than by sheer material transformation: as the 1980s progressed Brazil became increasingly powerful vis-à-vis its neighbors. By the end of the Cold War it accounted for approximately 30 percent of regional GDP; by the year 2000 it accounted for over half the wealth and the population of South America.

The existing literature on regionalism shows that regions are social constructs contingent on the perceptions of key players inside and outside the region. The notion of "region" is often politically contested among major players, who set out to define regional borders with a view to advancing their own interests and values. Brazil's readings of its own region's boundaries are a case in point. Starting just after the fall of the Berlin Wall arguments began to circulate within the foreign ministry that questioned the utility of defining Brazil's region as "Latin America." Part of the problem was Mexico – both as a source of division as it moved towards the US and as a source of financial instability. In Brazilian eyes, Mexico had chosen to adapt to the end of the Cold War by relinquishing an independent foreign policy and a "national project" for economic and social development. As Brazilian leaders saw it, Mexico had "sold out," challenging Brazilian notions of "self-reliance" in the face of increasing levels of globalization and interdependence. Historically, Brazil and Mexico have not had particularly close diplomatic relations but available documents show the very deep impression that Mexico's turn to the US, in the early 1990s, left in the minds of Brazilians. If Brazil was to succeed in its new international environment, then the region could be a useful construct to manage the transition to unipolarity. In redressing the regional space, Brazilian leaders were both seeking greater protection and increasing their relative power in a changing global environment.

There were two major ideas that coexisted about the region in late 1989 and the early 1990s. The first one held that regional integration in South America may have worked as a shield. The argument was most sophisticated with reference to nuclear proliferation and trade: from this perspective, the longer-term goals behind Brazil's regional policy were to mitigate US pressures, control neoliberal globalization and protect the national economy against external shocks. Note that here the emphasis was on regionalism as a tool to facilitate national, not shared goals. As a response to Carter's proliferation push the Brazilians since the late 1970s had begun to develop the argument that it was in Brazil's interest to close rank with

Argentina in resisting US pressures, and perhaps consider a major nuclear agreement with Buenos Aires.[31] In the mid-1980s they had been willing and able to move forward. By the end of the Cold War they thought a close coalition with Argentina – even if Argentina was severely weakened after a disastrous dictatorship and a conventional war against a NATO power – was the safest conduit to preserve Brazil's national autonomy in the new global order. The same went for trade: to a significant degree Mercosur, a regional integration agreement formalized in 1994, was a response to President George H. W. Bush's proposal for a free trade area for the Americas that same year.

The second major idea went in a different direction by highlighting that the region could be an important source of power accretion to Brazil. Being an increasingly powerful economy in the region since the early 1980s, Brazil could use the regional grouping to shape regional politics, manage disagreement within the region, and leverage its influence and bargaining power with the industrialized world. It is difficult to come by explicit references to this vision because the tenor of discourse tends to highlight Brazilian weaknesses and frailties. Not until the 2000s was there an explicit recognition that

> even a country as big as Brazil is a small country in a world like this ... we do not have the capacity to speak alone ... I believe that Brazil does not have full existence without being united [with South America].[32]

The underlying logic that saw the region as a launch pad for Brazil dates back to the days immediately after the end of the Cold War.

Yet, Brazil's regional behavior, right after the global revolutions of 1989, should not be seen as a mere attempt to undercut US influence: when it comes to regional management, Brazilians are always aware of the imperative to keep Washington engaged in the debate rather than alienate it. Take, for instance, the creation of the Rio Group in the 1980s – from Brasilia's standpoint this was an initiative to provide Brazil with a venue to defuse potential US interventions, ensuring that its interests were not overridden, and assist with the building of security cooperation. But the emphasis was on a multilayered system where close consultation with the US remained crucial, as it does to this day.

Brazil was relatively tangential to the global narrative of the Cold War. And yet, that global struggle shaped its politics, its political economy, and its foreign policy strategies for several decades. Life at home was deeply affected by what was going out in the wider world. The dramatic changes of 1989 had a profound impact in Brazil, even if they were indirect and came through several layers of perceptions, institutions and dynamics that were predominantly domestic. What we gain from studying Brazil in and around 1989 is a sobering awareness of the Cold War's powerful grip on societies that sat at a distance from its major battlefields.

Notes

1 This chapter offers a preliminary assessment of Brazilian estimates of the end of the Cold War, on the back of existing evidence. Most documents pertaining to this period remain closed for research or are very scarce. This is why in writing this chapter I have drawn extensively on a collection of personal archives and oral histories belonging to high-ranking diplomats that have been deposited at Fundação Getulio Vargas in Rio de Janeiro in the past few years. Most of these files are now undergoing sanitation and organization before being opened for public research and the interviews are classified until release. When these materials become available for research they will be available, online, at www.fgv.br/cpdoc.

2 Vernon Walters to Kissinger, "Brazil," *c.* January 1969, Nixon Presidential Materials Papers, NSC Files, HAK Office Files, HAK Administration and Staff Files, Transition, Box 1, NARA. For a treatment of this period see M. Spektor, *Kissinger e o Brasil* (Rio de Janeiro: Zahar, 2009).

3 John Gerard Ruggie, 1982. "International Regimes, Transactions, and Change: Embedded Liberalism in the Postwar Economic Order." *International Organization*, Vol. 36, No. 2 (1982).

4 Silveira, Política Externa Brasileira: Seus Parâmetros Internacionais, mimeo secreto, Rio de Janeiro, 16 January 1974. I wish to thank Luiz F. Lampreia for facilitating this document.

5 Silveira, Política Externa Brasileira: Seus Parâmetros Internacionais, mimeo secreto, Rio de Janeiro, 16 January 1974.

6 Exposição secreta do Ministro Silveira à Escola de Comando e Estado–Maior da Aeronáutica, Rio de Janeiro, 25 October 1976, AAS 1974.05.27.

7 MRE a Silveira, secreto, Brasília, 12 November 1980, ns.1860, 1862, and 1863, AAS 1979.08.02.

8 Geraldo Cavagnari, "Atlântico Sul: introdução ao debate," 35th Pugwash Conference on Science and World Affairs, Campinas, Brazil, 3–8 July 1985.

9 MRE a Silveira, secreto, Brasília, 12 November 1980, ns.1860, 1862, and 1863, AAS 1979.08.02.

10 Veja, 25 February 1981, pp. 28–9; Veja, 4 March 1981, p. 26. Armony, Argentina, the United States.

11 MRE a Silveira, secreto, Brasília, 28 August 1981, n. 1295, AAS 1979.03.19; MRE a Silveira, Brasília, 14 October 1981, n.1548, AAS 1979.03.19.See also Paulo Kramer, "Diálogo de surdos: as relações Brasil-Estados Unidos," Política e Estratégia, 3 (1), Jan-Mar, 1985.

12 MRE a Silveira, secreto exclusivo, Brasília, 5 November 1981, n.1660, AAS 1979.09.11.

13 Figueiredo a Reagan, unofficial translation, Brasília, 4 May 1982, AAS 1982.01.21. REF Esposito thesis.

14 Silveira a MRE, secreto urgentíssimo, Washington, 1 November 1982, n. 3475, AAS 1982.10.23.

15 Estado de São Paulo, 19 April 1981.

16 For memo see Gazeta Mercantil, 7 February 1984.

17 Washington Post, "Bush, in Brazil, Announces Nuclear Cooperation Effort," A24, 17 October 1981.

18 Silveira a MRE, secreto urgentíssimo, Washington, 22 October 1981, n. 3685, AAS 1979.03.19.

19 A. Fishlow, "The United States and Brazil: The Case of the Missing Relationship," *Foreign Affairs*, Vol. 60, No. 4 (1982), pp. 904–23.

20 Silveira a MRE, secreto exclusivo urgentíssimo, Washington, 15 February 1983, n. 499, AAS 1979.03.19.; Silveira a MRE, secreto exclusivo, Washington, 18

February 1983, n.534 AAS 1979.03.19.; Silveira a MRE, secreto exclusivo, Washington, 18 February 1983, n.533 AAS 1979.03.19.

21 Silveira a MRE, secreto exclusivo, Washington, 17 February 1983, n. 524, AAS 1979.03.19.

22 Guerreiro a Figueiredo, Informação secreta para o Sr. Presidente da República, Brasília, 21 February 1983, n. 55, AAS 1979.03.19.

23 Guerreiro a Figueiredo, Informação secreta para o Sr. Presidente da República, Brasília, 21 February 1983, n. 55, AAS 1979.03.19.

24 Andrew Hurrell, "Latin America in the New World Order: A Regional Bloc of the Americas?," International Affairs, Vol. 68, No. 1 (1992) pp. 121–39.

25 Celso Lafer, "Reflexoes sobre a insercao do Brasil no contexto internacional," Contexto Internacional, 11, Jan.–Jun. 1990, pp. 33–43.

26 Celso Lafer, "Reflexoes sobre a insercao do Brasil no contexto internacional," Contexto Internacional, 11, Jan.–Jun. 1990, p. 37.

27 Celso Lafer, "Reflexoes sobre a insercao do Brasil no contexto internacional," Contexto Internacional, 11, Jan.–Jun. 1990, pp. 33–43.

28 Celso Amorim, "O Brasil e a ordem internacional pos-Golfo," Contexto Internacional, 13, 1, Jan.–Jun. 1991, pp. 25–34.

29 Piece reprinted in Celso Amorim, "Os frageis pilares da nova ordem," in Renato Baumann, org., *O Brasil e a Economia Global* (Rio de Janeiro: Campus, 1996).

30 Celso Amorim, "Os frageis pilares da nova ordem," in Renato Baumann, org., *O Brasil e a Economia Global*.

31 Silveira Interview, tape 10, side B. Silveira a Geisel, Informação secreta para o Sr. Presidente da República, Brasília, 18 July 1978, n. 169, AAS, 1976. See also Legação em Buenos Aires ao MRE, telegrama confidencial, n. 165, 22 February 1978, AHMRE, caixa 159.

32 Celso Amorim, speech at the III Meeting of South American Foreign ministers, Santiago, Chile, 24 November 2006.

11 Were the Soviets "selling out"?

Vladimir Shubin

"Soviets selling out?" was the title of an article on Soviet policy towards Southern Africa, published in the *New Era* magazine by its editor, Guy Berger, in June 1989.[1] As harsh as this title was, it reflected the worries of the anti-apartheid forces caused by the international and local mass media reports about a new Soviet approach to the region in the final stages of the Cold War. This chapter will challenge the perception that Moscow was "selling out," in the latter half of the 1980s by looking at Soviet involvement in Southern Africa during that period. Although the Soviet Union came to play a crucial role in the political settlement of the Angolan Civil War, Soviet support for political solutions was neither absolute nor exclusive of military action. Rather, Moscow made use of both approaches and saw both as vital – both before Mikhail Gorbachev came to power and for several years after. The relaxation of tensions – as well as several shifts in the political situation – made a successful diplomatic resolution more likely. Only later, in the Soviet Union's final years, when its foreign policy was increasingly oriented towards Washington, did Moscow start to turn away from its friends in Southern Africa.

This chapter also argues that the Soviet Union did not attempt to dictate policies, either in the armed struggle or at the negotiating table, to its allies. As Anatolii Adamishin, the Soviet diplomat who led the negotiations on the Angolan conflict, noted in his memoirs, he and his team followed a very principled line: "What will suit Cuba, Angola, SWAPO [South West Africa People's Organization], ANC [African National Congress] – in various combinations of these four parties – will suit the USSR as well" and this line "was maintained to the end."[2] Adamishin's statement could be extended to broader questions of coordination and cooperation with these parties. The Soviet Union did not set itself the goal of playing puppet-master with its Southern African allies, nor could it have played that role even if it had tried. What Moscow tried to do was facilitate the national liberation struggle in these countries, not only by providing military supplies and training but also by helping to facilitate diplomacy and conflict resolution.

This chapter explores the Soviet role in the tripartite accords, which led to the end of the Angolan conflict with South Africa, and to the independence of Namibia. Moscow, far from twisting the arms of its allies to affect a quick settlement, played an important role, as a pillar of support, for both the Angolans and the Cubans, in the peace talks, which would have taken a course much less favorable for both Luanda and Havana were it not for the Soviet involvement and aid, political and military. Furthermore, this chapter considers reasons behind the establishment of contacts between Moscow and Pretoria, arguing that the ANC was aware of these contacts, and supported a broader Soviet policy towards the South African government. Soviet relations with the ANC developed and prospered until very late in Gorbachev's tenure as Soviet leader. However, the loss of this support in the wake of political changes in the Soviet Union in 1990–1991 proved detrimental for the ANC and the cause of struggle against apartheid in South Africa.

The Angolan case: the interconnection between military success and diplomatic success

That Soviet diplomats played an increasingly important role in resolving conflicts in Southern Africa in the 1980s is well known. Their involvement, however, did not mean the end of Soviet support for other forms of struggle. The more active participation of Soviet diplomats in the attempts to resolve the conflicts in Southern Africa was logical, primarily because the chances for them to succeed became higher in the second half of the 1980s. However, it was (and still is) important not to counterpoise talks to other forms of struggle. Discussing Moscow's interests in the region, Adamishin writes in his memoirs about the "demounting of apartheid in [South Africa] ... by peaceful means" [because] "reliance only on armed struggle as the method of achieving it has no prospect and is counterproductive."[3] In fact, the anti-apartheid forces there did not regard armed struggle as the only method of effecting change; the ANC spoke about "the four pillars" of the battle to end apartheid, and the armed struggle was just one of them, the other three being mass movement, underground structures and international solidarity. As for Angola, Luanda's talks with South Africa continued for several years (though with interruptions) against the background of Pretoria's intervention in the Angolan Civil War on the side of the União Nacional para a Independência Total de Angola (UNITA).

Thus, under Gorbachev, Moscow sought talks to resolve regional conflicts, but this did not mean the end of support for armed struggle. When the situation in Southern Africa was discussed by the Politburo on 13 November 1986, this highest Soviet political body supported "the line on strengthening the role of political factors at the expense of military ones."[4] However, it did not mean that military support to the liberation movements and independent African countries was to be decreased. In fact, the Soviets were on the ground in Angola, with equipment and advisers, as the civil war intensified in 1987–1988. Soviet advisors were involved in the preparation for, and during, the offensive of the Forças Armadas Populares de Libertação de Angola (FAPLA) against UNITA strongholds in September 1987, although the final decisions in this case as always were taken by the senior Angolan leadership.

The failure of the FAPLA offensive, and subsequent developments in the civil war, showed the existence of differences between Moscow and Havana, especially between their commanders in the field, towards the military strategy in Angola. However, these were differences between comrades-in-arms, and not between rivals. I believe that the Soviet–Cuban differences are exaggerated nowadays, after the political changes in Russia and Moscow's turn away from former allies. As Fidel Castro stated:

> We trained tens of thousands of Angolan soldiers and acted as advisers in the instruction and combat operations of Angolan troops. The Soviets advised the military high command and provided ample supplies of weaponry to the Angolan armed forces. Actions based on the advice given at the top level caused us quite a few headaches. Nonetheless, great respect and strong feelings of solidarity and understanding always prevailed between the Cuban and Soviet military.[5]

Indeed, the Soviets did not limit themselves to supplying weaponry and advising the military high command.[6] They also trained thousands of Angolans, both in training establishments and in the field, serving just like the Cubans, as "advisers in the instruction and combat operations of Angolan troops," sometimes down to battalion level.

When the Soviets advised senior Angolan commanders about the September 1987 offensive against UNITA in the southeast, in the direction of Mavinga and Jamba, they probably underestimated the scale of possible intervention on UNITA's behalf by South African forces. General Pavel Gusev, the chief Soviet military advisor in Angola during that period merely wrote in his memoirs: "In case of interference of South African troops we, in cooperation with Cuban troops, had to do away with intruders."[7] Yet, initially, the Cuban forces were not expected to take part in the operation. Their involvement was the result of FAPLA's retreat in the face of the South African advance, and the resultant siege of Cuito Cuanavale, an outpost in the wilderness of Southeastern Angola whose defense by the Cubans, in 1987–1988, turned the tide of war. In any case, the very heavy and overt military intervention by Pretoria gave the Cubans the "moral right" to proceed south from the Mocamedes–Lubango–Menonge line and to advance towards the Namibian border.[8]

Although a number of authors[9] have claimed otherwise, this Cuban advance was not opposed by Moscow, certainly not by those who were dealing directly with Southern Africa. Adamishin, who, as a diplomat, was more cautious than, for example, officials of the International Department of the Communist Party of the Soviet Union (CPSU) or the military, writes that at his meeting with the US negotiator, Chester Crocker, in Lisbon in May 1988, the latter was worried by the Cubans' advance towards the Namibian border, calling it a "dangerous game." However, Moscow's interests were different, that is to say – "not to hamper it, even help it in every possible way, but to see to it that it does not get out of control."[10] He reveals: "We had a secret understanding with the Cubans that they would not cross the border with Namibia. But it was also agreed upon that there was no reason to declare it publicly."[11]

Cuban Communist Party official Jorge Risquet writes that "it was more obvious than ever [by May 1988] that the military situation had compelled the South Africans to accept a solution that would prevent the liberation of Namibia from being achieved through war..."[12] Indeed, the debacle of South Africa and UNITA at Cuito Cuanavale and the advance of Cuban, Angolan and SWAPO forces towards the Namibian border created a favorable atmosphere for the completion of talks on conditions acceptable to Luanda and Havana and for the signing, in December 1988, of the New York agreements.

The Soviet contribution to the success of the peace talks was made, mostly, by Adamishin and another Soviet Africanist, Ambassador Vladlen Vasev. According to Adamishin, Washington's "program-maximum" at the talks included not only the withdrawal of South Africans and Cubans from Angola, and independence for Namibia, but "an additional prize" as well, that is – "bringing [UNITA's leader Jonas] Savimbi to power or at least power-sharing." However, the US finally had to "lower the stakes." He goes on to argue:

> To us it was easier in a certain sense. We always proceeded from the point that what is suitable for our friends will be suitable for us as well. We'll not ask for anything beyond it [...] And we didn't ask.[13]

Adamishin correctly points out that Soviet involvement in the peace talks was immensely important for the positive outcome; in the absence of Moscow's support for the Angolans and the Cubans, it would have been considerably easier for Washington and Pretoria to dictate the terms of the settlement. Indeed, Soviet support for Luanda continued even as Angola, Cuba and South Africa signed an agreement in New York in December 1988 to bring to an end foreign interference in the Angolan Civil War and to grant independence to Namibia. Russian archival documents indicate, for instance, that on 7 February 1989 the Politburo discussed "additional measures" needed in order "not to allow the weakening of the defense capability of Angola as Cuban troops withdraw from the country."[14]

At the same time, soon after the signing of the New York agreements, Moscow's attitude towards its allies in Southern Africa began to change. The difference between Soviet policy and that of the liberation movements and their African supporters became obvious and caused political complications for Moscow. During the talks on the implementation of these agreements Soviet diplomats supported the US proposal to cut down the number of UN troops to be deployed in Namibia in the pre-election period (elections were held in November 1989). The reason was not political but financial, and subsequent events showed that this reduction did not affect the functioning of the United Nations Transition Assistance Group (UNTAG), especially since the number of UN police officers was increased. But, indicatively of the changing times, this agreement was reached without the knowledge of either Cuba or SWAPO.

This Soviet action was a forerunner of several other decisions taken by the Foreign Minister Eduard Shevardnadze, acting single-handedly, or at best by agreement with Gorbachev, but behind the back of other members of the Soviet leadership. Thus, in December 1990, just days before his resignation, Shevardnadze met Savimbi at US request. It appears that he took this decision single-handedly as well, without the preliminary consent of the Soviet leadership. Vladimir Kazimirov, who was the Soviet Ambassador to Angola from 1987 to early 1991 and then the Head of the African Department of the Foreign Ministry recalls:

> After the meeting between Shevardnadze and Savimbi vacillations nearly appeared in Moscow [rather, in the MFA] – whom to orient ourselves to? Our embassy defended the orientation towards [José Eduardo] dos Santos in defiance of the fashion of those days and to spite various "democrats." Shevardnadze's assistants and even our press began showering praise on Savimbi, pointing to his intellect, sense of humor, etc. This reminded how Americans praised him to me, underlining in our discussions that he was quoting Rousseau is French, Mao Zedong in Chinese, etc. However the champions of democracy must have seen that, in addition to Savimbi's cult, witchcraft, corporal punishments and other "democratic" pearls of the Middle Ages were flourishing in UNITA.[15]

Unfortunately, the New York agreements did not mean the end of hostilities in Angola. Many observers, in Africa and beyond, expected that these agreements, and the independence of Namibia in 1990, would facilitate a political settlement in Angola as well. In June 1989 the then-President of Zaire, Mobutu Sese Seko, managed to convene a meeting in his native Gbadolite, and, in the presence of 16 African heads of state, to have dos Santos and Savimbi shake hands. The ceasefire between the government troops and UNITA was announced; however, Savimbi quickly changed his mind and withdrew his concessions.

Moscow supported the Gbadolite Declaration and went as far as sending Adamishin to Paris in early July for a special meeting with Mobutu to save the situation, but it was in vain.[16] Hostilities continued until a peace agreement was signed in Bicesse, Portugal, almost two years later, on 31 May

1991. A discussion of the developments that led to Bicesse is beyond the scope of this work. However, one point should be emphasized: apart from the geopolitical changes and reforms within the Angolan political system, the peace process was facilitated by successful FAPLA action against Savimbi's forces. In February 1990, when Cuban troops had already left southern Angola, government forces carried out "Operation Zebra" and finally reached their long-term goal of capturing Mavinga.

There is no doubt that the Cold War heavily affected developments in Angola. Much later, in 1995, dos Santos said: "The Cold War superpowers who once used our differences in their proxy battles are now trying to forget their old differences. But they must not forget old obligations. We look on them now as partners."[17] Yet, the civil war and foreign intervention in Angola cannot be regarded as Cold War "proxy battles." True, close relations between Luanda and Moscow were of concern to Washington and its allies. Yet, it is also true that, as Iko Carreira, the then-Angolan Defence Minister, put it in May 1976:

> We have to understand that our opting for socialism has brought us into confrontation with imperialism, and imperialism is going to use every possible means of fighting us, from sabotage to the supplying of small armed groups [later big ones] to try to create instability amongst our people.[18]

Most importantly, "opting for socialism" was the choice of the MPLA leadership, and not imposed by Moscow or elsewhere.

Political settlement: South Africa and Soviet relations with Pretoria and the ANC

Just as for Angola and Namibia, the changes in the world in the second half of 1980s facilitated the reach for political solutions in South Africa. But, just as in the previous case, the developments in that direction had begun much earlier. After the signing of the Lusaka Agreement with Angola in February 1984, followed by the Nkomati Accord on Non-Aggression and Good Neighbourliness with Mozambique in March, the South African government, apparently, hoped that it could press the ANC into talks.[19] In May 1984 the South African Ambassador to Paris, Robert du Plooy, said that due to rapid changes in the political situation in Southern Africa "anything is possible – even the rapprochement with the ANC."[20] But, the talks could start only after Pretoria's preconditions were met: the cessation of armed struggle, the recognition of the "sovereignty of the South African government," and the renunciation by the ANC of links with the Soviet Union.[21]

The ANC leadership publicly rejected such preconditions. Still, Oliver Tambo, the ANC President, clearly stated that the ANC would be ready to meet President P. W. Botha, although only after making sure that there would be a "serious dialogue aimed at bringing an end to apartheid."[22] The ANC had its own preconditions for such a meeting: the release of Nelson Mandela and other leaders and their participation in the talks. All of these statements and counterstatements at least made it obvious that the ANC could not simply be ignored or wished away. At the same time, the ANC leaders did not rule out the possibility of unofficial preliminary contacts and agreed to meet Professor Hendrik van der Merwe, of the University of Cape Town, who was close to some important figures in the South African National Party, when he came to Lusaka in August 1984, because he was regarded an "individual of apparently good faith."[23] The visits of Van der Merwe were aimed at promoting a political settlement in South Africa, and took place over several years. In parallel, discussions began, in prison, between Nelson Mandela and high government officials in 1985, followed later by covert "talks about talks" between ANC representatives, mostly Thabo Mbeki and Jacob Zuma, and Pretoria's emissaries.

Moscow supported the ANC efforts to put an end to apartheid by political means, but it never pushed it. In the words of Adamishin, "we never taught them how to live."[24] I cannot guarantee that each and every Soviet representative maintained this approach, but, having been present at all top level discussions in Moscow from 1982 to 1991, I can testify that there was always a common approach to the problems of the region and there was never any pressure on the ANC.

This was well demonstrated by the meeting (the first and last) between Oliver Tambo and Mikhail Gorbachev in November 1986. In their communiqué, the two leaders appealed "to all who are interested in the peaceful and free future of the peoples of Southern Africa to collectively search for ways to solve the problems."[25] At the end of the discussion Gorbachev informed Tambo, confidentially, that P. W. Botha was "knocking on our door through a third, even a fourth, party." "But," Gorbachev added, "we are not in a hurry." He assured Tambo that contacts with Pretoria could take place only after consulting the ANC leadership.[26] Alas, he did not keep his word.

Indeed, Pretoria used any excuse, often inappropriate, to involve Moscow in bilateral relations. The meeting between Gorbachev and Tambo in the Kremlin took place on 4 November 1986, after the death of Mozambique's Samora Machel, whose Tupolev-134 with a Soviet crew crashed on South African territory next to the Mozambican border. When an official of the Soviet Embassy in Maputo went to South Africa to visit a Soviet flight engineer who had been admitted to hospital there, the Foreign Minister, Roelof (Pik) Botha, received him personally and tried to send through him a political message to Moscow. Pretoria also sent a senior official from the Department of Foreign Affairs to accompany the technical specialists who went to Moscow to investigate the black boxes.

Later the South Africans tried in vain to find out what the Soviet response was to the matters raised by their emissary.

There is an opinion, shared in particular by Adamishin, that the lack of contact with Pretoria was detrimental to Moscow's efforts to facilitate a political solution in South Africa. This argument carries weight, but we have to keep in mind that any kind of contact, for example a visit to the Soviet Union by Helen Suzman, a South African liberal MP and an anti-apartheid campaigner, who accompanied her husband to a congress of cardiologists, was advertised by the Western media as proof of the turn in Soviet policy. And later, when such contacts did take place, Pretoria would, as a general rule, break an agreement on their confidentiality and blow them out of proportion.

One can also find many distortions, either deliberate or caused by the lack of knowledge, in reports about the discussions on Southern Africa between the Soviet Union and the US. For example, Stephen Ellis, a British academic, and his co-author "Sechaba," a renegade from the ANC and South African Communist Party (SACP), claim that at the Gorbachev–Reagan summit in Reykjavik, in October 1986, the two sides were "redefining zones of influence" and Moscow committed itself "to withdraw its forces or to refrain from seeking the overthrow of the existing order [in South Africa], leaving the field to the USA and its allies on the ground." They also allege that South Africa was included in Reykjavik "in the category of countries where the Soviet Union would henceforth refrain from aggression" and that it would no longer "throw its weight behind the effort by the ANC and the SACP to ferment a revolution in South Africa."[27] In fact, the published minutes of the Reykjavik summit do not contain a single word about South Africa![28]

The reality at that stage (though it did change later) was quite different. The Gorbachev-Tambo meeting in 1986 was not only the first summit of the leaders of the Soviet Union and the South African Liberation movement, but also brought about the further development of bilateral relations in both the political and the military spheres. At the subsequent meeting with the ANC delegation the CPSU Secretary and former Ambassador to the US Anatolii Dobrynin assured Tambo and his comrades of the Soviet Union's "100 percent support" for the ANC – and, "if you want it, 120 percent support."[29] Dobrynin fully supported the ANC proposal to explore the possibility of joint Soviet–American actions against apartheid. By that time Washington had been forced to change its attitude to the ANC. But, even if, theoretically, the main goal of official policy in both countries was the same – putting end to apartheid – the US administration declined the relevant Soviet proposals. Washington's approach could be summed up as: "What is mine is mine, and what is yours – let us discuss how to divide it." Angola was close to the Soviet Union, so it was possible to discuss the changes there, but South Africa was regarded by Washington as its "domain."

Soviet assistance to the ANC in the military sphere also increased early in Gorbachev's tenure. In accordance with a request from the ANC leadership, which believed it was time to train cadres for the future armed forces of free South Africa, even before the Gorbachev–Tambo meeting, the training of regular motorized infantry officers began, and, starting in 1987, full-course training was organized for helicopter and, later, jet aircraft pilots, naval and communications officers. At the same time the annual quota of ANC members coming for training in "Military Combat Work," a highly specialized course for organizers of the armed underground, was increased as well.[30]

During confidential consultations in Moscow in September 1987 Soviet, Cuban and ANC representatives discussed the situation in South Africa and the broader region, confirming their common approach to the question of the political settlement. Although the Soviets had been cautious about possible contacts with Pretoria, by that time the situation had changed. We, in the International Department, saw how, during the Angola/Namibia peace talks, the Luanda government had to face not only Pretoria, but also Washington in the supposed role of a mediator (both in fact were hostile), while Moscow was initially absent altogether. So we felt that, with regard to South Africa, with the prospect of a political settlement growing (primarily due to the upsurge of the anti-apartheid struggle), it was essential to establish a line of communication between the Soviet Union and the South African government, all the more so because the ANC was already in covert contact with it. However, this could be done only after consultation with the ANC.

A proposal to that effect was put forward, in May 1987, by those of us who dealt with Africa in the CPSU International Department and, after a short delay, it was endorsed by the leadership. The tripartite consultations in Moscow gave a good opportunity to discuss the issue of Soviet relations with South Africa with the ANC leaders, and Dobrynin confidentially raised it with Tambo. There was no objection, though Tambo suggested waiting a short while to get a better idea as to what the regime's intentions were. In the meantime, he expected Pretoria's informal go-between to come to Lusaka. It remains to be added that later the informal participation of the Soviet representatives in the talks on Angola and Namibia made contact with South Africa essential and the issue of establishing such contact as positively resolved.

Adamishin complains that when the decision to establish contact was taken, "various limitations were imposed on the Foreign Ministry. Contact should not be made public, initiative should be provided only by the RSA, every time contact had to be agreed upon by friends [ANC and SACP]."[31] However, his own experience proved the need to be cautious: when he finally met Pik Botha and the South African Minister of Defence, Magnus Malan, in Brazzaville on 3 December 1988, during one of the very last rounds of peace talks, the South Africans immediately made the encounter public and distorted the nature of the discussion. The ANC, for its part, correctly assessed the situation. Shortly after the September 1987 tripartite consultations in Moscow, the ANC National Executive Committee decided to publish a statement and to brief its membership, the Mass Democratic Movement in South Africa, African states, and socialist countries, on the issue of negotiations. The Executive underlined the fact that the international mood was to find political settlements and that the process had been started in Angola. However the ANC would resist the pressure "to negotiate on the least favorable terms ... with all the might at our disposal."[32]

While strengthening ties with the ANC, in 1985–1986 Moscow also undertook efforts to establish relations with legal anti-apartheid organizations in South Africa, mostly through the Soviet Afro-Asian Solidarity Committee and other Soviet "NGOs." We requested and received from the ANC a list of such organizations and personalities to invite to the Soviet Union; the ANC proposed to initially invite "moderates" to avoid Pretoria's repressions. These steps were discussed particularly when Thabo Mbeki visited Moscow in October 1985 as the head of the ANC Department of Information and Publicity. In our discussions he expressed a very important thought, that the ANC leadership was taking the Soviet Union's support for granted even as it expended a lot of efforts to win support for the ANC in countries which were hostile to it.[33]

Unfortunately, this recognition of the need to be more proactive in relations with Moscow was never properly carried out in practice, even when the necessity for a more dynamic ANC policy grew in the following years with the political changes in the Soviet Union. For example, one of the after-effects of Tambo's 1986 visit was the opening of the ANC Mission to the Soviet Union. From the very beginning the Mission enjoyed all diplomatic privileges, which included, for example, diplomatic immunity as well as the right to hoist the ANC flag on the mission's premises and use it on the official car.[34] Unfortunately, the ANC delayed the opening of the Mission and never used it to its full extent. Again, the ANC was beginning to take Moscow's support for granted and concentrating on improving relations with the West.

The cost of neglecting their Soviet supporter was demonstrated for the ANC when reports surfaced, first in the West and then in South Africa, about alleged changes (unfavorable for the ANC) in the Soviet approach to the question of political settlement. These speculations resulted from a number of episodes, including the appearance of a paper presented by Professor Gleb Starushenko, who, calling for "comprehensive guarantees for the white population" in South Africa, even proposed a future South African parliament "possessing the right of veto, on the basis of the equal representation of four communities [Africans, whites, coloreds and Indians]."[35] This was followed by reports that the Deputy Director of the Africa Institute, Victor Goncharov allegedly told a visiting South African Sovietologist, Philip Nel, in August 1987, that there was disagreement in

Moscow as to what policy to adopt with regard to the ANC, with some voices in favor of asking the Congress to renounce violent struggle. The *New York Times* wrote, in this connection, of the "easing of Soviet policy on South Africa."[36] In fact, no significant political figure in Moscow knew about these remarks.

The Soviet Union's actual policy towards South Africa was underlined in November 1987, when Andrei Gromyko, the head of state, awarded the Order of People's Friendship to Oliver Tambo, in the Kremlin. In his speech Moscow's support to the ANC actions, including the armed struggle, was reaffirmed.[37] Relations between Moscow and the ANC reached their zenith in 1987–1988, about half-way through *perestroika*; and the growing Soviet political and practical assistance to the ANC was strengthening its position and increasing the chances of an acceptable political settlement. This coincided with a general relaxation of international tensions, which was also beneficial to the ANC. Close cooperation between Moscow and the ANC continued through 1989, even as the Soviet Union was pulling back from its commitments elsewhere in the world.

Thus, it should be underlined that Moscow did not apply any pressure on the ANC to withdraw from Angola and this issue was never a part of the New York agreements. As Adamishin puts it:

> the issue of ANC members in Angola was not a theme of the four-party [Angola, Cuba, South Africa and the US] talks. Nothing is said about it in the signed agreements either. The matter was a direct arrangement, not even written, but oral, between Pretoria and Luanda.[38]

Indeed, when the ANC Secretary General Alfred Nzo visited Moscow, in November 1988, he not only confirmed that the movement was planning to leave Angola but also requested Soviet assistance in transferring ANC personnel and equipment from there. He was quite satisfied with the Soviet response, but appreciated our concerns:

> Soviet comrades were concerned lest their [unilateral] participation in transfer operations should spark off anti-Soviet campaigns. They would prefer countries of the region to be seen to be involved ... The Soviets had said that though they had air transport means, it was in the hands of Angolans.[39]

Then, in December 1988, representatives of the ANC leadership, headed by the Commander of the ANC People's Army, Umkhonto we Sizwe, Joe Modise, visited Angola. He reported to the ANC National Executive Committee (NEC): "The Soviet instructors were also briefed and they expressed willingness to continue serving the ANC."[40] In truth, some Soviet officers remained in Angola for two more years with the ANC cadres who stayed there, presumably to take care of the remaining war materials.

The common approach to the situation in South Africa was confirmed during the visit of the ANC delegation, headed by Tambo, in March 1989. This time he and his colleagues were met in the Kremlin by Anatolii Lukyanov, the first deputy to Gorbachev in the Supreme Soviet. When Tambo stated: "We want the Soviet Union to be a part of the solution of the problem; the South African situation should not remain only the concern of the US, UK and other Western states," Lukyanov confirmed that the Soviet Union was firmly in favor of preserving the international isolation of the racist regime through the broadening of economic and other sanctions. He underlined that discussions between Soviet representatives in the Joint Commission on South Western Africa and the South Africans were limited to questions concerning the implementation of the New York agreements.

> The attempts by South Africans to move the discussion to the questions of bilateral relations were resolutely rebuffed by us. We want full clarity. If there will be any moves, you would be the first we consult, seek advice from.[41]

The ANC leaders also sought advice from Moscow on a number of important questions. After the NEC meeting, in June 1989, a confidential draft paper spelling out the ANC's position on possible talks was prepared, and when Alfred Nzo together with the head of the ANC office, Sipho Makana, visited the International Department on 22 June, they asked us for our written opinion on it.[42] Nzo was leaving Moscow the next morning and there was no time to give an official response, approved by the top leadership. So that night Dr. Andrei Urnov, then Deputy Head of the International Department, and I prepared what we called "Informal notes by a friend." We supported most of the concrete proposals, though doubting whether all of them were realistic, for example a demand to install an interim government before general elections.[43] This very ANC document became the basis for the Harare Declaration of the Organisation of African Unity's Ad hoc Committee on Southern Africa, adopted on 21 August 1989 and later approved by the Conference of the Non-Aligned Movement and the UN.

Oliver Tambo also requested our practical assistance in the creation of a new underground network for the purpose of an armed uprising in South Africa, headed by one of the top leaders, Mac Maharaj, which later became known as Operation Vula.[44] Far from seeing the Soviet Union as "sellouts," the ANC leadership felt that Moscow was the safest place for Oliver Tambo and Joe Slovo of the South African Communist Party to meet, in July 1989, with the head of the Operation Vula, Mac Maharaj, who came from South Africa clandestinely with Soviet assistance. A new decision of the CPSU Central Committee followed to continue support for the ANC underground machinery in South Africa.

Meanwhile, due to the constitutional changes in the Soviet Union in 1989–1990 more concrete issues of bilateral relations with the ANC became the domain of the Ministry of Foreign Affairs, a shift that created some problems. Unfortunately, since MFA officials had barely dealt with the ANC earlier, they could not fully appreciate the complexity of the South African situation. As Joe Slovo put it once, "Soviet diplomats may have their heart in the right place, but they look at South Africa as at a chess board where some politicians were playing; they don't understand the role of the mass struggle."[45] Now and then they relied on the Western and South African media or were influenced by discussions with Western diplomats and even by meetings with South African whites abroad.

However, more dangerous was a general trend in the policy of Gorbachev and Shevardnadze. The talk of "de-ideologization" of almost everything, including international relations, and of the supremacy of "universal human values" became a disguise for the process of "re-ideologization" in the spirit of "free market" and the acceptance of Western values both in internal and external policies at the expense of Moscow's old friends. Speaking at the UN General Assembly in late 1989 Shevardnadze called for opposition to "all kinds of violence, whatever the motives or excuses for it."[46] In the conditions of South Africa this statement could not but be interpreted as a refusal to support the ANC armed actions and other acts of defiance. Nevertheless, Shevardnadze was able to easily adapt his language. When he met ANC leaders, including Alfred Nzo, Joe Slovo, and Thabo Mbeki in Lusaka in March 1990, he assured them of the continuation of Soviet assistance and suggested that they would continue to "consult, talk and co-ordinate our actions," adding: "We are ready to work with you in your revolutionary work." Referring to material aid, he confirmed that "the obligations we have pledged we will fulfil."[47] He properly sought their opinion of the advisability of his meeting with South African President de Klerk (both of them were coming to Windhoek for celebration of Namibia's independence) and received their consent.

Unfortunately, Shevardnadze did not keep his promise to consult and coordinate. At best, the ANC was informed (usually briefly) about the diplomatic initiatives and actions, and even US diplomats, who were in a hurry to build bridges with the ANC, often gave its representatives a more detailed (though biased) version of their discussions with the Soviets than we did. In any case, the importance of the Moscow–Washington contacts on South Africa should not be overestimated. Dr. Pallo Jordan, at the time a member of the ANC's National Executive Committee, rightly wrote in his paper on Soviet–South African relations in early 1990: "If today it appears that a negotiated settlement is likely, this owes more to the struggles waged by the South African people than to the strategies devised by policy-makers in either Moscow or Washington."[48]

Shevardnadze's contradictory policy was convincingly revealed when in August 1990, contrary to the boycott policy, he gave his approval for a visit to the Soviet Union of Kent Durr, South African Minister of Trade, Industry and Commerce, without any preliminary consultations with the ANC. Ostensibly Durr was to discuss assistance in overcoming the Chernobyl disaster, but this was just a cover-up for boycott busting. A big propaganda campaign followed in the South African press.[49] Durr met a couple of ministers, though not of the Soviet government, but of the government of the Russian Federation, formed by Boris Yeltsin in June 1990 after his election to the post of Chairman of the Russian Supreme Soviet. Thus, Pretoria resorted to the "Russian card" in dealing with the Soviet Union.

To be fair, however, it should be said that at this stage, the ANC, having broadened its international contacts, also did not use all the facilities offered by the Soviets. For example, the Soviet Afro-Asian Solidarity Committee was prepared to allocate at least 30 scholarships annually for academic studies in the Soviet Union. But, in spite of promises, no candidates were sent, while hundreds of South Africans were leaving for studies in the West, where various forces, including governments, were in a hurry to establish friendly relations with the ANC. Another difficulty emerged with the transfer of the ANC headquarters to Johannesburg by mid-1990, which created serious problems in communications solved later by establishing liaison missions between the Soviet Union and South Africa, attached to the Austrian Embassies in Pretoria and Moscow. The Soviet MFA underlined in a press statement: "The creation of the sections of interests does not mean the establishment of diplomatic or consular relations ... and [they] are deprived of the right to use the national flag, emblem and other state symbols."[50]

By mid-1990 another distressing issue appeared in Moscow's relations with the ANC – the visit of Mandela to the Soviet Union. An invitation "on behalf of the USSR leadership" for Nelson Mandela was sent to him via the ANC headquarters in Zambia and was repeated by Shevardnadze during his meeting with the ANC leader in Windhoek during Namibia's independence celebration. That meeting took place soon after the unbanning of the ANC and SACP and release of Nelson Mandela from prison. By the way, contrary to many reports, these events were a surprise neither to their leaders nor to us in Moscow.[51] However, the visit was postponed for various reasons. On the surface all of them looked administrative and technical, but the main reason was a fundamental change in Gorbachev's policy. His assistant Anatolii Cherniaev wrote in his memoirs:

> Gorbachev had a kind of good nose for the persons who had no prospects and were "useless for us" ... He "froze" his meeting with Mandela, though both academics and MFA officials (true, with some resistance from my side) more than once argued wordily that it must be done: that one [Mandela] traveled all over the world, everywhere – at the highest level – and yet could not come to Moscow! Gorbachev did not believe that by feeding up the ANC and supplying it with arms

> we were assisting the correct process in the RSA. He did not stop it "automatically"; he had no time to do it. And he realised that it was one thing to receive Mandela even in Washington and another thing in "red" Moscow, suspected of the expansion of communism.[52]

This phrase is nothing but a distortion of the truth, because Gorbachev, as a CPSU Politburo member voted for all the decisions in support of the ANC, he did not hesitate to receive Tambo in 1986, when Moscow was still very "red." On the other hand Gorbachev could hardly be suspected of fostering the "expansion of communism" in the last years of his rule.

I could feel Mandela's concern when he received me, a guest of the first legal ANC conference, in Durban, on 3 July 1991. I told him that there were no political reasons for the delay in his invitation (I thought so at the time) and, having received pledges from Gorbachev's staff before my visit, did my best to assure him that the visit will take place very soon.[53] But, by now, Gorbachev was playing a double game. Having forgotten his pledges, in a vain hope for economic assistance and probably a positive reaction from the West, he established covert contacts with Pretoria, in particular with its special services, through the KGB. This was done without informing either the ANC or us in the International Department of the party that he was (at least on paper) still heading. Kazimirov recalls how Niel Barnard, head of South African National Intelligence Service, asked for a meeting when he was "a guest of the KGB" in Moscow in May 1991. They had lunch in the KGB mansion, the same house where so called State Committee for the Emergency Situation had a founding meeting several weeks later.[54]

The actions of this "Committee" on 19–22 August, a so called "coup" and Yeltsin's counter-coup dramatically changed the political situation in the Soviet Union, and not in favor of the ANC and its friends. Pik Botha paid a "private and unofficial" visit to Moscow and signed a protocol with the then Soviet Foreign Minister Boris Pankin on 9 November 1991, formally restoring consular relations between the two countries. The establishment of full diplomatic relations was expected soon as well, and Pankin promised, publicly, that the Soviet Union would "certainly not be the last" to abandon sanctions against Pretoria.[55] Then it was announced that President F. W. de Klerk would also undertake an "unofficial and transit" visit to Moscow, but it had to be postponed because of the Soviet Union's disappearance in December of that year. The story of the further spoiling of Moscow's relations with ANC during Yeltsin's rule, which included the establishment of diplomatic relations with Pretoria in February 1992, and the welcome of F. W. de Klerk to the Kremlin in May, are beyond the scope of this chapter: the Soviet Union was no more.

Conclusion

The end of the Cold War, just as the war itself, undoubtedly influenced the developments in Southern Africa, though this influence was contradictory. There is a tendency to explain the cessation of Pretoria's intervention in Angola, achievement of Namibia's independence and the end of the institutionalized apartheid primarily with reference to the end of the global confrontation. However, to do this means to neglect regional and local dynamics. Besides, let us not forget that the political solution of the "Rhodesian conflict," that is the achievement of independence of Zimbabwe, was reached a decade earlier, at the very height of the Cold War. Most probably, Pretoria's former political, military and security establishment, unable to admit their defeat, found consolation in trying to explain their retreat by global changes. It is more surprising when academics follow them in those views.[56]

The assessment of the effect of the end of the Cold War on Southern Africa depends on what we mean by those words. If we mean the relaxation of international tension, the end of the East-West confrontation, the consequences were undoubtedly positive. However, if we mean the collapse of the Soviet Union, the emergence of a single superpower and the alleged disappearance of an alternative to capitalism, then it is hardly the case. On the contrary, the cessation of both political and practical assistance from Moscow to the ANC in late 1991 had a negative effect on the talks on the political settlement, whereas Pretoria adopted a less flexible position in 1992 after the assurances given to De Klerk in Moscow by Boris Yeltsin. Besides, the collapse of the "second world" harmed prospects of deeper social and economic transformation in the interests of the majority in South Africa.

One wonders as to who won and who lost in the Cold War in the southern part of the African continent. US diplomat Chester Crocker writes in his book: "This book tells the story of peacemaking in Africa the 1980s. It is a record of an American diplomatic strategy which helped us to win the Cold War in the Third World."[57] Yet, whose friends are in power nowadays? Who is ruling in Namibia now: SWAPO or the so-called Democratic Turnhalle Alliance? Who became President of South Africa: Mandela or Buthelezi? Of Angola: Dos Santos or Savimbi? Answers to these questions, as obvious as they are, may help us understand the deeper meaning of the Cold War in Southern Africa, which, for us in the Soviet Union, never had the simplistic character of a strategic chess game but that of a struggle for liberation from racism and social inequality.

Notes

1 G. Berger, "Are the Soviets selling out?" *New Era (Cape Town*, 1989), pp. 16–18.
2 A. Adamishin, *Beloe solntse Angoly* (Moscow: Vagrius 2001), p. 26.
3 Ibid., p. 25.
4 Ibid., p. 63.
5 Fidel Castro, "Speech by Dr. Fidel Castro Ruz, President of the Republic of Cuba, at the ceremony commemorating the 30th anniversary of the Cuban Military Mission in Angola and the 49th anniversary of the landing of the 'Granma,' Revolutionary Armed Forces Day," 2 December 2005.
6 From 1976 to February 1989 these supplies amounted to 3.7 billion rubles and arms for 600 million rubles were to be delivered in 1989 and 1990. RGANI: F. 89, Op. 10, D. 20, Ll. 2.
7 P. Gusev, *Ishchi Svoiu Sud'bu: Vospominani'ia Nachal'nika Shtaba PrikVO (1951–2001)* (Izhevsk: Udmurti'ia, 2004).
8 Referring to his meeting with Castro on 28 March 1988 in Havana, Adamishin mentions another date. He quotes Fidel's words: "[South Africans are] such fools, they attacked us [at Cuito Cuanavale] on 23 March, while from 18 March we were advancing south, getting into their rear." Adamishin, *Beloe solntse Angoly*, p. 98.
9 Even such a knowledgeable historian as Piero Gleijeses claims that "the Soviets staunchly opposed the Cuban offensive launched in 1988." (H-Diplo Review Essay. Piero Gleijeses on Vladimir Gennadyevich Shubin – The Hot "Cold War": the USSR in Southern Africa. 12 June 2009).
10 Adamishin, *Beloe solntse Angoly*, p. 117.
11 Ibid., p. 110.
12 J. Risquet, "Prologue, Post-Prologue and Continuation of the book by Professor Gleijeses," p. 35.
13 A. Adamishin, *Beloe solntse Angoly*, p. 194.
14 RGANI: F. 89, Op. 10, D. 20, Ll. 2.
15 Vladimir Kazimirov, "Moi MGIMO". Available online at www.vn.kazimirov.ru/d002.htm (accessed 1 August 2009).
16 Adamishin, *Beloe solntse Angoly*, p. 194.
17 Cited in George Wright, *The Destruction of a Nation: United States Policy Towards Angola Since 1945* (London: Pluto Press, 1997), p. 193.
18 Ibid., p. 90.
19 The Lusaka Agreement provided for the withdrawal of the South African troops from Angola. The price for it was the withdrawal for SWAPO units from areas adjacent to the Namibian border.
20 *Citizen* (Johannesburg), 12 May 1984.
21 Ibid.
22 *Zimbabwe Herald* (Harare), 7 July 1984.
23 *ANC Weekly News Briefing (London)*, No. 2 (1985), p. 3.
24 Adamishin, *Beloe solntse Angoly*, p. 161.
25 *Pravda*, 5 November 1986.
26 Author's notes of a conversation between Mikhail Gorbachev and Oliver Tambo, 4 November 1986.
27 S. Ellis and T. Sechaba, *Comrades against Apartheid: the ANC and the South African Communist Party in exile* (Bloomington, IN: Indiana University Press, 1992), p. 182.
28 *Mirova'ia ekonomika i mezhdunarodnye otnosheni'ia*, 1993, No. 4, pp. 79–86, No. 5, pp. 81–90, No. 7, pp. 88–104, and No. 8, pp. 68–78.
29 Author's notes of Anatolii Dobrynin's conversation with Oliver Tambo, 5 November 1986.

30 Much later, in March 1991, I received a message from Ronnie Kasrils, future South African Minister, who was at the time underground in South Africa: "The three little words have been our safeguard."
31 Adamishin, *Beloe solntse Angoly*, p. 139.
32 Mayibuye Centre Historical Papers, ANC Lusaka Collection, Decisions of the National Executive Committee Meeting 5–9 October 1987, pp. 1–2.
33 Author's discussion with T. Mbeki, Moscow. 15 October 1985.
34 Mayibuye Centre Historical Papers, ANC Lusaka Collection, Rules, governing the privileges and immunities granted to the Mission of the African National Congress (ANC) of South Africa.
35 Gleb Starushenko, *Problems of Struggle against Racism, Apartheid and Colonialism in South Africa* (Moscow: Africa Institute, 1986), p. 12.
36 John D. Battersby, "Easing of Soviet Policy on South Africa is Seen," *New York Times*, 27 September 1987, p. 19.
37 The author took part in drafting this speech.
38 Adamishin, *Beloe solntse Angoly*, p. 157.
39 Mayibuye Centre Historic Papers, ANC Lusaka Collection, meeting of NWC, 2 December 1988, p. 2.
40 Mayibuye Centre Historic Papers, ANC Lusaka Collection, minutes of the Special Meeting of NWC, 21 December 1988, p. 3.
41 Author's notes of a conversation between Anatolii Lukyanov and Oliver Tambo, 29 April 1989.
42 Author's discussion with A. Nzo and S. Makana, Moscow, 22 June 1989.
43 During the actual negotiations a compromise was found: though the "old" Pretoria government was not dissolved, in several fields its functions were controlled by a new Transitional Executive Council.
44 The Soviet role is described in detail in V. G. Shubin, *ANC: a View from Moscow* (Cape Town: Mayibuye, 1999) (Johannesburg: Jakana, rev.edn., 2008). As other decisions on assistance to the organizations which were acting underground it was kept highly confidential, the MFA officials were not informed.
45 Author's discussion with Joe Slovo, 10 January 1989.
46 "Shevardnadze's address to the UN General Assembly," *BBC Summary or World Broadcasts*, 28 September 1989. Part 1 The USSR; A. INTERNATIONAL AFFAIRS; 1. GENERAL AND WESTERN AFFAIRS; SU/0582/A1/1.
47 Mayibuye Centre Historic Papers, ANC Lusaka Collection, report on the ANC Meeting with the Soviet Foreign Minister, 20 March 1990, pp. 4–6.
48 Cited in *Asia and Africa Today*, No. 2 (1991), p. 8.
49 *Citizen* (Johannesburg), 14 August 1990.
50 *Pravda*, 28 February 1991.
51 Ellis and "Sechaba" commented: "The unbanning of the SACP and the ANC came as a surprise to the exiled leaders of both organisations ... The fact that the Communist Party was caught unawares threw it off balance." Ellis and Sechaba, *Comrades against Apartheid*, p. 189.
52 Anatolii Cherniaev, *Shest' Let s Gorbachevym* (Moscow: Progress-Kultura, 1993), p. 195.
53 Author's notes of a conversation with Nelson Mandela, Durban, 3 July 1991.
54 Vladimir Kazimirov, "Moi MGIMO."
55 N. Anderton, "From Gorbachev to Yeltsin: Moscow-Pretoria Relations at a Time of Change," Unpublished Paper (1994), University of Stellenbosch, p. 11.
56 I was astounded to find, in a South African journal, a calendar of negotiations on South Africa, which begins with: "November 1989. The Berlin Wall

collapses, signaling the end of Marxist-Leninist ideology." *Towards Democracy*, Durban, First Quarter 1993, p. 8.

57 Chester Crocker, *High Noon in Southern Africa: Making Peace in a Rough Neighbourhood* (New York and London: W. W. Norton, 1993), p. 17.

12 The ending of the Cold War and Southern Africa

Chris Saunders

As the Cold War ended, in 1989 South African troops withdrew from Namibia, after an occupation of that territory that had lasted almost three quarters of a century, and Namibia moved towards independence. Parallel to that, Cuban military forces began withdrawing from Angola, and, in February 1990, the South African President announced that apartheid would be dismantled and his government would enter negotiations that would lead to a transition to democracy. What role did the ending of the Cold War play in bringing about those dramatic changes in southern Africa? By the time they took place, the region had long been deeply involved in the Cold War, which had exacerbated many local struggles, so logic suggests that the ending of the Cold War would have significantly affected the region, but how did it? The relationship between the global and the local is not as direct as was suggested by one senior South African diplomat, who replied, to my asking why the South African government had agreed in 1988 to withdraw from Namibia, with a one word answer: "Gorbachev."[1] While it is, of course, important to explore how the General Secretary of the Communist Party of the Soviet Union influenced decisions taken in Pretoria, it should always be borne in mind that those decisions were influenced by a range of considerations, and that the Cold War is only part of the local story and may not be the main component.[2] In this chapter I explore the relationship between the ending of the Cold War and the changes that took place in southern Africa by examining the impact of the different events that made up the end of the Cold War and by keeping the sequence of those events clearly in mind. As I will show, that relationship was not a simple one.

The end of the Cold War was, of course, a process, in which key moments were the breaching of the Berlin Wall, on 9 November 1989, and the unification of the two Germanys, on 3 October 1990, while the dissolution of the Soviet Union in late December 1991 provides a convenient symbolic closing moment. Here 1989 will be taken as the key year and the main focus for discussion, but by then the Cold War had been winding down for some years, from soon after Mikhail Gorbachev became General Secretary in 1985. Some see this winding down as the beginning of the end, but treating the winding down separately from the end, as I shall do, allows for a reading that does not see the one as inevitably leading to the other.[3]

The winding down of the Cold War, 1986–1988

In the early 1980s South Africa's white rulers saw Soviet Communism, not the growing internal resistance to apartheid, as their main enemy. The Soviet Union, they believed, was actively working to take over all of southern Africa, by the revolutionary overthrow of the white minority regimes and the installation of Marxist-Leninist regimes in their place. It was feared that the Soviet Union would use as local agents both the Cuban military force that had been stationed in Angola since late 1975 and the various liberation movements, which were seen as puppets of Moscow. As evidence that the exile-based African National Congress (ANC) was a Trojan horse for Soviet imperialism, the South African government maintained that most of the members of its executive were members of the South African Communist Party (SACP), while the South West Africa People's Organisation (SWAPO), which was fighting to force South Africa out of occupied Namibia, was said to be planning to create a socialist society there that would also be under Moscow's hegemony. Such beliefs chimed with the anti-Communism of the Reagan administration, which saw the apartheid regime as a Cold War ally and pursued a policy of "constructive engagement" with it.[4] Under cover of that policy, South Africa was able to conduct, as part of its "total strategy" against its enemies, a major war in southern Angola against SWAPO, while attempting to move towards a unilateral settlement of the Namibian issue that would place a client regime in power in Namibia.

When Gorbachev came to power in the Soviet Union, Cold War allegiances remained strong throughout the region, and superpower competition there was as intense as ever. It was at this time that the US stepped up its support to the rebel Union for the Total Independence of Angola (UNITA), which the US viewed as a Cold War ally because it opposed the Marxist Movement for the Popular Liberation of Angola (MPLA) government in Luanda. But, while the renewal of Cold War tensions in the early 1980s helped buttress apartheid by providing de facto US support for it, the easing of superpower tensions after 1985 contributed to apartheid's eventual collapse, as we shall see. Superpower rapprochement – seen most visibly in the Reagan-Gorbachev summits from 1986 – was key to the Namibia/Angola settlement reached in 1988 and also helped make possible political transformation in South Africa itself.

It did not take long for the "new political thinking" in Moscow to make its impact felt in southern Africa. Gorbachev realized that South Africa and the US retained a strong influence across the region and he wanted to resolve conflicts in the Third World so that the Soviet Union could improve relations with the US. He and others in the Soviet Union now began to question what was being gained by continuing to provide vast amounts of military aid to the MPLA government of Angola and to support the armed struggles of SWAPO and the ANC, and some in Moscow now encouraged the ANC to think of a negotiated settlement.[5] When Gorbachev met the Cuban leader Fidel Castro, in March 1986, he agreed that it was necessary to maintain support for the MPLA in Angola, but in discussions with Reagan at the Reykjavik summit, in October of that year, he disavowed any long-term Soviet ambitions in southern Africa.[6] As the Kremlin moved towards withdrawing from Afghanistan, it reviewed its policy of giving massive military support to Angola. Though the Soviet Union did supply another $1 billion of arms to Angola in 1987, in part as a response to the weaponry, now including Stinger anti-aircraft missiles, that the US supplied to UNITA, Gorbachev announced, at a meeting of the Central Committee of the Communist Party in December 1986, that the Soviet Union would both withdraw from Afghanistan and, in future, reduce its military support for Angola. Gorbachev informed his colleagues that he was prepared to make compromises in the Third World and would use Soviet leverage to resolve regional conflicts by peaceful means.[7]

Along with this reassessment by the Soviets of their southern Africa policy went a growing appreciation in Washington and London that the ANC and SWAPO were first and foremost nationalist movements, open to negotiated routes to power, and not puppets of Moscow. There was an increasing awareness in Western political circles that the assistance and support these movements obtained from the Soviet Union was not primarily due to shared ideological beliefs, but was, at least in part, a consequence of the West's unwillingness in the past to support these movements in their challenge to colonial regimes in southern Africa. As the Soviet Foreign Ministry and others in the Kremlin began to think of encouraging the ANC to accept the idea of a negotiated settlement, the US Secretary of State, George Shultz, met Oliver Tambo, the ANC leader in exile, in Washington for the first time, against the background of rumors that the jailed Nelson Mandela was talking to the South African government in Cape Town.[8] These realignments began to undercut the South African government's mantra that it was fighting a war against Communism on behalf of the West and that the liberation movements would introduce socialist systems of government if they were to come to power.

A second major Cuban intervention in Angola – the first had taken Cuban forces there in late 1975[9] – then tipped the balance towards accelerated change for Namibia and South Africa itself. Encouraged by its Soviet military advisers, and against the advice of the Cubans, the Angolan army had launched another major offensive against UNITA in mid-1987, believing that the anti-aircraft system recently installed in southern Angola would deter a South African response. In September, however, this offensive was routed by the South African Defence Force (SADF) on the Lomba

River in southern Angola. To prevent an even larger defeat of the Angolan forces that had retreated to the small town of Cuito Cuanavale, Castro now sent 15,000 of his best troops there. The successful defense of that town by Angolan and Cuban forces against a series of South African onslaughts, together with the advance of Cuban forces to near the Namibian border for the first time in March/April 1988, fundamentally altered the military balance of power in southern Angola and northern Namibia. With the Cubans now flying Russian fighters from airstrips in southern Angola, the SADF lost air superiority in the area. This set-back further weakened the influence of the "securocrats" in Pretoria, who had believed in a military victory, and boosted that of the Department of Foreign Affairs, which had long sought a new era of cooperation with other states in the region. Events in southern Angola did much to persuade the South Africans to begin negotiations with Angola and Cuba at the conference held in London, under the mediation of the US Assistant Secretary of State for African Affairs, Chester Crocker, in early May.[10]

The Cuban decision to mount an offensive in southern Angola was a calculated risk, for while the South Africans had not admitted that they had developed nuclear weapons, it was widely – and correctly, as later revealed[11] – suspected that South Africa had a nuclear arsenal. The South Africans feared that the Cuban force advancing south might not stop at the Namibian border and anticipated that a major conflict between their forces and the Cubans would mean at least hundreds of white deaths on the South African side. A US threat to withhold satellite information on Cuban troop movements in southern Angola from the South Africans played a part in bringing South Africa to the negotiating table.[12] Under Crocker's able mediation at different venues, from May 1988, the series of talks between South Africa, Angola and Cuba led to the eventual signing, at the UN in December, of the Angola/Namibia Accords. These provided for the process leading to the independence of Namibia to begin on 1 April 1989 and for the withdrawal of all the Cuban troops from Angola within 27 months. Though the Accords did not explicitly say that the ANC's military bases inside Angola had to be dismantled, that was implicitly part of the agreement. In the course of the negotiations in 1988, South African officials, meeting their Soviet counterparts for the first time, found them working for similar goals, for the Soviets put pressure on Cuba and Angola to continue talking and negotiate an agreement.[13] South African fears of the "Red Menace" quickly dissipated. And the new spirit of cooperation between the US and the Soviet Union, seen in the cordial atmosphere at the Reagan-Gorbachev summits, fed into the secret discussions that took place in 1988, in both South Africa and the UK, between South African government officials and leading members of the ANC, though precisely how cannot be documented, for no transcript of what was said in these discussions is accessible to scholars.[14]

Before 1989, then, the winding down of the Cold War played a key role in the settlement that was to lead to the arrival of a UN force in Namibia, a democratic election, and Namibia's independence. During the winding down phase, both SWAPO and the ANC shifted their rhetoric from a commitment to Soviet-style socialism to an acceptance of a mixed economy and a liberal democratic multiparty system. The election manifesto that SWAPO drew up in early 1989 spoke of a mixed economy in a future Namibia and played down any suggestion of a socialist future for that country.[15] This was before the victory of non-Communists in the Polish election, in June 1989, signaled the beginning of a radical move away from socialism in Eastern Europe. The first democratic election in Namibia, held under UN auspices at the end of the first week of November that year, and declared by the UN Secretary-General's Special Representative to be substantially free and fair, took place before the breaching of the Berlin Wall. The Namibians were too caught up in their election to take notice of the peaceful, non-violent demonstrations in Leipzig that began in October, and, as Namibians voted in their first democratic election, those demonstrations had still to lead to the downfall of the German Democratic Republic (GDR).

Although Thabo Mbeki and other leading ANC officials had received training at the Lenin School in Moscow and become members of the SACP, they revealed themselves, in the secret talks held in 1988 with whites with ties to the South African government, to be pragmatists, keen to work for a negotiated settlement, even if some within the ANC still hoped for a victory through armed struggle. Until the events in Eastern Europe in late 1989 there was still considerable ambiguity in the position even of Mbeki, for not many months before, in September of that year, he and Jacob Zuma had met officials of the South African intelligence service in Switzerland, and he had been a key player at a SACP congress in Cuba that had approved a document calling for a "seizure of power" through "mass insurrection." In August 1989, however, some months before the collapse of the Communist regimes of Eastern Europe, the ANC formally accepted the idea of a negotiated settlement, on condition that apartheid was ended, in a declaration approved by the Organisation of African Unity in Harare, Zimbabwe.[16]

While a book with the title *Endgame in South Africa* was published as early as 1986,[17] and it seemed unlikely that apartheid South Africa could stand out against the history of decolonization and survive, it was not clear in the mid and late 1980s how it might end, given that the white minority regime could rely on its powerful security forces to maintain it in power. Though the winding down of the Cold War reduced fears of a Communist threat among white South Africans, it did not eliminate them. In 1989 the central pillars of apartheid remained in place,[18] and though State President P. W. Botha agreed to meet Nelson Mandela for tea in July of that year, he was not prepared to enter into negotiations for a transfer of power with an ANC still thought to be under strong Communist influence. Nor was his successor, F. W. de Klerk, ready to contemplate such negotiations before the collapse of the Communist regimes of Eastern Europe, even though the ANC had been weakened by the removal of its camps from Angola after the Namibia/Angola settlement. It is important to note that De Klerk, coming under strong pressure for reform immediately after he took over as State President,[19] began a process of liberalization before the dramatic events in Eastern Europe. On 13 September 1989 he allowed an anti-apartheid march to take place through the streets of Cape Town, and in early October all the key ANC leaders still in jail except Mandela himself were released. But it was the ending of the Cold War that gave him the opportunity to make the key break-through to a negotiated settlement and a transfer of power. An "act of God," the stroke that led P. W. Botha to relinquish the leadership of the National Party in January 1989, had brought F. W. de Klerk to power. Now, within months of his becoming State President, he was able to benefit from what seemed to him another "act of God," the collapse of Communism in Eastern Europe.

The ending of the Cold War, 1989–1991

As the Berlin Wall was breached on 9 November, Namibians waited to see if SWAPO had won the election and whether by the two-thirds majority that would allow it to write the constitution, for the newly independent country, on its own. As the last South African troops retreated to South Africa after the election, the South African-appointed Administrator-General was left to rule the country until independence. The foreign correspondents in Windhoek for the election now itched to be in Berlin. After SWAPO was declared the winner, though without a two-thirds majority, it had to grapple with the fact that it would no longer be receiving any aid and support from the GDR, which had given it major economic and military assistance. The collapse of the GDR regime came as a great shock to SWAPO, which hurriedly arranged for the Namibian refugees still living there, including a number of children at school, to be sent back to Namibia.[20] The events in Eastern Europe as a whole in late 1989 strengthened the hand of those in SWAPO, like Theo-Ben Gurirab and Hage Geingob, who had always preferred links with the West than with the East. The future now seemed to lie with Western investment rather than any continued assistance from socialist countries. The collapse of Eastern European regimes helped persuade SWAPO members in the Constitutional Assembly, which met from November 1989 to February 1990, to accept what the UN, and the three South African-based lawyers tasked with preparing drafts of the new constitution, suggested should go into it.[21] In February 1990 Namibia acquired a constitution that was generally regarded as the most liberal democratic one on the entire continent. Once Namibian independence came in March 1990, there was no nationalization and the new government made every effort to attract Western foreign investment.

The events in Eastern Europe in late 1989, together with the Angola/Namibia agreement of 1988, the relatively peaceful election campaign that followed in Namibia, and the knowledge that that country would soon become independent with a liberal democratic constitution, made it possible for South African State President, F. W. de Klerk, to announce, at the opening of Parliament on 2 February 1990, that the ANC, SACP and other organizations were to be legalized, and that negotiations would begin that all knew must lead to the end of apartheid and the advent of a post-apartheid era. In his speech on that day De Klerk emphasized the importance of the events in Eastern Europe in leading him to do what he then announced. "The year of 1989," said De Klerk, "will go down in history as the year in which Stalinist Communism expired." This, he continued, would "weaken the capability of organizations which were previously strongly supported from those quarters." "It was as if God had commanded a turnabout in world history. We had to seize the opportunity." "The risk that the ANC was being used as a Trojan horse by a superpower had drastically diminished," he added later.[22]

As the Cold War ended, the US in particular had less reason to hold back from exerting pressure on the South African government to end apartheid.[23] Anti-Communism had played a major role in justifying the position taken by Western governments to the apartheid regime and once this ideological justification began fading away, these governments came under new pressure to take steps to bring about an end to apartheid.

To many white South Africans the breaching of the Berlin Wall seemed to symbolize the triumph of Western values over Communism, and residual fears that a Communist tyranny would be imposed if the ANC were to come to power now rapidly evaporated. Many non-Communist black South Africans also read the fall of the Berlin Wall as a victory for freedom over oppression. In a rousing public speech soon after the Wall fell, Archbishop Desmond Tutu insisted that if that could happen the walls of apartheid could fall too.[24] The question then became how they would fall. The idea that apartheid might collapse, as the Eastern European regimes had, through popular pressure was of course anathema to De Klerk, who hoped, by his bold move on 2 February 1990, to be able to control the process, and that his National Party (NP) would emerge with a significant role in the new order. The collapse of the Eastern European Communist regimes, Gorbachev's *glasnost* and *perestroika*, and the settlement providing for the withdrawal of the Cuban forces from Angola, together seemed to suggest to De Klerk and the ruling white elite that there was no longer any threat of Soviet domination of the region.

Hermann Giliomee and others argue that De Klerk thought that the events in Eastern Europe removed the threat of a Communist future for South Africa and so provided him with the justification to unban the SACP along with the ANC, its ally. "In the last months of 1989," writes Giliomee, "the external environment improved dramatically from the government's point of view," meaning that the ending of the Cold War gave De Klerk the opportunity to act.[25] That he was able to take his supporters with him in his quite radical shift of policy suggests that the impact of the ending of the Cold War went far beyond the leadership of the NP. Though Adrian Guelke queries the argument that the ANC had been weakened by the events of 1989, on the grounds that it was to emerge as the main beneficiary of the negotiated settlement, there is really no reason why the two are incompatible. The South African government's perception, in early 1990, was of ANC weakness because of the ending of the Cold War. The way the negotiations played out thereafter – and they certainly did not go as De Klerk had hoped they would – is a separate story.[26]

Whereas much that happened in Eastern Europe in 1989 went unreported in southern African media, the iconic photographs of young people using home tools to dismantle the Wall, followed in December by images of the people of Romania turning against Nicolai Ceauşescu, had a dramatic and wide-spread impact. In Zambia and Mozambique, the collapse of the Eastern European socialist regimes, as the result of mass pressure, helped promote the move away from a one party state to multipartyism and political pluralism. When Ceauşescu had visited those and other countries in the region not long before, he had been received as a hero. Now the leaders of countries in the region feared the example set by his execution. It is said that Robert Mugabe of Zimbabwe could not eat for days after he heard the news of what had happened in Romania.[27] The end of the Cold War pushed the region as a whole in the direction of multiparty, market-friendly regimes, and for many the sudden transformation of Eastern Europe suggested that anything was now possible, and that a new age had dawned.[28]

The ending of the Cold War encouraged the ANC, which had witnessed from its exile headquarters in Zambia, the failure of attempts at socialism in the independent states bordering South Africa, to abandon support for the idea of a command economy for South Africa. Mbeki, a key figure in the ANC advocating a negotiated settlement, now let his membership of the SACP lapse.[29] Mandela remained in his house at Victor Verster prison while the Eastern European regimes collapsed, but he was able to access news and was in contact with the wider world. The dramatic developments in Eastern Europe seem to have affected him less than his colleagues. On the day of his release and for at least a year thereafter he continued to say that nationalization remained the policy of the ANC, until he too accepted in 1992 that in the new post-Cold War neo-liberal economic order there was no place for what by then seemed out-dated policies.[30]

Within the SACP, now formally allied to the ANC, there was much heart-searching. Joe Slovo, the SACP's leading theoretician, published a widely read article asking "Has Socialism Failed?" His answer, in an article in *The African Communist*, was that while the state socialism of Eastern European states had failed, the socialist ideal remained.[31] The SACP, acquiring a public face for the first time, in 1990, won new recruits, despite what had happened in Eastern Europe and the Soviet Union, because of its role in the struggle, but though it retained its name and its commitment to an advance from the national democratic revolution to a socialist one, its spokespeople increasingly defined such a socialist future in social democratic terms. The pragmatism shown by Slovo and other SACP officials during the negotiation process of the early 1990s must have been, in part, a consequence of the dramatic undermining of much of what they had long believed in.[32]

What happened in Eastern Europe in 1989 had both an immediate impact in southern Africa and a longer-term one. The mass protests that took place in Leipzig from October of that year and played a major part in the collapse of the GDR were relatively little reported in South Africa at the time, but the "Leipzig way" was very frequently evoked in mid-1992, after the first phase of the multiparty negotiations, the Convention for a Democratic South Africa, had broken down. To those who wanted to put pressure on the government to stop the political violence and make concessions in the negotiations, "Leipzig" symbolized the power of mass action, using peaceful means. In South Africa what the ANC called "rolling mass action" on the Leipzig model, meaning street marches and demonstrations, was stopped by the killing of 28 unarmed ANC demonstrators by Ciskei militia at Bisho in September 1992, but the Bisho massacre led directly to the Record of Understanding, between the government and the ANC, that opened the door to the renewal of multiparty negotiations. Until those negotiations were completed, the Leipzig example remained a possible way to put pressure on the government, which knew that the ANC derived much of its legitimacy from its mass support. That example may still return as a model to be followed by the new social movements that are now, more than 15 years later, challenging the ANC government's social and economic policies.[33]

Conclusion

By late 1989 South African scientists had constructed six nuclear weapons, and were building a seventh, as a possible deterrent.[34] Without the ending of the Cold War and the removal of the fear of the Soviet Union, De Klerk would have been very unlikely to have ordered, soon after becoming State President, the ending of the program. By then he had come under pressure from the US, in particular, fearing nuclear proliferation, to do that, and he announced, publicly, in 1993, that the weapons had been destroyed. But in this case, as in others, the precise connection between the ending of the Cold War and what happened in southern Africa remains difficult to trace. There is no doubt that the ending of the Cold

War had a greater impact on the region than some of the historiography suggests,[35] but the continuities should not be forgotten. It would be wrong to over-emphasize the impact of the end of the Cold War on the region, and the extent to which it marked a dramatic break from the past. The ANC's covert Operation Vula, to insert key ANC operatives within South Africa to support an insurrection, a move which Oliver Tambo authorized before the events of 1989, continued after them, as if they had not occurred.[36] Echoes of Cold War-type thinking, in which the world remained divided into antagonistic "imperialist" and "anti-imperialist" camps, were still to be found in the region long after the Cold War had come to an end.

During the Cold War southern Africa was not a priority for either the US or the Soviet Union. Both had sought to prevent the region being dominated by the other. While the West was able to maintain its influence, despite its long support for minority regimes, the influence of the Soviet Union in the region declined sharply from 1988, as the West emerged ideologically victorious in the superpower conflict. Had a major conflict taken place between the Cuban and South African forces on the Angola/Namibia border in mid-1988, the superpowers might have been sucked in, and that would probably have brought the winding down of the Cold War to an abrupt halt, but, in the event, there was no such clash, and instead, as has been noted, an agreed settlement for Namibia/Angola.[37] The ending of the Cold War helped pave the way for a negotiated settlement in South Africa in which both the ANC and the National Party government agreed to a liberal democratic future for the country.

This is not to say that the end of the Cold War was the main reason for the end of apartheid. It is now generally agreed among historians that the growing internal resistance, which made the threat that the country would become ungovernable a real one, was more important than any other single factor. But the ending of the Cold War was an important secondary factor in bringing apartheid to an end. As we have seen, it made it possible for De Klerk to open the door to a negotiated settlement based on the end of apartheid and a transition to democracy.[38] The ending of the Cold War profoundly shaped the context in which the major changes in the region, discussed above, took place.

Notes

1 Andre Jaquet, in discussion with the author, Union Buildings, Pretoria, October 1994. In places, in what follows, I draw upon the chapter that I co-authored with Sue Onslow for M. Leffler and O.A. Westad (eds.), *The Cambridge History of the Cold War*, Vol. 3 (Cambridge: Cambridge University Press, 2010). See the Bibliography in that volume for the relevant literature up to 2008.

2 Cf. esp. O. A. Westad, *The Global Cold War*.

3 In his 1990 New Year address, Gorbachev declared 1989 the "year of ending the

Cold War" and President George H. W. Bush, on 6 July 1990, formally announced that the Cold War was over.

4 The most recent analysis is Zachary Kagan-Guthrie, "Chester Crocker and the South African Border War, 1981–1989: A Reappraisal of Linkage," *Journal of Southern African Studies*, Vol. 35, No. 1 (2009), pp. 65–80.

5 The first suggestion of this came in a Soviet–Angolan statement of May 1986 that said that "the situation in southern Africa requires an immediate political settlement": V. Tikhomirov, *States in Transition: Russia and South Africa* (Bryanston: International Freedom Foundation, 1992), p. 46. But others influential in the Soviet Union remained committed to the ANC's armed struggle: interview with Irina Filatova, Cape Town, 2006.

6 The official records of the summit do not reflect this, but cf. e.g. Anatolii Cherniaev, Robert English and Elizabeth Tucker, *My Six Years with Gorbachev* (Philadelphia, PA: Penn State University Press, 2000).

7 A. Adamishin, *Beloe solntse Angoly* (Moscow: Vagrius, 2001); V. Shubin and A. Tokarev, "War in Angola: a Soviet Dimension," *Review of African Political Economy*, Vol. 28, No. 90 (2001), pp. 607–18.

8 For the history of Mandela's secret discussions with government officials see A. Sparks, *Tomorrow is Another Country: The Inside Story of South Africa's Road to Change* (Chicago, IL: University of Chicago Press, 1994).

9 Edward George, *The Cuban Intervention in Angola, 1965–1991: From Che Guevara to Cuito Cuanavale* (London: Cass, 2005); P. Gleijeses, *Conflicting Missions*.

10 A sign of the times was that the South African Defence Minister, Magnus Malan, in March 1988, suggested a bilateral agreement with the Soviet Union over Angola, an offer that was rejected. See M. Malan, *My Life with the South African Defence Force* (Pretoria: Protea Book House, 2006), p. 206.

11 There is now a large literature on this. See e.g. H. Steyn, R. van der Walt and J. van Loggerenburg, *Armament and Disarmament: South Africa's Nuclear Weapons Experience* (Pretoria: Network Publishers, 2003).

12 Interview with Robert Frasure, assistant to Chester Crocker, Washington, DC, 1990.

13 Transcripts of most of these discussions are to be found in the DFA archives, Pretoria. Cf. *Cape Times*, 26 June 1988, and my interview with Vladlen Vasev, the Soviet Foreign Ministry's Africa specialist, Moscow, 1996.

14 Cf. R. Harvey, *The Fall of Apartheid. The Inside Story from Smuts to Mbeki* (London: Palgrave Macmillan, 2001).

15 SWAPO, "Election Manifesto. Towards an Independent and Democratic Namibia," July 1989.

16 M. Gevisser, *Thabo Mbeki. The Dream Deferred* (Johannesburg: Jonathan Ball, 2007), p. 528. But, as Allan Boesak has recently written, Mbeki saw the fall of the Berlin Wall coming earlier than most of his colleagues: Boesak, *Running with Horses* (Cape Town: Joho, 2009), p. 181.

17 R. Cohen, *Endgame in South Africa* (London: UNESCO and James Currey, 1986).

18 There had been some not insignificant reforms in apartheid in the mid-1980s, most notably the repeal of the pass laws, which had controlled the movement of black Africans to the towns, in 1986. Merle Lipton, in my view, over-emphasizes the early collapse of apartheid, wishing to argue that big business played a vital role in the collapse of apartheid: Merle Lipton, *Liberals, Marxists and Nationalists: Competing Interpretations of South African History* (London: Palgrave Macmillan, 2008).

19 These came partly from within the Commonwealth, and were relayed especially by Robin Renwick, the British High Commissioner. Cf. R. Renwick, *Unconventional Diplomacy in Southern Africa* (London: Palgrave Macmillan, 1997).

20 Hans-Georg Schleicher and Illona Schleicher, *Special Flights, the GDR and Liberation Movements in southern Africa* (Harare: Sapes, 1998); C. Kenna (ed.), *Homecoming: the GDR kids of Namibia* (Windhoek: New Namibia Books, 1999); T. Weis, "Shaping the Discourse on Africa: the Concept of 'Solidarity' in East German relations with SWAPO," M.Sc dissertation, Oxford University, n.d. (2005?).

21 J. Diescho, *The Namibia Constitution in Perspective* (Windhoek: Gamsberg Macmillan, 1994). The lawyers were Arthur Chaskalson, Marinus Wiechers and Gerrit Erasmus.

22 Quotations from J. Kane-Berman, *South Africa's Silent Revolution*, 2nd edn (Johannesburg: Southern Book Publishers, 1991), p. 88 and P. Waldmeier, *Anatomy of a Miracle* (London: Penguin, 1997), pp. 136–7.

23 Interview with F. W. de Klerk, Cape Town, 2004. Cf. F. W. de Klerk, *The Last Trek – A New Beginning. The Autobiography* (London: Macmillan, 1988). Howard Wolpe led a Congressional mission to South Africa in January 1990 that concluded that sanctions should be intensified, and George H. W. Bush himself apparently told De Klerk in the same month that sanctions would be strengthened if he did not release Mandela and unban the ANC.

24 The clip of him saying this is in the film made for the Nobel peace prize exhibition *Strengths and Convictions.*

25 H. Giliomee, "Democratization in South Africa," *Political Science Quarterly*, 110:1 (1995), p. 86.

26 Cf. A. Guelke, *South Africa in Transition. The Misunderstood Miracle* (London: I. B. Taurus, 1999), esp. ch. 2. Cf. A. Guelke, "The Impact of the End of the Cold War on the South African Transition" and J. Daniel, "A Response to Guelke: the Cold War Factor in the South African Transition," both in *Journal of Contemporary African Studies*, 14:1 (1996).

27 *Work in Progress*, 65, March 1990, p. 25.

28 See esp. D. Anglin, "Southern African Responses to Eastern European Developments," *Journal of Modern African Studies*, 28:3 (1990). Moves in that direction had begun before the fall of the Berlin Wall: in Mozambique, for example, a process of accommodation with the IMF and other Western agencies had begun two years before, and steps had been taken towards an accommodation between FRELIMO and RENAMO, which would lead eventually to the peace settlement providing for the democratic election that took place in 1994. But in Zimbabwe the events in Eastern Europe helped prevent Mugabe from imposing his wish for a one-party state.

29 Cf. M. Gevisser, *Thabo Mbeki. The Dream Deferred.*

30 Personal recollection of hearing Mandela speak in Cape Town in early 1991. He does not mention Eastern European developments in his *Long Walk to Freedom* (London: Abacus, 1995).

31 Joe Slovo, "Has Socialism Failed?," *African Communist*, January 1990. As Slovo did not live to complete his autobiography, we do not have his account of the impact of the end of the Cold War on his thinking. The *African Communist*, which had long been published in the GDR, was now published from London.

32 It is certainly not correct to suggest that "communism ... vanished in the blink of history's eye" in southern Africa: D. Arbel and R. Edelist, *Western Intelligence and the Collapse of the Soviet Union 1980–1990* (London: Frank Cass, 2003), p. xi. Cf. S. Adams, *Comrade Minister: the South African Communist Party and the transition from Apartheid to Democracy* (Huntington, NY: Nova, 2001).

33 Cf. R. Ballard *et al.* (eds.), *Voices of Protest: Social Movements in Post-apartheid South Africa* (Pietermaritzburg: University of KwaZulu-Natal Press, 2006).

34 See esp. J. Richelson (ed.), "U.S. Intelligence and the South African Bomb" (National Security Archive Electronic Briefing Book No. 181), available on the National Security Archive website. De Klerk's Minister of Defence, Magnus

Malan, was later to write that the fall of the Berlin Wall "resulted in the Soviet Union withdrawing its nuclear potential from Southern Africa," and that made it possible for South Africa to end its nuclear weapons program: M. Malan, *My Life with the South African Defence Force*, p. 217.

35 In his memoir, *High Noon in Southern Africa* (New York: Norton, 1992), Chester Crocker plays down the impact of the winding down of the Cold War, to give himself maximum credit for the independence of Namibia. Vladimir Shubin also appears to discount its impact, perhaps because he is unsympathetic to the consequences of the winding down of the Cold War on the Soviet Union: *The Hot "Cold War." The USSR in Southern Africa* (London: Pluto, 2008).

36 On Vula see especially P. O'Malley, *Shades of Difference. Mac Maharaj and the Struggle for South Africa* (New York: Viking, 1998).

37 Cf. C. Saunders, "The Angola/Namibia Crisis of 1988 and its resolution," in S. Onslow (ed.), *Cold War in Southern Africa* (London: Routledge, 2009).

38 G. Evans, "The Great Simplifier: the Cold War and South Africa, 1948–1994" in A. Dobson (ed.), *Deconstructing and Reconstructing the Cold War* (Aldershot: Ashgate, 1999), pp. 148–9.

13 "The battle of Cuito Cuanavale"

Media space and the end of the Cold War in Southern Africa

Sue Onslow, with Simon Bright

The impact of the Cold War in Southern Africa was particularly complex, involving a multitude of international and local actors, each with their own agenda.[1] This, of course, was also true of many other parts of the world, such as the Middle East and Southeast Asia. In Southern Africa, the principal process at play was decolonization: this took the form of nation-state construction in the newly independent Southern African states, attempting to address the flawed political and economic legacies of the European colonial era, and the continuing struggle between rival liberation movements and white minority regimes. The wider Cold War environment enabled these political parties and mass movements to call on external financial assistance, military support and rhetorical solidarity. Given this particularly complicated combination of superpower agendas, the process of decolonization, and the ensuing contest of systems and ideas, the region became "a cauldron" of the Cold War. Just as the Cold War had different meanings for different actors and agencies during this struggle, so too its conclusion – or the complex progressive evaporation of the climate of fear and misperception that had indelibly marked the outlook of white minority governments, and external players – emerged at different times for different actors, and in different places.[2]

One of the integral components of the unraveling of these international tensions, and regional power politics, was the "battle of words and images": this was particularly true in Angola, the crucible of the Cold War in the region since 1975. This chapter looks at the contestation over "the battle of Cuito Cuanavale," and its connection with wider media developments, and news networks, as this "battle of words and images" was directly associated with the particular configurations of the new global space at the time.

A new phenomenon since the end of the Cold War has been the globalization of international communications and media. Over the past 20 years, this particular process of globalization has given greater choice through privatization of news outlets, less government direction of the news, and reduced regulatory controls, especially over the electronic media.[3] This dramatic expansion has been accompanied by a parallel shift in "news-frames" – "the interpretive structures which set particular events within their broader context" – and media networks. Just as in the Cold War era, journalists and audiences organize their thinking, their attitudes and their values as the lenses through which they view and understand complex events. Then, as now, narrative flows were structured, simplified with constructed priorities, and the resulting interpretation might – or might not – have any "real" relationship to the chronology. During the Cold War era this process of selection, and interpretation, was shaped by both elite and popular perceptions of the global ideological contest and the producers of news.[4] The Cold War framework provided "a clear and simple way for reporters to select, structure and prioritize complex news about international affairs," helping to cue journalists and consumers of news about friends and foe.

Given the multiplicity of information sources in the current global media age, it can be difficult to remember the contemporary media "space" during the winding down of the Cold War. This chapter seeks to highlight the importance of more research on the "gate keepers of news," the sources and their providers, in furthering our understanding of the ending of the Cold War in the Third World. Historians need a greater understanding of what policy makers there, and their advisers (as well as their political constituents) were reading.[5] By the 1980s there was also the vital aspect of the growing importance of television for policy-makers – what they were seeing – as this provided a key popular source of information which framed their "unspoken assumptions." This was as true in the Third World as the "First" – although television coverage and size of audience varied from country to country. Even though thoughtful political commentators readily appreciated that the choice of news stories for television was highly selective and simplified, television news was seen as "authoritative" and, therefore, trustworthy.[6] Ian Hargreaves and James Thomas reporting on the British Broadcasting Standards Commission and Independent Television Commission, described TV news as "the supreme news medium," in that it could be accessed and was respected by almost everyone. Unlike individual newspapers/journals it could be accessed right across the entirety of society.[7] Television imagery transcended linguistic, cultural and geographic barriers, and formed a critical part of the "ideological furniture" of the time.

During the Cold War, therefore, interpretive frameworks were both propagated and constructed, as a combined conscious and subconscious process. The global struggle of systems and ideas, between varying forms of Western liberal democratic capitalism and Soviet-inspired socialism, provided ideological lenses through which to interpret developments and events, and prompted differing cultural and political responses. These cultural effects have been analyzed from the point of view of the "refolutions"[8] in Eastern Europe in 1989, and the associated extraordinary images of "people power" that contributed to the collapse of Soviet-led socialism.

The kaleidoscope of "constructed perception" and manipulation was nowhere more present than in Southern Africa, reflecting a bewildering combination of inputs and standpoints. Here the essence of the contest between differing paths to modernity can be distilled into one between race and class. Television news was a key element in this as the visual image was playing a critical part of "the struggle" in the region – made manifest by the extraordinary visual impact in the international sphere of images of communal violence and regime suppression in South Africa dating back to the Soweto riots of 1976.[9] Television news had the ability to reach an extraordinary and diverse range of opinion, far above the narrower circulation and readership of newspaper reporting. It was one of the "unarmed forces,"[10] both during and in the resolution of the Cold War competition in both Europe and the Third World: a permutation of "trans-national relations," where a non-state agent interacted with a state actor or inter-governmental organization.[11]

Events in Angola in 1988, which saw the culmination of superpower competition in the Third World and its peaceful resolution, reveal the importance of understanding this overlooked dimension in the final resolution of the global Cold War: the power of visual imagery, and the role of television and the global news-scape. In this regard, foreign and local actors tried to use media networks to shape those thought processes, and were acutely conscious of carrying the battle of ideas to the "global North." While there have been detailed studies on South Africa's long-running propaganda campaigns in the 1960s and 1970s, the role of South African and Rhodesian lobbying groups, particularly in the US, and UNITA's use and exploitation of the Western media,[12] there has been very little research on how independent television networks – internationally – both picked up on each other's stories, and feeds, and how far they were also used, in turn, as "a force multiplier" by governments, and liberation movements. In the Angolan civil war, these news stories and their dissemination were used as a weapon of war, not just by UNITA, but also by the MPLA, exploiting the power and influence of Western news.

In Southern Angola, the site of the most intense military confrontation on the continent in the entire Cold War, the role of television news represented a harbinger of what soon became "the CNN phenomenon" in the First Gulf War of 1991 – the power and role of television news and its particular presentation of "the story" of conflict. However, the late 1980s in Southern Africa was not simply an era that predated the television coverage phenomenon of CNN and its "infotainment" of conflict coverage. Neither was it simply a question of television imagery and presentation of argument at home.[13] As the Cold War also constituted a propaganda battlefield on the international and the home fronts, each of its antagonists sought to claim veracity and moral justice in their ideologies and self-justificatory rhetoric. Therefore, the role of the international news media – both as contested space and as individual and composite elements of the complex chess board of the broader Cold War environment – require closer examination. This is particularly true in the case of Southern Africa, since the rhetoric and propaganda of the South African apartheid government was an integral part of its concerted effort to manipulate domestic and international public opinion to maintain its legitimacy against the challenge of radical African nationalist movements. Equally, "owning" the story was an important aspect of state sovereignty and equal status for recently independent Southern African states, and presenting or claiming a victory could be as vital as actual military prowess in the field in sustaining external support and solidarity.

Therefore, in contrast to the parallel opening up of the media news-scape in the "global North" during the later part of the 1980s, in Southern Africa there were fundamental structural and existential differences. The expansion of the media "space" in the "global North," and the proliferation of news media, in visual and written coverage, did not lead to a global homogeneity, but, instead, alternative news-scapes. At the same time, in Southern Africa, it is notable that a "Cold War atmosphere" still invaded media activities. There continued a pattern of state ownership and control of media sources – television broadcasting and print journalism, and a parallel proliferation of independent film makers. Therefore, in this geographic region, news reporting and film making – as a cultural expression of independence and national identity – was a contested space, with a particular range of actors and "sub-actors." There was also the wider ideational contest of the New World Information Order (NWIO), represented by newly independent African governments, and their struggle against the dominance of Western "imperialist" reportage. The campaign associated with the NWIO had long criticized the framing of Western news from developing countries only in terms of "coups, earthquakes and disasters." John Marcum's report for *Foreign Affairs,* in 1988, was symptomatic of this Afro-pessimism: in his article "Africa: A Continent Adrift," the opening sentence ran "For Africa, this decade has been a period of ominous economic, social and environmental decline."[14]

The NWIO was also directly connected to the racial struggle in Southern Africa, the key aspect of which was a vitriolic and long-running propaganda war.[15] There has been a considerable amount written about Pretoria's sustained covert and sophisticated media campaigns, which culminated in the scandal of "Muldergate" – the revelation that the South African Ministry of Information had spent $100m on a secret slush fund to buy foreign influence (including the planting of stories, payments to foreign journalists, and to establish *The Citizen,* the only major South African English language newspaper favorable to the National Party and the system of apartheid). From 1984 onwards there were increasingly draconian South African government press restrictions, part and parcel of the growing State of Emergency. As a direct product of the upsurge of violence surrounding the Township revolt, the state first instituted restrictions on reporting, then laws to suspend newspapers which published content of which it disapproved and, finally, by July 1988, the Minister of Home Affairs Stoffel Botha was drafting legislation to require journalists to register with the government, and to withhold registration from "unreliable" journalists. Thus, there was a progressive "gagging process" in the government's determination to manage the "story" at home, while it instituted cautious reform. (Stoffel Botha was thwarted by a "surprising alliance of journalists and newspaper editors, businessmen alarmed at the possible response in Western capitals and the possibility of further economic and financial sanctions, and Western diplomats").[16] As the South African media "space" contracted in the contest between the apartheid regime and its opponents inside South Africa,[17] so the media space outside the country "became another battleground."[18]

Within the Front Line States, this associated media space "battleground" was, therefore, influenced by the Cold War, but was not defined by it. It was directed against the apartheid state, but it intersected with the Cold War environment and the atmosphere that pervaded international media reporting. But – and this third point is very important – it was also defined, principally, as liberation from white imperialism – i.e. against Western-dominated, US-centric production of news and entertainment media. It was part of a subtle battle to fight the English-language mass media, and to promote African cultural expression and cultural diversity as part of a nation building project, to avoid a global homogenization, and also sterile stereotyping of media presentation: a wider cultural movement to avoid a market dominated and capitalist driven international media culture, which appeared to be driving global communication. This translated into a drive for African "ownership" of news, and resentment that African stories/African views were not being reported accurately from the politics on the ground.

Therefore, despite this media space "battleground" in the late 1980s, the "Cold War atmosphere" still pervaded international media reporting about Africa generally, and Southern Africa in particular. This had produced a paradoxical effect.

> On one hand, it (had) brought certain African issues, such as unrest in Angola, Congo, and the Horn of Africa, to the forefront of US foreign policy concerns. On the other hand, public interest in the East-West aspects of the African conflicts (came) at the expense of the relevant local political issues.[19]

Foreign reporting was also inherently limited, and subject to bias. It is always legitimate to ask how much knowledge a foreign national press corps actually has when following complex foreign news stories: what were their sources of local information, what were their language skills, what was their basic cultural awareness? All of this is vital in the preparation and presentation of foreign news stories. At the time, reporting on Southern Africa tended to be haphazard, and negative: the Angolan war fell neatly into the category of "parachute journalism." The international news media tended to rely upon the network of independent news agencies – e.g. Agence Press, Reuters, UPI – which employed stringers and provided regular feeds. *The London Times* was unusual in having a long-standing Africa editor.

This sense of under-reporting and distortion by foreign journalists and media networks was acutely felt by a number of independent film makers outside South Africa within the so-called Front Line States, and members of the Angolan and Mozambican intelligentsia who felt this pattern of news feeds still produced a Western-centric slant to news analysis. Their consequent determined drive to open up the media space was actively supported by the Zimbabwean, Angolan and Mozambican governments. The agenda of this informal network was to work to try to build a Southern Africa media space from a Southern Africa point of view.[20] This, therefore, did not necessarily conform to the Western agenda and style of coverage, nor to perceptions and methods of news gathering and reporting. It was based on an informal network of state-sponsored media and cultural creative film-making and news reportage – in all countries there was a pattern of state-ownership of national broadcasting, and like-minded foreign independent actors. This approach of cultivating a "pan African media space" was being supported at the time by various NGOs, the Canadian government, the Netherlands, and the Scandinavians, as part of a wider sharing of concern by non-aligned and neutral governments over issues of media coverage and unbalanced flows of media influence. Indeed, one white Zimbabwean independent film maker on his first trip to Luanda was met on his arrival by the Swedish Ambassador to Angola, and put up in an embassy flat.

The manner in which the civil conflict in Angola was reported typifies this "battle of images and ideas." Again, here, the colonial experience had formed the "initial conditions." Indeed, by the late 1980s decolonization in Angola appeared, to external observers, to be a striking combination of the continuities of the past, rather than the transformation of the present – in the view of the veteran historian David Birmingham, the Angolan state did not fit into "received models of decolonization," with the capital city forming the hub of the political, social and economic life of the new nation-state. Rather, the direct consequence of Portuguese bureaucratic authoritarianism, different missionary traditions, language divisions, and the communications network, were "three rival sets of sub-national leaders," based on three different urban hubs. Independence from Portuguese colonial rule had been won on behalf of the workers and the peasants, but whilst in the 1970s the workers rebelled against the post-independence popular-movement government of the MPLA, by the 1980s "the peasants did so with even greater persistence."[21]

The Angolan MPLA state retained marked similarities to the authoritarian and bureaucratic Portuguese colonial state; expectations at independence of the creation of a popular-movement government, based on mass politics, were thwarted as the continuing civil war forced the concentration of power into a narrow circle of decision makers, increasingly dominated by the army, whilst the ideological and economic struggle between urban and rural communities continued. "By 1987 the conflict between town and countryside had spread to the entire nation,"[22] as the civil war between the MPLA government and its urban supporters, versus UNITA and its rural supporters in the Ovimbundu region, was enmeshed with wider and multilayered racial and ideological conflict in Southern Africa: the South African regional struggle against the radical nationalist movements of the ANC, and SWAPO in South West Africa/Namibia, extended to South African Defence Force (SADF) attacks against Pretoria's ideological enemies, the MPLA and its Cuban/Soviet supporters, assisted by UNITA and its American backers.

This interplay of Cold War antagonists and regional actors produced highly complex diplomacy and a parallel, confusing, and hotly contested, military/strategic landscape in the Angolan theatre. The Reagan Administration's policy towards Angola was ambivalent and ambiguous, nominally aiming at the complete withdrawal of Cuban troops, and assistance to UNITA, whilst ostensibly aiming, in the long term, at a negotiated settlement between the MPLA government in Luanda and UNITA forces.[23] (The account of the Assistant Secretary of State, Dr Chester Crocker, contains some supremely condescending statements, which also reflected Crocker's determination that America should play a leading role to direct the outcome: for example, "April 1988: United States decides parties nearly ready for face-to-face talks, with US mediation."[24]) US policy towards Southern Africa was refracted through a combination of Orientalism and Cold War lenses: Jonas Savimbi was lauded for his intellect, his fluency, his multilingual abilities, as well as his declared anti-Marxist political views – the implication being Savimbi represented everything his MPLA opponents were not. (It has to be said that Savimbi was extremely adept at both exploiting international media contacts, and charming Western politicians.) For the Soviet Union, support for the MPLA liberation movement had been far from smooth, and their experience of the South African (SA) military also had ambiguous aspects: examples are South African leaflets politely urging Soviet military advisers attached to FAPLA forces to withdraw from Cuito Cuanavale, followed by the use of poison gas.[25]

From the US–Soviet Washington summit of December 1987, there was increasing evidence of a radical change in Soviet dealings with Washington in Third World affairs.[26] Meanwhile, South Africa interpreted this superpower detente, and renewed US support for UNITA, as an opportunity to solidify its regional policy of destabilization to destroy the National Party's ideological foes: the MPLA, SWAPO and the ANC. In Angola, the

MPLA position had been fortified by Cuban troops, requested and subsidized ($500–$800m p.a.) by the MPLA government. Removing Cuban troops from Angola had been the sine qua non for South African implementation of UNSC Resolution 435 on the independence of Namibia. From early 1988, Cuba was admitted into the negotiations and thereafter Fidel Castro pursued a two-pronged strategy of war and negotiations, sending reinforcements against four sustained South African/UNITA assaults on the defensive stronghold, and key airstrip at Cuito Cuanavale. These events in Southern Angola produced the last crisis – arguably one of the most dangerous – of the Cold War in the region: the US was intensely concerned that Cuban forces might attack across the Angolan–South West African border, producing possible South African nuclear retaliation; whereas the Soviets were more sanguine, believing that Moscow could restrain Havana. The rising number of South African casualties, and the growing voice of politicians advocating peace within the National Party hierarchy, coalesced with those within the SADF leadership who favored withdrawal.[27] Through an extraordinary process of "mini-lateralism" – a series of meetings in European and African capitals between the MPLA, South Africa, and Cuba, supported and facilitated by the US, the Soviet Union and the UK, between early May and December 1988 the superpower competition in Southern Africa was resolved.

Other authors have examined the interplay between the intense fighting on the ground in Southern Angola[28] and the parallel course of these high level meetings between the antagonists, which culminated in agreement on the independence of Namibia, and multiparty elections, and the withdrawal of Cuban troops from Angola. Embedded within the historical analysis is the continuing popular controversy over the relative importance of the "battle at Cuito Cuanavale." In the opinion of Chester Crocker, who headed African affairs at the US State Department during the Reagan Administration, the decisive positive shift in the process of negotiations on the political settlement took place before the major battle started. President Fidel Castro declared that the history of Africa would be divided into two parts: before and after Cuito Cuanavale.[29] For his part, a former top SADF commander claimed, in his memoirs, that his forces had no intention whatsoever of taking Cuito Cuanavale.[30] Former South African Foreign Minister, R.F. "Pik" Botha hotly disputes that South Africa was defeated at Cuito Cuanavale, arguing that the more important military confrontation was elsewhere at the Lomba river.[31]

This time-honored (and also heavily gendered) pastime of re-fighting old battles is not the purpose of this chapter. What is significant is the representational value of "Cuito Cuanavale" to another Angolan "battle" going on at the same time, closely associated with conceptions of decolonization, the anti-imperial struggle, neo-colonialism, state sovereignty and entitlement of independence outlined above. This process was also, in part, the dynamic of "core and periphery," using the expanding global media space as both vector and medium of diplomacy, to manipulate image and shore up prestige. Studying reporting on the war in Angola/Namibia in the early months of 1988 illustrates this point of informal networks, and determined presentation of the news to serve a power-political/ideological point.

By the start of 1988, there had been an intense battle between the defending Angolan army, FAPLA and its supporting Cuban forces, and the SADF/UNITA formations on the Lomba river. This had begun in October 1987 and became centered around the strategic airstrip and settlement at Cuito Cuanavale in Southeastern Angola. This intense conflict on the ground – described as the most significant military engagement in Africa in the Cold War era – was marked by four repeated SADF/UNITA assaults on Cuito Cuanavale. The military battle was matched by an equally intense contest in the presentation of the story by both sides. On 25 January, the Independent Television News (ITN) in London,[32] picking up a feed from the state-run South African Broadcasting Corporation (SABC), reported on secret talks between Jonas Savimbi of UNITA, President P.W. Botha and the West German Christian Democrat politician, Franz Josef Strauss. The ITN report on these clandestine discussions was dignified, emphasizing discussions on the possibility of ending the Angolan civil war and resolving the long-standing issue of Namibian independence. The clip included a quote from Savimbi remarking that Strauss had been sent by Chancellor Helmut Kohl on a fact finding mission, and

> will carry the message and the information we have given him. Moreover, he has been in touch with the Russian(s) ... (on) the problem of Angola especially. We believe that the Russian(s) also have a role to play in order to find the solution.

There was no mention of Cuban forces, nor even of a Cuban presence at the negotiations.

Three days later, on 29 January, using Angolan Television footage, ITN reported on "the resumption of US and Angolan peace talks as a month-long battle for the strategic garrison city of Cuito Cuanavale continued between government forces and the South African backed UNITA." (Again interestingly, there is no mention of Cuba, which by this time had approximately 50,000 troops and support personnel in the Angolan theatre). The news footage in the ITV archives is accompanied by the feed description:

> Angolan television broadcast film showing soldiers defending Cuito Cuanavale, in an attempt to refute claims by the rebel movement UNITA that government forces had fled the city after a three-week siege. But a spokesman for UNITA insisted government troops had retreated ... and said a fierce battle continued for the city and its

> strategic airstrip. The Angolan government says a force of 6,000 South African soldiers using tanks, planes and heavy artillery was attacking the city.

Western diplomats commented that the continued fighting was likely to hamper the efforts of the Assistant Secretary of State, Chester Crocker, to get a commitment from the Angolans to allow "an estimated 35,000 Cuban troops stationed in Angola to leave."

Again, on 19 February, using Angolan Television footage, ITN reported on UN Secretary General Pérez de Cuéllar's visit to Luanda as

> the Angolan government announced it had repelled a big South African offensive near the strategic town of Cuito Cuanavale. The offensive began on 14 February, and the Angolan Ministry of Defence said it involved 7,000 South African troops. The Ministry, quoted by the Angolan official news agency, ANGOP, said that 70 South African troops were killed and two South African planes were shot down before the attack was repulsed. Cuito Cuanavale is a key garrison Town in Cuando-Cubango province, and has been the scene of heavy fighting. Angola maintains that South Africa does most of the fighting, but UNITA rejects this, claiming its forces have killed 92 government troops and 17 Cubans in the area. South Africa has admitted that its forces are in Angola, but says that they are being withdrawn.

Arguing about battlefield casualties, and "kill rates," was a time-honored past-time between contesting militaries and their governments; and, although the South African military prided itself on the veracity of its reporting, these casualty figures only concentrated on SADF losses. However, this news clip demonstrates that the independent British television channel was taking its source from the state owned Angolan Television Corporation.

Parallel to this attempt to feed the "correct" story to the outside world, the Angolan government facilitated a visit by the first group of foreign journalists to visit Southeastern Angola since the previous August. Filing in the *Washington Post* on 1 March 1988, the American journalist Margaret Knox reported Major Armando Moreira of FAPLA announcing "We brought you here to show you that we still control Cuito Cuanavale." The report continued that morale was high. The Provincial Commissioner repeated that "the situation was still threatening but ... we are beating them." This message was confirmed by a representative of Angolan President Eduardo dos Santos in *The Windhoek Advertiser* on 6 March 1988. The South African Press Agency (SAPA) reported his statement that

> South Africa, in addition to having four battalions of its army stationed in the Angolan province of Cunene since 1981, had launched a major

> attack against the province of Cuando-Cubango with the aim of occupying the town of Cuito Cuanavale and its airfield, from which it intended to attack the provincial capital Menongue and setting up a UNITA government there. South Africa was reported to have about 9,000 troops occupying parts of Angola and continued to devastate Cuito Cuanavale in a "classic battle" that had cost hundreds of young lives and destroyed tanks, aircraft, helicopters and sophisticated military equipment.

During the following month, on 11 March, this time using Soviet Television (TSS) footage, ITN reported on a Soviet news team's coverage of fierce fighting between government and rebel forces around Cuito Cuanavale. "Government commanders say they will not give up, despite heavy artillery attacks." (The Soviet Union had an established pattern of using TASS or other East European news reporters as a means of acquiring independent intelligence on Angola, to supplement the paucity of detailed political and intelligence coverage.) The ITN report went on to note a report from UNITA, which is "backed by the United States and South Africa, states that UNITA forces have captured the strategic town of Nova Sintra, smashed a military convoy and killed 11 government troops and two Cubans." This is an interesting choice of language, selected to give an aura of progressive invincibility, and autonomous activity.

Clearly, the MPLA and UNITA were both using international news space to contest the legitimacy and strength of their movements in the ongoing Angolan civil war, just as the South African government was also managing the presentation of its case. The Front Line States were also close observers of the battle on the ground, and the presentation of the media "story." Two weeks later, while SABC radio was reporting South African Foreign Minister, Pik Botha's pessimism of an early agreement on South West Africa and Angola,[33] on 25 March a summit meeting of the Southern African Front Line States was held in Lusaka. Reuters in Lusaka reported

> Southern Africa's front line states and liberation movements, closing ranks behind Angola in its bid for a regional peace settlement, have thrown down a challenge to South Africa.... Angola is proposing an accord to be signed by itself, South Africa, Cuba and SWAPO, with the US as mediator. The accord would exclude pro-Western UNITA rebels. The agreement, which the Angolans say is being drafted, foresees withdrawal of the 40,000 Cuban troops in Angola in return for Namibian independence and other conditions aimed at ending Angola's civil war.

By mid-April (against the background of clandestine diplomatic arrangements for the South Africans, Cubans, Angolans and Americans to meet, for the first time, in London), ITN put out a special report (this time using Reuters footage) entitled "Military Successes by UNITA rebels may bring Angola closer to Peace Negotiations." It began with the announcement that Savimbi had recently declared himself president of a rival government – "a move seen by observers as a political gambit, capitalizing on military successes won for him by South Africa." "UNITA with significant South African support, had contained the Marxist government's strongest offensive yet against Savimbi's bush headquarters at Jamba in the southwest, and extended its control to the north." Savimbi told reporters, in March, that it was the military victories that now brought his country closer than ever to a negotiated settlement in its 13-year old civil war. He said there had been a flurry of diplomatic activity, including contacts between the Soviet Union and Cuba – which back the Angolan government – South Africa, Angola and Washington. This represented another excellent example of Savimbi using international media space to ensure that UNITA was not shut out of the proposed direct negotiations between the Angolan government and South Africa, to replace the separate talks the US had been holding with Angola and South Africa; and a rebuke to his US and South African backers. (US and South African aid to UNITA was reported to be at its highest level ever).

> We are officially informed by the South African government that they will start negotiations with the MPLA. Then taking account of all those movements, UNITA has to understand exactly what's going on because UNITA is a key player in the situation of this conflict in Angola and in Southern Africa.[34]

By the end of April, ITN had changed its editorial line. On 29 April, the ITV news reported (in contrast to the BBC's coverage, which was taking its feed from SABC, of continued military success in South Eastern Angola by UNITA and South African forces) that "Angolan troops supported by Cuban advisers beat back an invasion force from South Africa." The import of this story may seem slight, but it is intriguing. The MPLA government had become increasingly frustrated that the international news story was not reflecting their presentation of the news – despite the feeds from Angolan television mentioned above. In the view of the MPLA militariat, which dominated MPLA decision making, this was corroding the legitimacy of the MPLA government, and they took active steps to remedy this. Apparently, "at the time the international press pack was following Princess Diana in Uganda, photographing her kissing Aids babies and ignoring what the Angolans were putting out." Carlos Enrique, the FAPLA white Angolan running the weekly current affairs program on the war, "Opxale," on Angolan television, consequently contacted Simon Bright, an independent film maker in Zimbabwe with whom he had worked on a project in Angola in 1985, filming the SA/UNITA siege of the US-owned

Gulf Oil installation, then being guarded by the MPLA and Cubans. The Angolan representative to SADC, in charge of the energy portfolio made the visa and transport arrangements, while Enrique made the arrangements to get Bright and his cameraman to Cuito Cuanavale (by armored personnel carrier, and a helicopter flying at tree top level to avoid South African artillery fire.) Tim Leach, ITN's link in Harare, then arranged for Bright to take this scoop to London. Coincidentally, the news story – the first by an independent Western film crew from the Angolan front for several months – was broadcast in the run up to the first meeting between the Angolans and Cubans at the London Bell Hotel.

Simon Bright's film, which survives in the ITN archives in London, is itself rich in visual and linguistic symbols: the state-of-the-art military technology of Cuban MiGs flying in tight formation over a local festival and its street dancers in the provincial capital Menongue; the sang-froide of the highly articulate FAPLA lieutenant[35] showing Bright and his cameraman around the Cuito Cuanavale airfield and its defenses; FAPLA troops acting as human landmine detectors as they took the increasingly nervous Bright to see the wreckage of four massive SADF Oliphant tanks; the reality of the sustained South African artillery bombardment, which resumed half way through the film footage, and Angolan determined defiance. Bright and Carlos Enrique were extremely satisfied with the result – FAPLA particularly because, in their view, the news story struck a decisive blow against the international SABC-led narrative of South African military invincibility. Three days later, on 2 May, as another example of the complex interplay between international media sources and reporting, a front page article appeared in Granma, the official Cuban newspaper, praising "the audacious and unstoppable movements of the Cuban-Angolan-SWAPO forces." This was picked up by The *New York Times* special correspondent, who formed part of another group of foreign journalists visiting the Angolan theatre, who noted that a high-ranking Angolan army officer reacted with annoyance when shown this article: "I wish they wouldn't write that." South West African guerrilla units, he said, do not fight alongside Angolan troops.[36]

This is not to say that the breaking of Bright's Cuito Cuanavale news story (broadcast over ITV and Channel 4 news as a major scoop, in sharp contrast to the BBC line), played a seminal part in the outcome of the increasingly intense struggle in Southern Angola. The military contribution of the Cuban forces, augmented by the emergency airlift of the entire Cuban reserve in a determined bid to ensure that Cuba remained undefeated in Southern Africa, to bolster its prestige and standing against the hardline Reagan Administration and to underline Castro's position as the premier revolutionary leader in the Third World, played a central role in the military outcome.[37] The instructions of the Cuban Politburo, that Cuban forces should by-pass the SADF/UNITA defensive position, and advance towards the Angolan–Namibian border in a three-pronged phalanx, combined with the critical loss of South African domination of airspace in Southern Angola, were the key aspects. The dominance of the securocrats in Pretoria was severely shaken by military events in Southern Angola, leading to a re-assertion of the South African Department of Foreign Affairs line of a negotiated settlement. The prospect of substantial casualties in Southern Angola, the need for total mobilization at a time when the urban mass-violence, civic and trade union militancy was rendering the South African state increasingly ungovernable, proved key considerations in encouraging the National Party government to negotiate. The Cairo meeting in early June 1988, between Cuban, South African and MPLA delegates, provided the critical diplomatic breakthroughs.[38]

The war in Southern Angola has been described as "the last Cold War conflict which could have sucked in the superpowers, and which risked a possible nuclear exchange"; indeed, the "battle" over the historical narrative and significance of Cuito Cuanavale continues to this day. The Cuban Politburo certainly presented Cuba's military contribution to the Angolan theatre as decisive to the South African decision to negotiate, and the ultimate independence of Namibia.[39] The MPLA government in Luanda, and its state-led broadcasting station, had wider interests concerned with the image of a successful and militarily capable liberation movement/quasi-political party of government[40] against its domestic as well as foreign opponents.[41] "Getting the story out" may seem a clumsy ideological and foreign policy tool, but it is interesting to reflect on the diverse and, indeed, contradictory ways in which Simon Bright's original footage of this siege of a dusty Angolan airstrip has been used since.[42] The internationalized war of words between the MPLA and UNITA continued throughout the summer, matched by television footage,[43] until the signing of the peace agreement in New York, which formalized the independence of Namibia after UNSC Resolution 435 and the simultaneous withdrawal of Cuban forces. Robin Renwick, the British Ambassador to Pretoria, remarked in his memoirs that his experience of formal treaties and their implementation from Rhodesia/Zimbabwe's path to black majority rule in 1980, told him that the implementation phase of the agreement was critical.

Therefore, a more detailed understanding of the complex dynamic of the ending of the Cold War in the Third World, and in Southern Africa in particular, requires an intellectual framework combining Cold War cultural studies and traditional diplomatic history: the inter-play between political forces and cultural processes as an examination of relationships of power. It poses as an example of the role of new actors (film makers and newsmen), reinforcing the need for Cold War historians to keep culture and environment firmly in mind during the analysis of complex past events. It is also a manifestation of the role of Angolan nationalism and national identity; breaking down prevailing racial stereotypes that still permeated external Cold War perceptions in Southern Africa, rather than the self-belief of realist geo-political imperatives that were believed to frame American policies to the region. In the Angolan theatre, in particular, news-making itself was both war-making, and liberating, reminding us that the region's political and ideological struggles were also "profoundly shaped by a social and cultural world far beyond the conference table or the battle-field."[44]

In the Angolan case, it is clear that there were multiple relationships which were much more complex and which shifted depending on the actions of the various actors; that these were directly related to the role of the media, and the perceived – and actual – way it was used. The Angolan war, just as in the later case of external intervention in Somalia in 1993 (both in the run up to the US deployment and the subsequent Battle of Mogadishu), demonstrated the use of the media as an asymmetric weapon. It was deliberately used by the MPLA government to act as "a force multiplier" for FAPLA by extending the contest to broadcasting space. This was to assert the role of the MPLA government against its domestic opponents, Jonas Savimbi's UNITA, and by reasserting the support of Cuba, rather than its dominance in the military theatre. Targeted media output also acted as "a force multiplier" in the battle against the SADF. It undermined the South African state's traditional power over organizations and information on the war. (The success of this was made manifest in the anger of General Geldenhuys, when he was recalling this period at the oral history conference on Southern Africa in the Cold War era, in Ruimsig, South Africa, in January 2009, arguing that the MPLA printed "such lies.")[45] The South Africans found, just as their reluctant former Rhodesian allies had found to their intense frustration in the Rhodesian bush war of 1972–1979, that they were losing the propaganda war in the international press. The relative bias against South Africa in the international news media was, therefore, more akin to the US experience in Vietnam than the Gulf War when the international news corporations were decidedly on the side of the US-led coalition. The South African government's ability to manage the story, via the South African Broadcasting Corporation, was, thus, constrained.

Angola, before Somalia, showed that "sub-actors" could feed information to the international news media as fast as, or faster than, national governments; that "a global media then can hurt states," in particular when the growing lack of order inside South Africa was added into the equation. It can be seen as part of the so-called "boomerang effect" whereby relative local weakness is overcome by stimulating civil society overseas, to act as a reverberative source of pressure on the home government, to compensate for relative lack of power at home.[46] Examination of the intersection of state and independent media demonstrates clearly how "the news" was being used, manipulated and exploited. It points to trends which are valuable today when thinking about the media in a global age, and its relationship with a wide range of actors involved in modern conflict.[47] The Angolan war was not a scenario where the media forced a democratic government to intervene (for example, the US intervention in Somalia). Nor was this a story of the media "making" the story, seen in the deliberate editorial decision by the BBC to make the Ethiopian famine a centerpiece of its reporting in 1984. A more detailed study needs to collate the amount of television time given by the international news media (BBC/ITV/CNN/SABC) and the major national networks, to the Angola story and comparing those figures with the key political business taking place in Washington; or gauging the level of interest in the subject in the print media. All of these are very valid approaches.[48]

However, rather than simply looking at official key actors and their private deliberations via the documents, the end of the complex Cold War struggle in Southern Africa should also be seen as a case study in the role the media plays in unraveling the ideological contest in the region. In the context of the time in Southern Africa, in the struggle between the last white minority government and its black majority opponents, the media – and in particular, the international visual and print media – provided a key space which all actors sought to exploit; and which was itself, by its individual components, neither neutral nor passive. It was not simply that Western – particularly US – reporting was biased and viewed the Angolan war through Cold War lenses. At one level, the events and participants involved in the filming of the battle of Cuito Cuanavale represent a small snapshot of minor players in a much larger game. But the view from the ground showed that local actors were using external assistance and support, international networks of the burgeoning global media space, and the visual impact of television, expressly for their own agendas. The media were being used as explicit weapons of war by the MPLA (and Cuba), as well as UNITA.

This was not a Third World contest which suffered from under-reporting; nor a case of the "path dependency" of news wire services dictating the story. Just as economic globalization, information globalization, far from enhancing homogeneity, opened up networks. The New World Information Order debate in the 1960s and 1970s about international communication increasingly centered on UNESCO, proved to be an integral part of the story in that the Cold War in Southern Africa was also "the anti-imperialist" struggle. Certain political constituencies, expressing concern about the impact of the global economy and Western culture, expressly supported non-commercial media systems (and seriously opposed both Hollywood and the impact of Western music).[49] By the late 1980s, this NWIO debate was matched by a new wave of privatization and liberalization, and an emphasis on entrepreneurship and market forces, and a drive for mergers and acquisitions. This posed challenges but also – as the MPLA, Angolan Television and ITV showed – opportunities provided by the expansion of the global media space. This communications globalization is part of a structural shift in the international system that has paralleled economic globalization dating back to the 1970s; far from enhancing homogeneity, it opened up networks, proving to be one of the fundamental forces which led to the end of the Cold War in the Third World.

Notes

1 Chris Saunders and Sue Onslow, "The Cold War in Southern Africa 1975–1990," in M. Leffler and O.A. Westad (eds.), *The Cambridge History of the Cold War,* Vol. 3 (Cambridge: Cambridge University Press, 2010).

2 I. Tredten, "US Policy towards Angola since 1975," *The Journal of Modern African Studies,* 30:1 (1992), pp. 31–52. C. A. Crocker, F. O. Hampson and P. Aall (eds.), *Herding Cats. Multiparty Mediation in a Complex World* (Washington, DC: United States Institute of Peace Studies, 1999); See also Linda M. Heywood, "Unita and Ethnic Nationalism in Angola," *The Journal of Modern African Studies,* 27:I (1989), pp. 47–66; W. M. James III, *Cuban Involvement in the Angolan Civil War: implications for a lasting peace in Southern Africa* (Pretoria, 1988); Mike Hough, "The Angolan Civil War with Special Reference to the Unita Movement," in ISSUP Strategic Review (Pretoria), November 1985; and K. K. Virmani, *Angola and the Superpowers* (Delhi: University of Delhi Press, 1989). Also A. Tokarev and V. Shubin, "War in Angola: A Soviet Dimension," *Review of African Political Economy,* 28:90 (2001), pp. 607–18.

3 T. Phail, *Global Communications: Theories, Stakeholders, Trends,* 3rd edn (London: Blackwell, 2006).

4 Pippa Norris, "The Restless Searchlight: Network News Framing of the Post Cold War World," *Political Communication,* 12:4 (1995) pp. 357–70.

5 The importance of media sources in key decision making has a well established history. One very powerful example of the subtle influences of media sources upon key decision makers: in the growing Munich crisis between March and September 1938 the British Prime Minister, Neville Chamberlain, was drawing his understanding of Sudeten opinion in Czechoslovakia from the British Ambassador in Berlin, who himself was relying on German (i.e. anti-Slav) media comment and reporting. Chamberlain considered his Ambassador in Prague to be a non-entity and did not consult him at all. Hence, in the long-running Czech crisis, the British Prime Minister never got that side of the picture. The Runciman Commission's report of August 1938 failed to correct the Prime Minister's biased perceptions of Slav opinion on the Sudeten issue. I am grateful to Professor Anita Prazmowska, International History Department, London School of Economics, for this point.

6 S. Iyengar and D. Kinder, *News that Matters: Television and American Opinion* (Chicago, IL: University of Chicago Press, 1987).

7 Quoted in D.K. Thusu and D. Freeman, *War and the Media: Reporting Conflict 24/7* (London: Sage, 2003).

8 The term "refolution" was coined by Professor Timothy Garton Ash, to describe the demise of socialism in Eastern Europe in the late 1980s as a combination of elements of "revolution" from below, in the form of mass popular rejection of an ideologically bankrupt system, and "reform" by political elites.

9 The South African Broadcasting Corporation first began television coverage within South Africa in 1976.

10 M. Evangelista, *Unarmed Forces: the Transnational Movement to End the Cold War* (New York: Cornell University Press, 2002).

11 Ibid.

12 Elaine Windrich, *The Cold War Guerrilla: Jonas Savimbi, the US Media, and the Angolan War* (Orlando, FL: Greenwood Publishing Group, 1992).

13 The problem with the sound and film archives of Southern Africa is part and parcel of the fragility of archival material in Southern Africa in the Cold War era. The remaining SABC sound archives have only three surviving entries for Angola – not because this issue was unimportant, but because there was a deliberate destruction of film footage and recordings in the frenetic period leading up to elections for black majority rule in 1994. Reporters working at SABC at the time recall reels of film footage being dumped in rubbish bins in the frenzied political climate of the unraveling of the apartheid era, and spiraling internal communal violence within South Africa, 1990–1994.

14 John Marcum, "Africa: A Continent Adrift," *Foreign Affairs*, 68:1(1988/1989), pp. 159–79.

15 For an examination of the public and private propaganda of the South African state, see G. Hull, "South Africa's Propaganda War: A Bibliographic Essay," *African Studies Review*, 22:3 (1979), pp. 79–98.

16 Restrictions on the media. A reflection on journalism by Mono Badela and David Niddrie. Was available online as a webcache file, on 16 January 2011, at http://webcache.googleusercontent.com/custom?q=cache:xKK8mr1epJQJ:www.sahistory.org.za/pages/library-resources/online%2520books/culture-anotherSA/restrictions-media.htm+restrictions+media&cd=1&hl=en&ct=clnk.

17 The British Ambassador to South Africa, Sir Robin Renwick, (1987–1991) made a deliberate effort to cultivate links with the Afrikaner press in South Africa. This was a radical innovation: previously, British Ambassadors had not done this. (Robin Renwick, *Unconventional Diplomacy in Southern Africa* (London: St Martin's Press, 1999).

18 Simon Bright, Zimbabwean independent film maker, to the author, 25 September 2009.

19 R. Govea, *Africa's Media Image* (Santa Barbara, CA: Praeger, 1992), p. 94.

20 Simon Bright to Sue Onslow.

21 D. Birmingham: "Angola Revisited," *Journal of Southern African Studies*, 29:1 (1988).

22 Ibid.

23 Ronald Reagan, diary entry: Tuesday 24 March 1981, D. Brinkley (ed.), *The Reagan Diaries.*

24 C. A. Crocker, F. O. Hampson and P. Aall (eds.), *Herding Cats: Multi-party Mediation in a Complex World.*

25 V. Shubin and A. Tokarev, "War in Angola: a Soviet Dimension."

26 O. A. Westad, *The Global Cold War*, p. 385.

27 Ibid.

28 Piero Gleijeses places greatest emphasis on a Cuban military victory. Piero Gleijeses: "From Cassinga to New York. Cuba and the Independence of Namibia," in S. Onslow (ed.), *Cold War in Southern Africa: White Power, Black Nationalism* (London: Routledge, 2009). See also C. Brundenius, "Revolutionary Cuba at 50: Growth with Equity Revisited," in *Latin American Perspectives* 36:2 (2009), pp. 31–48; and E. George, *The Cuban Intervention in Angola 1965–1991: From Che Guevara to Cuito Cuanavale* (London: Cass, 1991); whereas V. Shubin, *The Hot "Cold War,"* (London: Pluto Press, 2009), p. 112, believes "Cuban military pressure brought about equilibrium on the battlefield.".

29 Unsurprisingly, the US viewed Castro as "clinging to his role of leader of the Third World Revolution." Chester Crocker interview in *The Financial Mail*, 19 August 1988.

30 V. Shubin and A. Tokarev, "War in Angola: a Soviet Dimension."

31 R. F. Pik Botha interview with Sue Onslow, July 2008.

32 This, and the following quotations, are taken from the Independent Television News sound archives, at www.itnsource.com.

33 *The Windhoek Advertiser*, 24 March 1988. The news report included comment from the Washington Post, that

> the United States is full of hope that the Angolan Government will soon propose an acceptable timetable for the withdrawal of the Cuban troops. The newspaper quotes a spokesman for the American State Department, who said that Dr Chester Crocker and his Soviet counterpart, Mr Anatoli Adamiskin (sic), had agreed in general on a possible solution to the Angolan problem.

34 www.itnsource.com, 12 April 1988. Ref. BGY509180025.

35 "He really was a media star." Simon Bright to Sue Onslow, September 2009.

36 James Brooke, Special Correspondent to the New York Times, *New York Times*, 31 May 1988.

37 By April 1988, there were 57,000 Cuban troops in Southern Angola. The Angolan Government denied any increase in Cuban forces, saying that the only change was the movement of Cuban troops from North to South. The *Sunday Times*, 26 June 1988.

38 R. F. (Pik) Botha to Sue Onslow, July 2008.

39 Ernesto Escobar, Cuban Communist Party Central Committee,

> An ill-fated move by the Angolan army, supported by the Soviet Union but against Cuban advice, allowed Cuba to reassert its pre-eminence in the conflict. An offensive earlier this year by 9,000 Angolan troops against UNITA positions in south-eastern Angola exposed them to the prospect of annihilation by the South African Army. The subsequent Cuban mission, involving 15,000 and leading to the four-month battle of Cuito Cuanavale has been portrayed by President Castro as the turning point in the Angolan war.
>
> (Havana. The Independent News Service, quoted in *The Star*, 23 August 1988)

For the South African perspective in the "war of perceptions," see T. Papenfus, *Pik Botha and His Times* (Pretoria: Litera, 2010), pp. 541–84; P. Stiff, *The Silent War – South African Recce Operations 1969–1994* (Alberton: Galago, 2004), pp. 547–52. See also Simon Barber, "Fidel Castro and the Legend of Cuito Cuanavale," *Business Day (S.A)*, 28 March 2008.

40 Key Cuban commanders were placed within Angolan units to enhance discipline and military capability. Vladimir Shubin to Sue Onslow, "The Year of Africa Conference," Institute of African Studies, Moscow, 31 March 2010.

41 Jonas Savimbi's visit to Washington, in June 1988, was sponsored by the Cuban National Foundation, a Washington-based anti-Castro group. *The Sunday Times*, 26 June 1988.

42 For an alternative presentation of the military conflict in Southern Angola, see Jihan El-Tahri, *Cuba! Africa! Revolution*, part 1&2, BBC storyville.

43 Angola: rebel leader Savimbi says he supports current four-party talks on ending country's civil war. ITV (Reuters footage) 19 June 1988. Savimbi also put on display of two captured Cuban soldiers, and claimed that UNITA has achieved considerable military successes in Angola over the last few months.

44 C. G. Appy (ed.) *Cold War Constructions: The Political Culture of US Imperialism 1945–1966* (Boston, MA: University of Massachusetts, 2000) p. 4, referred to in R. Griffiths, "Review: The Cultural Turn in Cold War Studies," *Reviews of American History*, 29:1 (2001), pp. 150–7.

45 In contrast to the information and news coverage of the Angolan Civil War outside South Africa, families of South African conscripted troops had no

knowledge of their relatives whereabouts. See G. Baines (ed.), *Beyond the Border War* (Pretoria: UNISA, 2008).

46 *The Citizen* (Namibia) reported, on 5 May 1988, that a new book "proved" that the Cubans, with Soviet support, were the first to intervene in Angola in 1975. J. R. Thackrah, *Encyclopedia of Terror and Political Violence* (London: Routledge & Paul Kegan, 1988).

47 I am grateful to Andrew Marshall, Masters student of Warfare in the Modern World, King's College, London, for this point.

48 See for example, J. Mermin, "Television News and American Intervention in Somalia: The Myth of a Media-Driven Foreign Policy," *Political Science Quarterly,* 112:3 (1997) pp. 385–403. M. Mandelbaum, "The Reluctance to Intervene," *Foreign Policy,* 95 (1994), pp. 3–18.

49 This culminated in the publication of the MacBride report on the imbalance of media flows. Eventually the debate reached such intensity that, in 1985, the US and the UK withdrew from UNESCO.

Bibliography

Abbas, Hassan, *Pakistan's Drift into Extremism* (London: M. E. Sharpe, 2005).

Adamishin, Anatolii, *Beloe solntse Angoly* (Moscow: Vagrius, 2001).

Adams, Simon, *Comrade Minister: the South African Communist Party and the transition from Apartheid to Democracy* (Huntington, NY: Nova Science Publishers, 2001).

Adamsky, Dima, *The Culture of Military Innovation: The Impact of Cultural Factors on Revolution in Military Affairs in Russia, the US and Israel* (Stanford, CA: Stanford University Press, 2010).

Alacevich, Michele, *Le origini della Banca Mondiale. Una deriva conservatrice* (Milano: Bruno Mondatori, 2006).

Aijazuddin, Fakir Syed, *From a Head, through a Head, to a Head: The Secret Channel between the US and China through Pakistan* (Karachi: Oxford University Press, 2000).

Ahimeir, Yossi (ed.), *Yitzhak Shamir kesela eitan* (Tel Aviv: Yediot Sfarim, 2008).

Amidror, Yaacov, *Hirhurim al tzava ve bitahon* (Tel Aviv: Misrad haBitahon, 2002).

Amorim, Celso, "O Brasil e a ordem internacional pos-Golfo," *Contexto Internacional*, 13:1 (1991), pp. 25–34.

——, "Os frageis pilares da nova ordem," in Renato Baumann (ed.), *O Brasil e a Economia Global* (Rio de Janeiro: Campus, 1996).

Amer, Ramses, "Sino–Vietnamese Normalization in the Light of the Crisis of the Late 1970s," *Pacific Affairs*, 67:3 (1994), pp. 357–83.

Anderton, N., "From Gorbachev to Yeltsin: Moscow-Pretoria Relations at a Time of Change," Unpublished Paper, University of Stellenbosch, 1994.

Andrew, Christopher and Mitrokhin, Vasili, *The World Was Going Our Way* (New York: Basic Books, 2006).

Anglin, D., "Southern African Responses to Eastern European Developments," *Journal of Modern African Studies*, 28:3 (1990), pp. 431–455.

Arbel, D. and Edelist, R., *Western Intelligence and the Collapse of the Soviet Union 1980–1990* (London: Cass, 2003).

Arens, Moshe, *Milkhama veshalom be mizrah hatikhon 1988–1992* (Tel Aviv: Yediot Sfarim, 1995).

Bakhitov, R. M. and Kazakov, S. A., "Rasprostranenie Marksizma v Latinskoi Amerike. Vli'ianie Velikogo Oktiabria na Obrazovanie Kommunisticheskikh Partii," in Kudachkin, M. F. (ed.), *Velikii Oktiabr i Kommunisticheskie Partii Latinskoi Ameriki* (Moscow: Nauka, 1978).

Baines, Gary and Vale, Peter (eds), *Beyond the Border War* (Pretoria: UNISA, 2008).

Bar-Joseph, Uri, *The Best of Enemies: Israel and Trans-Jordan in the War of 1948* (London: Routledge, 1978).

——, "Military Intelligence as the National Intelligence Estimator: The Case of Israel," *Armed Forces and Society*, 36:3 (2010), pp. 505–25.

Ben-Ami, Shlomo, *Hazit le lo oref: masa el gvulot tahalikh hashalom* (Tel Aviv: Yediot Akhronot, 2004).

Bar-Zohar, Michael, *Shimon Peres: Biografia* (Tel Aviv: Sifrei Maskel, 2005).

Beilin, Yossi, *Madrikh leyona haptzuah* (Tel Aviv: Yediot Akhronot, 2001).

——, *Lagaat beshalom* (Tel Aviv: Yediot Akhronot, 1995).

Ben Eliyahu, Eitan, *Haotzma haavirit shel Israel likrat shnot 2000* (Tel Aviv: JCSS, 1998).

Ben-Meir, Yehuda, *Civil Military Relations in Israel* (New York: Columbia University Press, 1995).

Birmingham, David, "Angola Revisited," *Journal of Southern African Studies*, 15:1 (1988), pp. 1–14.

Biersteker, T. (ed.), *Dealing with Debt. International Financial Negotiations and Adjustment Bargaining* (Boulder, CO: Westview, 1993).

Blasier, Cole, *The Giant's Rival: The USSR and Latin America* (Pittsburgh, PA: Pittsburgh University Press, 1983).

Boesak, Allan, *Running with Horses* (Cape Town: Joho, 2009).

Brinkley, Douglas (ed.), *The Ronald Reagan Diaries* (New York: Harper Collins, 2007).

Brun, Itai, " 'While You're Busy Making Other Plans' – The 'Other RMA,' " *Journal of Strategic Studies*, 33:4 (2010), pp. 535–65.

Brundenius, Claes, "Revolutionary Cuba at 50: Growth with Equity Revisited," *Latin American Perspectives*, 36:2 (2009), pp. 31–48.

Brzezinski, Zbigniew, *Power and Principle: Memoirs of the National Security Advisor, 1977–1981* (New York: Farrar, Straus and Giroux 1983).

Carazo, Jaime Morales, *La Contra* (Mexico D. F.: Planeta, 1989).

Castro, Fidel, *Vindicación de Cuba* (Havana: Editora Política Publishers, 1989).

Cavagnari, Geraldo, "Atlântico Sul: introdução ao debate," 35th Pugwash Conference on Science and World Affairs, Campinas, Brazil, 3–8 July 1985.

Cherniaev, Anatolli, *Shest' Let s Gorbachevym* (Moscow: Progress-Kultura, 1993).

Christensen, Scott R., "Thailand in 1989: Consensus at Bay," *Asian Survey*, 30:2 (1990), pp. 178–86.

Cohen, Robin, *Endgame in South Africa* (London: James Currey, 1986).

Coll, Steve, *Ghost Wars: The Secret History of the CIA, Afghanistan, and bin Laden, from the Soviet Invasion to September 10, 2001* (New York: Penguin, 2004).

Colosimo, Antonello, *Il debito estero dei Paesi in via di sviluppo* (Padova: CEDAM, 1991).

Cook, Susan E. (ed.), *Genocide in Rwanda and Cambodia: New Perspectives* (New Haven, CT: CIAS, 2005).

Cricco, M., Guasconi, M. E. and Napoletano, M. L. (eds), *L'America Latina tra Guerra fredda e globalizzazione* (Firenze: Polistampa, 2010).

Crocker, Chester, *High Noon in Southern Africa: Making Peace in a Rough Neighbourhood* (New York and London: W. W. Norton, 1993).

Crocker, Chester A., Hampson, Fen Osler and Aall, Pamera R., (eds), *Herding Cats. Multiparty Mediation in a Complex World* (Washington, DC: USIP Press, 1999).

Daniel, John, "A Response to Guelke: the Cold War Factor in the South African Transition," *Journal of Contemporary African Studies*, 14:1 (1996), pp. 101–104.

Del Pero, M., *Libertà e impero. Gli Stati Uniti e il mondo 1776–2006* (Roma-Bari: Laterza, 2008).

Dobson, Alan (ed.), *Deconstructing and Reconstructing the Cold War* (Aldershot: Ashgate, 1999).

Dominguez, Jorge I., "US–Latin American Relations During the Cold War and its Aftermath," in V. Bulmer-Thomas and J. Dunkerley (eds.), *The United States and Latin America: The New Agenda* (London: Institute of Latin American Studies and David Rockefeller Center for Latin American Studies, 1999).

Ellis, Stephan and Sechaba, Tsepo, *Comrades against Apartheid: the ANC and the South African Communist Party in exile* (Bloomington, IN: Currey, Indianapolis: Indiana University Press, 1992).

Eran, Oded, *Mediniut hutz shel brit hamoatzot mi lenin ad gorbachev* (Tel Aviv: Open University Press, 1993).

Evangelista, Matthew, *Unarmed Forces: the Transnational Movement to End the Cold War* (New York: Cornell University Press, 2002).

Evans, Grant, *A Short History of Laos: The Land in Between* (Crows Nest (NSW): Allen and Unwin, 2002).

Frieden, Jeffry, *Global Capitalism: Its Fall and Rise in the Twentieth Century* (New York: Norton, 2006).

Fishlow, Albert, "The United States and Brazil: The Case of the Missing Relationship," *Foreign Affairs,* 60:4 (1982), pp. 904–23.

Forbes, Dean, *et al.* (eds), *Doi Moi. Vietnam's Renovation: Policy and Performance* (Canberra: Department of Political and Social Change, Australian National University, 1991).

Gai, Carmit, *Bar-Lev Biografia* (Tel Aviv: Am Oved, 1998).

Gazit, Shlomo, *Hamodiin vetahalih hashalom* (Jerusalem: Hebrew University in Jerusalem, 1994).

George, Edward, *The Cuban Intervention in Angola 1965–1991: From Che Guevara to Cuito Cuanavale* (London: Cass, 1991).

Gevisser, Mark, *Thabo Mbeki: The Dream Deferred* (Johannesburg: Jonathan Ball, 2007).

Giustozzi, Antonio, *War, Politics and Society in Afghanistan* (London: Hurst, 2000).

Giliomee, Hermann, "Democratization in South Africa," *Political Science Quarterly,* 110:1, (1995), pp. 83–104.

Gleijeses, Piero, "From Cassinga to New York: Cuba and the Independence of Namibia," in Sue Onslow (ed.), *Cold War in Southern Africa: White Power, Black Liberation* (London: Routledge, 2009).

——, *Conflicting Missions* (Chapel Hill, NC: University of North Carolina Press, 2002).

Goodman, Allan E., "Vietnam and ASEAN: Who Would Have Thought It Possible?" *Asian Survey,* 36:6 (1996), pp. 592–600.

Gold, Dore (ed.), *Iahasei Israel-suria: la'an?* (Ramat Gan: Bar Ilan University, 1996).

——, *Haastrategiia hatzvait haamerikait bemizrah hatikhon* (Tel Aviv: Misrad haBitahon, 1993).

——, *Iran, Hizbullah, Hamas and Jihad globali: gishot iasod hadashot nohah tmurot astrategiot bemizrah hatikhon* (Jerusalem: Hamerkaz haerushalmi le inianei tzibur ve medina, 2007).

——, *Mirutz hatilim hahadash bemizrah hatikhon* (Jerusalem: Hamerkaz haerushalmi le inianei tzibur ve medina, 2000).

Gordon, Shmuel, *Keshet pireus* (Tel Aviv: Ramot, 1998).

Govea, Rodger, "Reporting African Violence: Can American Media Forget the Cold War," in Beverly Hawk (ed.), *Africa's Media Image* (New York: Praeger, 1992), pp. 94–108.

Gowan, Peter, *The Global Gamble: Washington's Faustian Bid for World Dominance* (Chicago, IL: Verso, 1999).

Grandin, G., *Empire's Workshop: Latin America, the United States, and the Rise of the New Imperialism* (New York: Owl Books, 2007).

Grandin, Greg, *The Last Colonial Massacre: Latin America in the Cold War* (London: Chicago University Press, 2004).

Griffith-Jones, S. (ed.), *Managing World Debt* (New York: St. Martin's Press, 1988).

Guégan, Francois, "Historical perspectives on development assistance to the Lao PDR." Available online at www.sono.ens-cachan.fr/IMG/pdf/article_guegan.pdf.

Guelke, A., *South Africa in Transition: The Misunderstood Miracle* (London: Macmillan, 1999).

——, "The Impact of the End of the Cold War on the South African Transition," *Journal of Contemporary African Studies*, 14:1 (1996), pp. 87–100.

Gunn, Geoffrey C., "Laos in 1989: Quiet Revolution in the Marketplace," *Asian Survey*, 31:1 (1990), pp. 81–7.

Gusev, P., *Ischi Svoiu Sud'bu: Vospominam'ia Nachal'sika Shtaba Prik VO* (1951–2001) (Izhevsk: Udmurti'ia, 2004).

Gwin, Catherine, *US Relations with the World Bank, 1945–92* (Washington, DC: Brookings Institution Press, 1994).

Halevi, Efraim, *Adam Betzel* (Tel Aviv: Matar, 2006).

Handelman, H. and Baer, W. (eds.), *Paying the Costs of Austerity in Latin America* (Boulder, CO: Westview, 1989).

Harvey, David, *A Brief History of Neoliberalism* (New York: Oxford University Press, 2005).

Harvey, Robert, *The Fall of Apartheid: The Inside Story from Smuts to Mbeki* (London: Palgrave, 2001).

Herring, George C., *From Colony to Superpower; US Foreign relations since 1776* (New York: Oxford University Press, 2008).

Herzog, Chaim, *Derekh Khaim: Autobiografia* (Tel Aviv: Ma'ariv, 1997).

Heywood, Linda M., "UNITA and Ethnic Nationalism in Angola," *The Journal of Modern African Studies*, 27:1 (1989), pp. 47–66.

Hirschfield, Yair, *Oslo: Nusha le Shalom – masa umatan leheskemei Oslo astrategiia vemimusha* (Tel Aviv: Am Oved, 2000).

Horn, Robert C., "Vietnam and Sino–Soviet Relations: What Price Rapprochement?," *Asian Survey*, 27:7 (1987), pp. 729–47.

Hough, Mike, "The Angolan Civil War with Special Reference to the Unita Movement," in *ISSUP Strategic Review (Pretoria)*, November 1985.

Hull, Galen, "South Africa's Propaganda War: A Bibliographic Essay," *African Studies Review*, 22:3 (1979), pp. 79–98.

Hurrell, Andrew, "Latin America in the New World Order: A Regional Bloc of the Americas?," *International Affairs*, 68:1 (1992), pp. 121–39.

Ivry, David, *Ma'arachot shlita vepikud lemivtzaim* (Tel Aviv: Fisher Institute, 2003).

Chen, Jian, *Mao's China and the Cold War* (Chapel Hill, NC: University of North Carolina Press, 2001).

Chen, Jinghua, *Guoshi yishu* (Beijing: Zhonggong dangshi, 2005).

Kagan, Robert, *A Twilight Struggle: American Power and Nicaragua, 1977–1990* (New York: The Free Press, 1994).

Kagan-Guthrie, Zachary, "Chester Crocker and the South African Border War,

1981–1989: A Reappraisal of Linkage," *Journal of Southern African Studies*, 35:1 (2009), pp. 65–80.
Kalinovsky, Artemy, "Decision-Making and the Soviet War in Afghanistan: From Intervention to Withdrawal," *Journal of Cold War Studies*, 11:4 (2009), pp. 46–73.
——, "Politics, Diplomacy and the Soviet Withdrawal from Afghanistan: From National Reconciliation to the Geneva Accords," *Cold War History*, 8:3 (August 2008), pp. 381–404.
Kam, Ephraim, *Iran mi terror le gar'in* (Tel Aviv: Misrad haBitahon, 2004).
Kapur, D., Lewis, J. and Webb, R. (eds), *The World Bank. Its First Half Century*, Vol. 1, *History* (Washington, DC: Brookings Institution Press, 1997).
——, *The World Bank. Its First Half Century*, Vol. 2, *Perspectives* (Washington, DC: Brookings Institution Press, 1997).
Karsh, Efraim, "Cold War, post-Cold War: does it make a difference for the Middle East?," *Review of International Studies*, 23, (1997), pp. 271–91.
Kaspit, Ben, *Ehud Barak: Biografia* (Tel Aviv: Alfa Tikshoret, 1998).
Khan, Riaz, *Untying the Afghan Knot: Negotiating Soviet Withdrawal* (Durham, NC: Duke University Press, 1991).
Kenna, Constance (ed.), *Homecoming: the GDR kids of Namibia* (Windhoek: New Namibia Books, 1999).
Kiernan, Ben (ed.), *Genocide and Democracy in Cambodia: The Khmer Rouge, the United Nations, and the International Community* (New Haven, CT: Yale Council on Southeast Asia Studies/Orville H. Schell, Jr. Center for International Human Rights, 1993).
Kirkpatrick, Jeane, *Dictatorships and Double Standards: Rationalism and Reason in Politics* (New York: Simon & Schuster, 1982).
Kober, Avi and Ofer, Zvi (eds), *Ikhut ve Kamut bebenian hakoakh* (Tel Aviv: Ma'arachot, 1985).
Kornbluh, P., *The Pinochet File: A Declassified Dossier on Atrocity and Accountability* (New York: New Press, 2003).
Kotkin, Stephen, *Armageddon Averted: The Soviet Collapse 1970–2000* (New York: Oxford University Press, 2001).
Kroef, Justus M. van der, "Cambodia in 1990: The Elusive Peace," *Asian Survey*, 31:1 (1991), pp. 94–102.
Kunz, Diane, *Butter and Guns: America's Cold War Economic Diplomacy* (New York: Free Press, 1997).
Lee, Boon-Chye, *The Economics of International Debt Renegotiation* (Boulder, CO: Westview, 1993).
Leng Rong and Wang Zuoling, *et al.*, *Deng Xiaoping nianpu, 1975–1997* (Beijing: Zhongyang wenxian, 2004).
LeoGrande, William, *Our Own Backyard: The United States in Central America, 1977–1992* (Chapel Hill, NC: University of North Carolina Press, 1998).
Levin, Arieh, *Envoy to Moscow: Memoirs of an Israeli Ambassador, 1988–1992* (London: Cass, 1996).
Levite, Ariel, *Hadoktrina hatzvait shel Israel: hagana vehatkafa* (Tel Aviv: Hakibutz hameuhad, 1988).
Liakhovskii, Aleksandr, *Tragedi'ia i doblest' Afgana* (Moscow: Nord, 2004).
Lipton, Merle, *Liberals, Marxists and Nationalists* (London: Palgrave, 2008).
Lissakers, Karin, *Banks, Borrowers, and the Establishment* (New York: Basic Books, 1991).
Lorini, Alessandra and Basosi, Duccio (eds), *Cuba in the World, the World in Cuba: Essays in Cuban History, Politics, and Culture* (Firenze: Firenze University Press, 2009).

Loveman, Brian, *Chile: The Legacy of Hispanic Capitalism* 3rd. edn. (Oxford: Oxford University Press, 2001).

——, "'Protected Democracies' and Military Guardianship: Political Transitions in Latin America, 1978–1993," *Journal of Interamerican Studies and World Affairs*, 36:2 (1994), pp. 105–189.

Macmillan, Margaret, *Nixon and Mao: The Week that Changed the World* (New York: Random House, 2007).

MacIntyre, Andrew J., "Interpreting Indonesian Foreign Policy: The Case of Kampuchea, 1979–1986," *Asian Survey*, 27:5 (1987), pp. 515–34.

Mahler, Gregory S. and Mahler, Alden, *The Arab–Israeli Conflict: An Introduction and Documentary Reader* (London: Routledge, 2009).

Malan, Magnus, *My Life with the South African Defence Force* (Pretoria: Protea Books, 2006).

Mandela, Nelson, *Long Walk to Freedom* (London: Abacus, 1995).

McPherson, Alan, *Intimate Ties, Bitter Struggles: The United States and Latin America since 1945* (Washington, DC: Potomac Books, 2006).

Mehta, Harish C. and Mehta, Julie B., *Hun Sen: Strongman of Cambodia* (Singapore: Graham Brash, 1999).

Michael, Kobi, *Madua kashal hamodel shel shituf hapeula habitkhoni-tzvai bein Israel le Reshut hapalestinit?* (Jerusalem: David Institute for International Affairs, 2003).

Moghadam, Assaf, *Globalization of Martydrom: Al Qaida, Salafi Jihad and Diffusion of Suicide Attacks* (Washington, DC: Johns Hopkins University Press, 2008).

Netanyahu, Benjamin, *Makom takhat shemesh* (Tel Aviv: Yediot Akhronot, 2005).

——, *Milkhama be Terror* (Tel Aviv: Yediot Akhronot, 2004).

Niksch, Larry A., "Thailand in 1988: The Economic Surge," *Asian Survey*, 29:2 (1989), pp. 165–73.

Nocera, Raffaele, *Stati Uniti e America Latina dal 1945 a oggi* (Roma: Carocci, 2005).

Nove, A., *An Economic History of the USSR* (London: Penguin, 1989).

O'Malley, Padraig, *Shades of Difference: Mac Maharaj and the Struggle for South Africa* (New York: Viking, 1998).

Pankin, Boris, *The Last Hundred Days of the Soviet Union* (New York: I. B. Tauris, 1996).

Pastor, Robert A., *Not Condemned to Repetition: The United States and Nicaragua* (Oxford: Westview Press, 2002).

Paszyn, Danuta, *The Soviet Attitude to Political and Social Change in Central America, 1979–1990: Case Studies on Nicaragua, El Salvador and Guatemala* (New York: St. Martin's Press, 2000).

Pearce, Jenny, *Under the Eagle* (London: Latin America Bureau, 1981).

Peng, Chin, *My Side of History* (Singapore: Media Masters, 2003).

Peres, Shimon, *Mizrah hatikhon hahadash* (Tel Aviv: Yediot Akhronot, 1993).

Pérez de Cuéllar, Javier, *Pilgrimage for Peace: a Secretary General's memoir* (New York: St. Martin's Press, 1997).

Phail, Thomas, *Global Communications: Theories, Stakeholders, Trends*, 3rd edn. (London: Blackwell, 2006).

Rabinovich, Itamar, *Hevlei shalom: Israel vehaaravim 1948–2003* (Or Ehuda: Dvir, 2004).

——, *Sof hashalom: Israel vesuria 1992–1996* (Tel Aviv: Mishkal, 1998).

Raymont, Henry, *Troubled Neighbors: The Story of US–Latin American Relations from FDR to the Present* (Cambridge, MA: Westview Press, 2005).

Reagan, Ronald, *An American Life* (New York: Simon & Schuster, 1990).

Renwick, Robin, *Unconventional Diplomacy in Southern Africa* (London: St Martin's Press, 1999).

Robinson, William I., *Promoting Polyarchy: Globalization, US Intervention, and Hegemony* (Cambridge: Cambridge University Press, 1998).

Rodrik, D. (ed.), *In Search of Prosperity: Analytic Narratives on Economic Growth* (Princeton, NJ: Princeton University Press, 2003).

R'oi, Yaacov and Morozov, Boris, *The Soviet Union and the June 1967 War* (Stanford, CA: Stanford University Press, 2008).

Rosen, F. (ed.), *Empire and Dissent. The United States and Latin America* (Durham, NC: Duke University Press, 2008).

Ross, Robert S., "China and the Cambodian Peace Process: The Value of Coercive Diplomacy," *Asian Survey*, 31:12 (1991), pp. 1170–85.

Rubin, Barnett, *The Fragmentation of Afghanistan: state formation and collapse in the international system* (New Haven, CT: Yale University Press, 1995).

Rubinstein, Dani, *Camp David 2000: ma beemet kara sham?* (Tel Aviv: Yediot Akhronot, 2003).

Rubinstein, Elyakim, *Derkei hashalom* (Tel Aviv: Misrad haBitahon, 2000).

Ruggie, John Gerard, "International Regimes, Transactions, and Change: Embedded Liberalism in the Postwar Economic Order," *International Organization*, 36:2 (1982), pp. 379–415.

Sagi, Uri, *Orot bearafel* (Tel Aviv: Yediot Akhronot, 1998).

Savir, Uri, *Miakhorei haklaim shel hakraa historit* (Tel Aviv: Mishkal, 1998).

Saunders, Chris and Onslow, Sue, "The Cold War in Southern Africa 1975–1990," in Melvyn Leffler and Odd Arne Westad (eds), *Cambridge History of the Cold War*, Volume 3 (Cambridge: Cambridge University Press, 2010).

Saunders, Chris, "The Angola/Namibia Crisis of 1988 and its resolution," in Sue Onslow (ed.), *Cold War in Southern Africa* (London: Routledge, 2009).

Schleicher, Hans-Georg and Schleicher, Ilona, *Special Flights, the GDR and Liberation Movements in southern Africa* (Harare: Sapes, 1998).

Segal, Gerald, "The USSR and Asia in 1987: Signs of a Major Effort," *Asian Survey*, 28:1 (1988), pp. 1–9.

Sela, Aviad, "Hashpaat artzot habrit al haitron haikhuti shel tzakhal," *Ma'arachot*, No. 383, (May 2002), pp. 42–9.

Schweizer, Peter, *Reagan's War: The Epic Story of His Forty-Year Struggle and Final Triumph over Communism* (Westminster, MD: Doubleday, 2003).

Shamir, Yitzhak, *Sikumo shel Davar* (Tel Aviv: Eidanim, 1994).

Sher, Gilad, *Tahalih hashalom: hazon mul matziut* (Tel Aviv: Tel Aviv University Press, 2001).

Shubin, Vladimir, "From the History of the Liberation Movement in South Africa," paper presented at the seminar on African nationalism at the Institute of General History, Moscow, 1985.

——, *The Hot "Cold War"* (London: Pluto Press 2009).

Shubin, Vladimir and Tokarev, Andrei, "War in Angola: A Soviet Dimension," *Review of African Political Economy*, 28:90 (December 2001), pp. 607–18.

Slocomb, Margaret, *The People's Republic of Kampuchea, 1979–1989: The Revolution After Pol Pot* (Chiang Mai: Silkworm Books, 2003).

Slovo, Joe, "Has Socialism Failed?," *African Communist*, January 1990.

Sklar, Holly, *Washington's War on Nicaragua* (Boston, MA: South End Press, 1988).

Sparks, Allister, *Tomorrow is Another Country* (Sandton: Struik, 1994).

Spektor, Matias, *Kissinger e o Brasil* (Rio de Janeiro: Zahar 2009).

Smith, Joseph, *The United States and Latin America: A History of American Diplomacy, 1776–2000* (London: Routledge, 2006).

Stallings, Barbara and Kaufman, Robert (eds), *Debt and Democracy in Latin America* (Boulder, CO: Westview, 1989).

Starushenko, G., *Problems of Struggle against Racism, Apartheid and Colonialism in South Africa* (Moscow: Africa Institute,1986).

Steenkamp, Willem, *South Africa's Border War 1966–1989* (Gibraltar: Ashanti, 1989).

Steyn, Hannes, van der Walt, Richard and van Loggerenburg, Jan, *Armament and Disarmament: South Africa's Nuclear Weapons Experience* (Pretoria: Network, 2003).

Stuart-Fox, Martin, "Laos in 1997: Into ASEAN," *Asian Survey*, 38:1 (1998), pp. 75–9.

——, "Laos: The Chinese Connection," *Southeast Asian Affairs*, 2009, pp. 141–69.

Szalontai, Balázs, "The Diplomacy of Economic Reform in Vietnam: The Genesis of *Doi Moi*, 1986–1989," *Journal of Asiatic Studies*, 51:2 (2008), pp. 199–252.

Thussu, Daya and Freedman, Des, *War and the Media: Reporting Conflict 24/7* (London: Sage, 2003).

Tian Zengfei, *et al.*, *Gaige kaifang yilai de zhongguo waijiao* (Beijing: Shijie zhishi, 1993).

Tikhomirov, V., *States in Transition: Russia and South Africa* (Bryanston: International Freedom Foundation, 1992).

Tira, Ron, "Shifting Tectonic Plates: Basic Assumptions on the Peace Process Revisited," *Strategic Assessment*, 12:1 (June 2009), pp. 11–107.

Tlaas, Mustafa (ed.), *Haplisha haisraelit lelevanon* (Tel Aviv: Misrad haBitahon, 1988).

Torres-Rivas, Edelberto, "Crisis and Conflict, 1930 to the Present," in Leslie Bethell (ed.), *Central America since Independence* (Cambridge: Cambridge University Press, 1991).

Tosi, Luciano and Tosone Lorella (eds), *Gli aiuti allo sviluppo nelle relazioni internazionali del secondo dopoguerra* (Padova: Cedam, 2006).

Tvedten, Inge, "US Policy towards Angola since 1975," *The Journal of Modern African Studies*, 30: 1 (March 1992), pp. 31–52.

Tzabag, Shmuel (ed.), *Ehudim, isrel ve astrategiia gariinit: asufat maamarim pri eto shel profesor Yval Neeman* (Ariel: Mihlelet ehuda veshomron, 2007).

Van Tooch, *International Aid and Democracy Building Process: Cambodia.* Available online at www.fletcher.tufts.edu/research/2004/Van-Tooch.pdf.

Varennikov, Valentin, *Nepovtorimoe'* (Moscow: Sovetskii Pisatel, 2002).

Virmani, K. K., *Angola and the Superpowers* (Delhi: University of Delhi Press, 1989).

Wang Taiping (ed.), *Zhonghua renmin gongheguo waijiaoshi, 1970–1978* (Beijing: Shijie zhishi, 1999).

Ward, John, *Latin America: Conflict and Development since 1945* (London: Routledge, 1997).

Weis, Toni, "Shaping the Discourse on Africa: the Concept of 'Solidarity' in East German relations with SWAPO," M.Sc dissertation, Oxford University, (2008).

Weizman, Ezer, *Rut, sof* (Tel Aviv: Yediot Akhronot, 2001).

Westad, Odd Arne (ed.), *Reviewing the Cold War. Approaches, Interpretations, Theory* (London: Cass, 2000).

Westad, Odd Arne, *The Global Cold War: Third World interventions and the making of our times* (Cambridge: Cambridge University Press, 2005).

Westad, Odd Arne and Quinn-Judge, Sophie (eds), *The Third Indochina War: Conflict between China, Vietnam and Cambodia, 1972–79* (London: Routledge, 2006).

Williams, Michael C., "New Soviet Policy toward Southeast Asia: Reorientation and Change," *Asian Survey*, 31:4 (1991), pp. 364–77.

Williamson, J. (ed.), *Latin American Adjustment: How Much Has Happened* (Washington, DC: Institute for International Economics, 1990).

Windrich, Elaine, *The Cold War Guerrilla: Jonas Savimbi, the US Media, and the Angolan War* (Orlando, FL: Greenwood Publishing Group, 1992).

Womack, Brantly, "Sino–Vietnamese Border Trade: The Edge of Normalization," *Asian Survey*, 34:6 (1994), pp. 495–512.

Wright, George, *The Destruction of a Nation. United States Policy Towards Angola Since 1945*(London: Pluto Press, 1997).

Ya'alon, Moshe, *Derekh Arukha ktzara* (Tel Aviv: Yediot Sfarim, 2008).

Yang, Kuisong, "The Sino–Soviet Border Clash of 1969," *Cold War History*, 1:1(August 2000).

Yang, Meihong, *Yingsu huagong: wo zai miangong shiwu nian* (Hong Kong: Tiandi, 2001).

Yariv, Aharon, *Haarakha zahira* (Tel Aviv: JCSS, 1998).

Zaira, Eli, *Mitus mul metziut* (Tel Aviv: Yedtio Akhronot, 1998).

Zamora, Augusto R., *La Paz Burlada: Los Procesos de Paz de Contadora y Esquipulas.* (Madrid: SEPHA, 2006).

Zubok, Vladislav, *A Failed Empire: The Soviet Union in the Cold War from Stalin to Gorbachev* (Chapel Hill, NC: University of North Carolina Press, 2007).

Index

Made in the USA
Las Vegas, NV
01 November 2024

9cf89ed4-1bd8-4c69-ba48-9cf1519763daR01